INTERNATIONAL MANAGEMENT BEHAVIOR

INTERNATIONAL MANAGEMENT BEHAVIOR

Prof. Sunil Tiwari and Dr. Richa Tiwari

SOCIETY Publishing

www.societypublishing.com

International Management Behavior

Prof. Sunil Tiwari and Dr. Richa Tiwari

Society Publishing
4164 Lakeshore Road
Burlington, ON L7L 1A4
Canada
www.societypublishing.com
Email: orders@arclereducation.com

ISBN: 978-1-83441-043-2 (Hardcover)

ABOUT THE AUTHORS

Prof. Sunil Kumar Tiwari is a professor and head at Awadhesh Pratap Singh University in Rewa, Madhya Pradesh. He has 16 years of experience in academia and administration. Prof. Tiwari holds a Ph.D. in Economics from Awadhesh Pratap Singh University. He has held various administrative positions, including Dean of Faculty and Executive Council Member. Prof. Tiwari has published books and articles in national and international journals. He has participated in conferences and presented on topics related to higher education and human resource development. He has consulting experience, including conducting management development programs. He has received awards and fellowships for his contributions to education and research. Prof. Tiwari has successfully guided 17 Ph.D. and 20 M.Phil. scholars. He has also visited Oxford University in London and the University of Malaya in Kuala Lumpur for academic purposes.

Dr. Richa Tiwari is currently working as Assistant Professor in Centre for Management Studies, Jain Deemedtobe University, Bengaluru (IN). Her research areas include work culture, organizational productivity, and employee engagement. Prior to the role, she worked as Academic Associate at the Indian Institute of Management, Ahmedabad in the Human Resource Area and along with a rich corporate experience in diverse roles of assistant manager human resources, public relations and editorials. She is an FDP alumnus of Indian Institute of Management, Ahmedabad and MBA from Devi Ahilya University, Indore. She holds certification in Industrial Relations and Personnel Management and other certifications in management areas from institutes like Academy of Management, USA, IIM Ahmedabad, IIM Indore, NIIT, INDAM to name a few. Her research work has appeared in multiple international ABDC indexed & Peerreviewed journals. She also presented her work in conferences across the management world for events of IITs, IIMs, EDII, INDAM, AOM, KJ Somaiya. Dr. Richa has also been invited for a series of lectures on transformational leadership, Research Analytics and other emerging fields in multiple institutions in India.

TABLE OF CONTENTS

LIST OF FIGURES

PREFACE

International business exposes people who approach, behave, and decide in different ways. What constitutes a compelling argument in one culture is deficient in another; a clear-cut “no” can be revered in one setting and avoided in another; the clock can control some meetings and relationships control others. Leaders must deal with differences in time frames, risk tolerance, hierarchy styles, and fairness. These differences are not problems to be removed but realities to be understood and used appropriately. When managers are aware of how values and context influence action, they sharpen judgment, communicate truthfully, and build organizations that act as one across boundaries.

Global management behavior is hence a practical field. It is about the way real people coordinate in the face of distance, culture, language, law, and technology to achieve shared results. It asks how to build trust when groups don’t meet in the same space, how to motivate performance when rewards are different from one culture to another, how to make an informed decision when facts are incomplete and groups are dispersed, and how to resolve conflicts without losing face or future cooperation. It challenges managers to look inward too: knowledge of their own biases, willingness to learn, and ability to change a point of view from another direction. The discipline is rewarded with curiosity, systematic observation, and practice in translating cultural knowledge into better decisions about structure, strategy, and day-to-day work.

International Management Behavior has been designed to make these ideas practical the same day. The book builds from principles to application, switching between concepts and tools and illustrations that can be applied on the same day. Every chapter has explicit objectives, offers a succinct set of frameworks, and then shows how to apply them by utilizing short cases, decision aids, checklists, and questions for reflection. Throughout, the emphasis is on transfer: how to transfer understanding from one cultural situation to another responsibly, how to turn an abstract model into a meeting agenda, a job description, or a negotiation script, and how to learn from experience so the next decision is improved on the last.

Chapter 1 presents the foundations of international management behaviors. It defines culture, norms, values, and identity; distinguishes among national, professional, and organizational cultures; and sets up why context matters to coordination, control, and cooperation. The chapter also introduces the key competencies of perspective taking, self-monitoring, and cultural humility, and it provides a starter toolkit for reflection on one’s current strengths and development needs.

Chapter 2 addresses the subject of learning about culture and global mindset. Readers contrast common cultural frameworks and learn how to use them wisely without stereotyping while still gaining insight. The chapter extends the idea of a global mindset as a mix of cognitive complexity, social awareness, and business sense. Practice exercise sharpens the ability to change frames, detect weak signals, and integrate what at first glance seems contradictory expectations into sound plans.

Chapter 3 considers individual behavior in cultures. Motivation, perception, attribution, and personality are briefly mentioned in relation to how they manifest in hiring, rating, giving feedback, and career development. The chapter illustrates differences in what people find fair, respectful, and motivation-generating; the chapter offers means of setting goals, praising or giving feedback, and designing jobs that balance autonomy and direction for multicultural teams.

Chapter 4 covers communication in cross-cultural situations. Topics covered are high- and low-context communication, directness vs. indirectness, silence and interruption, turn-taking, and employing nonverbal signals. The chapter offers tools for building up messages, measuring understanding without humiliation, using interpreters professionally, and selecting media—email, conversation, video, or face-to-face—based on task and relation requirements. Additional emphasis is given to listening as a performance skill.

Chapter 5 discusses leadership in cultures in international management. It contrasts common expectations of leadership—charisma, concern, involvement, decisiveness—and illustrates how the expectations of followers shape the effectiveness of a leader's style. One learns how to establish credibility, create psychological safety, and shift influence tactics to indigenous norms without sacrificing ethics and performance. The chapter concludes with guidelines for multicultural project team leadership and global communities of practice leadership.

Chapter 6 outlines cross-border and organizational strategic behavior. It mediates structure (global, networked, regional, transnational) and information flows, coordination mechanisms, and decision rights. The chapter addresses knowledge transfer, control systems, alliance governance, and headquarters–subsidiary relationships. Learners can diagnose strategy vs. structure misalignment and design simple rules in a way that flexibility does not create confusion.

Chapter 7 expands decision-making to global management. It returns to rational, bounded, and evidence-based approaches and shows how time pressure, cultural norms, and power distance influence who speaks, who makes decisions, and when to stop analysis. Techniques include stakeholder mapping by country, bias checks, premortems, and decision protocols that balance consultation with clarity. The chapter provides templates for noting down decisions so learning is compounded over time.

Chapter 8 addresses cross-cultural conflict resolution and negotiation. Preparation aids walk readers through clarifying alternatives, issues, and interests to a style that accommodates formality differences, time budgeting, and the use of third parties. Distributive and integrative styles, face-saving methods, and face-saving "no"s are discussed in the chapter. It also shows how to mediate conflicts, manage escalation paths, and save relationships after contentious episodes.

Chapter 9 deals with human resource management in global organizations. Staffing policy (ethnocentric, polycentric, geocentric), global talent pipelines, and competency models are linked with development paths like international assignments, virtual mobility, and short rotations. The chapter deals with selection for expatriation, preparation for departure, support on-assignment, and repatriation planning. The chapter also speaks of total rewards, performance appraisal across borders, and compliance with labor standards while building inclusive teams.

Chapter 10 deals with technology, digitalization, and virtual global work. It explains how tools—from everyday documents to AI-based translation—reshape workflows, team-building, and management. They learn to build digital rituals, manage time-zone spread, be present in virtual meetings, and ensure data privacy and security. The chapter also explores algorithmic bias, surveillance risks, and the human skills that make virtual collaboration humane and productive.

The book is intended for MBA and master's students, management and international business undergraduates, and first-career managers assuming work requiring coordination across nations. Senior managers will find frameworks and checklists useful for training purposes as well as for designing global initiatives. HR professionals and learning professionals can use the assessment and exercises to develop programs in cultural competence, global teamwork, and leadership development. Teachers and students will appreciate the clear structure for a semester course, with material to support cases, simulations, and project-based work. The only prerequisite is a curiosity and commitment to question one's own biases.

Chapter 1

Foundations of International Management Behaviors

Contents

INTRODUCTION

With business operations becoming more and more interconnected in a global setting, the dynamics of management behaviors require a sophisticated understanding of several determinants of successful international leadership. This is due to the mix of different cultural backgrounds as well as organizational practices that highly affect managerial decision-making and employee interactions. In this regard, the contribution of globalization cannot be overstated since not only does it facilitate cross-border exchange of goods and services but also accelerates the convergence of social norms and corporate ethics across borders. Theories of management have correspondingly reflected this phenomenon, gaining traction in order to keep pace with increasing heterogeneity within world marketplaces. Recognition of the ways in which globalization reshapes paradigms for management allows leaders to weather difficulties and take advantage of opportunities for growth and innovation, driving the overall effectiveness of global management practices. A second critical component which needs to be followed carefully in international management is culture. Recognition of cultural sensitivities is crucial since it directly affects behavior, communication styles, and organizational decision-making. The cultural management interface manifests itself in numerous configurations and has the tendency to influence the success of leadership strategies and employee motivation initiatives. For instance, high-context or low-context communication and individualism or collectivism cross-cultural dimensions determine team members' expectations and behaviors in various geographies. Furthermore, as a business expands its geographic reach, recognizing differences in culture becomes essential while developing tailored management programs that foster teamwork and avoid misunderstandings. Thus, managers who become culturally aware and sensitive are better suited to manage multicultural teams and enhance cross-border collaboration. The course of international management behaviors is also influenced by faster technological progress, which is transforming organizational structures and operating processes. Technological innovations such as artificial intelligence and data analytics have transformed managerial practices by making decision-making faster and resource allocation more effective. As industries mature, it is critical that practitioners learn to use these technology tools to remain competitive. Riding on this, the effects of technological disruptions cannot be understated; they not only transform internal management processes but also redefine customer interactions and models of service delivery across industries. By the integration of these innovations into their strategic plans, organizations can create value and succeed in the midst of the ever-changing global world, digging deeper the foundations of successful international management behaviors.

Definition of International Management

As time passed, with the evolution of international business, International Management gained greater prominence as businesses sought to expand beyond domestic markets for opportunities. It is the description of an array of practices aimed at managing operations, assets, and human resources in a multinational environment. As globalization transforms the economic landscape, the value of effective international management cannot be overemphasized. Companies not only have to deal with diverse regulatory complexities, but also with diverse consumers' needs and competitive forces shaping the world market. The importance of this discipline is that it can render organizational flexibility feasible, so that companies can use their capabilities outside boundaries without facing risks associated with cultural, economic, and political differences. The impact of globalization extends far beyond mere market expansion; it greatly alters the way management is conceptualized and implemented. In light of such circumstances, the demand for strategic international human resource management (SIHRM) emerges as a requirement factor for businesses seeking to maximize their global presence. SIHRM is an organizational framework that assists companies in managing the intricacies of dealing with an ethnically diverse workforce. Through the analysis of international human resource typologies, organizations are able to place their people management strategy within the context of greater organizational goals. In recognizing SIHRMs role in advancing management theory and practice, organizations can identify possible areas for shortcomings and work towards removing these in order to seek an ultimate competitive advantage in an increasingly globalized marketplace (Cieri et al., 1998). Cultural dimensions are critical when looking at international management behaviors, as they greatly influence organizational dynamics and employee relationships. It is important that managers working within multicultural environments study how cultures guide managerial styles and employee expectations. For instance, transformational leadership has been linked with organizational knowledge enhancement through developing good cultural practices within a company (Ghasabeh et al., 2017). By virtue of their function as change agents, transformational leaders are able to cross cultural differences that otherwise become problematic issues in global settings. Such ability to foster a unified organizational culture not only enhances employee commitment but also encourages innovation, enabling firms to remain agile and resilient in the face of global adversity. From this viewpoint, international management is a term that has changed its meaning, placing emphasis on how culture intelligence can be the vital asset for shaping organizational behavior beyond borders.

Importance of Studying Management Behaviors

Effective organizational behavior management has been a prime area of research, especially with the world's continued transformation. Coupled with the additional complexities from globalization, understanding management behavior is now a key consideration in fostering cooperation among cultures. With handling diverse expectations and norms, recognizing such behavior helps in identifying underlying motivations and impediments, enabling leaders to modify their approaches in turn. This demand is further encouraged by the dissemination of management theories that aim to standardize organizational practices worldwide while preserving the unique cultural diversities of every nation. Therefore, learning about management behaviors is not only relevant but also necessary because it provides information that guides strategic decision-making in multinational organizations, ultimately ensuring a standardized work environment harmonized with both global and local needs. The interplay between management behaviors and culture cannot be overstated either. With worldwide expansion of businesses comes the employees' underlying cultural frameworks affecting day-to-day operations as well as inter-employee relationships. Having an awareness of such facets of culture results in further knowing of management styles and their effectiveness in different regions. Research has indicated that management success largely depends upon leaders' capability to adapt their styles according to local communication and cultural expectations. By studying these behaviors, managers are then empowered to create not only but also culturally nuanced ones, maximizing their employees' engagement and satisfaction. As companies transition to cultivating talent in the global setting, this adaptability becomes a critical competency for effective international management. Lastly, as companies respond to the intricacies of a globalized economy, the evolving dynamics of management behaviors will have an ever-growing effect on outcomes. The dynamic interplay of agency and structure within management practice highlights the need for ongoing research in the discipline. Scholars urge the establishment of a strong structuration theory framework and suggest that combining both individual agency and large-scale socio-cultural constructs can enable a deeper level of knowledge of management behaviors (Elbasha et al., 2017). These questions enable organizations to form strategies that are sustainable amidst rapid change. For instance, interdisciplinarity, as exemplified by the cooperation between Purdue University and Sapienza Università di Roma, significantly illustrates how different disciplines can unite to create more engaging learning outcomes and prepare next-generation leaders to be better equipped to perform in an era of international integration (Fedele et al., 2019). Emphasizing the importance of learning management behavior ensures that organizations can position themselves to be responsive to the demands of international environments effectively.

1.1. SCOPE OF INTERNATIONAL MANAGEMENT

International management is an innovative set of practices that evolve with the intricacies of international business. The coverage of this domain is not just the execution of business models across borders; it also involves understanding how international markets function differently due to varying political, economic, and cultural contexts. As businesses expand globally, they must face regional-specific regulation and socio-economic conditions, so adaptability is necessary to succeed. This globalization-driven process of evolution calls for an interconnected approach that blends various management practice and theory for embracing the unique requirements of different geography areas. The establishment of multinational corporations has also brought into focus the added value from an extensive knowledge of international management as a subject. This knowledge is vital in developing strategies that not only work but are also adaptable to the diversified environments in which multinational companies conduct business (N/A, 2004). Globalization has significantly altered the nature of conducting business, with the relevance of global management practice rising tremendously. With decreasing trade barriers and improved communication and logistics through technology, corporations are not confined to local markets anymore. This shift compels managers to develop global strategies responsive to various consumer needs and competitive situations. As organizations stretch themselves territorially, they typically confront issues of cross-border alliances, investment decisions, and resource allocation. All these complications require a high sensitivity to global trends and the ability to develop strategies that embrace diversity but promote oneness in the organization (Figure 1.1).

Figure 1.1. Managerial function of international management.

Source: https://media.geeksforgeeks.org/wp-content/uploads/20230728112804/International-management-copy.webp.

Thus, the emphasis on international management has expanded to encompass not only strategic frameworks but also account for ethics and sustainability in a more globalized world (Belk et al., 2019). Cultural dimensions are at the heart of framing manager behaviors within international environments. Each country possesses distinctive cultural characteristics that influence business practices, communication styles, and models of leadership. It is essential to comprehend these cultural differences in developing effective teamwork and facilitating successful business operations worldwide. Cultural intelligence has to be cultivated by managers so that they can effectively cope with the complexities of the global workplaces, which involves adapting leadership styles to suit local behavior and conventions.

Awareness of culture at this level extends beyond protocol and involves inspiring employee motivation and satisfaction through values and beliefs. Because globalization encourages cross-cultural exchange, it then is a challenge for global managers to build integrated teams with varied backgrounds, and this demands cultural sensitivity to how the conflicts of cultures may ensue as well as how to effectively reduce such conflict. Ultimately, the integration of cultural understanding into the system of international management is a foundation for building cooperation and innovation in international business contexts (N/A, 2004).

1.1.1. Areas of Focus in International Management

In the intricate global context of management, it is essential to actualize the scope and relevance of the field to global business realities in order to function in the global business environment. Forging itself quickly with technology growth and expanding markets, international management is about integrating differing organizational practices across different cultural contexts. International management as a discipline entails strategic compatibility between local adaptation and worldwide objectives, addressing issues and opportunities generated through cross-border interactions.

With growing globalization, firms face problems that are intricate in nature, ranging from regulatory compliance to competitive strategies, which require a comprehensive understanding of international management concepts. This evolution of the subject also compels managers to be agile, forming an adaptive mindset to cope with evolving market needs and cultural nuances. Thus, the origin of international management practices must possess a keen instinct for such dynamic environments in order to enable sustained success in home and international markets together. Globalization has certainly redrawn the framework of management, with threats as well as challenges for organizations that have an international presence. With business ventures spreading their horizons beyond boundaries, they are confronted with a myriad of issues concerning regulatory authorities, economic crisis, and unstable customers' needs (Figure 1.2).

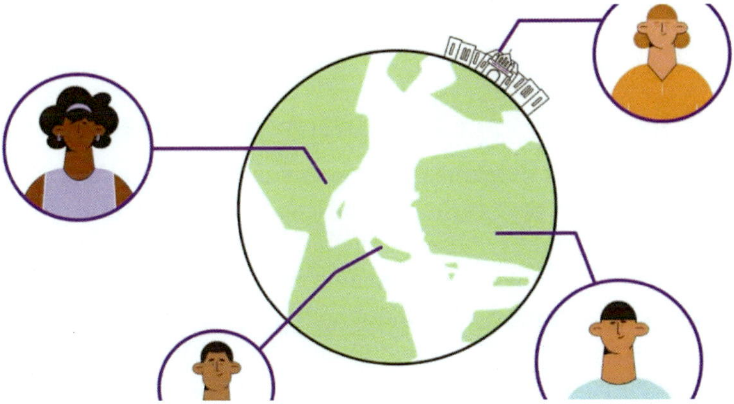

Figure 1.2. Technological advancements and the expansion of international management.

Source: https://www.alliancembs.manchester.ac.uk/media/ambs/content-assets/images/undergraduate/bsc-international-management.webp.

Here, international management has to be able to manage global supply chains, talent acquisition from various geographic areas, and the application of technology in collaboration and communication. Moreover, the companies must continue to innovate as a way of gaining the upper hand in the global market, which in most cases involves adopting practices that increase agility and resilience. By accepting these complexities, organizations are able to position themselves better to play the complexity of international business. Therefore, careful examination of globalization and its effects on management practices is a central area of focus that supports the conceptual behaviors of international management. Culture is a fundamental element that affects managerial behavior and organizational practices in foreign environments. The crossing of different cultural backgrounds holds the potential to produce both profitable cooperative opportunities and challenging obstacles, considering that cultural misunderstandings can adversely affect global operations. Managers need to cultivate cultural intelligence—a cultural difference awareness and knowledge—to facilitate effective communication and build diverse workplaces. Cultural awareness has a significant influence on decision-making, negotiation, and inter-group relations, in addition to organizational performance. In addition, during the era of social responsibility when companies are focusing more on social responsibility, cultural awareness enables managers to engage positively with local stakeholders and communities. The underlying behaviors for international management, therefore, must integrate cultural factors into organizational policies and leadership strategies since this is capable of driving employee satisfaction and powering long-term growth in an increasingly globalized globe.

1.1.2. Key Challenges Faced by International Managers

International management dynamics must be managed with a keen eye on the forces remaking contemporary business landscapes. With globalization drawing apart economies and cultures closer into one another, international managers need to contend with different regulatory environments and economic conditions. Compounding this is the pace of technological change, which demands agile leadership that can identify new opportunities even as it defends against new perils. The development of digitalization renders it intensely relevant for managers to create strong structures of collaboration and communication through and through. It increasingly becomes evident that policy-making—and execution—should be carried out with strategic vision, particularly when constructing collaborative relationships at an international level. The emphasis on creating multi-dimensional, creative solutions beyond geographical boundaries makes the efficient management international in the nature of imperatives (N/A, 2018). The role of culture cannot be overstated as regards its influence on international management behaviors. Cultural settings shape the expectations and behaviors of stakeholders, and it becomes crucial to understand regional values and norms. International managers are often saddled with the difficult burden of reconciling these cultural differences as they guide their organizations towards mutually reinforcing operating efficiencies (Figure 1.3).

Figure 1.3. Becoming a global manager with a global mindset.

Source: https://imageio.forbes.com/specials-images/imageserve/61fa85ee9ee76d358e1fe0fa//960x0.jpg?height=452&width=711&fit=bounds.

The delicate art of balancing respect for local customs and practices against carrying the general organizational culture consists not only of sensitivity but also a proper framework for cross-cultural communication. In addition, global managers are confronted with the risk of cultural misunderstandings, which can lead to conflict that erodes productivity and cooperation. With globalization offering a mosaic of organizational worlds, the ability to navigate through cultural worlds is the foundation of successful international management strategies (Margaret et al., 2018). Furthermore, operational challenges for international managers are exacerbated by ever-evolving economic worlds that delineate global markets. As organizations expand to new frontiers, they expose themselves to evolving economic circumstances, geopolitics tensions, and shifting consumer preferences. This necessitates active market monitoring, risk assessment, and planning. Managers must cultivate an adaptive mindset, such that they can rapidly adjust to evolving conditions through adaptive decision-making processes. In this environment, insights from data are paramount, in that they enable managers to be cognizant of both macroeconomic trends and local market details. Lastly, the ability to foresee issues and craft effective solutions relies on a combination of analytical rigor and creative imagination—key competencies for any international manager wanting success in an expanding global world (N/A, 2018).

1.1.3. Emerging Trends in the Field

In today's environment of global management, there is a convergence of forces that is remodeling the schools of management practices. With businesses going global, incorporating different cultural views becomes essential. This change makes managers go beyond learning about cultural sensitivities, which has implications for communication, decision-making, and teamwork. Emerging trends indicate that organizations are paying attention to cultural intelligence as a critical competency, enhancing teamwork and lowering conflict arising from cross-cultural miscommunications. Also with increased virtual communication, managers are employing more virtual interaction management strategies for managing geographically distant teams. The evolution of these dynamics unfolds the importance of adaptive management practices, which not only consider cultural factors but also leverage them towards better organization and innovation. Globalization becomes a driver as well as challenge for contemporary management practices, remapping traditional paradigms. The expansion of global markets established a competitive environment in which companies are required to be adaptable in their strategy. Increasing trends are showing that companies are increasingly and increasingly willing to go for global sourcing and outsourcing based primarily on cost reduction and efficiency. The offshore outsourcing market, for example, was worth more than $55 billion USD in 2008 with a projected 20% yearly growth rate, reflecting a glaring shift towards leveraging global capabilities and talent (Griffiths et al., 2009). When companies adopt such strategies, their managers are confronted with the double imperative of making organizational objectives align with several stakeholder interests while managing the complexities of country-level regulatory environments. Adapting a multifaceted strategy demands an understanding of international market dynamics, which emphasizes adopting adaptive management models in a globalized environment.

The rapid rate of technological advancements is also revolutionizing the game of global management practices, encouraging innovative tactics among companies. The innovation of digital software and platforms has revolutionized business processes, enabling real-time communication and teamwork across geographical regions. This digital revolution underscores the need for flexibility in management as firms strive to harness technology for competitiveness. Another important trend that has been observed is the increasing popularity of new collaboration methods, such as game jams, that promote the rapid development of ideas and innovative solutions by tapping into collective creativity (Galloway et al., 2015). Not only are these sessions defying conventional norms, but they also contribute to inspiring communities in the workplace, reinforcing the need for managers to create experimentation and risk-taking cultures. Implementing these new strategies can make managers more efficient and introduce a culture of ongoing improvement, pushing international organizations to greater achievement in a rapidly evolving global economy.

1.2. RELEVANCE OF INTERNATIONAL MANAGEMENT

The international management environment has been revolutionized as business dynamics have been reengineered by globalization. Increased interconnectedness gives companies a window into different markets, and this translates into the need for management practices beyond traditional paradigms. Global expansion demands organizations deal with complexities in cultural differences, regulatory frameworks, and competitive forces inherent in international markets. This expansion necessitates management strategy that incorporates both global and local sensibilities to avoid pitfalls. International management comes into play as specialists must learn to acquire skills necessary for managing teams and decision making in multilayered environments. According to previous research, how transformational leaders develop an adaptive and knowledge-based culture matters, as indicated by the fact that transformational leaders influence organizational culture and knowledge as mediators in effective international management (Ghasabeh et al., 2017) (Figure 1.4).

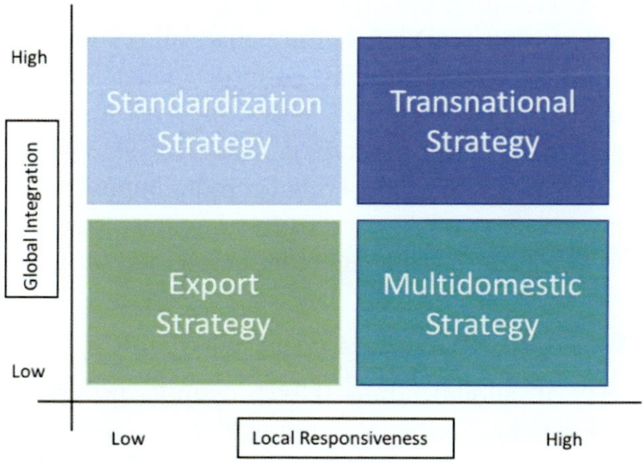

Figure 1.4. Importance of international management.

Source: https://library.fiveable.me/_next/image?url=https%3A%2F%2Fstorage.googleapis.com%2Fstatic.prod.fiveable.me%2Fsearch-images%252F%2522Impact_of_globalization_on_business_strategies_international_management_global_value_chains_and_market_adaptation.%2522-mod_16_strategies.png&w=750&q=75.

Globalization has profoundly influenced global management, causing a necessity for organizations to adopt integrated approaches sensitive to the fast-evolving economic landscape. Growing competition, increased sensitivity among consumers, and technological changes compel firms to constantly innovate and possess an adaptive operating system. With businesses venturing into new markets, they not only face competing institutions but also grapple with diverse expectations from distinct constituencies. It then becomes critical to understand the integration of supply chain management and strategy because it is what creates the basis for upholding competitive dominance in the global market. Strategic SCM literature shows that its adoption can greatly enhance the position of the company in the market and its operating efficiency (Koufteros et al., 2015). The evolution of global management practices signals the importance of balancing business strategies with a deep understanding of cultural differences and sectoral norms that function on the global level. Cultural consideration is a deciding factor in shaping managerial behaviors and overall organizational practices in global management. As much as businesses venture into new cultures, managers must move beyond their own biases to develop culture competence so that they can communicate effectively with various employees. Such malleability encourages collaboration and innovation, essential drivers for pushing performance in a globalized setting. The challenge lies not just with determining cultural dissimilarities but also with leveraging them to create a common working culture that values various thoughts. By developing a common organizational culture, leaders are more likely to influence worker behaviors and draw upon collective knowledge, ultimately leading to organizational better outcomes. The relevance of learning cultural impact is significant since it offers insights for reducing misunderstandings and enhancing greater cooperation between global teams, hence reinforcing the pillars of effective international management behaviors.

1.2.1. Impact on Global Business Operations

The complexities of globalization have deeply influenced the global management environment, compelling organizations to reshape their operations for wider reach and better performance. With borders disappearing and markets converging, firms are open to diverse sets of cultural conditions that necessitate an intimate understanding of domestic mores, consumption habits, and regulatory frameworks.

Figure 1.5. The importance of global business perspectives.

Source: https://fastercapital.com/i/Cambist-Chronicles--Simplifying-Cross-Border-Transactions--Managing-Currency-Risks-in-Global-Business-Operations.webp.

This synergistic relationship between global strategy and local adaptability emphasizes the importance of adaptive management techniques because companies strive to hold competitive advantage while being responsive to cultural awareness. Transformational leadership then emerges as a prime catalyst of the process because it establishes a culture of creativity and flexibility within companies. They facilitate the exchange of knowledge and can be agents of change who reshape organizational culture and enhance the effectiveness of operations across borders, hence mediating the relationship between transformational leadership and organizational performance, as the literature in organizational knowledge and leadership theories would indicate (Ghasabeh et al., 2017). Lastly, the significance of understanding the cultural elements influencing the behavior of management cannot be overstated, particularly global operations. As organizations' global presence grows, employees' and consumers' diverse cultural origins play a critical role in guiding business practice. Managing therefore involves cultural intelligence to enable executives to properly handle cultural diversity and reap its advantage to the organization (Figure 1.5).

This understanding helps to work out strategies that communicate universally in multiple cultural paradigms, thereby making the workplaces inclusive and achieving maximum employee engagement. Furthermore, the inclusion of knowledge from cross-cultural research can lead to more effective decision-making processes and problem-solving campaigns, endorsement of which reveals that managerial effectiveness within the globalized context depends on the ability to harmonize organizational objectives with cultural sensitivities (Fiennes, 2016). The ever-evolving global business landscape continues to challenge the traditional management philosophies, necessitating creative strategies in order to foster long-term growth. As organizations seek to respond to shifting economic conditions and emerging technologies, the need for flexible business models is greater than ever. The implementation of digital transformation and data analytics is imperative in rationalizing operations and optimizing efficiency. Moreover, the organizational culture, as driven by transformational leadership, initiates a culture which facilitates change. This two-way relationship charges organizations to become more agile in their operations, allowing them to anticipate the needs and shocks in the marketplace. As management practices continue to evolve in response to these forces, the foundations of global management are definitely being reshaped, with a focus on the absolute necessity of culture and leadership to success on the world stage (Ghasabeh et al., 2017).

1.2.2. Importance for Multinational Corporations

The organizational setting is continually influenced by shifting patterns of management practice and theory. Multinational corporations (MNCs) stretch out across borders, generating an array of dilemmas that necessitate an astute understanding of worldwide management conduct. This shift towards globalism not only highlights the importance of cultural abilities but also emphasizes the importance of managing, based on various circumstances. With globalization redesigning how organizations work, management frameworks that regulate the conduct of organizations need to keep pace. A critique of how culture and management practices influence each other shows that conventional, essentialist methods of understanding culture fall short in solving the issues of MNCs. These perceptions foster a more engaged, politically aware sense of cultural diversity that is crucial in functioning on the sophisticated terrain of global management in multinational companies (Angouri et al., 2009) (Figure 1.6).

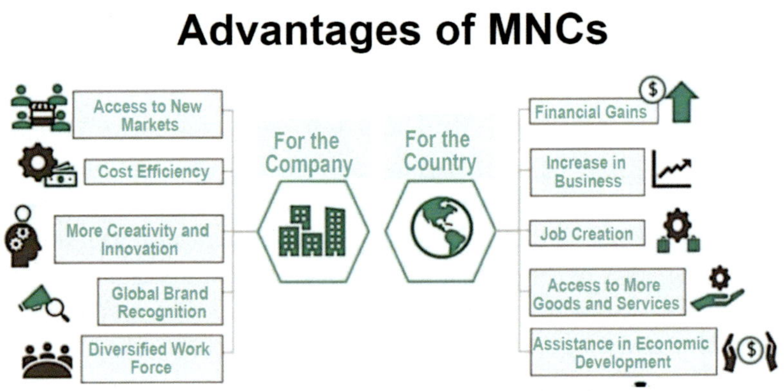

Figure 1.6. Advantages of multinational corporations (MNCs).

Source: https://www.wallstreetmojo.com/wp-content/uploads/2021/06/MNCs-Advantages-1024x553.jpg.

The cultural environment under which MNCs operate has far-reaching consequences for decision-making and operational effectiveness. Out of respect for variations in cultural identities, organizations can operate more effectively to the needs of the host country and thus more sustainably build relationships with various stakeholders. The evolving terrain of strategic international human resource management (SIHRM) addresses this need by making the incorporation of knowledge about culture part of management conduct. This blend of strategic imagination and cultural awareness enables MNCs to build effective teams that enjoy a broad base of experiences and skill sets. In doing so, however, it raises important questions regarding theory building and the threat of intellectual imperialism in management practice. While businesses take advantage of cross-cultural interactions, they must be careful to pay attention to how cultural narratives shape their organizational practices and policies (Cieri et al., 1998). For MNCs to thrive in an increasingly interconnected economy, they have a responsibility to concentrate on building a culture that fosters diversity and supports inter-border partnerships. Cultural adaptability is a key way of stimulating organizational strength and stimulating innovation. With an understanding of the variations in regional cultures, firms can implement workplace practices that are not only aligned with local conventions but also that support a corporate culture as a whole. As firms integrate divergent perceptions into their operational models, they are in a stronger position to accommodate changes in the global market. Lastly, the compliance with understanding and embracing cultural variation is not a passing trend but an integral part of successful international management practice. A richer incorporation of these aspects of culture will ensure multinational organizations are robust and adaptable to a rapidly changing world and hence further their commitment to sustainable world practice (Cieri et al., 1998).

1.2.3. Role in Economic Development

The intricate interplay between management action and economic development remains a subject of discussion, especially given the reshaping of the market by globalization. The contemporary environments require organizations to negotiate a paradigm with increased interconnectedness. Multinational enterprises bring a competitive landscape in which management action plays a critical role in determining national and international economic realities. Managers are therefore faced with ensuring effective governance institutions, and trust building with stakeholders. This demand stems from an awareness that control and trust are increasingly being conceptualized as complementary mechanisms for organizational frameworks. Through the advocacy of trust in managerialism, organizations not only promote economic development but also facilitate smooth collaborations that bridge geographical space, facilitating developmental plans across countries, as elucidated in the explanation of Fords Assets Program portfolios worldwide (N/A, 2004). Cultural influences play a significant role in shaping managerial behaviors and, by implication, economic development outcomes. Culturally astute organizations are well placed to adapt their strategies to various contexts, aware that culturally attuned management practices can yield greater operational effectiveness and responsiveness to local markets. This renders it essential in a global economy, where standardization of strategy risks overlooking critical local nuances. When considering trust and control dynamics, culturally-based attitudes towards both such notions come forward as significant facilitators or constraints of cooperative undertakings within and between organizations. With evolving collective behavior, an understanding of cultural dimensions can guide managers to formulate policies promoting sustainable economic advancement, thereby highlighting the culturally-sensitive nature of international management behavior (Costa et al., 2007). In addition, the issue of scaling up successful projects is central to ensuring considerable economic progress in developing areas. Efficient management behavior tends to be pivotal to ensuring that innovative concepts may effectively be applied at a large scale. Through knowledge of the basis of global management behavior, organizations are able to manage issues around resource distribution, partnership formation, and stakeholder interaction in diverse environments better. Systems that demonstrate scalability, like those derived from Fords work, show the significance of long-term planning by managers and collaborative frameworks focused on sustainable practices. Such methodologies not only enhance economic development but also enhance organizational resilience to global challenges. By recognizing that control and trust mechanisms can be instrumental to such processes, managers can align their strategies to larger economic objectives, ultimately fostering a more unified and dynamic world economy (N/A, 2004).

1.3. EVOLUTION OF INTERNATIONAL MANAGEMENT

With the dynamic paradigm of global business, international management has never been as essential as it is today. Globalization has ushered in complexities that have forced management practices to adjust to various regulatory and cultural setups. With companies venturing across home borders, the intersection of trust and control becomes a determinative factor of organizational performance. Of specific importance, research determines that control and trust are not dichotomous concepts but rather evolve based on interrelated processes of how multiple different mechanisms of governance interact. This recognition allows for the opportunity to develop subtle management methods of prioritizing trust building in inter-organizational relations together with adaptations to local environments for readjustment of control measures (Costa et al., 2007). Thus, learning the intricate interdependences that define global management practices promotes flexibility and adherence to shifts in the market. Globalization is an agent of change in global management practices that compels organizations to constantly develop and innovate. Interdependence of global markets guarantees competitiveness, which later necessitates embracing sophisticated management frameworks. Consequently, firms are more challenged to traverse complex cultural landscapes, since cultural differences present threats and possibilities for international managers (Figure 1.7).

Figure 1.7. The ability of international management.

Source: https://images.squarespace-cdn.com/content/v1/5b1735dd8ab722a791596d79/1584464594362-Y61HFLQSJOVHJ8YWRUGI/Management+Systems+Integrated+Model+for+Organizational+Development.png.

The ability to understand and accumulate diverse cultural perspectives can make the building of organizational resilience as well as stakeholder relationship stronger. In this context, knowledge regarding how trust is established and reconstructed in these diverse environments comes into play (Ng et al., 2015). For example, the development of alternative food networks has illustrated how organizations can rebuild trust in times of crisis, evidencing the primacy of interpersonal relationships in consolidating a cooperative business culture in the wake of globalization threats. As management goes global, the role of culture in shaping managerial practices cannot be understated. It is both a lens through which global interactions are viewed and a template through which decision-making processes are organized. Cultural dimensions influence everything from the negotiation process to leadership style, demanding a adaptive management plan led by contextuality. Further, mixing and matching informal social mechanisms is most effective in complementing spaces for formal management styles, particularly during uncertain conditions. Informal structures have a tendency to create necessary trust channels that compensate for gaps within formal institutions, especially where extrinsic factors compromise conventional governance (Ng et al., 2015). A knowledge of these cultural sensitivities equips international managers with the necessary information that enables them to build cooperative relationships, which eventually result in organizations' long-term success in the global market.

1.3.1. Historical Context and Development

The management landscape of the world has evolved significantly, and traditional contexts served as the launchpad for contemporary practices. Throughout history, the concept of talent has been extensively studied with specific considerations in a multiplicity of linguistic and cultural frames. Scholars have engaged in critical reviews that not only indicate variations in conceptualizing talent but also examine its applied aspects in organizational settings. The philological proof provided by researchers reflects various applications of the word in various languages and illustrates that language plays a vital role in defining how talent management is conceptualized when various cultures are in question (Tansley et al., 2011). The evolution emphasizes the value of adaptability in management practice since successful global strategies must transform to fit culturally determined meanings and constructs of talent. Globalization has also complicated the international management's historical context by blending different management traditions and norms. While companies open their frontiers beyond their borders, they are confronted with a mosaic of values, which guide managerial decisions and employee attitudes. The fusion of cultures calls for a more sophisticated understanding of how leadership dynamics operate in different settings, such as the evolution of shared and distributed leadership theories. Understanding that leadership cannot be the sole province of formally appointed individuals, scholars identified ways in which collaborative approaches to management foster organizational strength and adaptability (Alvarez et al., 2011). Such evolution through time accents the necessity for management practices that originate out of culture, which focus on inclusiveness and collective responsibility, leading characteristics against an increasingly globalized business world. Basically, such recognition of historical context of international management practices also comes with critical examination of how the behavior has been conditioned by historical theories and methods. Shared and distributed leadership frameworks have evolved from the differences after decades of research, which contributes to efficient management knowledge. Each theoretical framework has something new to bring to the complex nature of leaderships, revealing contradictions and tensions in traditional approaches (Alvarez et al., 2011). By comparing these frameworks, organizations are better able to analyze their leadership styles and integrate practices that suit their specific cultural environments. Ultimately, examining management behaviors in a historical context enriches debate today while allowing organizations to develop management strategies that are both globally applicable and regionally sensitive so that they may better enhance their overall effectiveness in the global setting.

1.3.2. Influential Theories and Models

The constant changing of economic forces in the globe has resulted in a serious scrutiny of the theoretical paradigms that inform international management behaviors. As organizations are increasingly engaging multiple stakeholders from geography and culture, it has become imperative to understand how such meetings affect management behavior and practice. The effects of globalization are most applicable here because firms are now dependent on collaborative partnerships, which transcend the normal competitive paradigms. Today's research highlights that establishing trust, commitment, and cooperation between channel members is crucial in order to succeed in this diverse environment. Adopting the footsteps of Dooley et al. (2025), shifting from rivalry competition to cooperation is vital in order to transform supply chains to be effective and sustainable, and the need for new leadership styles adaptable to global environments and set for inter-organizational collaborations emerges. In the area of global management, culture strongly affects organizational behavior and how management's conduct expresses itself in varying contexts. The cultural nuances require managers to utilize flexible strategies that fit with the local customs and values while maintaining overall strategic objectives. The influence of cultural dimensions transcends communication styles; it affects decision-making, team performance, and organizational structure. The role of multi-level theories, such as those presented in conventional internalization theory, provides a framework for explaining these complex interactions. Such theories encourage a systems approach that integrates firm-level and industry-level analysis to allow management to navigate and take advantage of cross-cultural differences, as early international business studies research, e.g., (Alchian et al., 2018), demonstrates. Additionally, international management model and theory construction reflects the growing acceptance of the interdependent nature of global markets and the advanced challenges that they present. The more traditional models based on linear, hierarchical structures are rapidly becoming a relic of the past as firms scramble to fit into highly dynamic operating landscapes with technological innovation and changing consumer patterns. The emergence of collaborative models in which relationship-building and adaptive leadership are encouraged is a sign of the necessity to be resilient within the context of global uncertainties. Leadership behaviors that create inter-organizational networks are necessary in the sense that they enable organizations to respond pre-emptively to problems and opportunities within the global marketplace. The synthesis of the theories encourages a better understanding of international management practices, and the stage is set for novel practices that support sustainable development in diverse operating environments.

1.3.3. Changes in Management Practices Over Time

Through the centuries, the landscape of management practice has undergone an extraordinary transformation, hand in hand with broader societal shifts and technology. At the outset of the industrial era, management was centered on productivity and efficiency, often with an overlay of top-down mentality obsessed with hierarchical configurations. Afterwards, as globalization began to work its magic on the economic scene, managers were set in a responsive context that demanded more adaptable approaches. This move made it possible for organizations to use diverse assets and engage with a global labor force, in the end making it easier to develop more inclusive management processes. The ability to effectively scale cross-border initiatives has played a critical role, as seen with initiatives such as Fords Assets Program, which emphasizes the importance of considering dominant trends in the past over today's realities and opportunities in global management systems (N/A, 2004). The impact of globalization on management styles cannot be overstated. With companies working all over the borders, there was an immediate need for managers to understand and respond to various cultural norms. Such understanding has necessitated the use of more culturally sensitive methods in leadership and people management. By building intercultural skills, organizations are not only able to handle conflict fueled by misunderstandings at the cultural level but also enhance employee productivity and engagement. This shift toward a more global mentality has required managers to learn and adapt continuously to handle the complexity of the global marketplace. With the growing multifaceted workforce, the need for culturally sensitive management practices is still underscored, and as such, a multifaceted array of solutions that are answers to regional and global problems of business operations (Keys et al., 2012). With the ongoing evolution of the domain of management, identifying the vast impact culture exerts on behaviors within organizations is unavoidable. Embedding cultural competence in management practices is no longer optional but imperative in order to minimize misunderstandings and maximize effective communication. Managers today have to craft strategies that not only appreciate but maximize cultural diversity for competitive advantage. Thus, the evolution of management practices has been more and more focused on inclusivity and creating equitable working environments. Such organizations are better placed to address the needs and aspirations of their diverse stakeholders' population, thus enhancing organizational effectiveness. Looking back at these developments throughout history, it is clear that the foundations of global management behaviors must evolve continuously in order to accommodate the intricacies of an interdependent world.

1.4. GLOBALIZATION AND ITS IMPACT ON MANAGEMENT

With convergence of markets and economies integration in the contemporary period, the dynamics of global management practices have been profoundly altered. That is the message underscored by globalization as the force behind strategic international human resource management (SIHRM). As companies go out to expand beyond borders, they must cope more with different cultural practices and customs affecting operational effectiveness as well as motivating employees. The newly emerging field of SIHRM offers a holistic intellectual framework that allows scholars and professionals to manage such complexities in an effective manner. Examining the changing paradigms of SIHRM, one can observe that an understanding of these culture-bound practices is not only necessary for theory construction but also for eradicating essential gaps in existing management literature.

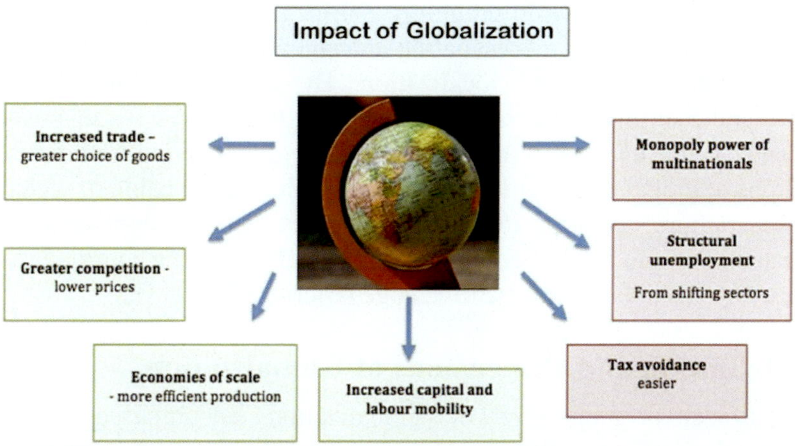

Figure 1.8. Globalization and its impact on management.

Source: https://xapotechsystems.com/public/uploads/blog/2021/04/week_2/Impact-of-globalization_1618295660.jpg.

This exploration of SIHRM reveals both a demand for new academic research and an invitation to transcend assumptions that would otherwise embed intellectual imperialism within the field (Cieri et al., 1998). As continued globalization reshapes the competitive landscape, management practice must also adapt to a complex mix of cultural influences. The intersection of indigenous customs and corporate policy emphasizes the necessity for organizations to apply culturally responsive management practices. Managers must recognize that the behavior and expectations of workers differ significantly in the context of different cultures, affecting motivation, communication, and work output. Therefore, it is important to incorporate a cultural focus into management frameworks to ensure inclusive workplaces where talents can perform their best without restriction. This advanced understanding will provide more suitable policy and practice design for specific cultural contexts to improve organizational performance. Lastly, appreciating the intersection of globalization and cultural forces is imperative in equipping managers with the tools required to foster global success (N/A, 2004) (Figure 1.8).

The importance of globalization extends beyond the cultural, reaching each and every level of management's strategic planning. As firms deal with the complexities of international markets, consciousness of the global economic landscape and its specifics is extremely critical. This necessitates a shift towards more adaptive and responsive managerial techniques that focus on innovation and adaptability to changing market demands. Second, the emphasis on strategic alignment between worldwide programs and local execution adds yet another dimension of complexity, necessitating managers to strike a subtle balance between standardization and localization. By cultivating an environment of agility and learning, organizations can place themselves better positioned to respond to the ever-evolving challenges of globalization. Therefore, the foundations of global management behaviors ought to be capable of welcoming this new paradigm, adopting integrated strategies that are adaptive to diverse settings and dynamic market conditions, ultimately resulting in organizational resilience and sustainable competitive edge (Cieri et al., 1998).

1.4.1. Definition and Dimensions of Globalization

The multifaceted geography of globalization encompasses numerous dimensions that reflect its large-scale scope and far-reaching implications. It is most appropriately labeled as a process with the accelerating interlinking of world economies, societies, and cultures. It has taken decades to evolve with impacts from expansions of technology and communications, and reconfigurations of political contexts. The importance of globalization to global management behavior is profound; it necessitates managers' understanding of various cultural contexts and economic environments, further impacting their strategic choices. By examining various aspects of globalization, including the economic, political, and cultural dimensions, organizations can be adequately positioned to capitalize on a more intricate global framework. As such, the importance of knowledge in these dimensions becomes essential for managers keen to promote competitive advantage within their organizations (Edgar et al., 2018). The effects of globalization can be observed in the ways with which organizations adapt to the challenges of an interconnected world. As businesses expand globally, they must navigate various regulatory environments and cultural values that necessitate a sophisticated appreciation of contexts. This adaptation gives rise to progressive management styles that are more sensitive and flexible to the trends of the world. The establishment of multinational organizations highlights cross-cultural skills and the necessity for management teams to use measures responding to divergent requirements in an efficient way. Globalization thus compels organizations to implement these practices into their organizational systems. It not only affects the strategic orientation of corporations but also organizational culture and workers' involvement in a multicultural workforce (Bouckaert et al., 2012). Culture also plays an important role in formulating management practices in the context of globalization. As a business firm faces different cultures, the management practiced is typically compatible with local norms, beliefs, and values. Such cultural contacts influence communication, leadership, and decision-making styles in a deep way. For instance, collectivism may be central in some cultures and demand that managers prioritize group consensus over individual effort. Elsewhere, in more individualistic cultures, assertiveness and individual achievement may be publicly encouraged and valued. The result is a rich interactive process in which not only does managerial practice become open to cultural demands, but employee performance and motivations also become affected. Thus, familiarity with the dimensions of culture is essential for managers who seek to encourage effective co-operation and build a unifying organizational culture in the wake of globalization (Edgar et al., 2018).

1.4.2. Effects on Organizational Structures

Organizational forms are naturally shaped by both external and internal realities, which impact the form under which an organization operates. As the world continues to globalize and transform the business landscape, organizations are compelled to continually evolve their forms in a bid to remain competitive globally. This ongoing change calls for a more flexible form of management, which is challenging firms to rethink traditional hierarchies and embrace more decentralized forms. For instance, as companies go global, they may opt to use organizational forms that are networked in order to facilitate speedy communication and decision-making across borders. The challenge is ensuring inter-alignment of various cultural expectations and working practices in such arrangements, illustrating the critical role played by strategic management in creating effective organizational arrangements. Lastly, the influence of globalization on organizational design highlights the imperative of a versatile management approach capable of coping with diversity and yet maintaining cohesiveness and effectiveness. Cultural forces form a decisive determinant of organizational designs because they directly determine worker behavior and expectations within the workplace. Cross-cultural environments produce varied responses to management practices, which can lead to significant variations in employee engagement and organizational performance. For example, collectivistic cultures may build a culture that emphasizes cooperation, and therefore has a flatter organizational profile. An extremely individualistic culture, however, may reinforce hierarchical structures, whereby clear lines of authority define organizational dynamics. This is why the ability of leaders to appreciate these cultural nuances is essential in building an environment of cooperation where one may be able to galvanize productivity (Figure 1.9).

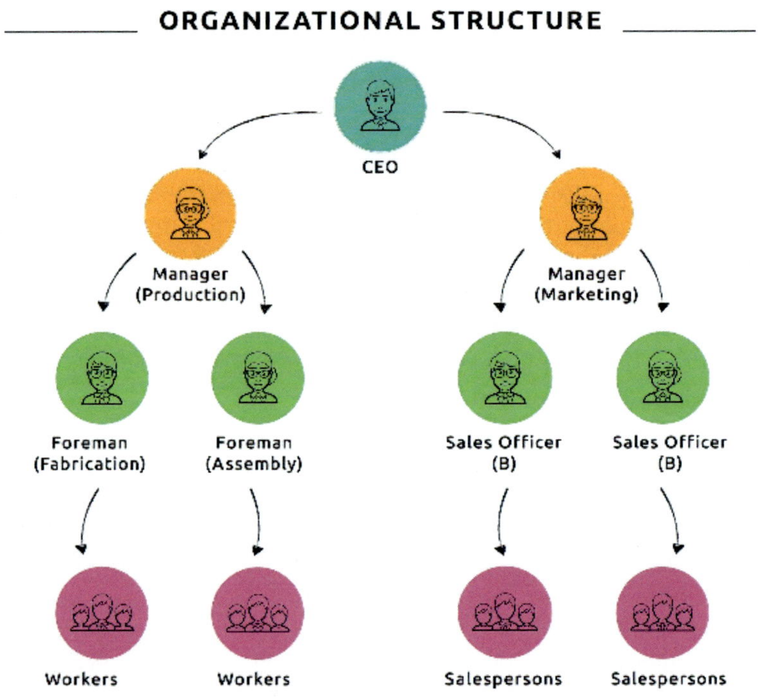

Figure 1.9. Importance of organizational structure.

Source: https://digitalleadership.com/wp-content/uploads/2022/11/Organizational-Structure.webp.

Since organizations are confronted with the imperative of adopting multiple views of culture, organizational structures and management behaviors become more complex, and it becomes increasingly imperative to recognize the role of culture in system interactions. Compensation systems are also a critical element that affects organizational structures since they lie at the heart of the employment relationship and significantly influence motivation and turnover among employees. The philosophies and practices of remuneration can reflect more deep-seated organizational values and make an impact on structural configurations. As per the employment exchanges literature, providing valuable inducements is vital in order to generate desired employee role conduct (Gerhart et al., 1991). But with all these compensation strategies now available—such as competency pay or team pay—organizations are faced with the challenge of critically examining which systems best complement their structural design and employee characteristics (Bloom et al., 1995). Through deliberate use of compensation programs, organizations can create a more coherent and committed workforce as well as facilitate alignment of their structures with strategic objectives. This reiterates the interconnectedness of reward practices, organizational structure, and culture as drivers in producing effective global management behaviors.

1.4.3. Challenges and Opportunities for Managers

In contemporary management, the interconnectedness of different factors requires that managers lead in a compound environment defined by globalization, technological advancement, and cultural diversity. The escalating interconnectedness of markets enables organizations to go beyond their typical boundary constraints, providing opportunities for expansion and innovation. This internationalization is marred by drawbacks, such as the acquisition of cross-cultural competencies and strategic adaptability in reacting to different market environments. Managers must respond to these dynamics with creative practice that not only captures emerging trends but also draws upon the creative resources of an international workforce. Confronting these challenges entails designing responsive strategies able to effectively integrate local knowledge and wider corporate objectives, hence linking innovation with globalized market needs (N/A, 2018).

Organizational crossing of borders necessitates a profound cultural influence understanding, framing managerial practices and worker relationships. Culture has a far-reaching impact on norms and behavioral expectations that require managers to employ culturally sensitive leadership styles that foster respect and inclusivity. Managers' awareness of culture enables them to build cohesive groups that not only acknowledge but appreciate cultural difference. The ability to negotiate the cultural intricacies of work can lead to improved employee motivation and organizational performance. Besides, it also offers an opportunity to innovate by crafting diverse perspectives that enhance creativity and problem-solving abilities. Managers who establish a culturally aware environment have the ability to reveal immense competitive advantage, leading to organizational success in the world (Margaret et al., 2018). Moreover, the technological advances are altering the managerial responsibilities, bringing both immense opportunities and daunting challenges. Technology facilitates effective communication, collaborative workspaces, and fact-based decision-making, giving managers a device for streamlining operations and raising productivity. The rapid pace of technological change requires managers to be continually adaptable, adding new skills and acquiring new techniques, as well. In order to optimize the application of these tools, managers must establish learning-oriented organizational culture that fosters flexibility and coping. By fostering a culture of continuous improvement and innovation, managers can facilitate the adoption of technology as a means of enhancing their performance. Ultimately, being adaptable to technological advancements will solidify managers' roles as important leaders in guiding the future of their firms in a more diversified global landscape (N/A, 2018).

1.5. THE ROLE OF CULTURE IN SHAPING BEHAVIOR

The intricate dynamics of cultural forces shape individual and collective behavior in organizational environments and underscore the need to understand culture in global management. With increasing globalization of the corporate landscape, organizations are faced with new challenges in cross-cultural navigation of diverse structures. Building multinational teams offers Varied perspectives that add power to issue-solving and innovation but demand a delicate balance of knowledge and adaptability. For instance, communication patterns, decision-making, and conflict management are shaped by culture and often vary significantly from those in the West. Management experts must then acquire cultural intelligence that will enable leaders to balance their plans with native customs but maintain organizational objectives. Disregard for these cultural differences can lead to misunderstanding and inefficiency that stifles cooperation and productivity and, in turn, affects organizational success in an age of globalization. One significant aspect of the cultural role is its role as a trust determinant in organizational relations. Trust constructs differ substantially across cultures, as evidenced by research into building trust among employees in Turkey and China. It demonstrated that while underlying precepts such as Ability, Benevolence, and Integrity were present, their expression of Benevolence was culturally conditioned and a chief contributor to building trust among various organizational dyads (Figure 1.10).

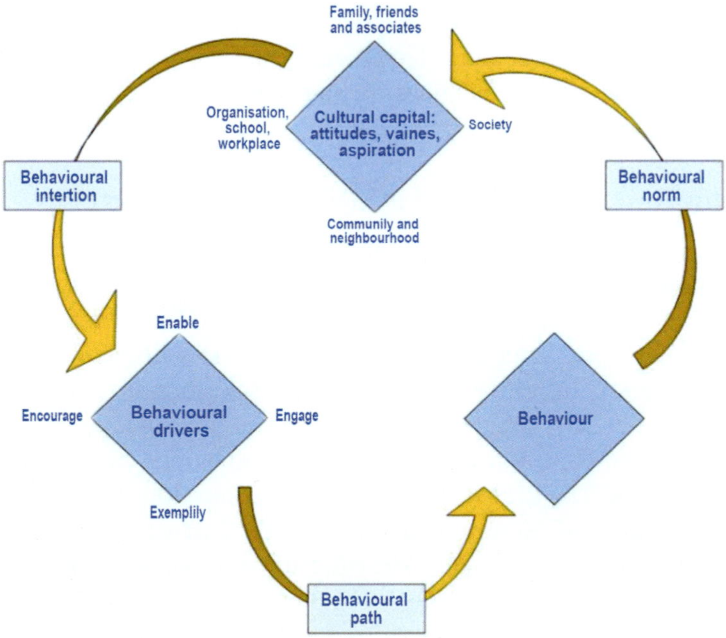

Figure 1.10. Cultural change in an organization.

Source: https://assets.coursehero.com/study-guides/lumen/images/boundless-management/shaping-organizational-culture/culture-change-model1.jpeg.

This comment points out the manner in which trust combines with more than merely professionally technical interactions, uniting individual experience and cultural values with the workplace. It also makes explicit the necessity for international managers to transfer their trust-building techniques in ways that resonate within local cultural paradigms so that management practices resonate with the underlying values and beliefs of various workers, resulting in conformity and commitment throughout the workforce. Furthermore, development of effective cultures in high-performance organizations tests the impact of culture on behavioral outcomes. From a decentered vantage, a full analysis of effective programs of cultural change, such as that of English Rugby Union's Leeds Carnegie, illustrates the subtle processes that shape organizational cultures. This case study provides an example of the managerial function of strategically impacting the psychosocial environment surrounding team dynamics indirectly, providing a context for healthy behavioral growth. Through power dynamics management and building a supportive context, leadership can in fact foster a shared culture that supports organizational goals. Therefore, the key takeout is that cultural awareness is not a theoretical endeavor; it is a hands-on imperative across the board for management. Organizations need to adopt these cultural drivers in order to create behavior toward sustainable performance and achievement in an increasingly globalized and dynamic marketplace.

1.5.1. Definition of Culture in a Management Context

In the changing context of international management, understanding what culture is all about is of great significance to managers. With companies spreading across frontiers, varied cultural traditions are encountered that influence management attitudes and business strategies. Culture, in this context, is not merely an environment but a core performance and employee engagement driver. The use of cultural nuances in management practice enhances communication and provides a sense of belonging for employees of different cultures. The knowledge allows leaders to adjust their strategy in turn. The recognition of culture as a fundamental part of the functioning of an organization is instrumental in addressing the complexities engendered by globalization, and leaders therefore learn to create inclusive environments that respect and benefit from cultural diversity. Leadership style plays a significant role in organizational culture development and maintenance in the global environment. Transformational leaders play a crucial role in establishing an effective culture that promotes knowledge sharing and innovation in diverse teams. They act as change agents to establish a sound organizational culture in conformity with international norms but with respect for local cultures. The complementary relationship between culture and leadership is also necessary because the latter directly influences workers' behavior and attitude toward organizational alignment and knowledge sharing. Such a complementary relationship is even more pressing as companies confront the rapid face of globalization that necessitates flexibility and broad acquaintance with cultural differences. Combining leadership strategy with cultural considerations thus gives rise to organizational knowledge and effectiveness, the secret of successful international management. In the case of family business, the cultural dynamics gain additional dimensions that further complicate the management complexities. Leadership styles within such firms tend to imitate family values and relational traits that affect knowledge sharing and organizational conduct. Empirical research has indicated that the family influence tends to affect beliefs on knowledge-sharing climates and differentiate them from other business models. This intersection between leadership intention and family dynamics occurs in various forms, generating contrasting styles, such as organization-focused participation versus family-led guidance. Such cultural stories must be decoded by family business leaders, as they highlight the role of context in playing a part in shaping management tendencies. By combining these cultural findings, leaders are best suited to sharpen their strategies with the aim of optimizing both organizational and family impacts for realization of sustainability and growth in the broader contexts of globalization.

1.5.2. Cultural Dimensions and Their Impact on Management

With the business internationalization, cultural dimension knowledge becomes crucial for successful management. Global managers must navigate different cultural expectations that affect behavior and organizational functioning. This not only enhances the ability to manage teams with contrasting cultural orientations but also sets up a facilitative context for collaboration and innovation. The study in Ghasabeh et al.)2017) emphasizes transformational leadership in creating an organizational culture embracing diversity of perspectives. By engaging proactively with such cultural elements, leaders can set the context for their organizational knowledge, ensuring that they foster an adaptability and learning culture required in the current global economy. This is a strategy that demands both leadership and cultural insight that prepares organizations to thrive despite the rising challenge of globalization. The effect of globalization on management schools of thought cannot be downplayed. As businesses expand across borders, they are exposed to an incredible diversity of cultural practices and societal norms that influence their policies of operation. The dynamic interaction of different dimensions of culture is likely to shape management practices, employee motivational strategies, and decision-making processes in multinational firms. Moreover, as Eaves et al. (2013) emphasizes, one must understand the complexity of knowledge creation in diverse settings in order to manage accordingly. It is required of leaders to integrate cultural knowledge into plans so that they can tap into local knowledge and facilitate innovation. Festivals of cultural diversity can provide competitive advantage through the exchange of ideas and enhancing flexibility in employees, ultimately leading to organizational effectiveness in the global market. In order to successfully serve the intricacies of international management, it is necessary to understand the role of culture in influencing behaviors and expectations in organizations. Coordination of management practices with culture enhances a cohesive work culture that values the differences among people, thereby building team cohesion and morale. From the evidence indicated in Ghasabeh et al. (2017), transformational leaders are key to enacting such cultural values in their respective organizations. Through developing open communication and learning culture, these leaders can easily ensure the connection between cultural dimensions and management practices. It is here that organizations can apply cultural insight to make their strategies locally appropriate, with a culture in which employees are empowered and appreciated, ultimately ensuring organizational prosperity in multicultural settings.

1.5.3. Strategies for Managing Cultural Differences

The expansion of globalization has played a revolutionary role in transforming management practices across cultures, demanding an intimate understanding of how cultural differences affect organizational dynamics. As businesses expand globally, they are confronted with dissimilar cultural practices, beliefs, and values that demand tailored management practices. To tackle these differences effectively, global managers must adopt an elastic approach in recognizing and embracing local practices while integrating them with corporate visions. This methodology shifts the emphasis from a rigid, essentialist view of culture to one that is sensitive to the complexity and permeability of cultural identities, as addressed in the critique of post-structuralist political theory in cultural management contexts (Angouri et al., 2009). This definition highlights the importance of identity, difference, and interaction in building management practices that are culturally attentive and responsive. Moreover, the role of intercultural learning plays a vital role in forming effective global partnerships. Continual learning on diverse cultural traditions may be able to enhance the efficiency of organizations, improve communication, and establish trust between multicultural teams. An intercultural learning model for the real world, developed based on extensive research, describes ways for managers to apply their knowledge of differences in culture in making decisions, thus fostering collaboration and cooperation (Reid et al., 2009). With cultural competence on the rise, organizations find themselves overcoming the barriers of divergent thinking, and thus transforming potential friction into potential for innovation. Consequently, creating a climate where employees are encouraged to become familiar and learn from other cultural backgrounds can enhance overall organizational performance and responsiveness. Last, employing strategic frameworks that focus on cultural consciousness not only enriches the culture of the organization but also fuels outward business relationships. Global managers must establish a culture where cultural differences are not perceived as liabilities but as assets. They must establish effective communication channels and foster sensitivity to cultural nuances that will affect negotiations and partnerships. By giving teams the capacity to identify and appreciate differences in cultures, corporations can enhance their positioning in a globalizing economy. As has been noted, the ability to manage cultural differences effectively is a direct factor in the achievement of competitive advantage, culminating in long-term expansion and success in international markets (Reid et al., 2009). In such a situation, strategy formulation that embraces cultural diversity stands as a key tenet in the context of international management practices.

1.6. ETHICAL CONSIDERATIONS IN INTERNATIONAL MANAGEMENT

In the globalized context of international management, the ethical dimensions are open to increasingly intense scrutiny, requesting an arrangement which involves corporate governance as well as sensitivity to cultures. Globalization, as it has entwined economies, has produced multi-dimensional challenges where firms operate in diverse cultural environments. These demands understanding the variation in ethical guidelines and the potential implications of decisions taken in one place or another. As organizations go global, they are confronted with varying regulatory needs and ethical expectations, which consequently make the process of moral decision-making more complex. Adequate consideration for these aspects means a commitment to ethical processes as opposed to just compliance to ensure genuine corporate responsibility in various markets. Establishing the organizational culture based on the fundamental values is essential to mitigate risks involved with cross-cultural miscommunications and eventual success in the international setting. The role that culture plays in affecting management practices cannot be overstated, as it necessarily influences ethical perception and conduct within diverse societies (Figure 1.11).

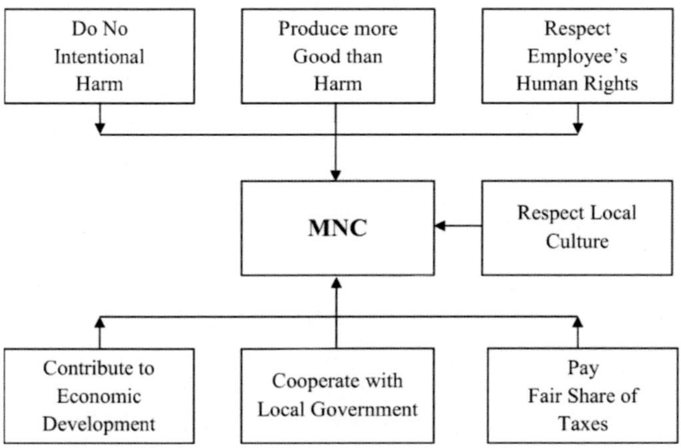

Figure 1.11. Socio-ethical issues and international management.

Source: https://media.springernature.com/lw685/springer-static/image/chp%3A10.1007%2F978-3-319-96622-9_2/MediaObjects/978-3-319-96622-9_2_Fig2_HTML.png.

An awareness of the cultural dimensions, i.e., power distance and individualism vs. collectivism, enables international managers to anticipate what the reactions of indigenous stakeholders are likely to be to their actions. Consequently, ethical dilemmas then often arise when corporate values of a firm meet with conflict with the indigenous norms and open up a potential space between usual practices and ethical responsibility. For instance, openness in a company may be at odds with cultures where establishing relationships requires confidentiality in matters of business. International managers are thus important to be considerate of cultural backgrounds while enhancing ethical congruence. Embracing diversity in non-culture entities not only enhances ethics but also enhances organizational flexibility and perseverance, essential in today's rapidly changing globalized business environment. Besides that, global management ethics also address broader effects of business activities on host communities and the environment. With businesses engaging with global supply chains, they must keep in mind the ethical consequences of their production and sourcing decisions, particularly in low- and middle-income economies. The application of concepts such as the circular economy is one potential path for organizations seeking to balance profitability with social and environmental responsibility. Any attempts at this, however, must be subject to close scrutiny to determine that they are not instances of greenwashing, whereby firms promote green programs with unforeseen but harmful impacts on communities and the environment. As these debates around health systems within such environments have pointed out, low-quality care has the potential to wreak havoc on populations, and international managers consequently have a mandate to seek not only economic objectives but also moral efforts that create shared value for all parties concerned (Velenturf et al., 2021; Margaret et al., 2018).

1.6.1. Importance of Ethics in Global Business

The dynamic business culture of international business increasingly emphasizes the central role of ethics in framing effective management models. With organizations expanding across the world, the similar cultural values and legal frameworks make it a demand for an expressed manner of making ethical choices. Business leaders must navigate their paths through these complexities by establishing ethical cultures that resonate across different settings. For instance, effective leadership is contingent on authentic and ethical practices' values, which directly impact organizational effectiveness. Ethical decision-making in this case does not involve a focus on compliance but involves looking into the long-term effects of business practices on stakeholders and communities. Authentic, ethical, and transformational leadership behaviors are necessary, whose substantial contribution to leader effectiveness and, by extension, organizational success cannot be overemphasized (Copeland et al., 2016). Lastly, global managers must integrate these ethical requirements into their vision plan, including a feeling of responsibility and integrity. The intersection of globalization and ethics brings into relief the importance of firms establishing sound structures that focus on ethical behavior. As firms extend their reach globally, they must confront varied ethical dilemmas depending on differences in customary and regulatory practices. To guarantee competitive advantage, not only must companies maintain legal frameworks, but they must also take up a sense of responsibility towards the enforcement of ethical values similar to their core business (Figure 1.12).

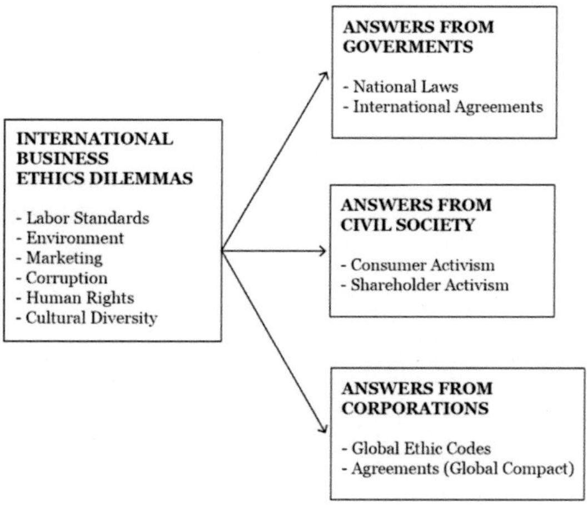

Figure 1.12. Answers from practitioners to the moral dilemmas of global business.

Source: https://cdnintech.com/media/chapter/60620/1512345123/media/F1.png.

Emphasis on environmentally conscious practices is important, especially in regions where ethical concerns will be minimized due to economic restrictions. It has been established through studies that ethical value underpins the achievement of sustainability in various industries, such that firms with a passion for ethical practice are expected to excel in competitive business (Hasani et al., 2025). By implementing ethical values at all levels of management, organizations can manage the intricacies of globalization while reinforcing their social obligations. The impact of culture in influencing ethical conduct cannot be underestimated since varying cultural values have a great bearing on corporate conduct in different regions. Recognizing these cultural sensitivities is important for successful international management since it enables businesses to develop strategies that capture local sentiments. World business ethics is not uniform; variations in perceptions of culture necessitate tailored responses in decision-making. There is a need for managers to cultivate cultural sensitivity and understanding of different ethical paradigms, which can encourage cooperation and harmony within multicultural teams. This is especially important in the establishment of a culture where employees feel at liberty to voice ethical concerns without fear of retribution. Through a more inclusive ethical culture, organizations can mitigate risks and enhance their global reputation, ultimately leading to long-term success and growth in an increasingly connected world.

1.6.2. Cross-Cultural Ethical Dilemmas

The intricacies of global management are directly affected by globalization, linking different cultures and economies into one global landscape. Under such a setting, firms normally experience cross-cultural ethical dilemmas that arise when competing cultural norms and values intersect. As firms expand to emerging markets, balancing local traditions and established corporate ethics is an essential challenge. The socio-economic drivers involved call for a sense of understanding of the way in which cultural context influences decision-making. Such sensitivity is able to facilitate the formulation of effective strategies for navigating ethical complexities, thus creating sustainable practice in different cultural contexts. Such adaptability is central to creating trust and credibility in global markets, thus ultimately realizing successful management results in an era of globalization (Hubert et al., 2004). Effective management is not only a matter of having knowledge of ethical standards but also of being able to engage in effective dialogue on diverse moral standards. Employees, particularly Western expatriates, may find themselves in liminal states where their notion of ethics is in contradiction to local tradition. Through this condition, knowledge of the transitional condition may help an instrumental use of coping strategies, easing individuals through the contradiction between local tradition and Western ethical standards. By situating such cross-cultural contact within rites of passage, companies can assist employees in developing the competencies required to navigate ethical dilemmas (Figure 1.13).

This approach can illuminate the paths to sustainable adaptation in multicultural settings, ultimately enhancing personal and organizational resilience in the context of competing ethical paradigms (Costa et al., 2025). On top of that, organizations which focus on cross-cultural training and ethical sensitivity can develop an organizational culture that appreciates diversity and fosters effective communication. This pro-active strategy not only alleviates the ethical dilemmas that are caused by differential cultural practices but also improves decision making by pooling varied wisdom. Appreciation of the consequences of cross-cultural variations for ethical frameworks is indispensable if managers are to forge inclusion and minimize conflict possibilities. As companies strive to thrive in a rapidly globalizing world, the capacity to cope with cross-cultural ethical challenges surfaces as a success factor determinant. Lastly, global management practices develop based on the assurance of ethical integrity across various cultures to ensure that companies can operate effectively in any foreign environment (Hubert et al., 2004).

Figure 1.13. Credibility in international markets.

Source: https://www.mci.edu/images/2024/08/19/mci-executive-education-header-mba-international-management-Cmci-christian-kasper.jpg.

1.6.3. Frameworks for Ethical Decision-Making

The interconnectedness and complexities of today's business environment necessitate a critical scrutiny of ethical models in global management. Globalization's ever-deepening expansion across various areas continues to drive organizations toward inevitable confrontations with global ethical challenges. Thus, ethical decision-making models have evolved to encompass the multifaceted pool of global cultural contexts and social norms to equip managers to deal with moral ambiguities more appropriately. The value of such frameworks lies not only in establishing effective management practices but also fostering organizational legitimacy within the global environment. The need for ethical accuracy is brought into focus by the rise in social and digital marketing, which has transformed consumer interaction and the moral responsibilities of brands, emphasizing the need for responsible conduct and communication, informing action that adapts to stakeholders' expectations (Yogesh et al., 2020). A systematic analysis of ethical decision-making models reveals their background role in establishing behaviors across different cultural settings. Systems are progressively recognizing the significant impact of cultural influences on ethical perceptions and decisions. Utilitarianism, deontology, and virtue ethics are a few of the models that present variegated perspectives which can be customized according to the unique requirements of global markets. Such frameworks not only facilitate ethical thinking but also foster a corporate culture founded on social responsibility and integrity. For instance, the moral implications of electronic marketing practices prompt managers to address issues of consumer privacy and brand representation in a culturally appropriate manner (Yogesh et al., 2020). By integrating these frameworks into global management policies, companies can develop a more ethical and inclusive method of conducting business, thereby enhancing their competitive advantage. Separately from the globalization factor, the relationship between ethical decision-making frameworks and cultural values demands keen observation. Culture affects people beliefs, values, and actions, which in turn determine their perceptions regarding what is ethical or unethical. Therefore, a method of universal ethical decision-making may be inadequate; organizational leaders must be attuned to regional cultural differences underpinning ethical norms. An integration of knowledge from social sciences can provide greater understanding of such human factors, which play a key role in implementing useful ethical policies and practices. By embracing cultural variation and applying ethical principles appropriate to distinctive contexts, international managers are able not only to manage ethical issues more effectively but also to establish a culture of ethical differentiation within their firms, achieving more legitimate and potent outcomes on the global stage.

SUMMARY

In examining the evolution of management behaviors globally, it is evident that management has been influenced significantly by cultural forces and globalization. When organizations expand their business globally, it is essential to understand various cultural frameworks in order to manage effectively. Cultural values and management practice shape employees' behaviors, decision-making patterns, and communication styles. This is compounded in the multinational firm where managers must cope with a multicultural weave of expectations. The foundation of international management behaviors must therefore change in order to move forward and meet these nuances; being aware that what is acceptable in one cultural context is not another. This integrated understanding not just facilitates smoother operations but also enhances organizational effectiveness, cultivating inclusive and respectful culture that has the potential to unleash the possibilities of diversified human capital. Organizational theory findings emphasize the importance of paradoxical practices in achieving ambidexterity, particularly in global contexts. By the practice of hybrid tasks and learning-evoking environment, individual ambidexterity beyond the traditional operating boundaries can be cultivated by management. The ability to balance exploitation and exploration is central to organizations that aim to ensure competitive advantage in different markets. Moreover, the emphasis on synergies among competing requirements is also compatible with the requirement for synthesizing organizational goals with culturally relevant practices. These models of strategic management can potentially ensure more adaptability and responsiveness to the altering needs of international markets. While organizations synthesize such approaches, they lay the ground for creative behaviors required in today's increasingly interconnected business world, ultimately cementing the relevance of merging cultural intelligence into management. In conclusion, the pillars of global management behaviors are constructed on an ever-evolving interrelation of globalization, diversity, and adaptive practices. With international business constantly evolving its form and shape, the necessity for managers to embrace a culturally empowered methodology is becoming ever more pressing. This requires the challenging of old-guard management models and embracing practices that celebrate diversity and leverage the strengths of different thinking. Lastly, the unification of these elements not just advances the field of international management but also produces responsive organizations that can thrive in the midst of change. With the ability to create an environment where paradoxical practices can thrive, businesses can optimize their potential so that the pillars of management behavior are strong, dynamic, and responsive to the needs of the global market.

The studies of international management behaviors have evolved very rapidly with the increasing complexity of global markets. To be understood properly, its scope and application should be subject to proper analysis keeping in view globalization. When companies expand globally, they must confront various regulatory systems, economic systems, and cultural norms that influence managerial practices dynamically. The interplay between these forces underscores the need for close examination of management practices to firms seeking success in an interconnected world. Beyond that, this change reflects the continuous evolution of management theory and practice that addresses new challenges and opportunities in an integrated economy, emphasizing the role of visionary strategies and adaptive leadership in global business. Of similar concern is the drastic impact of globalization on managerial practices that needs examination of the way different socio-economic factors determine organizational behavior. When firms are now operating globally, they are confronted with different expectations and norms of leadership as well as productivity. The need to develop culturally aware strategies is at the center, as the world not only might be opened up for business but also raise the stakes of managerial decisions across cultures. The organizations that realize and adapt to such differences are likely to achieve competitive advantage in the international business world. By integrating various visions and practices of different cultural settings, global management can foster creativity and organizational effectiveness, and thus reemphasize the importance of building cross-cultural agility in managers and teams. At the core of global management behaviors lies the role of culture as a driver of organizational and individual behavior. Culture not only dictates communication styles and negotiation techniques but, more significantly, underlying management doctrines and paradigms that dictate the way organizations operate. For instance, protocol analysis can further enrich these cultural influences by providing an understanding of the cognitive processes underlying problem-solving activities in different contexts (Nguyen et al., 2006). Secondly, identification and consideration of cultural variables enhance the viability of management strategies because leaders must constantly learn and adapt in order to effectively support their teams. As stressed by the literature, debriefing as an activity is essential in the construction of reflective learning and enhancing sensitivity to potential gaps in performance and thereby promoting a culture of improvement and safety within organizational environments (Alinier et al., 2017). Lastly, an understanding of the intricate tie between management behavior and culture is essential to optimizing performance within an increasingly integrated global world.

REFERENCES

1. Alchian, A. A., Klein, B., Kindleberger, C., Vaitsos, C., Warren-Boulton, F. R., MacDougall, G. D. A., Demsetz, H., et al. (2018). The theory of international business: The role of economic models. https://core.ac.uk/download/151259595.pdf (accessed on 24th September 2025).
2. Alinier, G., & Oriot, D. (2017). *Pocket Book for Simulation Debriefing in Healthcare*. https://core.ac.uk/download/159073196.pdf (accessed on 24th September 2025).
3. Alvarez, C., Arnone, M., Avolio, B., Avolio, C., Baligh, H., Balkundi, P., Benne, K., et al. (2011). Alternative approaches for studying shared and distributed leadership. https://core.ac.uk/download/9637547.pdf (accessed on 24th September 2025).
4. Alvesson, M., Bandura, A., Seaman, C., Davenport, T. H., McGuire, D., Dixon, M. L., et al. (2016). Perceptions of knowledge sharing among small family firm leaders: A structural equation model. https://core.ac.uk/download/293861880.pdf (accessed on 24th September 2025).
5. Amabile, T., Bentham, J., Foucault, M., Haslam, S. A., Heath, C., Kotter, J., Kotter, J., et al. (2013). Culture change in a professional sports team: Shaping environmental contexts and regulating power. https://core.ac.uk/download/16415365.pdf (accessed on 24th September 2025).
6. Angouri, J., & Glynos, J. (2009). Managing cultural diversity in the multinational corporate workplace: Solution or symptom? https://core.ac.uk/download/9341781.pdf (accessed on 24th September 2025).
7. Barney, J., Chen, G., Doney, P., Gargiulo, M., Gillespie, N., Hampden-Turner, C., Hofstede, G., et al. (2010). Antecedents of trust across foci: A comparative study of Turkey and China. https://core.ac.uk/download/pdf/11741788.pdf (accessed on 24th September 2025).
8. Belk, R., Garry, T., & Harwood, T. (2019). Design fiction diegetic prototyping: A research framework for visualizing service innovations. https://core.ac.uk/download/287585709.pdf (accessed on 24th September 2025).
9. Bennett, N., Roth, R., Klain, S. C., Chan, K. M. A., Christie, P., Clark, D. A., Cullman, G., et al. (2016). Conservation social science: Understanding and integrating human dimensions to improve conservation. Biological Conservation, 205, 93–108. https://doi.org/10.1016/j.biocon.2016.10.006 (accessed on 24th September 2025).
10. Bloom, M. C., & Milkovich, G. T. (1995). Issues in managerial compensation research. https://core.ac.uk/download/5128496.pdf (accessed on 24th September 2025).

11. Bouckaert, L., & Zsolnai, L. (2012). Spirituality and business: An interdisciplinary overview. https://core.ac.uk/download/12355661.pdf (accessed on 24th September 2025).
12. Buhalis, D., Harwood, T., Bogicevic, V., Viglia, G., Beldona, S., & Hofacker, C. F. (2019). Technological disruptions in services: Lessons from tourism and hospitality. *Journal of Service Management, 30*, 484–506. https://doi.org/10.1108/josm-12-2018-0398 (accessed on 24th September 2025).
13. Copeland, M. K. (2016). The impact of authentic, ethical, transformational leadership on leader effectiveness. https://core.ac.uk/download/81665710.pdf (accessed on 24th September 2025).
14. Costa, A. C., Arrow, K., Das, T. K., Deutsch, M., et al. (2007). Trust and control interrelations: New perspectives on the trust control nexus. https://core.ac.uk/download/337130.pdf (accessed on 24th September 2025).
15. Costa, N. G., & Cunha, M. P. e. (2025). The ethical dilemma of expatriates in emerging economies: A liminal perspective. https://core.ac.uk/download/pdf/6776156.pdf (accessed on 24th September 2025).
16. De Cieri, H., Cox, J. W., & Fenwick, M. (1998). Representing strategic international human resource management: Is the map the territory? https://core.ac.uk/download/5124432.pdf (accessed on 24th September 2025).
17. Dooley, L. B., & Luca, E. (2025). The role of inter-organizational leadership in agri-food value chains. https://core.ac.uk/download/pdf/6457696.pdf (accessed on 24th September 2025).
18. Dwivedi, Y. K., Ismagilova, E., Hughes, D. L., Carlson, J., Filieri, R., Jacobson, J., Jain, V., et al. (2020). Setting the future of digital and social media marketing research: Perspectives and research propositions. *International Journal of Information Management, 59*, 102168–102168. https://doi.org/10.1016/j.ijinfomgt.2020.102168 (accessed on 24th September 2025).
19. Eaves, S., & Walton, J. (2013). An introduction to STRIKE: STRuctured Interpretation of the Knowledge Environment. https://core.ac.uk/download/18407764.pdf (accessed on 24th September 2025).
20. Edgar, D., Sakkas, N., & Yfanti, S. (2018). Clustering tales from the Greek construction sector: Lessons from experience. https://core.ac.uk/download/293884200.pdf (accessed on 24th September 2025).
21. Elbasha, T., & Wright, A. (2017). Reconciling structure and agency in strategy-as-practice research: Towards a strong-structuration theory

approach. https://core.ac.uk/download/131316783.pdf (accessed on 24th September 2025).

22. Fedele, L., Brunese, P. A., McComb, S., & Simpson, V. L. (2019). An interprofessional, intercultural, immersive short-term study abroad program: Public health and service systems in Rome. https://core.ac.uk/download/196295637.pdf (accessed on 24th September 2025).
23. Fiennes, C. (2016). *Effective Philanthropy: Towards a Research Agenda–A White Paper*. https://core.ac.uk/download/75784407.pdf (accessed on 24th September 2025).
24. Galloway, D., Locke, R., Parker, L., Sloan, D., et al. (2015). The game jam movement: Disruption, performance and artwork. https://core.ac.uk/download/228178555.pdf (accessed on 24th September 2025).
25. Gerhart, B. A., & Milkovich, G. T. (1991). Employee compensation: Research and practice. https://core.ac.uk/download/5129129.pdf (accessed on 24th September 2025).
26. Ghasabeh, M. S., & Provitera, M. J. (2017). Transformational leadership: Building an effective culture to manage organizational knowledge. https://core.ac.uk/download/144553701.pdf (accessed on 24th September 2025).
27. Griffiths, C., Kotlarsky, J., & Willcocks, L. P. (2009). Beyond BRIC: Offshoring in non-BRIC countries: Egypt–A new growth market: An LSE Outsourcing Unit report January 2009. https://core.ac.uk/download/2799732.pdf (accessed on 24th September 2025).
28. Hasani, A., Mojaveri, H. R. S., & Mojaveri, M. A. (2025). An investigation of challenges in managerial ethics and its role in sustainable development of Iranian industries. https://core.ac.uk/download/pdf/6231460.pdf (accessed on 24th September 2025).
29. Heracleous, L. Th., & Papachroni, A. (2020). Ambidexterity as practice: Individual ambidexterity through paradoxical practices. https://core.ac.uk/download/287606241.pdf (accessed on 24th September 2025).
30. Hubert, B., Ison, R. L., Jiggins, J., Roggero, M., et al. (2004). The SLIM (Social Learning for the Integrated Management and Sustainable Use of Water at Catchment Scale) final report. https://core.ac.uk/download/248441.pdf (accessed on 24th September 2025).
31. Keys, T. R. (2012). Behaviors that eliminate health disparities for racial and ethnic minorities: A narrative systematic review. https://core.ac.uk/download/56703666.pdf (accessed on 24th September 2025).
32. Koufteros, X., Dabic, M., Gonzalez-Loureiro, M., Saenz, M. J., & Kiessling, T. (2015). Supply chain management as the key to a firm's

strategy in the global marketplace. https://core.ac.uk/download/30650361.pdf (accessed on 24th September 2025).

33. Kruk, M. E., Gage, A., Arsenault, C., Jordan, K., Leslie, H. H., Roder-DeWan, S., Adeyi, O., et al. (2018). High-quality health systems in the Sustainable Development Goals era: Time for a revolution. The Lancet Global Health, 6, e1196–e1252. https://doi.org/10.1016/s2214-109x(18)30386-3 (accessed on 24th September 2025).
34. Ng, C. N., Scott, S., Si, Z., Wang, Y., et al. (2015). The transformation of trust in China's alternative food networks: Disruption, reconstruction, and development. https://core.ac.uk/download/157835060.pdf (accessed on 24th September 2025).
35. Nguyen, L., & Shanks, G. (2006). Using protocol analysis to explore the creative requirements engineering process. http://hdl.handle.net/10536/DRO/DU:30008101 (accessed on 24th September 2025).
36. Reid, S. (2009). The learning process model for intercultural partnerships. https://core.ac.uk/download/46444.pdf (accessed on 24th September 2025).
37. Stetson, A., & Kramer, M. R. (2008). A brief guide to the law of mission investing for U.S. foundations. https://core.ac.uk/download/71341116.pdf (accessed on 24th September 2025).
38. Tansley, C. (2011). What do we mean by the term "talent" in talent management? https://core.ac.uk/download/30630257.pdf (accessed on 24th September 2025).
39. Toropova, A., Myrberg, E., & Johansson, S. (2020). Teacher job satisfaction: The importance of school working conditions and teacher characteristics. *Educational Review, 73*, 71–97. https://doi.org/10.1080/00131911.2019.1705247 (accessed on 24th September 2025).
40. Velenturf, A. P. M., & Purnell, P. (2021). Principles for a sustainable circular economy. *Sustainable Production and Consumption, 27*, 1437–1457. https://doi.org/10.1016/j.spc.2021.02.018 (accessed on 24th September 2025).

Chapter 2

Understanding Culture and Global Mindset

Contents

INTRODUCTION

In a more globalized world, the complexities of international management demand an intimate understanding of culture. This encompasses the patterns of behavior, values, and social norms which dominate in various groups. The subtleties of cultural frameworks extend beyond sensitization; they demand cognitive interaction with abstracted social and psychological forces that vary dramatically across regions. This interplay of dimensions impacts not just individual-to-individual relations but also strategic business decision-making within international business scenarios. As companies push into new markets, operating in cultural spaces becomes a necessity, and so the necessity to develop a global mindset that embraces diversity and facilitates easy cross-cultural communication. These measures are important to avoid businesses losing track and lagging behind in an evolving international market. Cultivating global mind involves cultivating an openness to diversity of opinions and sensitivity to the fine distinctions inherent in various cultures. It is not an abstract concept; it is an adaptive set of skills, with which one can successfully lead diverse work teams and innovate. As have been found in previous studies, curiosity drives cross-cultural knowledge development and competence acquisition to facilitate further interaction with cultural realities of the foreign markets (Mikhaylov et al., 2016). Interaction with such cultural diversities not only develops individual competences but also creates organizational capacity for managing cross-border operations. Thus, institutions that promote continuous learning and cultural exchange will be more likely to achieve success in today's global context, pointing to the strategic importance of building a holistic comprehension of cultural processes. Additionally, the importance of cultural sensitivity is again underscored while expanding into new markets with varying cultural and operational models. The various cultural interpretations of business, government, and technology can directly impact market entry strategy and business operations (Lambert et al., 2025). In response to these new cultures, organizations must adapt their strategies to fit new customs and norms. Flexibility is extremely crucial in conflict avoidance and leveraging market opportunity. Therefore, it is imperative that managers embrace a global mindset that not only acknowledges cultural variation but also seeks to leverage them for organizational growth. Summarily, the marrying of cultural awareness and international management strategies paves the way for efficient global engagement, underlining its utilization in contemporary business practice.

Definition of Culture

A concept so multifaceted as culture extends far beyond definitions or superficial traits. At its root, culture is the summed aggregate of patterning in behavior, belief, value, and symbol that characterizes a particular group. This rich tapestry is interwoven into the texture of social life itself and influences everyday practices, occupational modes of communication, and group identity. In global management, understanding these cultural dimensions is crucial, as different cultural settings can significantly impact operational success. The contemporary debate regarding culture is that it is both constant and fluid, continually redefining itself in accordance with globalization and technology. In order to fully appreciate the level of cultural influence, its status as a guiding principle that shapes people's and companies' identities in various international contexts needs to be understood, requiring strategizing around those differences. Additionally, the cognitive, social, and psychological dimensions of culture highlight its significance in international management. Cognitive factors deal with the way individuals perceive and construct their world, and in the process, they can formulate various visions of business behavior and human relations. Social factors include the customs, norms, and traditions that govern action within a culture and encompass patterns of communication, team dynamics, and leadership. Finally, psychological dimension accounts for group and individual sentiment, which in turn influence drives and decision-making processes. Through a global mindset, international managers are more capable of embracing and understanding these diverse cultural perspectives, enabling them to cooperate and innovate across the world. Culture in this context is not merely a backdrop but an imperative structure within which the prospects for organizational success within a globalizing world are delineated. Furthermore, for effective management of the complexities of culture in global management, there is a need to consider broader implications of strategic international human resource management (SIHRM). SIHRM is an evolving science that focuses on marrying the values of human resource management with extensive expertise in cultural diversity. By way of cautious integration of cultural awareness into managerial practices, organizations can develop policies that promote inclusivity and unity. SIHRM not only encourages theory building but also enhances the pedagogic context in which it occurs, asking managers to become reflective practitioners. Culture, as also previously noted, can be both enabler and constraint in international contexts and requires on-going debate about its evolving role in strategy development, practice, and international alliances (Cieri et al., 1998). Lastly, a highly educated approach to cultivation and a commitment to ongoing education will equip global managers to establish a truly equitable and productive international work environment (Chatterjee et al., 2006).

Importance of Culture in International Management

The international management-culture interface is profound and affects many organizational behaviors and decision-making styles. Culture consists of values, beliefs, and practices that define a group and affect not just individual identity but also collective norms that direct managerial conduct. There is a broad body of knowledge about culture that assists international managers in overcoming the complexity of international operations. The mental or intellectual components of culture inform how managers think and perceive and hence strategic decisions. For instance, in large multinational companies, diverse cultural viewpoints could lead to varied styles of problem-solving, offering room for innovation as well as challenges in ensuring goal congruence among teams. It is therefore important to detect and value cultural differences because effective management hinges on the competency of being in a position to integrate these differences into coherent operation strategies while establishing an enabling system that fosters growth. Moreover, building a global mindset is crucial for managers operating in diverse cultures. Not only does a global mindset facilitate flexibility but also enhance the capability to connect to local cultures in ways that matter. This mindset has cognitive, social, and psychological dimensions that equip managers to go global with an integrated approach. For instance, effective communication is primarily rooted in cultural sensitivity where sensitivity to the nuances of language, body language, and practices unique to a country can significantly improve stakeholder relations and team integration. Secondly, it fosters a culture of inclusiveness, inviting individuals with different perspectives to contribute, greater creativity, and problem-solving skills that are essential to competitive success (Figure 2.1).

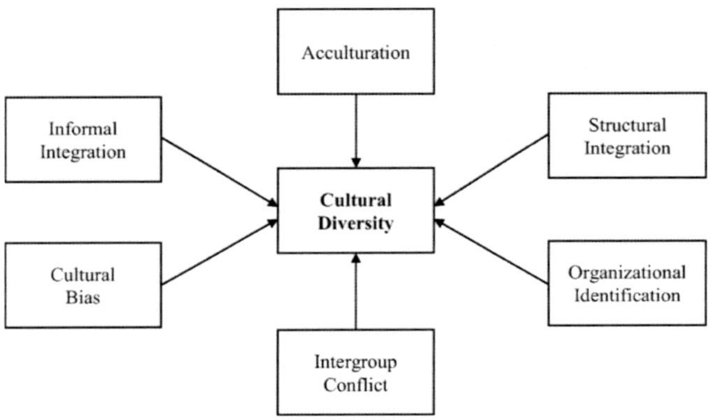

Figure 2.1. International management and the cultural context.

Source: https://media.springernature.com/lw685/springer-static/image/chp%3A10.1007%2F978-3-319-96622-9_3/MediaObjects/978-3-319-96622-9_3_Fig2_HTML.png.

Therefore, acquiring a global mindset is not just a personal issue; it is also an organizational imperative for those companies that want to thrive in the integrated international market. The issues facing international management situations highlight the necessity of constructing strong leadership pipelines, particularly when addressing cultural subtleties. In countries like China, local leaders are taking over from expatriates the roles they have played traditionally, and henceforth, there is a call for developing local leadership on a priority basis. Figures from Aon Hewitt's survey support the trend, with the percentage of multinational corporations (MNCs) replacing expatriates with local talent nearly doubled between the years 2007 and 2010, indicating the need for sustainable leadership development initiatives. Similarly, since turnover levels are much higher than global averages, firms must strategically focus employee retention through ethnically sensitive development programs. Emphasizing key competency demands can allow managers to not only conform to regional cultural sensitivities but also create a work environment where employees feel valued and encouraged, thereby gaining competitive edge in international markets (Kovack et al., 2015; Hackett et al., 2015).

Overview of Global Mindset

The intricateness of culture becomes central in building a global mindset, particularly international management. Culture refers to the common norms, values, and practices of a people, manifesting themselves in forms as varied as language to customs to systems of belief. Building a global mindset involves comprehending and respecting these various cultural characteristics, which are essential to effective collaboration across boundaries. Because globalization continues to make markets interdependent, managers must develop the cognitive, social, and psychological dimensions that will enable them to manage differences between cultures. The ability to identify with and adapt to varying cultural environments fosters communication and fewer misunderstandings, thus ensuring enhanced teamwork and organizational performance in multinational environments. Having a global mindset entails the integration of cognitive, social, and psychological capabilities that allow an individual to perform well in global settings. Cognitive capability involves understanding complex cultural frameworks and embracing how these are able to influence business practices and decision-making protocols. Social capability, on the other hand, addresses the importance of building interpersonal relationships and communication within multicultural settings. By building social awareness, managers are in a stronger position to collaborate and foster teamwork with a variety of groups of individuals. Psychological competence, the final dimension, is one's capacity to mentally and emotionally adjust to multicultural situations, cultivating the type of strength required for overcoming adversity. By going through this multi-dimensional process of constructing a global mindset, one is in a better position to navigate the depth of global management, generating more organizational success. The use of a global mindset is once again indicated by the evolving nature of emerging markets, where multinational corporations are becoming more interested in establishing a presence. As noted, globalization opened the door for multinational corporations to grow their businesses in emerging markets as well as for the local giants of developing countries to move into western markets. These markets offer both special challenges and opportunities, and therefore it is essential that managers possess the skills and knowledge necessary to deal with such environments. It is important for managers to be familiar with the business patterns and institutional settings that define these markets in order to succeed in their expansion efforts. Such an understanding not only enables the creation of sustainable relationships with local stakeholders but also enables strategic alignment with regional market forces, thus creating long-term sustainability in international operations (Serban, 2025). Further, these results complement the practice of the discipline of strategic international human resource management (SIHRM), which is imperative in the identification of the effectiveness of human resource practices in diverse cultural settings (Cieri et al., 1998).

2.1. THE ROLE OF CULTURE IN INTERNATIONAL MANAGEMENT

In the dynamic world of international management, the varied patterns of culture may exert a significant influence on organizational dynamics and strategies. Culture, typically defined as the common values, beliefs, and behaviors that define a group, plays an integral role in defining how businesses are communicated, negotiated, and conducted across boundaries. Understanding these cultural characteristics is crucial for managers who want to develop effective collaboration among different teams. Moreover, as companies go global, they are being asked more and more to consider differences in culture that could have an impact on worker motivation and customer relations. Cultural differences can be minimized by an understanding of them, and that will lead to more harmonious working relationships and eventually better organizational performance and globalization sustainability (Pucik et al., 1996). Building a global perspective requires exposure to multiple cultures but also demands a motivational vision that represents the cognitive, social, and psychological dimensions of cross-cultural relationships. The cognitive aspect involves an understanding of the schemes that direct cultural interpretation, while the social aspect represents the interpersonal dynamics that build up through diverse team relationships. From the psychological aspect, managers should foster emotional sensitivity and empathy to facilitate them handling differences in culture. It is this global mindset creation that allows managers to anticipate challenges and seize opportunities arising in international environments. This thinking ahead is not only useful; it is necessary for the leaders who wish to leverage the full capacities of their multicultural workforce in today's integrated business world (Mikhaylov et al., 2016) (Figure 2.2).

Figure 2.2. Psychological dimensions of cross-cultural interactions.

Source: https://www.businessbecause.com/uploads/default/news/images/1639574377.png.

Empirical research underscores the importance of curiosity in enhancing cross-cultural knowledge and competence sharing within international settings. Organizations that foster a culture of curiosity enable their members to engage more deeply with alternative perspectives, enhancing their consciousness and adaptability within international operations. Such dynamic exchange of cross-cultural knowledge plays a primary function in the support of creative problem-solving and decision-making activities, allowing business organizations to respond well to the quick changes characterizing global markets. Cross-cultural competency building is therefore not only beneficial for individual employees but also significant for business organizations striving to achieve a competitive edge. As globalization continues to redefine business landscapes, the promotion of cultural diversity through learning and inquisitiveness will be the driver of organizational success on the international stage (Pucik et al., 1996; Mikhaylov et al., 2016).

2.1.1. Cultural Dimensions Theory

As part of understanding the interconnectedness of markets in today's globalized economy, cultural appreciation is a requirement. Culture prescribes the values, norms, and practices peculiar to a group that, in turn, shape individual and organizational performance. This embedded framework is used to structure not just interpersonal relations but also international management's strategic decision processes. Having the knowledge of the contribution of cultural dimensions to global business practices can be utilized to design expatriate training and fill communication gaps. Managers can develop approached-tailored strategies taking into account local customs while developing a collaborative and innovation-friendly environment by being sensitized to such dimensions. With cultural dimensions theory, an organization thereby has a platform upon which it can empirically quantify its strategic goals and blend them with the cognitive requirements of different groups of stakeholders (Figure 2.3).

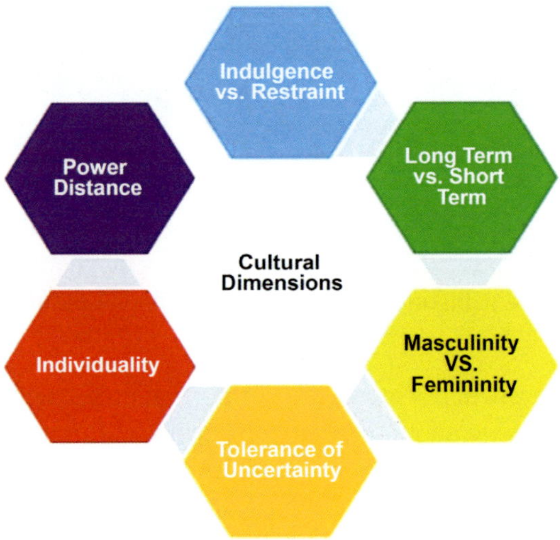

Figure 2.3. The basics of cultural dimensions.

Source: https://mmbgims.com/wp-content/uploads/2019/03/Understanding-Cultures-and-people-with-Hofstede-Dimensions.jpg.

Global mindset implies flexibility and openness to other cultural environments in a way that allows individuals and organizations to effectively operate across boundaries. It involves cognitive and psychological elements that facilitate the comprehension and leverage of various perspectives, and this is most critical when it comes to international management. Global mindset allows managers not only to appreciate multiple cultural orientations but also to leverage cultural intelligence to inform decision-making. This is especially fitting where cultural misunderstandings have the potential to bring about operational inefficiencies or conflict. The integration of cultural dimensions theory into leadership development challenges practitioners to embrace a more refined approach to cultural interactions, which fosters an open-minded climate that recognizes the value of diversity as an operational imperative essential to sustainably succeeding in global markets. Furthermore, when implementing strategic international human resource management (SIHRM), alignment of cultural dimensions is key. Some HRM systems such as global compensation and rewards highlight the importance of adopting a contextual approach to understanding how culture influences organizational effectiveness. The dynamics between HR practices and cultural nuances create windows of opportunity for increasing engagement and retention in multinationals. By identifying the factors revealed in cultural dimensions theory, organizations can develop policies that actually embody local expectations, and therefore guarantee employee satisfaction and performance. The ongoing discussion regarding the relative efficacy of SHRM highlights the importance of fine-tuning theoretical models to accommodate these cultural dimensions so that international management methods continue to be effective and relevant (Cieri et al., 1998; Bloom et al., 1998).

2.1.2. Impact of Culture on Business Practices

Today's globalized economy has prompted businesses to realize that culture is a primary factor in influencing their business strategy and practice. Culture is composed of shared beliefs, values, and traditions that characterize a group, and it influences the way individuals and organizations perceive their world and interact with one another. It is because of this realization that business executives must develop a robust global mindset—a mental framework for dealing with the complexities of several worlds of culture. By fostering such a mindset, leaders become more tolerant of several cultural dimensions, including cognitive, social, and psychological ones that influence behavior across settings. Thus, alteration of business practices to conform to cultural expectations not only makes communication easier but also strengthens relationships with foreign collaborators and, hence, makes negotiations and collaborations more comfortable.

Business globalism has also forced companies to rethink traditional management approaches. Cultural factors influence human resource management practice strongly, conditioning recruitment practice, training practice, and employee involvement practice cross-nationally. Organizational growth in international markets requires understanding the local customs and practices while framing HR policies and strategies. An adaptive approach is necessary, where HR policy and practice locally evolve to address the cultural context of each country. For instance, Pucik et al. (1996) emphasizes that as global interactions increase, organizations must continually review their human resource capabilities in a bid to effectively support extensive business globalization. This adaptability typically includes training programs based on cultural mindset, which enables employees to appreciate diversity as an organizational tool. Finally, as organizations shape global compensation and reward schemes, the impacts of cultural diversity become more pronounced. Differences in cultural attitudes to compensation, praise, and intrinsic motivation present a sensitivity to what drives employee satisfaction across regions. Implementing one remedy will lead to misunderstanding and dissatisfaction with employees, ultimately impacting organizational performance. Evidence shows that when organizations reconsider HRM practices, particularly in the global perspective, they must embrace fuller theories and contextual factors influencing organizational effectiveness and some HRM systems. In this perspective, it aligns with (Bloom et al., 1998), which advocates for a better grasp of how localized variables account for motivating employees across the world. With the adoption of cultural variations in compensation practices, companies are able to develop a diverse workplace culture that fosters commitment and high performance globally.

2.1.3. Case Studies of Cultural Misunderstandings

The complexities that arise as a result of cultural misperceptions largely stem from a lack of appreciation for the cognitive, social, and psychological dimensions of multicultural societies. As individuals with different backgrounds come into interaction, the significations they assign to communication cues, gestures, and context would vary significantly. Such variation can have negative implications in cross-cultural management contexts, where differing expectations can decide the success or failure of collaborative ventures. For instance, an American assertiveness-based business negotiation may be perceived as aggressive by Japanese partners who are focused on harmony and indirectness in communication. Such dissimilar attitudes not only undermine negotiations but may even instill resentment or distrust so that good professional relationships cannot develop.

Thus, an understanding of the intricate layers of culture is imperative in preventing misunderstandings that may interfere with international business activities and prevent the development of an integrated global mindset. Through in-depth case study examination of cultural misunderstandings, it is clear that the ramifications are not only at the interpersonal level but also extend to interfering with the broader organizational functions. An example involves multinational corporations undertaking advertising campaigns in foreign countries without undertaking a critical examination of culture. If an organization adopts promotion strategies that are much popular in Western settings but would end up being insensitive to countries like Asia or the Middle East, the return can be tremendous, and the organization will have public relations crises along with reduced brand perception. As is observed in the analysis of psychocentric development (Klein et al., 2017), the emphasis on a single mode of knowing human behavior doesn't consider the customized cultural contexts that affect consumer responses.

Due to this, firms must cultivate an advanced understanding of cultural values and norms so as to cope with these forces more effectively, ultimately enabling an effective global strategy. In addition, the pursuit of entering new markets calls for respect for the nature of cultural differences, especially where dominant stories are not dominant. As brought out by the technological market expansion discourse (Lambert et al., 2025), companies entering global markets need to understand that cultural systems vary significantly, affecting consumer behavior and business operations. If companies do not respect these cultural differences, they end up alienating their potential clients without realizing it, risking local market penetration initiatives. Without a world view informed by cultural awareness, organizations risk forcing their own reasoning upon unsuspecting markets. As a result, creating cultural competency and culturally informed strategies becomes a necessity for businesses seeking global success. By learning from past mistakes and taking intelligent steps, organizations can make sense connections, and so foster sustainable growth in a more interconnected economy.

2.2. BUILDING A GLOBAL MINDSET

The cultural idea plays a key position in building a global mindset, as it shapes the individual's way of perceiving, behaving, and relating to others in various environments. Culture refers to the collection of common values, beliefs, and norms among the group, and it determines how individuals interpret experiences and connect with individuals. When practicing international management, it is vital that leaders and professionals learn these cultural dimensions in order to work across borders. This understanding not only facilitates comprehension of complex social relationships but also fosters collaboration between multinational groups. As organizations go global, the ability to observe and value the variations in cultures becomes essential in leveraging the strengths of a multicultural workforce, ultimately enhancing organizational performance in competitive markets. Hence, a refined understanding of culture is the basis for building a global mindset that will empower leaders to guide cross-cultural relations within and among organizations. Global mindset development involves creating cognitive, social, as well as psychological dimensions that enable individuals to manage the complexities of the global business environment (Figure 2.4).

Figure 2.4. Developing a global mindset for successful international management.

Source: https://fastercapital.co/i/International-business-negotiation-Mastering-International-Business-Negotiation--Strategies-for-Success--Developing-a-Global-Mindset-for-Successful-International-Business-Negotiation.webp.

Cognitively, it requires openness to learn and adapt to other individuals' perspectives, enabling creative problem-solving as well as strategic decision-making. Socially, relationship-building across cultures facilitates teamwork and trustworthiness, which is crucial in cross-border business settings. Psychologically, resilience and flexibility have to be cultivated to weather problems that arise from cultural disagreements or misunderstandings. These dimensions converge to form a complete global mindset that allows leaders to respond ahead of the evolving needs of globalization. This more integrated form of leadership not only aligns with the sweeping ideas of contemporary business practices but also places importance on the necessity of companies to invest in developing their human resources in order to win in international markets (Pucik et al., 1996). The expansive characteristic of globalization requires a focus on strategic international human resource management (SIHRM) as a catalyst in the fostering of a global mindset for organizations. The increasing interconnectedness of the markets requires a transformation in the character of how organizations handle human resource strategies in order to make them culturally sensitive and global-aware. SIHRM can serve as a unified structure to bring together various human resources practices and develop an integrated organizational culture that spans geographical locations. The structure provides an environment where employees are forced to embrace diversity, hence allowing them to operate effectively in various cultures. As scandals and ineptitude have most times their origin in cultural insensitivity, the emphasis on SIHRM is more important than ever to correct current deficiencies and shape practices to address the increasingly globalized face of business (Cieri et al., 1998).

2.2.1. Definition and Significance of a Global Mindset

In the current global management context, the interplay between culture and global mindset has become a more focal concern. It is critical to comprehend that global mindset is not merely awareness of diverse cultures; rather, it is an all-encompassing cognitive, social, and psychological system that enables individuals to manage complex international environments effectively. Cultural intelligence is an essential part of this frame of mind because it allows managers to appreciate and engage with the intricacies of culture, thus enhancing collaboration and communication with global teams.

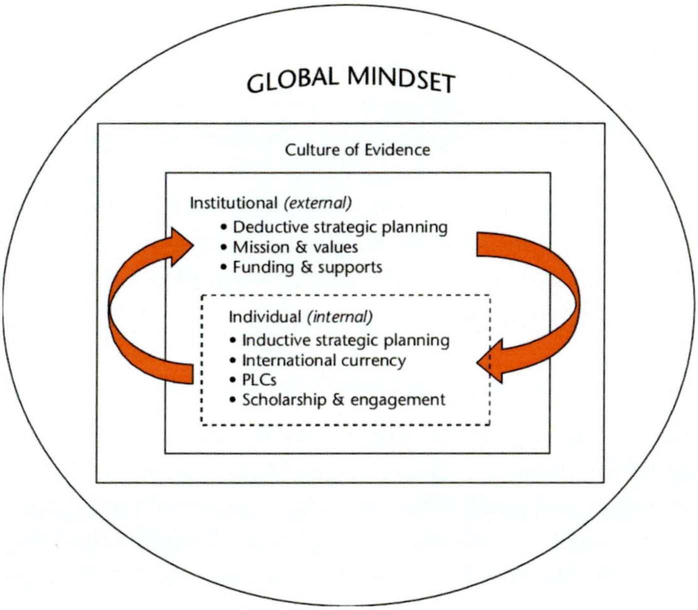

Figure 2.5. Evolution of a global mindset.

Source: https://www.researchgate.net/profile/Cynthia-Grant-2/publication/260334404/figure/fig1/AS:597760826953728@1519528695166/Development-of-a-Global-Mindset.png.

The emergence of new global economic powers such as the BRIC countries puts into perspective the need for global business leaders to embrace this frame of mind (Salmi et al., 2012). Without it, organizations will be at risk of misreading cultural contexts, thereby making poor decisions and poor leadership in an increasingly globalized world. It takes deliberate efforts at both the individual and organizational levels to develop a global mindset. This includes establishing an environment that allows cross-cultural contact and learning through experience, where individuals learn firsthand about alternative ways of thinking. Global mindset concepts are integrated into the curricula by international business teachers to equip future leaders with the sophisticated issues of global management (Salmi et al., 2012). Moreover, policies and practices need to be created that appreciate inclusiveness and cultural flexibility so that their workers are adequately trained to adjust in various cultures. These proactive actions contribute to establishing an agility and responsiveness culture in which diversity is not a hindrance but a path for innovation (Figure 2.5).

The significance of the global mindset is further extended to its applicability for organizational performance in general, particularly in the area of strategic human resource management (SHRM). Global mindset enables organizations to reconcile HRM strategies better with the complexity of international contexts. This reconciliation allows for the contextualization of human resource practices according to the varying employee cultural backgrounds. Thus, integrating a global mindset can make the company more efficient by encouraging stronger relationships, employee commitment, and productivity. Thus, acquiring and implementing a global mindset is not an optional plan but a necessity for success in the global economy, where cultural sensitivity is the key to obtaining sustainable competitive edges.

2.2.2. Strategies for Developing a Global Mindset

Culture dynamics are central in forming an individual's global mindset, the underpinning of international management. Culture as a set of shared beliefs, values, and practices in a group affects the manner in which individuals conceive and deal with the world. These dynamics should be approached from a multi-faceted perspective that involves cognitive, social, and psychological levels. Cognitive strategies involve developing a sense of awareness about various cultural perspectives, being tolerant, and critical thinking. Through exposure to other cultures, individuals will come to have a greater appreciation of diverse worldviews that will ultimately enhance their ability to operate effectively in complex international environments. With the globalization of organizations, accepting this broader definition of culture is essential to grow leaders that are effective in cross-cultural interactions and cross-cultural decision-making that is culturally sensitive (Pucik et al., 1996). It requires concerted efforts to reach out to global networks and diverse teams to acquire a global mindset. In the world today, one has to invest time and effort in building relationships across geographical boundaries. This can be achieved by being involved in international projects, collaborations, and expatriate turnovers that provide on-the-job exposure to multiple cultures. Also, it is important to develop intercultural competence in this process because individuals need to be taught how to adjust their ways of communication and behaviors to suit different cultures. Organizations have the mandate to facilitate this by building environments that encourage collaboration between individuals of different cultures (Figure 2.6).

Figure 2.6. Essential elements for a global mindset.

Source: https://spiceup.jp/en/service/g-ship/imgs/g-ship_factor.png.

These practices not only promote interpersonal skills but also foster innovation since cross-cultural teams draw on a wider range of experiences and ideas in resolving complicated situations (Bloom et al., 1998). Besides these methods, self-reflection and self-awareness are crucial components in building a global mindset. One should critically assess his/her own cultural assumptions and biases that might influence the way he/she treats other individuals. In this regard, reflective processes such as mentoring or journaling may facilitate individuals to develop by making them reflect on their experiences and adjust their behavior appropriately. Additionally, possessing a learning orientation makes one inquisitive and open to new ideas and hence resilient during difficult times. By developing an environment that emphasizes continuous learning and consideration, organizations can equip their leaders and employees with the knowledge necessary to thrive within the diversity of global settings. This comprehensive approach not only prepares people for the complexities of globalization, but it also allows them to positively contribute to their organizations and society (Pucik et al., 1996).

2.2.3. Role of Education and Training in Fostering a Global Mindset

Deeper cultural understanding is essential to effective global management because it informs the strategies that organizations employ to deal with multiple contexts. Learning is central to building leaders and employees with the cultural competencies to function across borders. Training programs can instruct people on how to be respectful of diverse cultural norms and values, creating a culture of inclusiveness and respect. This cultural awareness is not exactly a soft skill; it's a necessity for the formulation of strategies that can leverage opportunities across the globe. With more globalization redefining the business landscape, the incorporation of cultural education into training programs becomes vital in order to empower companies to move forward of intricate international market patterns. As such, education is no longer just a tool for individual development but also a beacon of organizational adjustment in the face of international challenges (Pucik et al., 1996). Cognitive, social, and psychological components of a global mindset are actually attained through formal education programs. Cognitive components include knowledge and information processing from different cultures, which plays a crucial role in sound decision-making and strategy formulation in foreign settings. Experiential learning-focused training—e.g., simulation and cross-cultural interaction—develops participants' ability to empathize with overseas perspectives. At the same time, social implications are based on the construction of interpersonal skills to facilitate teamwork across cultures. By creating a sense of global citizenship, training initiatives can prepare employees for psychological resilience in embracing ambiguity and adjusting to various cultural settings. In this way, education is a change agent, which allows people to make sense of worldwide management complexity and develop a deeper appreciation of cultural diversity (Cieri et al., 1998). In the end, the contributions of education and training towards instilling a global mindset are not contained within personal skills; it is critical to developing a global-oriented corporate culture. Organizations that invest in all-round education programs are able to create a culture-friendly and supportive organizational environment that facilitates innovation as well as cross-cultural collaboration. Such a constructive approach not only equips employees with necessary skills but also aligns them with the organization's strategy at a global scale. In their exposure to various cultures as well as ideas, these employees learn a skill to identify new market opportunities and reap them aptly. By prioritizing education and training that involves global competencies, organizations can position themselves very well in the ever-evolving international marketplace, eventually guaranteeing their competitive advantage while addressing the essential imperatives of a global economy (Pucik et al., 1996).

2.3. COGNITIVE DIMENSIONS OF CULTURE

Underlying international management is the complex intersection of cognitive, social, and psychological elements that shape the experience and the understanding of cultures. Culture has been typically defined as the shared values, norms, and customs of a group, and it permeates the way in which individuals perceive and interpret their worlds. This cognitive framework is a prism that filters through the managers' eyes the foreign markets and interprets the nuances of cross-cultural relations.

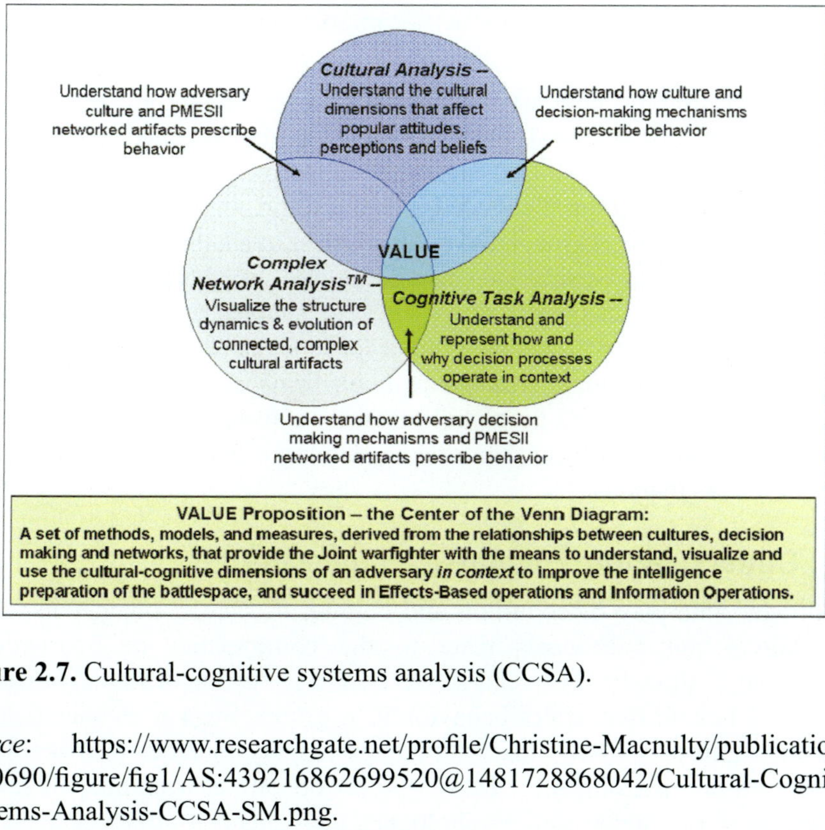

Figure 2.7. Cultural-cognitive systems analysis (CCSA).

Source: https://www.researchgate.net/profile/Christine-Macnulty/publication/235070690/figure/fig1/AS:439216862699520@1481728868042/Cultural-Cognitive-Systems-Analysis-CCSA-SM.png.

By developing an understanding of these cognitive realms, organizations can acquire a global mindset that facilitates effective decision-making across various contexts. Cognitive knowledge of culture allows leaders to comprehend not only the surface-level behaviors that typify different cultures but also the implicit assumptions and beliefs that influence them, and thus be better prepared to compete in a global marketplace. Inculcation of global orientation is at the heart of international management since it prepares individuals to accept and adjust to differing cultures. Flexibility in this regard is crucial in the current more globalized environment where various cultural backgrounds overlap. The cognitive elements of culture, which consist of cultural knowledge and awareness, are at the nucleus of such an adaptation and shape how managers respond to different management styles, communication patterns, and negotiation styles. Since organizations contend with pluralistic cultural settings, they must craft mechanisms that recognize and appreciate these cognitive differences. Successful global managers harness the power of curiosity—an intrinsic motivation that moves individuals to find out, understand, and value other cultures—hence capitalizing on their capability for cross-cultural communication and forming productive relationships in their organizations (Figure 2.7).

Moreover, cultural cognitive management goes beyond awareness to the stage of building cross-cultural competence and learning-oriented organizational culture. Mikhaylov et al. (2016) identifies curiosity as one of the individual attributes which fuels cultural knowledge creation and competence development for multicultural teams. Through the establishment of a culture that is curiosity-fostering, organizations can foster discussion and collaboration among team members from different backgrounds. These initiatives not only help extend cultural knowledge but also lay the ground for innovative problem-solving and adaptive behavior in global management. As firms navigate the uncertainty of globalization, the value of a global mindset informed by cognitive cultural dimensions is more important than ever in shaping organizational success and resilience across markets.

2.3.1. Understanding Cognitive Frameworks

The intricate interplay of cognition and culture affects the manner in which organizations and individuals react to the complexities of international management. Culture has been characterized as a collection of shared practices, values, and beliefs that affect behavior in a group. Such a characterization points to cognitive schemes that individuals employ in order to make sense of their cultural environments. These models operate at a number of levels, weaving cognitive, social, and psychological elements that influence decision-making behaviors. An appreciation of these dimensions through critical analysis sees how cultural meanings are produced and reproduced through experience and interaction. This is what is crucial to international managers who have to make their strategies effective in a range of cultures, as it facilitates better communication, reinforces relationships, and guarantees productive cooperation across borders. In order to acquire a global mindset, individuals must work with and study their own thought processes, most likely viewing cultural diversity as a result. A global mindset means a respect for the subtleties of culture and a mechanism to adapt one's behavior accordingly. A global mindset is comprised of a combination of local flexibility with a broader, international outlook, enabling social and informal connections to be established that span traditional organizational boundaries. As organizations operate increasingly in a matrix of local as well as global influences, the ability to access these mental frameworks becomes a sheer necessity. This highlights the reason why international business managers have to be attuned towards cultural aspects and hence enable their subordinates to navigate the hurdle posed by numerous stakeholders having dissimilar worldviews. By doing this, they will position themselves more strongly for strategic advantages as well as operational successes (Figure 2.8).

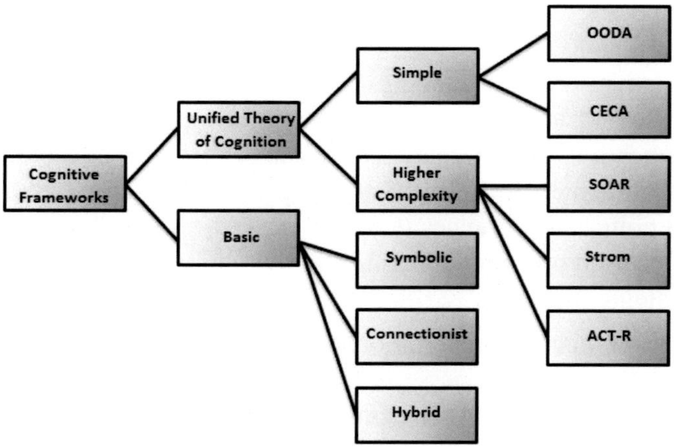

Figure 2.8. Classification of cognitive frameworks.

Source: https://www.researchgate.net/profile/Tahir-Mushtaq/publication/257255973/figure/fig6/AS:668357212786702@1536360185895/Classification-of-Cognitive-Frameworks-33.jpg.

Besides, understanding cognitive frameworks is at the heart of comprehending how best to exploit the benefits of global integration. By applying tools of analysis such as the Value-Chain, Culture, and Product (VCCP) matrix, managers can examine the multifaceted interdependencies that exist between organizational culture and structure. This makes possible a closer understanding of how human resource processes align with strategic objectives. As business corporations are expanding their operations in the emerging economies, the relevance is also high, particularly in nations such as the BRIC countries, where economic dynamism provides new opportunities for cooperation and development. Emphasizing global orientation in the leadership development and education is critical if the forthcoming generation of business leaders is to be able to deal with these complexities (Boudreau et al., 2002; Salmi et al., 2012).

2.3.2. Influence of Cognitive Biases on Decision-Making

The cross-section of cognition and culture are important to shaping decision-making in international management. With a globalized world, cultural differences act to increase the risk of cognitive biases, where managers make decisions from their own cultural paradigms rather than objective information. One such example is confirmation bias, where people like to receive information confirming what they already believe in, which can cause effective communication and collaboration in multi-cultural teams to be compromised. By recognizing and valuing these biases, managers can actively work towards a more inclusive decision-making process with cultural diversity values. Cognitive biases are not only an academic research topic but also have significant practical implications for international human resource management (SIHRM), affecting recruitment, selection, and training practices that must be sensitive to international cultural differences (Cieri et al., 1998). Also, the development of a global mindset involves recognizing the ways in which cognitive biases can penetrate strategic thinking.

A framework that can accommodate several epistemological perspectives can enhance the self-awareness of leaders to their own bias and strategic reasoning. With the internationalization of organizations, decision-makers must be mindful of the cognitive heuristics common that accompany rapid judgments of cultural contexts. For example, overconfidence bias might make an organization underestimate the intricacies involved in conducting international business. Excessive reliance on being familiar with one's own culture may have negative effects on decision-making and strategic errors. The application of holistic models, such as the Cynefin Framework developed by David Snowdon and his team, can potentially enable leaders to manage uncertain situations more effectively, thereby reducing the detrimental effects of cognitive bias on decision-making (Starr et al., 2018). Lastly, it is necessary to collectively work towards increasing the cultural awareness level and sensitivity of leaders and teams. Organizations must develop a culture that promotes reflection and critical discussion of decision-making processes. Training courses designed to develop cultural competency can rewire cognitive pathways and break established biases so that one can approach decisions with an open and fresh attitude. These initiatives not only enhance group dynamics but also enhance the organizations' ability to adapt to global challenges. Through the active management of cognitive biases, global managers can create more effective and complementary models of decision-making that value the subtleties of many world cultures, advancing the aims of strategic international human resource management (Cieri et al., 1998).

2.3.3. Cross-Cultural Communication and Cognition

Within the complex global management scenario, understanding culture in multidimensional terms is crucial. Culture not only comprises collective practices and beliefs but also cognitive systems through which individuals interpret their experience. These cognitive elements have a direct influence on cross-cultural communication by setting parameters on message construction, transmission, and reception across different cultures. The comprehension of language subtleties or non-verbal cues can vary significantly based on the cultural contexts, and this may lead to potential miscommunications. With different organizations worldwide facing diverse markets, an awareness of the role of cognitive schemas in the development of impressions is essential for effective interaction. A solid theoretical underpinning is required to deal with such complexities, as described in the emerging discipline of strategic international human resource management (SIHRM), which calls for comprehension of the consequences of culture for various organizational functions (Cieri et al., 1998). Building a global mindset involves not only cultural sensitivity but also the ability to deal with dissonance caused in cross-cultural interactions. This mind-set embodies flexibility and openness to other frames of reference, both of which facilitate improved communication and collaboration in a global environment. Such cognitive flexibility makes it possible to rise above own cultural bias and cooperate more smoothly with colleagues and customers who have backgrounds different from own. Social intelligence is most essential here because tuning into the affective and contextual cues that underpin communication becomes imperative. An awareness and higher-level thinking acquired through research on cognitive styles in learning emphasize the necessity of sustainable awareness and higher-order thinking in the acquisition of a global mindset by prospective leaders (Colás et al., 2018). Therefore, encouraging this global mindset becomes imperative in shaping professionals to address the challenges brought by cultural diversity to international management. Lastly, effective cross-cultural communication is built on being able to identify and work with the psychological factors that are involved in cultural interactions. Inbuilt biases and ingrained cultural norms could act as brakes to understanding and cooperation. This requires a system where individuals engage in reflective activities that improve critical thinking and awareness of one's cognitive process. As professionals become more aware of cultural influences, they acquire the capacity to empathize with alternative perspectives. These practices may improve interpersonal relationships, contribute to a positive impact in organizational dynamics, and enable adaptive strategies in global markets. Understanding the significance of cognition in the development of communication styles sustains the role of cultural competence even further in international management, unlocking opportunities for effective collaboration in diverse contexts. Hence, embracing such complexity is crucial in creating a uniting global organizational culture.

2.4. SOCIAL DIMENSIONS OF CULTURE

The sophisticated nature of culture exceeds simple definitions to require a deeper inspection of its many dimensions, particularly the social underpinnings that underlie interpersonal relationships. Culture requires an examination of its multi-faceted nature to encompass not just beliefs and values but relational interactions that shape collective behavior in societies.

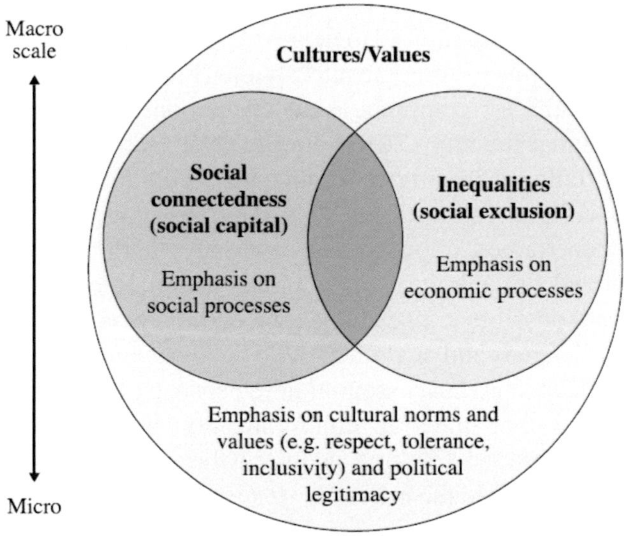

Figure 2.9. Dimensions of social cohesion, showing social, economic and cultural domains.

Source: https://www.researchgate.net/profile/Habila-Jerry/publication/344284344/figure/fig1/AS:936716219199489@1600341958094/Dimensions-of-social-cohesion-showing-social-economic-and-cultural-domains-Source.ppm.

Social dimensions of culture like norms, customs, and communal involvement are the pillars through which groups exchange and respond. Global management identifies the significance of these social dimensions because they are the core of developing a global mentality that supports diversity while promoting collaboration. Therefore, organizations that intentionally integrate these social aspects into their systems of operations can foster cross-cultural understanding and an inclusive culture that enhances innovation and adaptability (Mikhaylov et al., 2016). Global mindset is attained through a balance of cognitive, social, and psychological factors where people adjust their frames of reference to adapt to cultural differences. Cognitive aspects pertain to mental frameworks that guide perceptions, while psychological characteristics dictate emotional responses to cross-cultural circumstances. The integration of both dimensions enhances people's ability to handle complex global situations effectively. For instance, instilling curiosity regarding culture combines these cognitive and psychological elements to enable individuals to engage more earnestly with cross-cultural experiences and appreciate differences. This is particularly critical in the domain of international management, where effective teamwork often hinges upon a high-level understanding of social dynamics that shape intra-personal relationships across different cultures (Cieri et al., 1998) (Figure 2.9).

While interpreting social dimensions of culture, organizations must be aware also of the strategic implications these associations bear on strategic practices such as human resource management. Strategic international human resource management (SIHRM) underscores the significance of tailored approach to considering cultural differences in international operations. By assessing usually overlooked factors, organizations can craft sound plans that interact with various cultures, thereby increasing staff motivation as well as organizational effectiveness. Specifically, building a culturally competent workforce is also important in preventing possible confrontations and guaranteeing collaboration across geographical boundaries. As the world continues to become a global village, a growing need for systemic alignment that leverages recognition of social forces in transnational contexts continues to reveal itself, paving way for sustainable development and adaptive leadership in different markets (Cieri et al., 1998).

2.4.1. Social Norms and Their Impact on Management

A careful scrutiny of social norms brings them into focus, their profound influence on management practices across various culture contexts. Social norms as unwritten rules govern behavior in society, shaping expectations and interactions between people and organizations. In international management, an understanding of such norms is imperative because they highly impact communication styles, decision-making, and leadership styles. For instance, a firm founded on a collectivistic culture will most probably rely on group harmony and agreement, which is far from individualistic cultures in which assertiveness and personal achievement lead business relations. Therefore, those managers who are tasked with overseeing diverse teams will need to comprehend and monitor such disparate social norms so that they can unite individuals and make the company more efficient, particularly in situations involving uncertainty and cultural diversity (Bloom et al., 1998). On top of this, global mindset is more relevant to international managers. Cross-cultural understanding and appreciation that enables professionals to adapt their styles effectively is what this term means. Social norms play a key role in influencing the mindset since they influence how leadership, authority, and teamwork are perceived. For instance, a manager who embraces cultural diversity can employ local tradition to enhance local employee involvement and thereby boost overall productivity. In addition, as companies expand into new countries, they also have to embrace the unique social norms that govern those regions. Otherwise, organizations risk mistaken communication and incompetent management, potentially stopping their international endeavors (Figure 2.10).

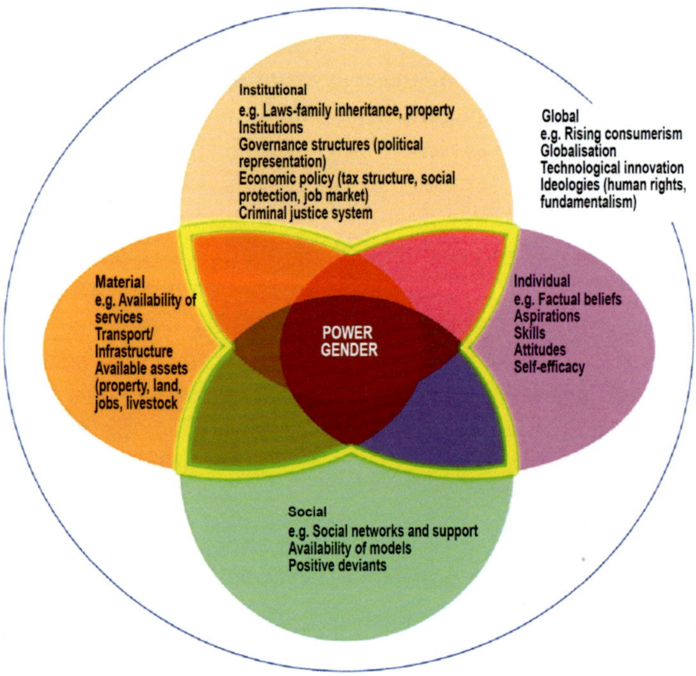

Figure 2.10. The influence of social norms visualized on the dynamic framework.

Source: https://www.researchgate.net/profile/Ben-Cislaghi/publication/323945763/figure/fig2/AS:607071368126470@1521748501583/The-influence-of-social-norms-visualized-on-the-dynamic-framework.png.

Thus, building a global mindset that is rooted in the understanding and appreciation of diverse social norms is essential to the application of sustainable international management practices (Lambert et al., 2025). To bridge social norms to effective management efforts, organizations must also consider cognitive, social, and psychological aspects that lead to cultural engagement. These factors shape individuals' perceptions of themselves and their role in global networks and influence motivation and workplace conduct. For example, cultural assumptions about hierarchy and authority influence how workers engage with leadership, such as where habits of respect and obedience within some cultures might clash with more egalitarian styles. Managers must be taught to establish inclusive dialogue that bridges these divisions, developing an environment where the worker is respected and heard no matter what culture. By being aware of these sophisticated dynamics, management can cultivate resilience and adaptability, key competencies for prosperity in the rapidly evolving global markets of today, hence the contribution of social norms towards crafting effective management practice in a globalized environment (Bloom et al., 1998).

2.4.2. The Role of Social Networks in International Business

The relationship between social networks and culture is pivotal in shaping international business operations. Given the increasing trend towards globalization in industries, cultural awareness is essential in ensuring effective communication and collaboration across borders. Social networks serve as conduits for transferring not just business operations but also cultural interactions, which enable firms to adapt to varying environments. For instance, differences in communication culture can generate misunderstandings, as there is a necessity to establish relationship that can accommodate such differences. Strategic social networks help organizations to adapt their strategies to fit local customs and practices, thereby propelling their global operations. Therefore, the influence of social networks extends beyond mere connection, that it is a building block that enhances intercultural capabilities and enhances business performance at the global level, increasingly important as firms compete in the international marketplace (Pucik et al., 1996). In addition, the development of global mindset is inextricably linked with the ability to use social networks effectively. Business leaders who cultivate connections between various cultural backgrounds are better placed to assimilate various perspectives, which eventually lead to innovative solutions and improved decision-making processes. This mental adjustment is all about grasping what social constructs impact behavior in different situations, necessary for the establishment of trust and credibility. With industries transcending national boundaries, the need for a robust social network becomes more eminent; social networks facilitate not only obtaining market intelligence but also aid organizations in perceiving and reacting to cultural change. Social networks, in this sense, can serve as a barometer of culture, thereby aiding companies to modify their strategy for sustainability and growth in today's competitive global marketplace (Cieri et al., 1998). Finally, the social networks' function in global business also apply in human resource management, albeit more intensely in strategic international human resource management (SIHRM). Firms that concentrate on developing global talent networks are able to coordinate their human capital better with organizational objectives and cultural expectations globally. The capacity to share best practices, experience, and culturally adjusted training within social networks ensures that employees have skills they need to excel in diverse environments. As articulated in contemporary discourse on SIHRM, an understanding of the dynamics of social networks is imperative for addressing the challenges created by globalization. Through the creation of an integrated workforce, organizations can best utilize dynamic pools of talent and ultimately set themselves up for success in an increasingly integrated international business environment (Pucik et al., 1996).

2.4.3. Cultural Diversity and Team Dynamics

In international management, culture is the foundation on which an understanding of teamwork becomes possible. Culture encompasses the shared beliefs and values as well as traditions that characterize a group, and how these impact interpersonal relations and decision-making within teams. The more inter-border an organization works, the more it has to understand the multi-dimensionality of culture. Cultural diversity in particular produces richer perspectives, enhancing problem-solving and creativity. But without a properly fostered global mindset, groups are bound to struggle, leading to miscommunication and ineffectual conflict. It is thus important for team members to develop cognitive approaches that enable them to navigate successfully cultural differences, thereby embracing their unique backgrounds to establish an integrated and high-performing team environment, as outlined in existing studies in a bid to de-mystify constructs of global mindset and how it may be applied in multinational corporations (Arora et al., 2007). Developing a global mind is not only a product of awareness but a product of effort along cognitive, social, and psychological axes. Cognitive complexity enables people to understand and interpret several cultures' norms and conduct as they navigate effortlessly in handling varied perspectives. Social aspects involve attempts at active communication plans and management of relationships that build trust and co-operation among members of various cultures. Furthermore, readiness of a psychological nature requires team members to be receptive to uncertainty and adaptability—key attributes in the modern fast-paced, globally competitive environment. As organizations aim to improve their efficacy across multicultural settings, the acquisition of this intricate interplay among cognitive, social, and psychological dimensions becomes a fundamental component. This places teams in a readiness state to adequately manage the rapidly changing demands of the global markets, thus making organizations remain competitive and relevant (Martin et al., 2010). To take advantage of the dividends of diversity in teams, leaders must come up with policies that support the creation of a friendly environment that encourages teamwork. The ideal way is through the implementation of virtual teams, in which individuals with diverse geographical and cultural backgrounds are brought together to collaborate on clearly defined tasks. The versatility of virtual teams allows companies to mobilize talent rapidly in response to fluctuating markets and, consequently, meet customer demands for customized solutions. This necessitates team members possessing cultural awareness and flexibility that defines a robust global mindset. As suggested in recent arguments, such teams can effectively overcome obstacles regarding intercultural collaboration to deliver enhanced performance. Hence, achieving a global mindset is essential not just for individual team members but for the success of teams as a whole that operate in different cultural contexts (Martin et al., 2010).

2.5. PSYCHOLOGICAL DIMENSIONS OF CULTURE

It is crucial to have a comprehensive understanding of culture in global management since it is the beliefs, values, and practices that direct the behavior and decisions of groups. Essentially, culture could be defined as a complex system of shared meanings that governs the manner in which individuals experience and behave toward their environment. When addressing the psychological dimensions of culture, one must consider how cognitive frameworks and social environments shape not only the behavior of individuals but also organizational operations. This is critical in strategic international human resource management (SIHRM) where cultural differences can significantly alter employee expectations and organizational dynamics. Thus, a study of the psychological underpinnings of culture offers insights into how managers need to handle cross-cultural interactions so as to have coordinated action, thus attaining alignment and reducing friction in global teams (Cieri et al., 1998). A global mindset does not only imply consciousness of geographical and cultural differences; it demands thorough comprehension of the psychological determinants that shape human behavior in cultures. Cognitive flexibility—the ability to redirect one's thinking to accommodate various cultural settings—is essential for global managers. Cognitive flexibility allows executives to redefine challenges in local terms more hospitable to indigenous cultures, facilitating cooperation and collaboration among multicultural teams. The combination of psychological readiness and cultural awareness is significant because it prepares international managers to apply tactics and make alliances.

Putting cross-cultural competence into action demands utilizing curiosity and open-mindedness that have the ability to widen one's worldview of different cultural paradigms and enhance problem-solving capacity (Mikhaylov et al., 2016). An important aspect of developing this global mindset is to cultivate curiosity, which triggers a rich cultural knowledge creation process. Curiosity plays the role of a catalyst in developing cross-cultural competence that enables individuals to bring themselves into and enjoy diversity rather than staying away from it.

This psychological factor can guarantee more significant interpersonal relationships and successful organizational performance in multicultural environments. International management companies and educational institutions must adopt frameworks that facilitate question-based learning experiences. Managers can guarantee environments conducive to cultural exchange and creativity by doing so. As can be seen in most study papers, not only individual learning is enhanced by creating a culture of wonder but also organizational resilience and flexibility in order to address global issues (Cieri et al., 1998; Mikhaylov et al., 2016) (Figure 2.11).

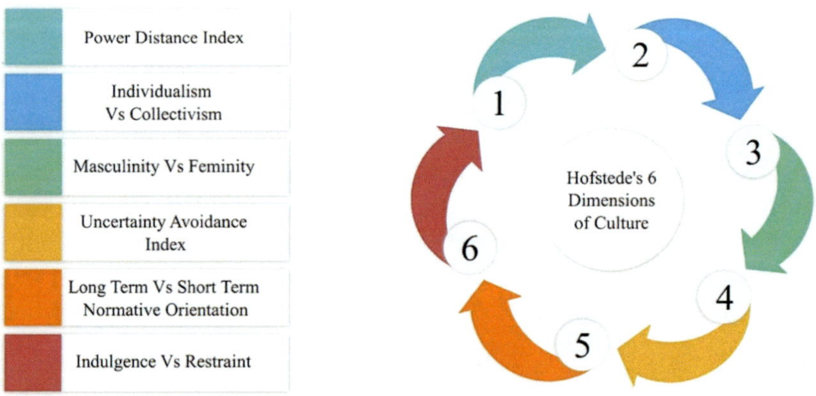

Figure 2.11. Hofstede's cultural dimensions theory.

Source: https://www.simplypsychology.org/wp-content/uploads/hofstede-cultural-dimensions.jpg.

2.5.1. Cultural Identity and Its Effects on Behavior

In examining the relationship between cultural identity and behavior, it is essential to keep in mind that culture encompasses shared beliefs, values, and practices of a groups worldview. This is the working definition of culture that can serve as the foundation for understanding how people navigate through their social worlds, particularly in multicultural settings. International managers benefit from this knowledge most of all, as it guides interaction among team members from varying cultural backgrounds. Cognitive dimensions of cultural identity—beliefs, assumptions, and mental models—play a significant role in workplace behaviors and responses.

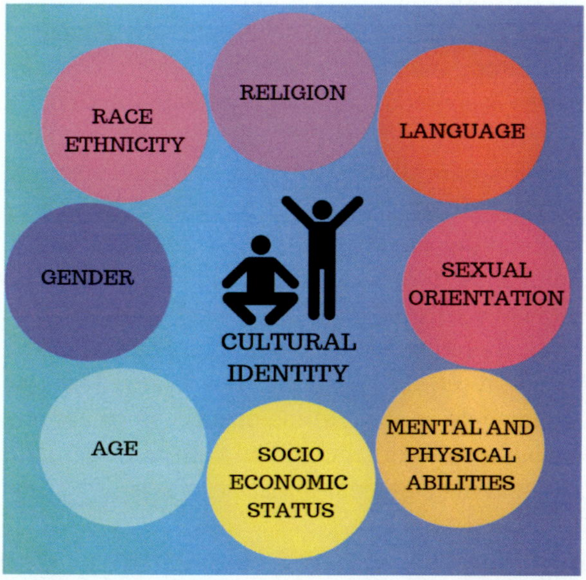

Figure 2.12. Examine the cultural identity and its effects on behavior.

Source: https://media.licdn.com/dms/image/v2/C4D12AQHuZv8UeQGI6w/article-inline_image-shrink_1000_1488/article-inline_image-shrink_1000_1488/0/1559884222951?e=1760572800&v=beta&t=Jqsx6-cUhbtMF4y70bpef9HZcXIz3x-rjG1lm6v4oTg.

Particularly, cognitive models can be useful in facilitating or hindering effective collaboration and organizational performance in a global economy. Therefore, a wise awareness of cultural nuances becomes a valuable asset for building an inclusive organizational culture that embraces diversity and fosters productive engagement. As organizations seek to develop a global mind, they must also tackle the social dimensions of cultural identity. Social conduct within diverse teams is highly influenced by cultural norms and learned habits that individuals bring from their cultures. These norms dictate how things are discussed, disagreements are managed, and friendships developed. For instance, collectivist cultures may emphasize harmony and consensus at the group level, and individualist cultures may emphasize personal initiative and assertiveness. Such differences in social behaviors can lead to misunderstandings and conflict unless leaders are cross-culturally competent, which allows them to explore and broker such differences. The development of this skill is not merely an organizational necessity, but a strategic advantage in the creation of a synergistic work environment to enhance overall productivity and innovation (Figure 2.12).

Moreover, the psychological dimensions of cultural identity are extremely important in shaping behavior, particularly how individuals see themselves as belonging to their cultural background and adapting to new surroundings. The concept of habitus, as is contended through contemporary research, emphasizes the embedded dispositions that affect management practice and decision-making habits within organizations. Besides, understanding the psychological and emotional bonds individuals possess towards cultural identity can assist managers in implementing effective plans that resonate with their respective staffs. Understanding these forces can also lead to the creation of a collaborative culture that is inclusive of cultural interest and knowledge-sharing—factors highlighted in the literature as essential for empowering cross-cultural competence (Mikhaylov et al., 2016; Hrotko, 2025). Thus, an awareness of the multi-faceted elements of cultural identity becomes not only significant to personal behavior but also to organizational culture construction and eliciting successful international management initiatives.

2.5.2. Emotional Intelligence in Cross-Cultural Contexts

With the globalized world of today, the intersection of cross-cultural dynamics and emotional intelligence has been especially in the limelight. Culture is a many-sided reality that has to be understood in its cognitive, social, and psychological implications that influence individual behavior and interactions. Emotional intelligence, wherein one can recognize, understand, and manage one's own and other individuals' feelings, plays a pivotal role in operating multicultural environments. This skill enables one to gauge emotional cues and respond appropriately, thereby ensuring better communication and collaboration across cultures. It also enhances one's capacity for adapting to numerous social mores and customs, thereby facilitating smooth interactions in multicultural environments. As businesses seek to cultivate global thinking, emotional intelligence emerges as a key skill that erases cultural boundaries and facilitates inclusive leadership (Mikhaylov et al., 2016). The expansion of global mindsets relies on building emotional intelligence in multicultural populations. With more multinational organizations relying extensively on global virtual teams consisting of employees from different backgrounds, cultural intelligence is a prerequisite (Figure 2.13).

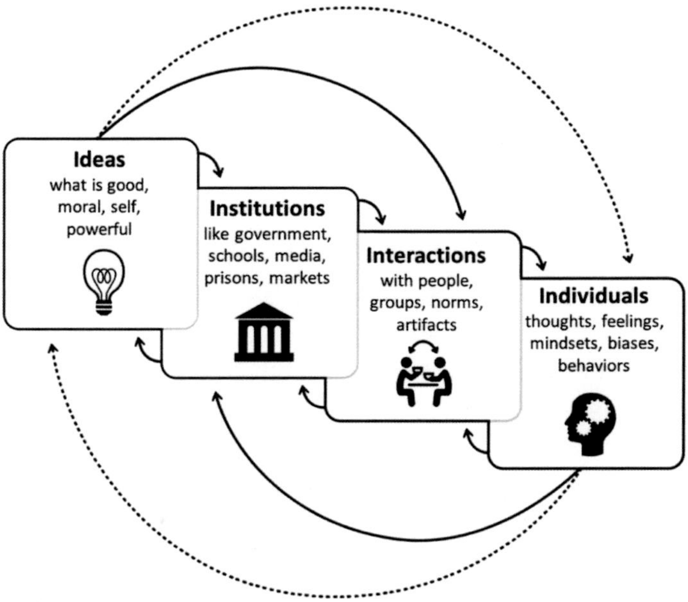

Figure 2.13. The interplay between international management and emotional intelligence in cross-cultural dynamics.

Source: https://www.frontiersin.org/files/Articles/379620/fpsyg-10-00700-HTML/image_m/fpsyg-10-00700-g001.jpg.

Emotional intelligence provides team members with the skills to participate effectively in meaningful collaboration, leading to teamwork and productivity. In an era of competition and fast-paced market changes, culturally intelligent individuals are able to adjust their communication strategies and styles to suit the needs of diverse stakeholders. Consequently, the formation of emotional intelligence in teams will create higher cross-cultural competence, and hence enable organizations to adapt to the demands of an international economy. Such cross-fertilization of cross-cultural consciousness and emotional intelligence then enhances organizational effectiveness and agility (Martin et al., 2010). Curiosity as a given-born trait that provokes questioning and exploration further supplements the development of emotional intelligence in cross-cultural contexts. Curious people are more receptive to different cultural perspectives, and this facilitates a better degree of comprehension of emotional cues for a given culture. Research indicates that curiosity is a key driver in cultural knowledge building because it gets people interested in experiencing new things. By the inclusion of curiosity within learning cycles of multicultural organizations, managers are able to create a setting where emotional intelligence can be nurtured. With such organizations navigating complex global contexts, the creation of curiosity along with emotional intelligence will be crucial to the successful development of tailor-made solutions for various consumer needs. Emotional intelligence, therefore, hand in hand with high curiosity levels, is critical in the achievement of cross-cultural competence as well as effective collaboration across global landscapes (Mikhaylov et al., 2016).

2.5.3. Psychological Safety in Diverse Teams

In order to create a culture of psychological safety in diverse teams, the intersection of a number of cultural dimensions needs to be appreciated. Diverse teams comprising people with different cultural backgrounds generally accompany challenges of miscommunication and variations in conflict management. By grasping the dimensions, the members of the team are able to establish a cohesive environment where intelligence and innovation flourish. The actual notion of psychological safety enables one to express varied opinions without apprehension of adverse consequences, thus enhancing the collective intelligence of the team. Organizations can develop global competencies and be more aligned with the multidimensional nature of international management by creating norms around openness and respect for diverse perspectives. It is through such initiatives that organizations can build a strong base of inclusion and diversity, which finally manifest into enhanced performance outcomes in global contexts (Nishii et al., 2007). When it comes to managing psychologically safe spaces, leaders occupy the forefront in determining team dynamics, particularly within multicultural contexts. They are tasked with balancing between maintaining operations as effective as possible and building an inclusive culture where all voices are heard. Strategies such as seeking feedback from quieter team members openly and offering constructive feedback help significantly increase psychological safety. Not only does this improve the morale of an individual but also teamwork amongst the members, which produces creative solutions that might not be seen in more isolated settings. Culturally sensitive leadership behaviors are central to spanning gaps because such leaders can diagnose and fix issues of team members related to their cultures, thereby creating a more united and productive team culture (Fink et al., 2019). As companies get increasingly global in character in their operations, psychological safety among multivalent teams becomes a critical component of good global management. The promotion of such a culture reinforces the principles of freedom of inquiry, where members are allowed to challenge each other's thoughts in a constructive manner and avoid fear of confrontation by not being judged. Such freedom is important as it spurs innovation and ensures that organizations remain competitive on the global scene. Furthermore, effective diversity management depends on a system that maximizes diverse interactions in addition to promoting a shared identity among team members, thus ensuring psychological safety. Thus, understanding these factors not only enhances team effectiveness but is also congruent with overall organizational goals, enabling companies to thrive in the challenging global economy (Nishii et al., 2007).

2.6. CHALLENGES IN MANAGING CULTURAL DIFFERENCES

The nuances of global management require an advanced understanding of culture, a complex weave composed of strands involving values, norms, behaviors, and expectations shared by a group. Managing dissimilarities in cultures becomes increasingly challenging with the onset of globalization, where firms venture into operations in other jurisdictions and employee backgrounds. Cultural miscommunication can lead to reduced cooperation and even conflicts among members. Aside from this, time perception, concept of authority, and work ethics also vary considerably from culture to culture, so they have to learn cultural intelligence. As organizations become increasingly aware of the reality that the HR function will be at the forefront of attempts toward globalization, effective management of these cultural differences is a necessity in order to develop an effective and pleasant work climate (Pucik et al., 1996). Forming a global mindset is what leaders who aspire to be successful in international markets require. This is beyond cultural sensitivity; it includes cognitive, social, and psychological dimensions that equip the ability in individuals to operate and interact effectively within a multicultural world. Cognitive aspects concern awareness of cultural constructs and thought patterns, while social elements are concerned with the ability to interact and communicate across cultures. Lastly, there is the psychological dimension that involves self-knowledge and the ability to be in a position to modify one's behaviors under multicultural environments. Missing this multi-faceted approach, managers risk losing important stakeholders and also discourage cooperative work within multicultural teams. Possessing a global mindset as a key competency has the potential to break cultural divides and enable more effective international management practices (Salmi et al., 2012). The challenges of managing cultural differences are perhaps most pronounced in rapidly growing economies, such as those represented by the BRIC countries. These nations possess unique cultural contexts that can stifle successful global business conduct. For instance, the dynamic between individualism and collectivism can affect staff motivations and expectations substantially, to the point of influencing managerial ability. In addition, the rich historical and socio-political contexts of these countries require international managers to have an understanding of local practices and norms. With these economies expanding and becoming part of the world business environment, the need for culturally aware leaders becomes more evident. It is only by effective negotiation of these barriers with not only awareness but also with an active educational and training strategy, that future managers are able to negotiate these complex cultural terrains (Salmi et al., 2012).

2.6.1. Common Challenges Faced by International Managers

The complexity of culture presents daunting challenges to global managers working across various work cultures. Culture is the beliefs, values, customs, and behaviors that distinguish various groups and influence styles of communication, decision-making, and conflict resolution. Global managers working abroad must evolve a global mindset to manage cross-cultural teams. This involves awareness of cognitive, social, and psychological dimensions of culture to allow leaders to span cultural differences and foster cooperation between employees. Also, cultural incompetence can lead to conflicts, low morale, and eventually organizational performance. Research underscores the increasing importance of global competence, and more particularly the capacity to manage culturally diverse teams, underlining the acute need for models that support managers in embracing and leveraging cultural diversity in their firms (Nishii et al., 2007). Without this preparatory knowledge, international managers will be unlikely to cope with their teams and interrupt cooperative organizational functioning. Also, adjusting to different legal and ethical demands in various countries is an extra challenge for international managers. Each country has a distinct legal framework governing business conduct, labor practices, and corporate governance. Having influence over such rules requires strong knowledge of the local laws as well as the power to plead corporate values that may not have compliance with host country norms. The interplay between top management team (TMT) characteristics, such as international orientation and education intensity, is key to countering such problems. International background and diversity TMTs are best equipped to handle operation complexities and decipher international regulations (Vallone et al., 2019). Mergers of different perspectives thus not only enhance the depth of decision-making but also equip managers with flexibility to cope with the ever-changing legal frameworks across the globe. The psychological and emotional aspect of managing global teams cannot be overlooked since it has a direct impact on shaping an organization's dynamics and overall performance. Managers typically experience cultural dissonance when team members anticipate diverse modes of leadership and communication. Emotional intelligence becomes the central function in such an environment, since managers have to navigate the varying emotional spaces of their employees while creating a sense of belongingness. This can involve talking about individuals' motivational drivers, communication style, and conflict resolution depending on their cultures. Moreover, the lack of a single diversity management framework for globally spanning nations impedes international managers' ability to comprehend systematically and implement approaches for their diverse workforce (Nishii et al., 2007). It is thus essential for international managers to foster emotional and cultural awareness for them to be effective leaders in a globalized world, maintaining the cohesiveness of their teams despite the challenges of culture.

2.6.2. Strategies for Overcoming Cultural Barriers

Managing across borders involves a holistic approach towards creating a deep appreciation of multicultural configurations. Culture can be seen as a set of shared beliefs, practices, and values that dictate the manner in which members of a group interact with one another and perceive the world around them. With this multiculturally composed setting, a global mind needs to be formed. A global orientation allows one to synthesize cognitive, social, and psychological elements necessary for successful cross-cultural interaction. This involves not only being aware of cultural differences but the ability to adjust strategies to fill in gaps and promote mutual respect. Through cultural intelligence training, organizations are able to equip their teams with the tools they need to move beyond cultural fences and establish a diverse working environment that takes into account differences in opinion and includes them. Beyond awareness, there are practical approaches that can help foster cooperation across cultures. One of the successful strategies used is through the application of virtual teams comprised of multiculturals. Such virtual teams tap into the various abilities held by their members, who utilize them to solve local market needs in a personalized way, as witnessed in current organizational practice (Martin et al., 2010). The success of these virtual teams is based on flexibility and cultural competence, which requires from its members not only the establishment of working skills but also culture sensitivity that influences teamwork. Facilitating open communication and trust in such teams can lead to better teams, reducing misunderstandings and overall performance improvement. Organizations must then concentrate on establishing venues that foster such virtual interactions, thereby fostering a culture of continuous learning and responsiveness across geography. In addition to cultural breakthrough, organizations would be better advised to invest in repatriated expatriates' knowledge because they bring applicable relational knowledge that can break workforce gaps. Evidence from research on expatriates within German multinational firms showed that returned country leaders have a unique understanding of cultural forces, which can enable organizations to increase significantly (Antal et al., 2025). But the challenge here is to translate this individual experience into collective organizational intelligence. Institutionalizing support systems for knowledge sharing and integrating expatriates' experience into training programs can put an organization on a stronger foundation as a whole regarding cultural competency. Enabling coordination among returning expatriates and in-country staff not only facilitates a learning culture but also enables bridging of that knowledge gap that normally occurs. By highlighting relational knowledge and creating an open, encouraging climate, organizations are able to be successful in bridging cultural variations and leveraging diversity as a resource in international management.

2.6.3. Importance of Cultural Sensitivity and Awareness

In today's globalized world, the intricate web of cultures greatly influences economic and social life on the international arena. Individuals and institutions operating across cultures are thus obligated to possess a refined understanding of the various aspects of culture. Culture is used to denote shared values, beliefs, practices, and social behaviors characterizing different groups. Understanding these differences in culture becomes essential for effective communication and cooperation in international management. Moreover, cognitive, social, and psychological dimensions of culture shape perceptions and interactions, and it is therefore crucial that managers learn to be culturally sensitive. Realizing the intricacy entailed in multicultural environments, firms can optimize their strategic potential and their international reach be as respectful and knowledgeable as possible, and address the challenges in the emerging literature on intercultural communication competence (Cieri et al., 1998). Cultural sensitivity is more than tolerance; it is an in-depth appreciation of the way cultural differences manifest in the course of daily life, particularly in the corporate world. With the globalization of organizations, cultural awareness is essential as a primary force in driving their human resource management policy and practice. Strategic international human resource management (SIHRM) emphasizes the significance of culture-sensitive approaches to recruiting, training, and organizational development. Such culturally aware practices not only facilitate transitions in operations but also mitigate likely clashes from miscommunications. The analysis of SIHRM draws attention to the significance of understanding multiple cultural models and situating interactions against such values. Greater sensitivity to these lacunas in cultural awareness, as sustained within the literature, positions organizations to answer questions that still go unanswered and navigate the complexity of global engagement (Cieri et al.,

1998). Also, a sound background in cultural sensitivity can also translate to increased cooperation between multicultural teams. In high-context cultures, communication relies on implicit messages and non-verbal cues, and hence requires the low-context culture members to modify their style of communication. Developing intercultural competence contributes to more effective cooperation, enabling team members to share knowledge and opinions that are instrumental in innovative problem-solving. By investing in cultural sensitivity training, organizations not only enhance human relationships but also build a global mind among the workforce. This evolution of consciousness, in turn, increases an organization's ability to adapt to diverse settings and respond sensitively to local traditions and mores. Ultimately, building a sensitivity-awareness culture in global management can lead to more resilient organizations that can survive despite global challenges (Zografi, 2025).

SUMMARY

The study of culture, particularly in a global management context, reveals a multifaceted construct greater than mere geography. It is a psychological, social, and cognitive system that determines how people and organizations think and interact with one another. What can be derived from varying experiences of culture holds the promise of increased understanding and appreciation of differences in behavior, decision, and leadership. Specifically, the acceptance of such diversity in organizational frameworks makes it possible to have more creativity and innovation, which helps companies create better problem-solving solutions in an increasingly globally interconnected world. This calls for a conscious attempt at cultivating cultural curiosity among employees, as established in evidence showing that curiosity fuels the construction of cultural knowledge and cross-cultural competence in multinational teams (Mikhaylov et al., 2016). Ultimately, an understanding of these factors enables businesses to master navigating complex global situations. In developing a global mindset, however, organizations must strive for an integrative strategy in which various cultural viewpoints are blended into central strategy. A global mindset involves a desire to learn and shape practice to suit varied cultural conditions, leading ultimately to more successful market penetration and relationship building across varied territories. Companies have the challenge of comprehending that operational strategies that succeed in one market may not suit another due to cultural variations. For instance, the development of new marketplace opportunities requires explicit understanding of sociopolitical frameworks and business tradition that inform behavior in foreign nations (Lambert et al., 2025). Companies that take up this process on an active basis can not only accumulate competitive advantages but also formulate stable alliances with local stakeholders, thus optimizing their overall performance in international management practices. In addition, cultivating a global mindset has an enormous impact on organizational performance and employee involvement at various levels. When employees get exposure to diversity in culture and soft skill acquisition is given priority, organizations cultivate an environment that is inclusive in essence and respectful of diversity of thought. This cultural alignment of a global mindset can contribute to the creation of innovative solutions better addressing global problems. Additionally, firms that undertake cultural competence training and offer opportunities for cross-cultural engagement are more likely to see enhanced inter-team collaboration, as well as enhanced employee satisfaction. Thus, as business firms engage in cross-cultural meetings resulting from curiosity and the need to be versatile, they solidify their versatility and punctuality within the global business world, and to make sure that cultural knowledge is integrated is a critical aspect of achieving long-term success as a global manager (Mikhaylov et al., 2016).

Multifaceted is crucial to understanding its implications in international management. Culture, traditionally defined as the body of values, beliefs, and practices held by a community, governs the behavioral context in which business is conducted across borders. This context regulates communication patterns, decision-making, and conflict resolution methods in diverse situations. Cross-cultural environments can cause confusion and inhibit effective collaboration if these cultural complexities are not managed. The BRIC countries demonstrate the significance of cultural intelligence, whose distinctive yet convergent identities determine international economic patterns (Salmi et al., 2012). The identification of these cultural factors is thus no mere academic pursuit but a practical necessity for contemporary international managers aspiring to excel in a globalized world. Developing a global mind is essential for international managers to excel in diverse cultural settings. This mindset entails not only understanding various aspects of culture but also mental flexibility to adapt one's leadership style and strategy accordingly. Managers must become aware of their own cultural orientations and consciously engage with values and practices of other cultures. This adaptation relies on social interactions creating mutual respect and learning, facilitating managers' ability to bridge cultural gaps more effectively. As the review in the literature on strategic international human resource management (SIHRM) has highlighted, cultivating such a global mindset can enhance managerial effectiveness and catalyze innovation among multicultural teams (Cieri et al., 1998). Finally, cultivating a global mindset is more than being sensitive; it entails active effort and ongoing learning in the ever-changing global business environment. The psychological, social, and cognitive dimensions of developing a global mindset emphasize the need for intentional educational practices in global management. Cognitive aspects involve reflective thinking of cultural differences, enabling the manager to strategize accordingly in different contexts. Social dimensions involve the establishment of relationships across cultures, which is vital in creating networks and collaborations that enhance business efficiency. Psychological aspects relate to emotional intelligence and adaptability—qualities that allow leaders to cope with the complexities of working with inclusive teams. The advent of the new economies, namely the BRIC countries, also highlights the imperative for leaders to grasp these dimensions, as intercultural contact is reshaping global business dynamics (Salmi et al., 2012). In short, it is the interaction of these dimensions that is crucial to effective management in a global environment, both of individual and organizational growth in a context of cultural diversity.

REFERENCES

1. Antal, A. B., Stroo, I., & Willems, M. (2025). Drawing on the knowledge of returned expatriates for organizational learning: Case studies in German multinational companies. https://core.ac.uk/download/pdf/6653947.pdf (accessed on 24th September 2025).
2. Arora, A., Bird, A., Chakravarthy, A., Ginsberg, A., Kefalas, A., Chandler, A. D., Goldberg, A. I., et al. (2007). What we talk about when we talk about "global mindset": Managerial cognition in multinational corporations. https://core.ac.uk/download/pdf/11738163.pdf (accessed on 24th September 2025).
3. Bloom, M., & Milkovich, G. T. (1998). A SHRM perspective on international compensation and reward systems. https://core.ac.uk/download/5128495.pdf (accessed on 24th September 2025).
4. Boudreau, J. W., Dowling, P. J., & Ramstad, P. M. (2002). Global talentship: Toward a decision science connecting talent to global strategic success. https://core.ac.uk/download/5131512.pdf (accessed on 24th September 2025).
5. Chatterjee, K. (2006). An evaluation study of the core courses of the master's degree in training and development with alignment of globalization. https://core.ac.uk/download/5066837.pdf (accessed on 24th September 2025).
6. Colás Bravo, M. P., Conde Jiménez, J., & Magnoler, P. (2018). Identification of levels of sustainable consciousness of teachers in training through an e-portfolio. https://core.ac.uk/download/190375526.pdf (accessed on 24th September 2025).
7. De Cieri, H., Cox, J. W., & Fenwick, M. (1998). Representing strategic international human resource management: Is the map the territory? https://core.ac.uk/download/5124432.pdf (accessed on 24th September 2025).
8. Fink, G. (2019). Freedom of science. https://core.ac.uk/download/286370703.pdf (accessed on 24th September 2025).
9. Hackett, A. (2015). What are the key practices that STEM & manufacturing-based companies are deploying to drive improvements in the diversity of their workforce? https://core.ac.uk/download/33606064.pdf (accessed on 24th September 2025).
10. Hrotko, T. (2025). Wash corporate heads! Business practice can be changed via the dispositions of executives: Re-socialization towards implicit eco-sustainability. https://core.ac.uk/download/pdf/7297047.pdf (accessed on 24th September 2025).

11. Klein, E., & Mills, C. (2017). Psy-expertise, therapeutic culture and the politics of the personal in development. https://core.ac.uk/download/187115787.pdf (accessed on 24th September 2025).
12. Kovack, K. S. (2015). What are the key competencies and skills required for leaders in China for the greatest ROI? https://core.ac.uk/download/33606057.pdf (accessed on 24th September 2025).
13. Lambert, J., Chanaron, J. J., & Klieb, L. (2025). When markets are unfamiliar: Comparing the market for presentation technology in the French and U.S. legal systems. https://core.ac.uk/download/pdf/7313815.pdf (accessed on 24th September 2025).
14. Martin, M. (2010). Developing global mindset and the impact on virtual teams. https://core.ac.uk/download/219376659.pdf (accessed on 24th September 2025).
15. Mikhaylov, N. S. (2016). Curiosity and its role in cross-cultural knowledge creation. https://core.ac.uk/download/46603917.pdf (accessed on 24th September 2025).
16. Nishii, L. H., & Özbilgin, M. F. (2007). Global diversity management: Towards a conceptual framework. https://core.ac.uk/download/219376625.pdf (accessed on 24th September 2025).
17. Pucik, V. (1996). Human resources in the future: An obstacle or a champion of globalization? https://core.ac.uk/download/5131465.pdf (accessed on 24th September 2025).
18. Salmi, A., & Scott-Kennel, J. (2012). Just another BRIC in the wall? The rise of BRICs and educating tomorrow's global managers. https://core.ac.uk/download/29200651.pdf (accessed on 24th September 2025).
19. Serban, E. M. (2025). Differences awareness model to fundament long-term strategy extension in a new emerging market. https://core.ac.uk/download/pdf/6523336.pdf (accessed on 24th September 2025).
20. Starr, L. (2018). Frameworks for Strategic Leadership. https://core.ac.uk/download/213441653.pdf (accessed on 24th September 2025).
21. Vallone, T., Elia, S., Greve, P., Longoni, A., et al. (2019). Top management team influence on firms' internationalization complexity. https://core.ac.uk/download/227452428.pdf (accessed on 24th September 2025).
22. Zografi, M. (2025). Relevance of intercultural communication for human resources management. https://core.ac.uk/download/pdf/6312382.pdf (accessed on 24th September 2025).

Chapter 3

Individual Behavior Across Cultures

Contents

INTRODUCTION

The international management environment is inherently complex with varying cultural norms governing the behavior of people in significant ways. Understanding how motivation, values, and personality characteristics work in diverse cultural environments is important for organizational and leadership effectiveness. Individuals are likely to bring their own psychological models to work, which may clash or complement the prevailing corporate culture of an organization. This dynamic is often vivid in multinational companies, where workers from different backgrounds need to work together to attain common objectives. Managers in such settings need to develop cultural intelligence as well as adaptability to efficiently navigate heterogeneous value systems, thus creating a convergent environment that promotes innovation and cooperation. By valuing the part played by individual characteristics, businesses are capable of optimizing the performance of their heterogeneous workforce to improve the bottom line. Cultural differences are likely to significantly influence decision-making and ethical concerns in international management. The nuance of individual behavior conditioned by cultures is likely to be reflected in varying styles of problem-solving and risk-taking. For instance, whereas there are cultures that prioritize collective agreement and building relationships in decision-making, others prioritize individual independence and tempo. Such variability could lead to miscommunication and poor communication if not addressed accordingly. The cultural norms that govern personal and professional conduct also vary across cultures and affect conflict resolution and negotiation practices. Management can then devise a plan that integrates multiple perspectives while pursuing organizational objectives by understanding the dimensions of this cultural variance. Leaders who recognize and learn to manage these intricacies will be most likely to develop smoother interfaces and establish a more harmonious workplace atmosphere. When comparing expatriate and domestic managers, the role of the cultural environment is even more intense. Expatriate managers frequently have to adjust their style of leadership to connect with local cultural norms, which can be quite different from their own. Expatriates' success relies not just on technical competence but also on how successfully they become involved with and learn the local culture. Evidence from experiments suggests that the alignment of values of personal leaders with cultural values would impact their performance in cross-cultural team leading. Expatriate experience also highlights the value in gaining cultural intelligence and self-knowledge, e.g., previous work on leadership value congruence with national culture values. By investing in learning about individual and local cultural patterns, organizations can enhance their leaders' competency to perform well within the contexts of different international settings, with the eventual result being enhanced overall performance and cohesiveness (Kelly et al., 2015; Mustafa et al., 2015).

Definition of Individual Behavior in the Context of International Management

In the context of global management, the necessity of understanding people's behavior calls for investigating the influences shaping motivation, values, and personality. These elements play a significant part in shaping people's performance within diverse environments. In fact, to managers and organizations, knowing the potential for the existence of differences in motivational drivers and values among people can be a significant difference in organizational outcomes. Curiously, motivation can either be extrinsic or intrinsic and tends to differ across cultures. For example, collectivistic cultures might strive for harmony in the community and collective success, while individualistic cultures might emphasize personal achievement and autonomy. Thus, global managers must acquire cultural sensitivity so that their motivational policies are such that they synchronize with the diverse aspirations of their subordinates, placing them all in a position to grow harmoniously with their innate values. Cultural differences also become fairly obvious when it comes to decision-making and ethical problems, which are such salient aspects of individual conduct within global management. Where challenging business problems crop up, problem-solving approaches between individuals may differ across cultures. For instance, individuals from high-context cultures may rely heavily on relational relationships and wholes-cognitive inclinations while making decisions, while those with low-context cultures may lean towards straightforward, analytic decision-making procedures. Such a difference may be a cause of confusion and inefficiency in cross-cultural communication. Cultural standards also dictate what behavior is acceptable in carrying out business through moral standards. Thus, creating an ethical decision-making model that is sensitive to cultural diversity is core to international managers as it fosters harmony and can de-escalate the tensions that can arise from differing moral codes among team members. The expatriate-manager-local relationship presents unique challenges and opportunities which also underscore the challenge of human behavior in a multinational management context. Expatriates, who are usually thought to be corporate culture bearers from their home countries, may unintentionally impose their values and styles on host-country teams, causing tension and resistance. Host-country managers possess innate cultural knowledge and sensitivity that contribute to organizational success. Best global operations occur when expatriates and local leaders collaborate, using their diverse strengths to facilitate smoother integration and knowledge transfer. It is absolutely crucial to understand the importance of cultural intelligence in this relationship; high-cultural-awareness individuals are best equipped to manage cross-cultural nuances, eventually establishing an environment that fosters collaboration and drives organizational cohesion in an increasingly interconnected global economy (Marcotte et al., 2019).

Importance of Understanding Cultural Differences

It is essential to understand the dynamic interaction of motivation, values, and personality in different cultural groups for the success of global management. It can significantly impact employee motivation and organizational performance in the current globalized world. Cultural contexts affect not just individual motivation, but also what success and achievement mean and how these are defined within a specific set of norms. This may result in varying leadership and management styles. As Van de Voorde et al. (2007) infers, though differences in practices observable at the national level are present, the reasons underlying these differences might be less marked than originally thought, placing a premium on looking more deeply for the common values that motivate these behaviors. This discussion encourages managers to adopt a more evolved perspective of how cultural background influences team behavior and individual contributions, ultimately resulting in a more diversified workplace that honors differences and maximizes collaboration.

Figure 3.1. The contrast between culture and differences.

Source: https://www.globalcoachcenter.com/wp-content/uploads/2024/09/Why-the-ICBI%E2%84%A2-is-Essential-for-Navigating-Cultural-Differences-in-the-Workplace.jpg.

Ethical decision-making and decision-making generally are tremendously influenced by cultural differences, thus emphasizing the importance of cultural competence in international management. Managers must steer through these complications in order to create contexts in which diverse views are appreciated so that varying ethical perceptions won't interfere with business processes. Knowing how cultures make decisions—via consensus or hierarchical means—can have a direct effect on the effectiveness of cross-cultural teams. For example, whereas certain cultures are inclined to favor individual decision-making, others might favor group consensus, and this influences speed and quality of results. As observed in Mustafa et al. (2015), value congruence of leaders with their cultural context can produce synergistic effects, informing decisions in harmony with organizational goals and cultural expectations. Such differences are crucial to note since they are capable of helping managers prepare for expecting conflict and employing approaches that reconcile opposing viewpoints, thereby fostering a more harmonious organizational culture (Figure 3.1). The distinction between domestic and expatriate managers also reflects the necessity of adapting cultural differences in foreign situations. Expatriates carry with them inimitable skills and experience but will succeed only if they are able to get along with the host nation's cultural milieu. Domestic managers possess natural familiarity with the culture of their nation, which gives them an advantage in aligning management practices with national values and expectations. But this can mean potential disconnection if expatriates fail to appreciate or respect local cultural practices. As is being argued in Van de Voorde et al. (2007), the differences in HR practices by country may not always be understood in terms of cultural differences but may also reflect more general institutional environments—asserting local knowledge can bridge divides. By promoting cross-cultural training and sparking debate between expatriates and indigenous managers, organizations can enhance cooperation and drive performance towards greater international operating success.

3.1. THEORETICAL FRAMEWORKS OF CULTURE

International management is intricately affected by underlying cultural frameworks that shape motivation, values, and personality profiles across organizational contexts. Effective management of diversity groups depends largely on knowledge of these cultural factors because individual behavior tends to significantly vary based on cultural origins. For instance, an expatriate manager from a high individualistic culture may have challenges in dealing with a team in a collectivist culture where decisions are very collaborative. Cultural values also shape ethical issues in decision-making because managers must address moral dilemmas arising from clashing cultural norms. By placing managerial practices within cultural theory contexts, organizations are able to efficiently deal with multicultural employees and translate their motivational methods into addressing the diverse values of their employees and also foster harmonious and improved work culture. In decision-making, cultural theories offer better understandings of managerial behaviors being influenced by values and ethics in societies (Figure 3.2).

High uncertainty avoidance societies, for example, prefer formal decision-making and risk avoidance, while those with low uncertainty avoidance are more flexible, tolerant of uncertainty. These variations will also result in ethical variations because managers operate on different sets of rules that determine what is acceptable business conduct. These studies have shown that such cultural variations exist frequently in multinational organizations, where local managers are more likely to cater to the welfare of the community, but expatriates will adhere to company regulations. Such variation needs detailed understanding of cultural frameworks so that different notions are synchronized, so that organizations can embrace decision-making systems which are culturally adapted as well as functional in meeting business objectives, thus enhancing overall performance within the global economy.

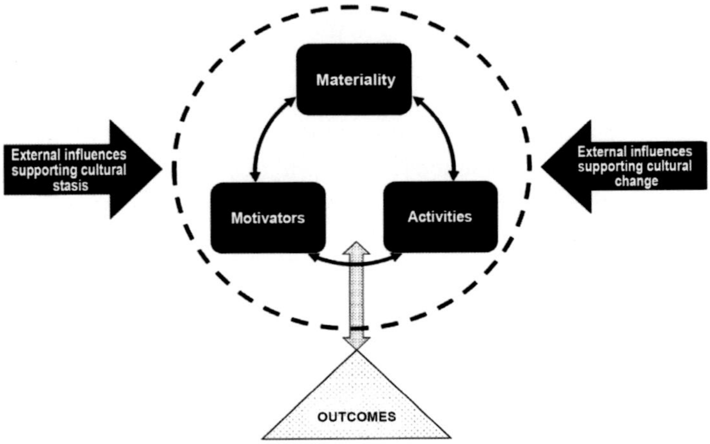

Figure 3.2. The complete cultures framework.

Source: https://media.springernature.com/lw685/springer-static/image/chp%3A10.1007%2F978-3-031-25515-1_4/MediaObjects/509568_1_En_4_Fig8_HTML.png?

In addition, the efficiency of international organization operations depends largely on local managers' and expatriate managers' interrelationship, that is to say, their management styles and leadership styles. Expatriate managers tend to have preconceived corporate values and practices in hand that might not necessarily be effective following national habits and expectations. An understanding of the theoretical models of culture, such as Hofstedes dimensions or Trompenaars cultural types, is effective in explaining how and why these differences manifest themselves in the behavior of people and attitudes towards management. Incorporating these models into training modules can facilitate communication and mutual understanding among expatriates and indigenous talent, leading to smoother transitions and improved collaboration. With companies shifting towards global integration, such cultural fusion of knowledge becomes essential not only for effective working, but also for creating an integrated organizational culture that honors and appreciates diversity, eventually leading to long-term development and innovation in global management practices.

3.1.1. Hofstede's Cultural Dimensions Theory

Understanding the strength of culture over individuals' conduct is vital to international management practitioners. Hofstedes Cultural Dimensions Theory is a collection of works that can be applied to describe how cultures affect values, motivations, and person-to-person interactions. The theory conceptualizes dimensions such as individualism versus collectivism and power distance, and they specify managerial and employee expectations. As various studies have established, these dimensions are far from being theoretical constructs but real realities that influence decision-making and ethical standards across various organizational environments. As organizations become global, a grasp of such cultural differences can mean enhanced cooperation and improved motivation among employees and ultimately a peaceful workplace environment conducive to various cultures. In the perspective of the complex nature of motivation across various cultures, Hofstedes model highlights significant observations. For instance, high-performing individualistic societies can foster personal achievement and autonomy, which could be radically different from collectivist societies that prioritize group harmony and social obligations. This disparity may be evidenced in varied motivational incentives and management practices (Figure 3.3).

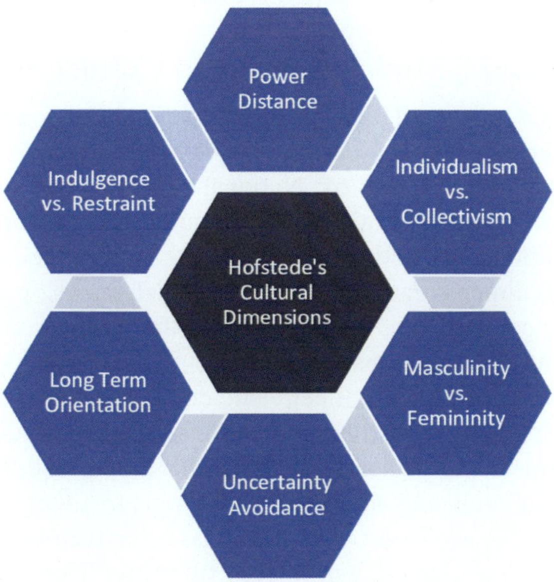

Figure 3.3. Hofstede's cultural dimensions.

Source: https://www.researchgate.net/profile/Dominic-Ligot-2/publication/377219185/figure/fig1/AS:11431281216219777@1704651994851/Hofstedes-Cultural-Dimensions.png.

In the global leadership context, being aware of these cultural dimensions could be the key to conflict resolution negotiation and developing motivation strategies that are appropriate to address the needs of indigenous employees. Additionally, the intersection of national culture with motivation theories emphasizes adaptive forms of leadership that can accommodate not just behavioral differences but also ethically situated frames of mind (Trampel, 2025). The interaction between the local managers and the expatriate also highlights the relevance of Hofstede's Cultural Dimensions Theory in global management. Expatriates are likely to have diverse cultural assumptions regarding power relations, communication, and decision-making that may not be compatible with the host nation's conventional practices. Such incongruence in compatibility may create misunderstandings and tension within the organization if not managed appropriately. Therefore, local managers can also possess cultural intelligence to handle such complexities so there are smoother interactions in multicultural teams. As organizations try to embrace effective management practices, discovering and integrating Hofstede's dimensions into training will bridge the gap between expatriate expectations and local realities so that a more harmonious working experience will be facilitated that leverages cultural diversity as a means of competitive advantage (Trampel, 2025).

3.1.2. Trompenaars' Model of National Culture Differences

With a more interconnected world, it is essential to comprehend human behavior in different cultures, particularly when it comes to management practices. Trompenaars Model of National Culture Differences provides a framework that explains how various cultural values impact managerial behavior and relationships between individuals. This model situates cultures within numerous dimensions, including universalism vs. particularism and individualism vs. collectivism, which describe the motivations and operating principles that inform decisions and actions in numerous diverse cultural contexts. For instance, in more collectivistic cultures, such as in certain Asian nations, group consensus tends to carry more weight than individual opinion, influencing organizational decision-making. This model highlights the critical imperative to get to know and adapt one's own style to adopt the cultural ways of one's units, and further foster organizational effectiveness and harmony in the more multiculture-oriented workplaces of today. The interplay between culture and ethics employed in decision-making is another evidence of the applicability of Trompenaars model to global management settings. Diverse cultural backgrounds bring forth diverse ethical concerns that decide how individuals perceive and respond to dilemmas. For example, in high-context cultures like Japan, indirect styles of decision-making may be the norm, with an emphasis on social relationships and harmony. By contrast, low-context cultures like the United States might focus more on directness and openness. Such cultural models create added layers of complexity regarding how expatriates—and even local managers—go about navigating ethical dilemmas and decision-making..." Here, Trompenaars model becomes a critical tool to establish the role played by values in forming ethical perspectives and behaviors and assist managers in establishing an environment of ethical openness and respect between heterogeneous groups of individuals and thus leading to improved decision-making. Secondly, these interactions between expatriates and home-country managers validate the practical usefulness of Trompenaars model for international management. Expatriates also have difficulties with cultural adjustments that affect leadership and relationships with local employees. The model clearly defines the varying dimensions of culture that may affect those relationships—such as the distinction between the presence of specific versus diffuse cultures, which affects the interactions of expatriates with their local counterparts. As domestic managers may be more attuned to organizational culture and cultural differences, it is very important that expatriates learn about the cultural differences. Organizations can start training programs using Trompenaars approaches to equip expatriates with proper cultural skills in order to successfully collaborate with local staff, encouraging cross-cultural collaboration and organizational performance in the global marketplace. Such information enables organizations to reduce the cultural gap that typically erodes the effectiveness of international management strategies.

3.1.3. GLOBE Study and Its Implications for Management

In global management, understanding the wealth of cultural differences is essential towards ensuring successful working conditions. The GLOBE Study provides significant data on how these dimensions of cultures influence management practices across countries. Emphasizing the interaction between national cultures and leadership behaviors, the GLOBE Study highlights the need for bringing managerial styles into harmony with values that are native to the regional settings. Thus, cross-cultural management becomes an essential factor in international cooperation, especially in the example of Turkey and America, as differences in leadership expectation and communication can potentially have a significant impact on cooperation. Theoretical approaches founded on Hofstedes dimensions of culture intertwined with GLOBEs findings are employed within this research to demonstrate how managers might achieve harmony and productivity by laying out strategically tailored plans while considering and acknowledging such differences in cultures (Halub et al., 2017). The other critical implication of the GLOBE Study is its examination of values, motivation, and personality across cultures. It posits that individuals' motivations are heavily influenced by their culture, consequently impacting organizational behavior. For instance, collective-oriented cultures tend to induce more participative decision-making practices, while individual-oriented cultures tend to induce more competitive culture. Understanding these variations is central to the work of leaders to properly motivate their employees. Additionally, the relationship between a leaders cultural orientation and society culture where they operate can have a critical impact on performance outcomes. The GLOBE Study makes clear the significance of leader-society value congruence, highlighting the fact that effective leaders must adapt their styles depending on the underlying values in society in a bid to enhance team dynamics and effectiveness (Mustafa et al., 2015). Besides, the expatriate challenges compared to host managers are likely to manifest in various decision-making and ethical standards, exacerbated by cultural alignment. Expatriates are likely to refer to the procedures of their home country, causing tension in host organizations where customs and ethical standards differ. The GLOBE Study has comparative analysis that expounds on these dynamics in further detail, suggesting that local managers will have a more intuitive understanding of ethnically embedded ethical systems than expatriate managers. Thus, organizations engaging in globalization need to actively attempt to bridge these cultural gaps by putting in extensive training and development programs directed at the cultivation of cultural consciousness for leaders. This aids the expatriates and local managers in synthesizing their decision-making with the organizational culture, thereby influencing overall performance and work satisfaction in international settings.

3.2. MOTIVATION ACROSS CULTURES

A recognition of the nuances of motivation culturally is relevant in the global management context, as this influences the manner in which organizations are able to effectively engage and motivate employees. Cultural values do shape what would motivate individuals, as this establishes work ethic and emotional satisfaction derived from working. For example, in high uncertainty avoidance cultures like those in some regions of Europe, workers might want structured settings and expectations, with intrinsic motivators closely linked to job security and predictability. Lower uncertainty avoidance cultures, on the other hand, might place a higher premium on innovation and creativity, causing different motivational approaches centered on autonomy and self-actualization. Thus, managers must recognize such cultural differences in order to change their motivational strategies so that they can attract various employee thinking and thus enhance organization-level productivity (Aiken et al., 2018). Decision-making activities, usually reflecting cultural tendencies, also become important for the sense of motivation. In collectivist settings, the need for harmony in the group and consensus may be the source of motivation, resulting in collective decision-making, while individualistic settings may emphasize individual success and reward (Figure 3.4).

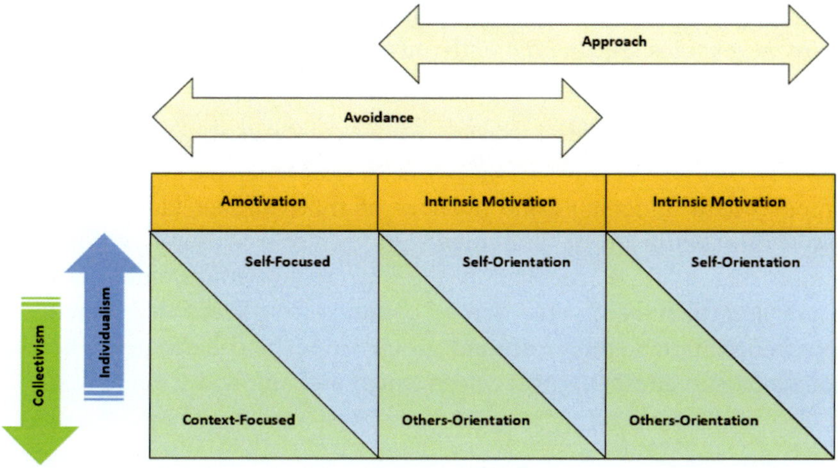

Figure 3.4. Orientations of approach & avoidance motivations across individualist & collectivist cultures.

Source: https://www.researchgate.net/profile/Amelie-Hanna/publication/277927193/figure/fig3/AS:885250498494465@1588071574875/Orientations-of-approach-avoidance-motivations-across-individualist-collectivist.ppm.

This difference can affect goal-setting and feedback systems among managers. For expatriates as well as domestic managers, addressing these cultural dimensions is crucial for establishing proper communication and motivational strategies. Without this, managerial efforts can mismatch employee expectations, leading to decreased motivation and overall performance. As evidence indicates, the recognition of cultural effects on context helps organizations to access a more harmonious workforce dynamic, which is imperative when it comes to enhancing individual behavior in multicultural settings (Karma et al., 2025). No less vital is the role played by cultural intelligence in managing diversity of motivation in international teams. Leaders with high cultural intelligence are better able to appreciate the nuances of diverse workforce values and behavior, enabling them to leverage the creative potential of their teams. As businesses continue to embrace diversity in the workplace, it becomes increasingly relevant to appreciate the multiple motivations driven by cultural environments.

Appreciation has the ability to influence not just employee performance but also retention strategies and team performance. Cultural sensitivity to motivational variation helps organizations come up with accommodating working environments in which the employees are made to feel valued and rewarded, promoting loyalty and enhanced employee satisfaction. Therefore, by prioritizing the management of cultural intelligence and incorporating it into management, businesses can efficiently motivate workers and establish success conditions beyond global frontiers (Karma et al., 2025).

3.2.1. Variations in Motivational Factors

It is important to understand the nuances of motivational factors to be able to control the behavior of individuals in different cultural environments. Motivation has a close correlation with personal values and personality, which are significantly diverse across cultures. In collectivist societies, for example, motivation revolves around group values and harmony, whereas in individualistic societies, personal achievement and autonomy come first.

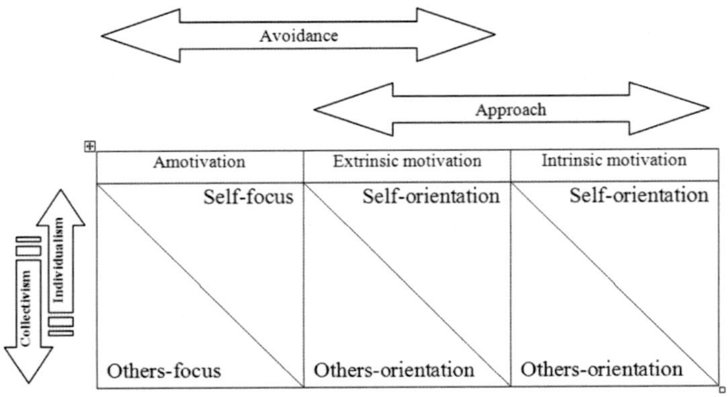

Figure 3.5. Self and others orientations in motivations across individualist and collectivist cultures.

Source: https://www.researchgate.net/profile/Amelie-Hanna/publication/277927092/figure/fig1/AS:885267204431873@1588075557053/Self-and-others-orientations-in-motivations-across-individualist-and-collectivist-cultures.ppm.

This value conflict can potentially influence not only organizational behavior in the workplace but also the process of decision-making among individuals in an organization. With expatriates engaging with domestic teams, intrinsic motivation in them can be at odds with domestic managers,' requiring a culturally sensitive strategy towards motivating teams. This creates an interesting dynamic in which being cognizant of and respecting differing motivational drivers can translate to productivity and communication. Cultural differences also encompass ethical differences as well as styles of decision making, necessarily shaped by the prevailing motivational drivers within a society. When cultures value relationship-building over the long term, decision making will be more consensual and consultative than in cultures with an emphasis on swift, individual decision making. These differences are capable not only of shaping the expectations levied on employees but also of affecting methodologies employed by managers to ensure operational success (Figure 3.5).

A careful critique of these cultural dimensions informs international management practices, enabling leaders to design motivational values that have synergy with the values of multi-cultural teams. Therefore, adopting culturally informed motivational strategies is essential in developing an inclusive culture in an organization, particularly in integrating expatriates into native contexts. In view of the mismatch between expatriates and native managers, motivational influences are clearly articulated. Expatriates, who are usually driven by career development and international experience, may unwittingly underestimate the motivational drivers of host country managers, who may highly prioritize job security and work-life balance compared to other drivers. This discrepancy can lead to misunderstandings and ineffective management strategies if allowed to proceed unchecked. Honest communication about motivations and expectations can bridge this gap and foster cooperation between different managerial competencies. Therefore, it is a tool to both enhance individual performance and align the company's overall objectives with its multicultural workforce. In controlling these differences on an international scale, international managers can leverage the strengths of each cultural perspective to fuel innovation and growth.

3.2.2. Impact of Cultural Values on Motivation

Cultural values significantly impact the motivational climate in organizations, defining how individuals are attached to work as well as employers' objectives. For example, collectivist cultures may value group triumph and consensus above individual success and therefore encourage people through their contribution to group success. In contrast, individualistic cultures emphasize more personal achievement and autonomy and hence motivational policies focusing on individual desire and personal achievement. These inherent contrasts are most important for global managers attempting to develop successful teams from a mix of cultural backgrounds. The challenge is to comprehend these distinct motivational drivers and integrate them into management practices that account for differing cultural values and norms, thereby raising overall organizational effectiveness. Motivation is strongly linked with individual values, and these may vary significantly between cultures. In Western cultures, the emphasis placed on achievement and self-actualization as motivators for motivation tends to create competitive work environments wherein people are stimulated to push themselves. In contrast, interdependent and social harmony-oriented societies can develop motivation on the basis of teamwork and common goals. This difference can be observed in how decisions are reached, with individualistic cultures possibly enjoying rapid decision rounds triggered by individual action and collectivistic cultures deciding through consensus and longer debate. Such nuances significantly impact expatriates and native managers since expatriates may experience cultural dissonance when applying motivation strategies common in their home culture to culturally plural global environments, leading to conflict and reduced morale among native members. Such cultural values also overlap with organizational theories of creativity and innovation, which are key to competitive success. There is also evidence that motivational dynamics differ across cultures in how they facilitate creativity and innovation, and this emphasizes the importance of a culturally sensitive approach to international management. In societies where hierarchical organization is in place, motivation may be based on authority and stability rather than risk-taking, and therefore suppress creative endeavors. By contrast, societies that encourage experimenting and flexibility are able to harness intrinsic motivation for innovation. An investigation of these differences from the perspective of cultural values gives us deeper insights into how organizations can effectively tap their workforce. Cross-cultural knowledge on motivational strategies is important in order to support an innovative culture between different groups to thrive in the fast-globalizing marketplace (Stevan et al., 2017; Anderson et al., 2014).

3.2.3. Strategies for Motivating Diverse Teams

In contemporary global management, an appreciation of the multifaceted nature of motivation is essential while managing heterogeneously composed groups. Personality and values have largely to do with how individuals respond to motivational strategies, especially most particularly in a multicultural environment. Collectivist cultures, for instance, may emphasize harmony within group members and collective achievement as compared to individual rewards, such that leaders invoke reward mechanisms that acknowledge collective achievement. Alternatively, individualistic culture members need autonomy, highlighting the need for differentiated approaches that cater to varying motivational drivers. Sensitivity to such cultural differences allows managers to use various motivation approaches that appeal to individuals from diverse backgrounds, optimizing team cohesiveness and performance. Decision making and ethics are central practices when managing diverse teams. Cultural variation typically affects the decision-making style of team members, some cultures stressing consensus styles while others may stress stronger styles. Leverage in differences can be an incentive tactic since collaborative decision-making styles can empower team members and legitimize their cultural perspective. Moreover, ethical models can look very different from one culture to another, and tolerance for such variation instills a trust and cooperation culture. Through the implementation of a culturally sensitive decision-making style, managers not only motivate their subordinates but also develop a more harmonious work environment, which ultimately leads to more productivity and innovation. The dynamics of motivational techniques are even more important considering the expatriate-local manager difference. Expatriate managers typically possess certain unique challenges, such as cultural adaptation and local team dynamics understanding, that can impact their potential to motivate. Leveraging local managers' cultural competence will enable expats to learn essential information regarding the motivational needs of their teams, so that strategies employed are context-appropriate. Additionally, integration of local managers into managerial roles will foster a sense of belonging and ownership among team members. As organizations become more willing to adopt various leadership styles, collaboration of expatriates with local managers is a powerful method of establishing effective motivational models acknowledging and leveraging cultural diversity within the framework of the team.

3.3. VALUES AND PERSONALITY IN INTERNATIONAL MANAGEMENT

Knowledge of how motivation interfaces with personality and values is central to effective global management. Individuals bring their own set of values shaped by cultural frames, which by definition influence behavior in the settings of the organization. The variability of motivation, for instance, can be traced to variability in societal norms regarding individualism and collectivism. Managers ought to realize that the variance in these values systems has the potential to energize the process of altering decisions and actions among employees. Closely related in significance is the role of personality traits, such as agreeableness and openness, which play a significant role in how individuals interact with individuals from other cultures. Based on (Kelly et al., 2015), individuals scoring high on these factors are likely to be higher on cultural intelligence, enhancing their capacity to work collaboratively with multicultural groups. Therefore, an inclusive understanding of personality and values will aid in fostering peaceful global workplaces. Decision-making within a multicultural setting is generally directed by variations in ethics and values between cultures. While dealing with such variations, international managers are tasked with reconciling opposing ethical expectations. For example, while there are cultures that will stress consensus and relationship harmony in decision-making, others will stress responsibility and results of the individual. This variation may lead to confusion and conflict and highlights the imperative for managers to become culturally attuned. Besides, the implications of the differences extend to organizational performance, as ethical mismatches can limit teamwork among diversified workers. Applying the principles of cultural intelligence, as expounded by Karma et al. (2025), allows managers to bridge the gaps, then relating workforce diversity to the organization's objectives. Through developing an inclusive environment that respects diverse ethical frameworks, international managers are able to foster collective decision-making. The difference between local managers and expatriates highlights the intricacies of personality and values in international management. Expatriates, coming from diverse cultural backgrounds, can find it difficult to fit into local norms and values, ultimately impacting their leadership efficacy. Local managers, however, have an innate cultural understanding of the terrain, which translates to superior communication and decision-making strategies among their teams. Expatriates, however, introduce fresh perspectives that can facilitate innovation, provided that they approach their work with awareness of local customs and traditions. It is important to ensure a mutual relationship between expatriate employees and local managers so that the power of cultural diversity in organizations can be fully realized. The added dynamic of personality traits, and in particular agreeableness, as highlighted in Kelly et al. (2015), can also complement such interaction, creating a more collaborative approach to management that honors difference while leaping on similarity.

3.3.1. Role of Personal Values in Decision-Making

International management decision-making is usually guided by intrinsic individual values of individuals. Such intrinsic guiding values, importantly, impact how managers frame situations, weigh options, and engage stakeholders. For instance, managers from collectivist cultures, where group harmony and concurrence are valued, may rate team input as more central to decision-making. Conversely, individualistic people are likely to adopt a more autonomous position, where individual effort and achievement are stressed. This difference serves to illustrate how cultural environments affect the prominence of values and how close attention to such cross-cultural variations is needed in effective international management. Examining the relationship between individual values and decision-making not only sheds light on leadership styles but also helps make predictions about managerial actions under different circumstances. By appreciating the significance of these values, organizations are more able to manage the dynamics of cross-cultural management (Figure 3.6).

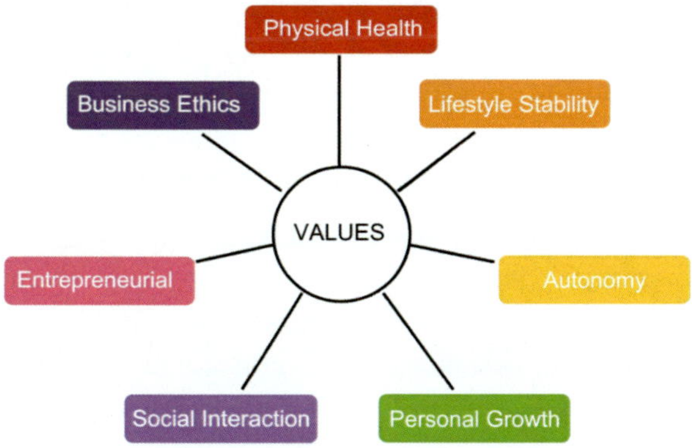

Figure 3.6. The integration of personal values in different cultural backgrounds.

Source: https://interact-global.co/wp-content/uploads/2022/11/Values-Clusters-1024x653.png.

The integration of individual values into decision-making situations becomes more critical as businesses operate in a variety of culturally different environments. Different cultural backgrounds contribute to conflicting ethical norms and decision-making processes among managers, making it more difficult to reconcile organizational goals with individual values. For example, expatriates are likely to encounter decision-making dilemmas when they face incompatibility between personal values and local culture. Research has also shown that alignment of personal values of the leaders with societal values is essential in building effective communication and cooperation within multinational settings. Awareness of these dynamics will enable organizations to create customized approaches to management and leadership such that personal values align with the company mission in different cultural contexts. Such alignment not only enhances the effectiveness of decision-making but also encourages organizational integrity in a global environment. Besides, the broader personal values implications lie with innovation adoption for global management. National culture influences levels of innovation penetration deeply, demonstrating how personal values blend with macro cultural determinants. receptiveness to innovation is due to core values differences held by stakeholders in organizations. For example, traditionally-oriented managers may resist adopting new technology, while those aligned with progressiveness may be ready to grab innovations enthusiastically. This person-organization and nation-person dynamics of cultural values underscores the importance of coordinating personal values with adoption models, as with organizational behaviors in cross-cultural contexts. As a result, locating these layers of values within decision-making is not only able to optimize innovation strategies but also to optimize overall organizational adaptability in a globalized economy, complementing further the effectiveness of global management strategies.

3.3.2. Influence of Personality Traits on Management Styles

Among the numerous determinants of management styles, personality traits come out as the primary determiners of leadership effectiveness and worker relationships. Managers are inclined to extrapolate their innate qualities such as extroversion, conscientiousness, and emotional intelligence into their management style.

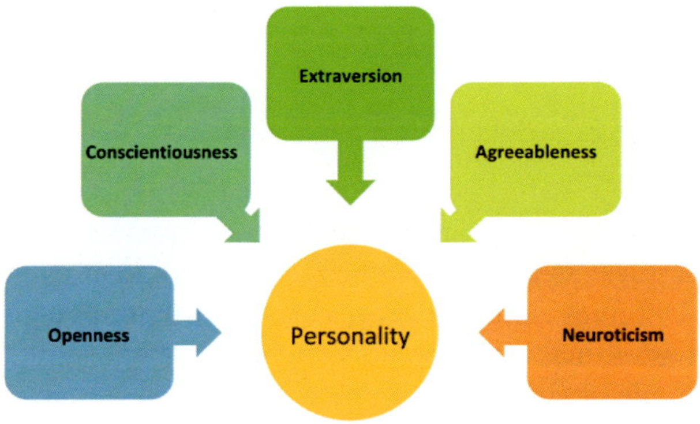

Figure 3.7. Understanding how personality traits shape management styles is crucial for organizations operating in multicultural environments.

Source: https://s3-us-west-2.amazonaws.com/courses-images/wp-content/uploads/sites/1972/2017/08/18224012/Big_Five_Personality_Traits.png.

For instance, an extraverted manager is likely to adopt a participative style of leadership that encourages open communication and cooperation. Alternatively, a more introverted manager might value a directive style, one that minimizes interaction and focuses on task achievement rather than team relations. Thus, the alignment between a manager's personality and his or her preferred management style can have a significant influence on organizational culture and team performance. Of special interest, cultural context can amplify or dampen these influences, as various cultures will place varying emphasis on varying traits, thus creating different expectations for managerial behavior and decision-making processes. It is essential for organizations operating in multicultural environments to recognize the impact of personality traits on management styles. As an example, expatriate managers must deal with the nuances of foreign cultures and yet be loyal to their own personality attributes. The challenge is achieving a syncretic blend of these personal attributes with an awareness of local mores, motivators, and codes of morals. Local managers, however, may have management styles influenced by shared cultural norms that may reinforce or oppose those of expatriates (Figure 3.7).

This distinction can be a source of confusion, particularly in the decision-making process based on differential ethical considerations along cultural orientation. Application of insights from personality study can assist in creating training techniques that bring about cross-cultural competency in managers in order to enhance effectiveness across multicultural contexts. Incorporating psychological elements, such as PsyCap, in management styles is a reflection of the dynamic interplay between personality and performance in leadership contexts. PsyCap comprises hope, efficacy, resilience, and optimism—a necessary set of strengths that facilitate a manager's capacity to inspire and motivate teams during tough times. Through an emphasis on positive leadership characteristics, managers are in a position to generate a positive climate to facilitate collaboration and innovation. This new emphasis on a motivational leadership style is particularly relevant in global management, where flexibility and emotional intelligence are paramount considerations. Focusing on the cultural sensitivities that come with these traits will help managers align their management strategies more appropriately with the expectations of local employees, boosting individual and organizational performance. Therefore, recognizing the direct influence personality traits have on management styles is important in creating effective positive organizational impacts among culturally diverse staff.

3.3.3. Cross-Cultural Personality Assessments

In today's globalized business world, it is important to comprehend the behavior of people from various cultures in order to manage internationally effectively. Personality testing is an important aspect here, as it helps one understand how values, motivations, and behavioral styles differ across people from different cultures. For example, dimensions like collectivism versus individualism can affect how personality traits are expressed at the workplace. Members of collectivist cultures will exhibit higher agreeableness and conscientiousness, prioritizing cooperation and harmony within groups over personal drive. Therefore, it is critical that the nuanced meaning of these traits be cross-culturally translated in measurement methods such that what is measured actually reflects the underlying values and behaviors found in a society, allowing managers to make more informed decisions regarding staff composition and team building. Furthermore, cross-cultural personality assessments are also demonstrated by the diverse approaches taken by expatriates and native managers. Expatriates, generally from individualist cultures, may be relying on dominant Western personality models, which may fail to identify culturally grounded traits predominant in collectivist environments, such as deep shared values and relational dynamics. Conversely, native managers possess rich contextual knowledge of their culture, which shapes their ethics and decision-making. This phenomenon testifies to the necessity of culturally sensitive assessments that consider the local values and norms to generate more effective management practices that resonate with the behavioral inclinations of the workforce. Hence, organizations must bridge these cultural divides using a variety of assessment methodologies that foster tolerance and inclusion of the local practices and customs. At the center of this controversy is also the significance of trust in cross-cultural settings, especially in multicultural teams. The evidence of trust relationships, as is observed in China and Turkey, is that relational dynamics extend outside the workplace into personal relationships as well. Trust development, pivotal in cross-cultural assessments, may vary considerably on the basis of beliefs in benevolence, integrity, and capability. As Barney et al. (2010) illustrates, benevolence becomes a key factor in trust development, enabling cooperative behavior and knowledge sharing among members. Consequently, global managers must be able to identify the cultural undertones of human relationships through the use of tailored personality tests that not only assess individual behaviors but also offer insight into the relational dynamics that enable successful team work in diverse cultural contexts.

3.4. CULTURAL DIFFERENCES IN DECISION-MAKING

In global management, decision-making in most instances is largely influenced by the values and motivations behind people's behaviors. These values can shape how managers view problems, assess risk, and rank various outcomes. For instance, individualistic cultures that the United States belongs to, in their essence, push decision-makers towards considering individual success and autonomy. Conversely, collectivistic cultures in most Asian countries emphasize group harmony and consensus, leading to more cohesiveness in decision-making. This dichotomy highlights that individual values shaped by cultural experiences have humongous implications for managerial effectiveness and the strategies employed within an organization. It is essential that expatriates and local managers understand these differences as they can cope easily with the complexities of multicultural work environments. The intersection of cultural difference and ethical issues in decision-making also has a significant contribution to make towards international management. Managers are frequently faced with decision dilemmas where organizational and personal ethics are pitted against cultural norms that vary heavily between contexts. In some cultures, historic priority for outcomes may override ethical issues, and decisions taken may prioritize short-term gains at the cost of integrity (Figure 3.8).

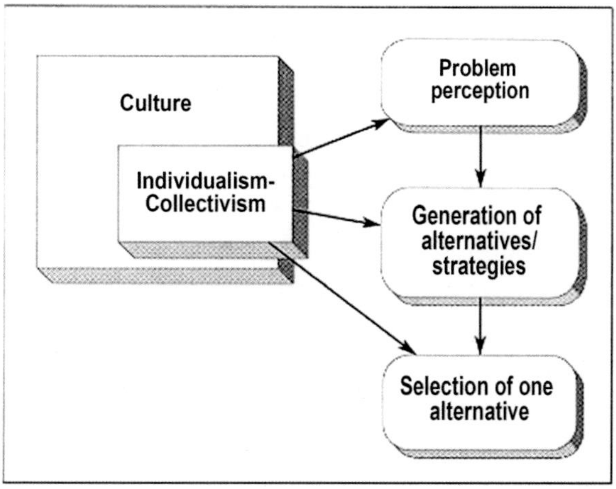

Figure 3.8. Cultural influences on decision making.

Source: https://www.researchgate.net/profile/C-Guess/publication/228759245/figure/fig3/AS:393607417745413@1470854729198/Cultural-influences-on-decision-making.png.

However, other cultures can place greater stress on ethics, leading decisions towards more socially conscious and transparent results. This is a challenge to multinational firms attempting to maintain a uniform ethical framework across their global operations. Companies must know about these differences in cultures so that they can devise training and policies supported by decision-making procedures, both ethical standards and cultural demands, resulting in organizational credibility and viability. Furthermore, the contribution of technology in bridging cultural variations in decision-making cannot be overlooked. Advances in information and communication technology (ICT) enable teams to bridge cultural variations, facilitating an atmosphere of inclusive decision-making. Cultural diversity can enhance decision-making by offering diverse perspectives and could also hamper communications (Shachaf et al., 2008). There are effective uses of ICT tools, such as video conferencing and collaboration platforms, which can improve communication between differing groups, hence their overall decision-making abilities. This technology support is most crucial in trans-boundary virtual teams where differences in culture might lead to misunderstanding unless well handled. By applying such tools, organizations are able to create a harmonious team culture that honors diverse inputs without making the decision process more complicated, allowing for efficiency and innovation in worldwide management scenarios.

3.4.1. Individualistic vs Collectivistic Decision-Making Processes

In international management, one needs to be able to comprehend the psychological foundation that informs decision-making strategies. Individualist cultures, which usually prefer personal freedom and autonomy, often have expressed decision-making tendencies in favor of personal interest over group interest. Collectivist cultures, on the other hand, prioritize group harmony and accord and have decision-making strategies that consider input from all members of the group towards the attainment of common good. This divergence has a significant impact on the manner in which managers working in expatriate settings engage with workplace interactions. Individualist expatriates will struggle to collaborate with indigenous teams that highly regard strong communal relationships and pooled contributions, as this is likely to cause a values conflict that drains the quality of teamwork. Decision-making dynamics further point to the significant role of underlying cultural values. Individualistic decision-makers would react to problems with an emphasis on innovation and personal responsibility. Collectivistic decision-makers use group knowledge and the necessity of keeping team members in check. The guideline holds true with Hofstede's cultural dimensions model, as analyzed in the discussion of tourist behaviors and how they underscored the individualism/collectivism aspect in relation to risk orientations. Remarkably, collective orientation in decision-making is found to bias risk perceptions and preferences with collectivistic decision-makers tending to choose options that enhance group comfort and security over personal profit, thereby revealing a rich organizational landscape of workplace decision-making influenced by cultural orientation (Manrai et al., 2025). Moreover, the interconnectedness between decision-making processes and leadership styles suggests the pivotal role of cultural congruence in management. Contextual culture shapes leaders' embodiment of values that are congruent with either individualistic or collectivistic philosophies; leaders from collectivistic cultures may employ democratic and participatory leadership styles that emphasize consensus, and leaders from individualistic cultures may employ more autocratic styles. This contrast tends to mediate the impact of leaders' articulation of visions and goals to subordinates on overall organizational performance. The value congruence complexity of leadership-society offers understanding for the enduring need for cross-cultural training in international management, with the aim of bringing leadership strategies into harmony with prevailing cultural norms. Cross-cultural training assures expatriates learn and execute decision-making strategies in accordance with the local level expectations, which results in more intensive cooperative relationships within multicultural business settings (Mustafa et al., 2015).

3.4.2. Risk-Taking Behaviors Across Cultures

In the context of international management, it is crucial to unravel the multifaceted web of risk-taking behavior in order to effectively function within diverse cultural contexts. Each culture possesses distinctive motivational drivers that influence individual choice mechanisms, particularly in the context of risk. For instance, while Western cultures value autonomy and individualism, encouraging risk-taking as a means to success, collectivist cultures would be more likely to encourage community interest, thus adopting more conservative approaches to risk-taking.

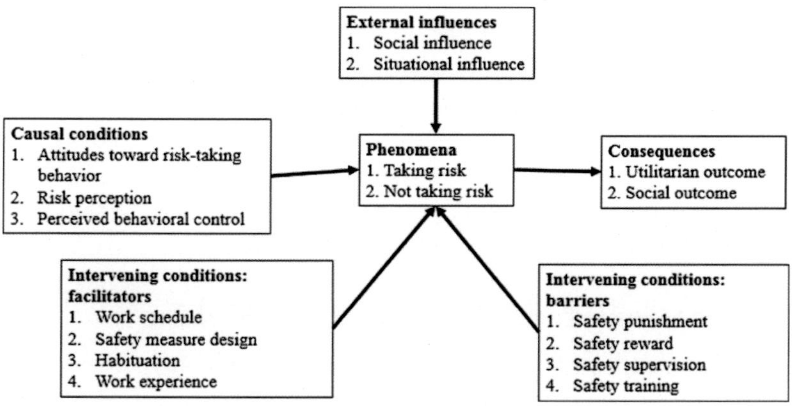

Figure 3.9. Risk-taking behaviors.

Source: https://ars.els-cdn.com/content/image/1-s2.0-S0925753516303071-gr1.jpg.

These cultural norms are fluid and can shift with globalization, creating a complex interaction wherein managers must redo their strategy to meet local requirements. The conflict between control and cooperation can have a significant impact on the success of an expatriate leader in such varied systems, and the necessity for culture awareness in managing perceptions of risk and risk behaviors becomes increasingly obvious. In addition, values form the core of defining risk-taking attitude in all cultures. The higher the uncertainty avoidance, say in most Asian cultures, the more cautious there will be in making decisions and taking risks (Figure 3.9).

Conversely, low uncertainty avoidance cultures would encourage experimentation and risk-taking as part of entrepreneurial culture. Such divergence becomes difficult for multinational firms, particularly when defining policy and procedures that regulate risk management. It is imperative to align management practices with such cultural dimensions; failure to adapt and cognize local values could lead to miscommunication and ineffective strategies. As Bromiley et al. (2015) also suggests, combining risk management with corporate governance competency and cultural dynamics can facilitate increased synchronicity in otherwise heterogeneous organizational environments. Additionally, the impact of people's personalities and values on risk-taking behavior cannot be overstressed. Culturally aware and flexible expatriates may be able to manage risks better than low-profile home-country managers with diminished visibility of international business intricacies. Conversely, indigenous managers have a better grasp intuitively of their cultural background, making them better suited to risk analysis in their respective settings. While both groups enjoy strengths that are unique to them, their approaches can be significantly different based on individual experience and ethical practices instilled by their cultural backgrounds. Understanding these behavioral nuances is important to multinational companies as they seek to establish a culture where risk can be positively debated. As the international business landscape continues to evolve, understanding these distinctions will be a component of optimizing management strategies in various settings.

3.4.3. Ethical Considerations in Decision-Making

In the complex setting of international management, where the intersection of individual behavior and cultural context necessitates a deliberate focus on ethics decision-making, dealing with varied cultural expectations as managers will have to navigate the subtleties of motivation, values, and personality traits that affect their decisions. The influence of values that are deeply rooted in culture can make a vast difference in ethical frames of reference between native managers and expatriates. For example, what constitutes appropriate behavior in one culture can be considered unethical in another, and this underscores the need for cultural sensitivity in leadership. Since they operate beyond borders, managers not only have responsibility for the immediate implications of their decisions but also for their consistency with the broader ethical norms that arguably exceed local norms, thus placing value on complexities that arise in making ethical judgments in a multicultural environment. Secondly, ethical myopia can also occur within organizational environments, especially during emergencies when short-term survival may override long-term ethical considerations. Under such circumstances, it is critical that decision-makers tap into ethical frameworks beyond nearby context. Research reminds us that micro-cultures of emergency are formed during crises, and this stimulates compressed ethical perspectives with overriding proximal values and preservation needs (Mumley et al., 2019). This is important because managers are in between their own interests to produce a setting in which ethical decision-making occurs. Transcendent value leaders can also act as ethical mentors, guiding their teams through challenges with an emphasis on recognizing the importance of ethical considerations. This emphasizes sensitivity to ethical considerations that can impact decision-making, particularly under pressure that comes with global management. The educational platform of project management also emphasizes the use of behavioral skills as well as technical skills to facilitate ethical decision-making. Soft skills like critical thinking, emotional intelligence, and cross-cultural communication are of utmost value when managers have to face complex ethical dilemmas (Kanabar et al., 2018). Preparing future leaders with proper skills to meet these challenges can assist institutions in enhancing project-related competencies that by nature may influence ethical behavior. These competencies allow leaders to think through decision-making in a holistic approach so that ethical considerations are incorporated into the process. Developing students who are not only technically proficient but also ethically responsive can ultimately lead to more informed decision-making within multicultural environments, enabling the superior need for ethical responsibility in cross-border management practices.

3.5. EXPATRIATES VS LOCAL MANAGERS

In the context of international management, understanding individual behavior worldwide becomes essential, particularly when comparing native managers with expatriates. Expatriates often possess a diverse set of skills and knowledge that can inspire organizations seeking international insights. They might struggle to manage local cultural nuances and operation habits, thus affecting their performance in the long term. For example, local managers would typically possess a natural understanding of the workings of the local market as well as cultural subtleties that would find expatriates lacking. This tried and tested fact makes local managers better equipped to manage complex interpersonal relationships and ethical considerations that resonate with their teams, and eventually foster a working environment that encourages cooperation and trust. Secondly, the compensation and incentive structures associated with different managerial roles have a strong influence on motivation and performance. Expatriates have traditionally been granted pay perks aimed at maintaining their economic balance overseas, tying their compensation to a global benchmark rather than domestic market rates. The practice, however, can create a sense of disconnection with which local managers, who have the unique compensation standards characteristic of reality in the culture, are in tune, noticing discrepancies in their own compensation relative to expatriates (Figure 3.10).

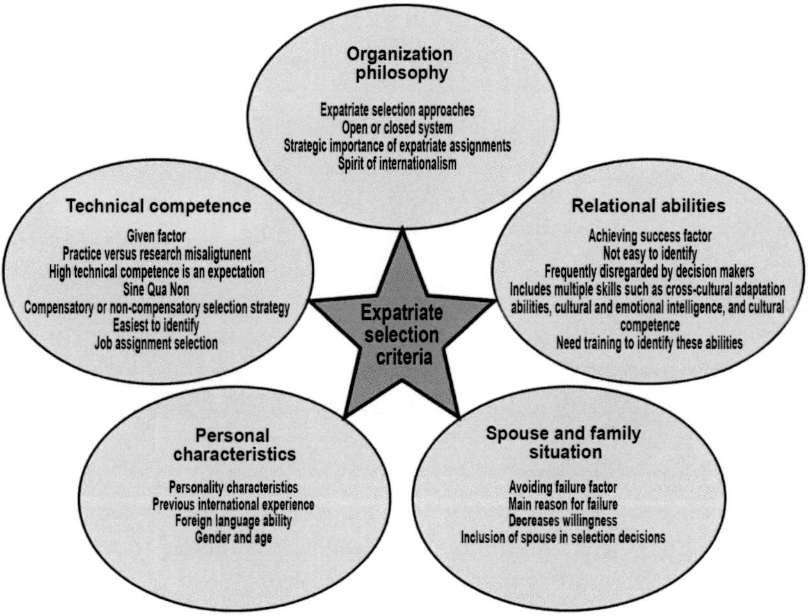

Figure 3.10. Expatriate selection criteria clustered by organization.

Source: https://www.researchgate.net/profile/Snejina-Michailova/publication/307879489/figure/fig2/AS:613961774923801@1523391302438/Expatriate-selection-criteria-clustered-by-organization-philosophy-technical-competence.png.

As articulated by Bloom et al. (1997), the new world economy is compelling businesses to rethink their compensation systems, thus discrediting current paradigms that have differentiated between expatriate and host-country compensation packages. Such shifts in trends emphasize international businesses' need to be responsive and sensitive to cultures in their management practices. Both domestic and expatriate managers' functions may also play roles in team dynamics in multinational companies. Research indicates that expatriates have the capability of bringing global best practices and strategic knowledge, but local managers tend to excel in exploiting local knowledge essential for project success. Teaming cosmopolitans (expatriates) and locals together has the capability of enhancing knowledge transfer, but team imbalance can hinder performance, as detailed in Haas et al. (2006). The right balance must be achieved; too many expats would lead to a disconnect with indigenous realities, yet too many domestic managers might limit innovative approaches. Thus, the right combination of these two managerial perspectives is essential to optimizing team performance and achieving organizational objectives in multicultural environments.

3.5.1. Challenges Faced by Expatriates in Foreign Cultures

Cultural adaptation is a primary concern for expatriates since it profoundly influences how they are received in international work environments and impact general organizational performance. The feeling of novelty in a new cultural environment gives rise to sensations of isolation and tension, which deter successful adaptation. When cultural values, expectations, and norms differ significantly from those of their home country, expatriates tend to have identity conflicts and moral conflicts. For example, expatriates working in the emerging markets could find themselves caught between local expectations and the home country's moral standards, thus developing cognitive dissonance. This intermediate experience requires expatriates to employ coping strategies as with rites of passage, which can make the transition between moral standards smoother, thus enabling effective engagement in the novel cultural setting (Costa et al., 2025). Finally, a lack of proper support mechanisms aggravates these problems, proving an extreme necessity for organizations to provide stringent preparatory training and ongoing support to their expatriate employees. Knowledge transfer also makes the life of expatriates more challenging in foreign cultures. While expatriates are typically sent to bring about valuable know-how, they typically encounter severe hindrances when attempting to transfer their individual expertise into organizational knowledge. Evidence indicates that a significant discrepancy exists between the individual learning achieved by expatriates on their assignments and organizational ability to leverage such knowledge productively (Antal et al., 2025). This is likely due to poor infrastructure for supporting knowledge sharing or corporate cultures opposing new concepts. As a result, expatriates can get their contributions dismissed or disregarded, becoming frustrated and disenchanted. These challenges need to be overcome in order to maximize the return on investment in expatriate assignments as well as to create a learning and adaptability culture within the organization (Figure 3.11).

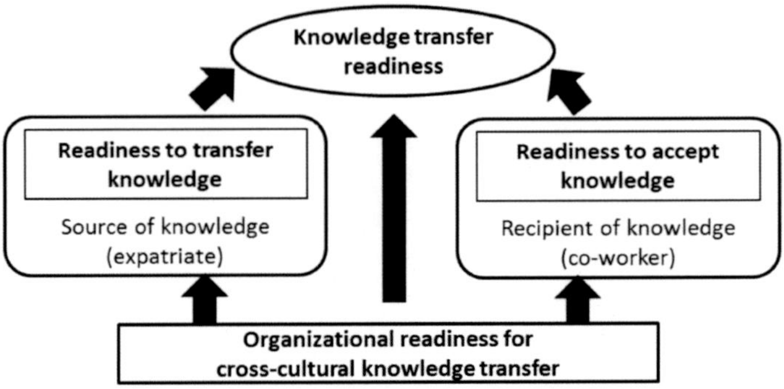

Figure 3.11. The changing nature of expatriation.

Source: https://media.springernature.com/lw1200/springer-static/image/art%3A10.1007%2Fs13132-021-00777-y/MediaObjects/13132_2021_777_Fig3_HTML.png.

The differential dynamics among expatriates and host managers also increase the problems in foreign cultures. Often, expatriates carry an arsenal of assumptions and values learned in their native culture, which can be at odds with host country customs and decision-making processes. Such disparity may cause tension, particularly when expatriates introduce Western management practices that are not compatible with host local habits or operating conditions. Furthermore, expatriates may also be perceived as aliens by host managers, and their leadership may be resisted. This conflict can inhibit collaboration and the development of effective working relationships. Organizations can prevent this from happening by creating inclusive cultures that emphasize teamwork through various styles of management. Through promotion of dialogue and respect for diverse opinions, organizations are able to promote the integration of expatriates into host country workforce, ultimately gaining from diverse ideas and experiences.

3.5.2. Advantages of Local Managers in International Settings

The intricacies of international management reveal a complex interdependence among variations in cultures and managerial practice. In this case, local managers serve as vital intermediaries who mediate the contradictions between international corporate strategies and regional operating realities. Their intimate understanding of local market dynamics enables them to approximate organizational practices that resonate with local consumer behavior, which sometimes improves customer satisfaction and brand loyalty. In addition, local managers tend to also possess information that expatriates lack regarding the socio-cultural conditions in the domestic site, leading to more effective decision-making. This cultural sensitivity is crucial, especially in multinational corporations where adapting to local practices and norms can have a tremendous influence on the outcomes of business, hence further cementing the critical role of local managers towards the success of international operations (Everdingen et al., 2025). The advantages of local manager use extend beyond operational efficiency; they also produce innovation aligned with local cultural settings. As suggested by innovation adoption studies across different national cultures, local managers are well placed to respect the factors that facilitate or hinder the penetration of new practices and technologies within their markets (Everdingen et al., 2025). Their exposure to local regulatory forces, consumers' preferences, and competitive horizons provides a specialized insight enabling them to innovate on dimensions that are attuned to regional requirements. Not just does this localized innovation capability enhance the adaptability of a multinational company in reacting to market fluctuations, but also creates a culture of innovation that can drive long-term growth. As such, local managers not only serve as tactical executors of corporate strategy, but also key drivers for innovation based on regional perception and experience. Moreover, local managers can help positively engage and retain the employee base of multinational companies. They are inclined to embody values and practices which the local employees accept and foster a work culture which is inclusive and respectful of cultural pride and identity. When local managers operate from within their environments, they create trust and loyalty among the workers, both of which are central to enhancing motivation and productivity. In mediating the contradictions between the global imperatives of multinational corporations and the local expectations, the job of local managers is to manage these forces effectively. Their ability to link organizational goals to local values not only fosters employee commitment but also improves the overall performance of the organization as a whole on a global scale (Bloom et al., 2000).

3.5.3. Strategies for Effective Collaboration Between Expatriates and Local Managers

Organizing successful cooperation among expatriates and local managers demands an awareness of the hidden culture dynamics influencing motivation, values, and personality orientations. When entering a new destination, expatriates are likely to carry with them cultural biases and assumptions that could significantly differ from those of local managers. This cultural difference is likely to lead to misunderstandings, affecting decision-making processes and ethical stances within the organization. Hence, it is important to establish open lines of communication. This can be achieved through regular team-building activities and workshops, cultural sensitivity, and through them, expatriates and local managers can exchange their values and ideologies. By creating a platform of communication, organizations can bridge gaps, thus enhancing cooperation and encouraging respect for one another, which are essential aspects of successful global management in terms of human behavior in different cultures. It is also important to implement systematic cultural competences training programs focusing on the special needs of expatriates and local managers on an individual basis. These courses must include tailored content designed to increase local practices and customs awareness, which will also ease the adaptation stage of expatriates. For local managers, understanding expatriate perspective as well is crucial. This two-way approach helps create a more diverse workplace with shared knowledge, and diverse views are valued. Incorporating collective learning methods can result in both gaining knowledge from each other's practice. Collective learning is an important aspect of knowledge transfer, especially in a global environment, and conforms to the emerging wisdom that embedded knowledge in groups can develop firm capabilities (Anand et al., 2001). By intentional fostering of such group environments, firms can leverage the strengths of both local managers and expatriates. Finally, reliance on technology to facilitate communication and cooperation can strongly advance the effectiveness of local manager-expatriate partnerships. Technologically advanced platforms have the ability to overcome geographical distances, facilitating real-time communication and feedback systems. These technologies facilitate the continuous exchange of thoughts, especially useful when addressing complex decision-making systems based on cultural differences. Adding these technologies not only facilitates the ease of communication but also creates a sense of relationship that otherwise proves difficult to maintain over distances. Besides, the organizations need to think about paying close heed to the development of inclusive structures that encourage all members to contribute, be it from diverse backgrounds. Emphasizing the role of expatriate and local manager contributions can foster an inclusive atmosphere, allowing the individuals to contribute sufficiently towards the organizational goals and recognizing personal challenges of each group (Janssens et al., 2025).

3.6. COMMUNICATION STYLES ACROSS CULTURES

Cultural differences in communication style are significant in influencing individual behavior in international management. Such differences arise from entrenched culture values that are the cause of determining interpersonal relations, controlling decision-making processes, and consequently influencing managerial performance. For instance, in certain cultures, communication will be more direct, clear, and concise, whereas in others, communication is indirect as a tool to sustain harmony and rapport establishment. Recognition of such varying inclinations enables managers to mold communication practices, making it a collaborative and innovative environment. Additionally, the congruence of leader values and societal values can enhance the efficiency of communication, as leaders who adjust styles to cater to the culture of their environment are more effective in their roles in diverse environments (Mustafa et al., 2015). Hence, these differences must be understood and addressed in cross-cultural management. Cultural communication style's biggest influence comes when considering the motivation and nature of people at the workplace. Different cultures instill distinct values that not only shape how people communicate but also why they communicate (Figure 3.12).

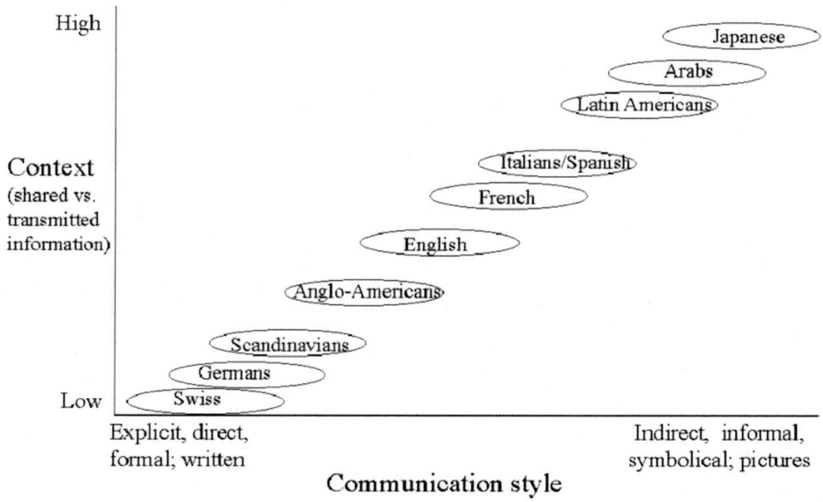

Figure 3.12. Cultural communication styles.

Source: https://www.researchgate.net/profile/Marc-Hermeking/publication/220438110/figure/fig14/AS:977037472829440@1609955294135/Cultural-communication-styles-according-to-Hall-Usunier-1991-modified.png.

For example, collectivist-orientated cultures can encourage communication with excess on group consensus, whereas individualistic cultures will emphasize personal achievement as well as being assertive in communication. This should make managers reflect rather critically on how various cultures influence team communication as well as decision-making. In the local managers vs. expatriates context, expatriates face challenges due to their lack of familiarity with the local communication norms, thus resulting in poor leadership and misinterpretations (Halub et al., 2017). Recognizing and conforming to these differences are critical to the creation of effective working relationships in foreign environments. Additionally, effective communication skills are essential for overcoming ethical dilemmas and decision-making situations in cross-cultural environments. Cultures differ in having varying systems of ethics that may influence decision communication and their execution. For instance, while some cultures view openness as the greatest virtue, others may value loyalty and secrecy, thus influencing the way information is shared among team members. The global manager needs to appreciate the presence of such ethical considerations because miscommunication may result in ethical breaches, loss of trust, and team conflict in multinational teams. Cultural context mediation, especially through self-construal and communication styles, is a key process that constitutes leader-society value congruence (Mustafa et al., 2015). Thus, cultivating an increased awareness of underlying cultural communication patterns will significantly influence the effectiveness of decision-making and ethical behavior in multicultural organizational settings.

3.6.1. High-Context vs Low-Context Communication

Effective communication is of utmost significance to international management, particularly when handling the subtle complexities of divergent cultural contexts. High-context and low-context communication strategies have far-reaching effects upon interpersonal relations and organizational activity in cross-cultural settings. High-context communication, most prevalent in collectivist cultures, primarily relies on implicit messages, non-verbal communication, and the surrounding context of the communication rather than the explicit nature of the message. This is a style of communication that assumes shared understanding among participants, and as good as this can yield robust relationships, it may equally lead to miscommunication for outsiders who do not understand the underlying cultural requirements. Without these nuances, expatriate managers, for example, might misinterpret intentions or meaning from behind their local counterparts' communications, undermining cooperation and performance in international teams. Low-context communication, common in individualist cultures, however, favors directness and clarity. In such a scenario, the surface meaning of the message is paramount as it is the paramount meaning that facilitates effective and unambiguous communication regardless of the relational context. Managers in such an environment typically prioritize openness and straightforwardness in their decision-making and negotiating processes. This style of communication can be particularly beneficial for expatriates or international managers who need to communicate ideas and directions unambiguously to heterogeneous teams. However, it would be too crude or even rude in high-context cultures where relationship building and implicit communication are more prevalent. Hence, the need to understand the variations between such communication styles so as to transpose management methods into embracing cultural differences and consolidating the organization to be more efficient. Further, incorporating cultural dimensions in global management is required for creating effective human resource practices. As suggested in current research, there is a growing awareness that cultural influences shape many dimensions of interaction in organizations, such as communication patterns. For instance, the application of low-context communication may cause some expatriates to overestimate the skills or work motivations of domestic staff, resulting in poor management techniques. Likewise, high-context communication can be hard to determine in performance reviews if not well understood in the context of the workforce's values and beliefs. If global managers can identify with these differences in communication styles, they can tailor their management styles more to the cultural dimensions relevant to their employees, and thereby establish greater cooperation, increase job satisfaction, and, ultimately, guide their organizations to success (Maitland et al., 1998; Van de Voorde et al., 2007).

3.6.2. Non-Verbal Communication Differences

In worldwide administration, it is particularly significant to know the variations in non-verbal communication since the subtle factors largely influence interpersonal relations and organizational actions. All cultures possess different gestures, facial expressions, and postures that may lead to misunderstandings unless navigated carefully. For instance, keeping eye contact has been generally accepted as a sign of confidence and honesty in Western culture, but is considered confrontational or even insulting in other cultures of Asia. These kinds of variations need a high level of awareness of cultural mores so that communication can function to prevent breakdowns, which is a requirement in order to meet organizational goals. The test is then stronger since leaders must shift their non-verbal cues to please varying workforce members, creating the significance of cultural intelligence as a part of effective global management practices. Understanding these differences is the foundation for the development of trust and rapport in multicultural settings. Further, research has established that leaders whose non-verbal cues are consistent with the cultural standards of their groups have better communication effectiveness, leading to enhanced group dynamics and decision-making performance (Mustafa et al., 2015). Such alignment, known as leader-society value congruence, suggests that leaders must identify how their individual cultural inclinations intersect with the broader societal standards of team members. This sensitivity not only increases relationships among individuals but also reduces conflicts that might develop based on misunderstanding (Figure 3.13).

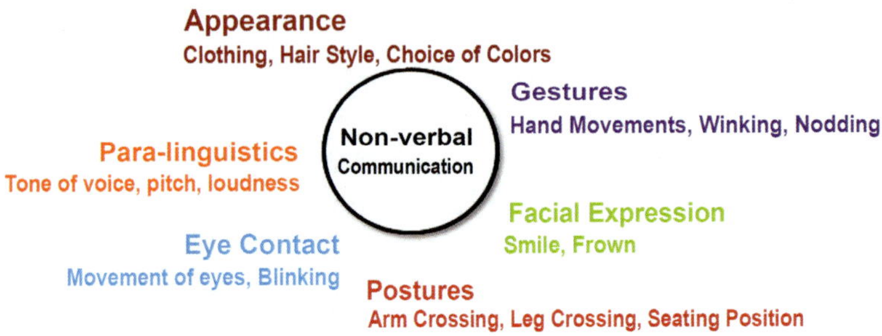

Figure 3.13. Non-verbal communication differences and organizational dynamics.

Source: https://commupower.weebly.com/uploads/5/0/0/5/50058577/7431464_orig.jpg.

As varied teams become the cornerstone of organizations in today's times, most especially in international settings, the capacity to get used to non-verbal communication patterns accordingly can greatly affect team performance as a whole. Therefore, developing a rich sensitivity for non-verbal cues in cross-cultural settings has become critical in the development of cohesive, high-performing teams in global management. In the context of the problem of cultural diversity, the integration of information and communication technology (ICT) has been a fundamental solution that has made non-verbal communication easy. Although verbal communication is hindered by language barriers, video conferencing, for example, and collaborative platforms facilitate such gaps because they open up possibilities for visual communication and articulation. Findings have indicated that such ICT can counteract some of the adverse impacts on intercultural communication while facilitating decision-making processes of multicultural teams (Shachaf et al., 2008). Through the efficient use of technology, managers are not only able to better comprehend but also extend a culture-friendly environment to perceive and honor various non-verbal cues. As companies are still grappling with the implications caused by globalization, applying ICT in promoting non-verbal communication will be crucial in facilitating effective management and team collaboration in a multicultural setting.

3.6.3. Barriers to Effective Cross-Cultural Communication

Adopting the finer nuances of human nature across various cultures is a deeper comprehension of the driving forces of communication behavior. Values and personality contribute significantly to how individuals receive and deliver messages, highly likely to cause cross-cultural miscommunication. For instance, indirect communication and group harmony are the focus for individuals in collective cultures, while directness is a desire for individuals in individualistic cultures (Bratianu et al., 2025). This variation can be an obstacle to working in a shared mode since expatriates tend to be faced with local communication style expectations. Moreover, cultural variations in conceptions of assertiveness and conflict resolution complicate affairs, producing misunderstandings that reverse managerial efficiency abroad due to its impossibility to please everyone worldwide. As global enterprises expand, it becomes more critical to grasp these motivational and value-based variations in order to create a flexible and integrated labor force. Decision-making differences are often a function of the underlying ethics reflecting cultural environments. Cultural distinctions not only determine how decisions are made but also what ethical concerns are emphasized during such decision-making. For instance, while Western cultures may consider decisions in terms of individual rights and evidence-based approaches, Asian cultures may emphasize group consensus and relational harmony (Todorova, 2024).

These deeply ingrained differences can become significant barriers when groups composed of individuals from varied backgrounds must reach consensus decisions together. Expatriates, generally accustomed to rapid decision-making, may have difficulty with a slower consensus-oriented approach to making decisions that exists in some cultures. Alternatively, host-country managers may find expatriate decision-making to be rushed or insufficiently considered. This divergence in ethical decision-making underscores the importance of cross-cultural training not only to better understand alternative approaches in the global business arena but to ensure effective cultural acclimatization in that context. Cross-cultural barriers in communication also appear in terms of disparate roles for expatriates and indigenous managers, especially within international management settings. Expatriates, though with a rich technical knowledge background and multiple outlooks, can experience difficulty in cultural acclimatization, paving the way for possible conflict within a local organizational setting. The union of local managers with their intimate familiarity with the nuances of culture can in turn increase tensions; different communication styles may counteract collaboration and erode organizational integration (Bratianu et al., 2025). Successful intercultural interaction relies on the ability to integrate and synergize these differing managerial styles. It is crucial that local managers and expatriates cultivate cultural intelligence because it enables them to learn skills of handling and filling communicative gaps. Organizations can, through cross-cultural competence training programs, create a smooth working environment that benefits maximally from the talents of local managers and expatriates.

SUMMARY

In understanding the intricate web of individual behavior in global management, cultural difference of motivation, values, and personality cannot be overemphasized. All these have a significant influence on the way decisions are made and how ethics are handled. Managers who are culturally sensitive have a greater potential for facilitating good communication and collaboration in diverse cultures. This is significant, since individuals from diverse backgrounds may share different values, or may see actions differently depending on personal cultural assumptions. Moreover, variations in the drivers for motivation between expatriates and local managers may lead to varying management styles impacting organizational performance. It is not merely a case of accepting these differences but adjusting managerial systems to harness the strengths of cultural diversity, ultimately resulting in enhanced organizational performance and job satisfaction. Decision-making and ethical considerations impose an additional layer of difficulty on international management. The organization is often confronted with conflicts where cultural conceptions of ethical conduct differ dramatically. In one culture, collective decision-making is favored, while in another, personal discretion is tolerated. This variation can lead to disagreements and misperceptions in multinational businesses, making it more difficult to collaborate.

Cultural standards also establish what is ethical or unethical, from bargaining approaches to corporate social responsibility styles. Understanding these variations is essential for managers who want to prosper in the global marketplace. Cross-cultural sensitivity methods can prevent potential conflicts and develop a more cohesive organizational culture. Against this context, the cross-cultural critical analysis of decision-making practice shows the imperative for successful leadership approaches that embrace and leverage diversity (Van de Voorde et al., 2007). Finally, the intersection of individual behavior in international management across cultures emphasizes the imperative for flexibility and ongoing learning in a more globalized business world. Organizational culture, on the other hand, is not static; it evolves along with behavior and is open to modification by individual actions, exemplifying the dynamic nature of cultural integration in multinationals (Indu, 2025).

Diversity leaders, when they commit to diversity, must also commit to equal creation of inclusive culture that values and acknowledges diverse origins. Such commitment not only augments the strength of teams but also organizational efficacy as a whole. By accessing the unique vistas of perspective which individuals from various cultures can provide, corporations can adapt and innovate more effectively to changes in market requirements. Thus, studies must continue to explore the various interdependent relationships between culture, conduct, and management practices as a stepping stone for more effective international management practices.

Dynamics of personal behavior in different cultural contexts have been an international management focus area. One critical area that has often been studied is motivation, and it tends to be influenced by cultural values and personal traits. Various cultures place emphasis on differing motivating factors as some highlight shared success whereas others reward individual success. This variation necessitates global managers not just being sensitive to their workers' driving forces but also to adapt their management approach accordingly. Further, an understanding of cultural factors that affect personality facilitates managers in establishing improved staff relationships and more productive teams. Lastly, an in-depth insight into the way that personality and motivation interact in diverse cultures can lead to enhanced organizational performance as well as job satisfaction, key requirements for international organizations operating in the complex cultural contexts. Ethics and decision-making constitute another critical dimension affecting individual behavior in global management. Cultural environments significantly influence decision-making, with some cultures promoting collectivism, the emphasis of consensus within a group, and others valuing independence and decision ownership on a personal basis. This contrast has the potential to cause confusion and ineffectiveness when working across multinational teams, particularly when ethical requirements are concerned. For instance, what is ethical in one society can be differently interpreted by another. Therefore, establishing a culture that appreciates and incorporates multiple ethical viewpoints can help minimize conflict and establish a harmonious workplace culture. It is essential for managers to manage these inherent cultural differences to ensure effective communication and enhance collaboration among workers, making cultural diversity a cornerstone and not a hindrance in international management situations. The diverging experiences of expatriates and indigenous managers also demonstrate the complexities of individual behavior in cross-cultural contexts. Expatriates are normally unable to adapt to new cultural environments, which has a negative impact on their performance as managers and their overall job satisfaction. They typically have difficulties with adapting to local norms, work culture, and customs, with varying degrees of success. In contrast, local managers typically possess valuable insights about staff behavior, cultural sensitivities, and deep-rooted networks that are able to drive organizational performance. Identifying the inherent strengths and weaknesses in each group can assist multinational firms in providing suitable support structures for expatriates while benefiting from local managerial know-how. Lastly, understanding the relationship between expatriates and local managers is crucial in order to promote cooperation, which can greatly facilitate international business operations and reinforce organizational objectives across cultures.

REFERENCES

1. Aiken, L. S., Alchian, A., Kim, A., Carberry, E. J., Fukuyama, F., Hofstede, G. H., et al. (2018). Employee stock ownership and financial performance in European countries: The moderating effects of uncertainty avoidance and social trust. https://core.ac.uk/download/299790960.pdf (accessed on 24th September 2025).
2. Alarcón del Amo, M. del C., Butkouskaya, V., Llonch Andreu, J., Rondán Cataluña, F., et al. (2017). IMC customer-based perception: Strategic antecedents and consequences on post-purchase customer behaviour. https://core.ac.uk/download/161254680.pdf (accessed on 24th September 2025).
3. Ali, M. (2009). Situated cultural approach versus predefined cultural archetypes models. https://core.ac.uk/download/336251.pdf (accessed on 24th September 2025).
4. Anand, J., Mitchell, W., & Zhou, J. (2001). Transferring collective knowledge: Collective and fragmented teaching and learning in the Chinese auto industry. http://www.wdi.umich.edu/files/Publications/WorkingPapers/wp420.pdf (accessed on 24th September 2025).
5. Anderson, N., Potočnik, K., & Zhou, J. (2014). Innovation and creativity in organizations. Journal of Management, 40, 1297–1333. https://doi.org/10.1177/0149206314527128 (accessed on 24th September 2025).
6. Antal, A. B., Stroo, I., & Willems, M. (2025). Drawing on the knowledge of returned expatriates for organizational learning: Case studies in German multinational companies. https://core.ac.uk/download/pdf/6653947.pdf (accessed on 24th September 2025).
7. Barney, J., Chen, G., Doney, P., Gargiulo, M., Gillespie, N., Hampden-Turner, C., Hofstede, G., et al. (2010). Antecedents of trust across foci: A comparative study of Turkey and China. https://core.ac.uk/download/pdf/11741788.pdf (accessed on 24th September 2025).
8. Bloom, M. C., & Milkovich, G. T. (1997). Rethinking international compensation: From expatriate and national cultures to strategic flexibility. https://core.ac.uk/download/5131309.pdf (accessed on 24th September 2025).
9. Bloom, M., Milkovich, G. T., & Mitra, A. (2000). Toward a model of international compensation and rewards: Learning from how managers respond to variations in local host contexts. https://core.ac.uk/download/5131305.pdf (accessed on 24th September 2025).
10. Born, M. P., Cem-Ersoy, N., Derous, E., van der Molen, H. T., et al. (2012). The effect of cultural orientation and leadership style on self-

versus other-oriented organizational citizenship behavior in Turkey and the Netherlands. https://core.ac.uk/download/55806965.pdf (accessed on 24th September 2025).

11. Boudreau, J. W., & Najjar, M. M. (1996). Extending social learning theories to collectivist cultures: The effect of behavior modeling training, service orientation and language skills on service skills and behaviors. https://core.ac.uk/download/5121941.pdf (accessed on 24th September 2025).
12. Bratianu, C., Paiuc, D., & Brancu, L. (2025). Exploring the connections between DNA, cultural intelligence and knowledge dynamics in multicultural business environments. *Business Process Management Journal*. https://www.semanticscholar.org/paper/d071e6884adcd7f6ee693eb86696bfda727e4470 (accessed on 24th September 2025).
13. Bromiley, P., McShane, M., Nair, A., Rustambekov, E., et al. (2015). Enterprise risk management: Review, critique, and research directions. https://core.ac.uk/download/322493756.pdf (accessed on 24th September 2025).
14. Choi, J. W., Lee, H., Lee, H. J., Sajjad, A., et al. (2014). The influence of national culture on the attitude towards mobile recommender systems. https://core.ac.uk/download/20496341.pdf (accessed on 24th September 2025).
15. Costa, N. G., & Cunha, M. P. e. (2025). The ethical dilemma of expatriates in emerging economies: A liminal perspective. https://core.ac.uk/download/pdf/6776156.pdf (accessed on 24th September 2025).
16. Demirgüç-Kunt, A., Klapper, L., & Singer, D. (2013). *Financial Inclusion and Legal Discrimination Against Women: Evidence from Developing Countries*. World Bank Policy Research Working Paper. https://doi.org/10.1596/1813-9450-6416 (accessed on 24th September 2025).
17. Dwivedi, Y. K., Ismagilova, E., Hughes, D. L., Carlson, J., Filieri, R., Jacobson, J., Jain, V., et al. (2020). Setting the future of digital and social media marketing research: Perspectives and research propositions. International Journal of Information Management, 59, 102168–102168. https://doi.org/10.1016/j.ijinfomgt.2020.102168 (accessed on 24th September 2025).
18. Everdingen, Y. M. van, & Waarts, E. (2025). A multi-country study of the adoption of ERP systems. https://core.ac.uk/download/pdf/6906031.pdf (accessed on 24th September 2025).

19. Haas, M. R. (2006). Acquiring and applying knowledge in transnational teams: The roles of cosmopolitans and locals. https://core.ac.uk/download/5121295.pdf (accessed on 24th September 2025).
20. Halub, H., Sauber, A., & Stück, J. (2017). The Turk and the Yankee: A cross-cultural comparison between Turkish and American managers. https://core.ac.uk/download/84885650.pdf (accessed on 24th September 2025).
21. Herrmann-Pillath, C. (2025). A 'third culture' in economics? An essay on Smith, Confucius and the rise of China. https://core.ac.uk/download/pdf/6387809.pdf (accessed on 24th September 2025).
22. Hobfoll, S. E., Halbesleben, J. R. B., Neveu, J. P., & Westman, M. (2017). Conservation of resources in the organizational context: The reality of resources and their consequences. Annual Review of Organizational Psychology and Organizational Behavior, 5, 103–128. https://doi.org/10.1146/annurev-orgpsych-032117-104640 (accessed on 24th September 2025).
23. Ithnin, N. B., & Olusegun, O. J. (2013). Enhancing the conventional information security management maturity model (ISM3) in resolving human factors in organization information sharing. https://core.ac.uk/download/42908059.pdf (accessed on 24th September 2025).
24. Janssens, M., & Steyaert, C. (2025). Reconsidering translation and language in an international business context: Beyond an instrumental approach. https://core.ac.uk/download/pdf/6468842.pdf (accessed on 24th September 2025).
25. Johnson, K. (2010). Virtual leadership: Required competencies for effective leaders. https://core.ac.uk/download/219377043.pdf (accessed on 24th September 2025).
26. Kanabar, V., Messikomer, C., & Thomas, A. (2018). Enhancing project-related behavioral competence in education. https://open.bu.edu/bitstream/2144/29016/1/Enhancing%20Project-Related%20Behavioral%20Competence%20in%20Education.pdf (accessed on 24th September 2025).
27. Karma, K., & Vedina, R. (2025). Cultural intelligence as a prism between workforce diversity and performance in a modern organization. https://core.ac.uk/download/pdf/6314774.pdf (accessed on 24th September 2025).
28. Kato, H., Inagaki, N., Takemi, Y., Special Advisors, Kido, Y., Miyazawa, T., & Shimizu, M. (2023). IUNS 22nd International Congress of Nutrition.

Annals of Nutrition and Metabolism, 79, 1–8. https://www.semanticscholar.org/paper/39d3adbe4945b09ad1f462f0f73556ab2e055737 (accessed on 24th September 2025).

29. Kelly, A., Li, M., & Mobley, W. H. (2015). Linking personality to cultural intelligence: An interactive effect of openness and agreeableness. https://core.ac.uk/download/151157090.pdf (accessed on 24th September 2025).
30. Luthans, F., & Youssef-Morgan, C. M. (2017). Psychological capital: An evidence-based positive approach. *Annual Review of Organizational Psychology and Organizational Behavior, 4*, 339–366. https://doi.org/10.1146/annurev-orgpsych-032516-113324 (accessed on 24th September 2025).
31. Maitland, C. (1998). Global diffusion of interactive networks: The impact of culture. https://core.ac.uk/download/pdf/12237594.pdf (accessed on 24th September 2025).
32. Manrai, A. K., & Manrai, L. A. (2025). Hofstede's cultural dimensions and tourist behaviors: A review and conceptual framework. https://core.ac.uk/download/pdf/6322905.pdf (accessed on 24th September 2025).
33. Marcotte, D., Rustambekov, E., & Trendowski, J. (2019). Importance of cultural intelligence: Cross-cultural examination and analysis. https://core.ac.uk/download/231818803.pdf (accessed on 24th September 2025).
34. Maurer, T. (2017). Motivations of Americans to be fans of non-U.S. sports teams. https://core.ac.uk/download/213032047.pdf (accessed on 24th September 2025).
35. Mumley, W. E. (2019). Organizational culture and ethical decision-making during major crises. https://core.ac.uk/download/223117464.pdf (accessed on 24th September 2025).
36. Mustafa, G. (2015). The emergence of leader-society value congruence: A cross-cultural perspective. https://core.ac.uk/download/144552158.pdf (accessed on 24th September 2025).
37. Rao, I. (2025). The behavioral equivalence of organizational culture. https://core.ac.uk/download/pdf/6443708.pdf (accessed on 24th September 2025).
38. Rietveld, J. (2013). Climbing the Great Wall: Linking teacher beliefs and learning styles in cross-cultural teaching–Observations from cross-cultural teaching in Mainland China. https://core.ac.uk/download/16272291.pdf (accessed on 24th September 2025).
39. Shachaf, P. (2008). Cultural diversity and information and communication technology impacts on global virtual teams: An exploratory study. https://core.ac.uk/download/11887687.pdf (accessed on 24th September 2025).

40. Suharnomo, S. (2010). Study on employee motivation in Indonesia: Does culture really matter?
41. Todorova, L. (2024). Cross-cultural aspects of teaching English in an international business environment. Social Pedagogy: Theory and Practice. https://www.semanticscholar.org/paper/0ba73f5953b221435332e2ad89199639798408d7 (accessed on 24th September 2025).
42. Trampel, J. (2025). To offshore or nearshore IT services? An investigation using transaction cost theory. https://core.ac.uk/download/pdf/9314617.pdf (accessed on 24th September 2025).
43. Van de Voorde, K., & Wright, P. M. (2007). Multi-level issues in international HRM: Mean differences, explained variance, and moderated relationships. https://core.ac.uk/download/5121553.pdf (accessed on 24th September 2025).

Chapter 4

Communication in a Cross-Cultural Context

Contents

INTRODUCTION

The growing complexity of global business highlights the need for good communication between different cultures. Business today, being a globalized world, tends to be in touch with cultures different from their own, resulting in different expectations and interpretations regarding communication. An appropriate distinction in this regard is the distinction between high-context and low-context cultures. High-context cultures, which are found in the majority of Asian countries, heavily rely on the context of a message and non-verbal cues in order to convey meaning. Low-context cultures, typical of Western countries, prefer straightforward and explicit communication. Managers who wish to successfully navigate cross-cultural encounters need to be cognizant of such differences. The inability to see these differences can lead to very deep misunderstandings, influencing the performance of an organization and the interaction of employees working in a multi-national environment. Cross-cultural communication is plagued by a number of challenges that can invalidate the success of international management systems. Communication breakdowns are not solely brought about by language differences but also by cultural assumptions and diverse non-verbal communication styles. Misinterpretations of gestures, eye contact, and body language can contribute to communication breakdowns in culturally diverse teams. Additionally, cultural disparities in conflict resolution and decision-making are some of the aspects that may complicate the process of interaction. This calls for greater cultural awareness and sensitivity from managers who are meant to bridge such differences in order to promote collaboration and innovation within their organizations. Practitioners should employ vast resources that provide information regarding diversity in the workplace, as illustrated in Bormann et al. (2001), to produce more inclusive and productive organizational cultures. When the subject of cross-cultural management is interrogated, post-structuralist political thought offers rich insight into the character of identity and cultural difference. The theory unveils a reconsideration of the essentialist methodologies that have a tendency to oversimplify cultural identities. According to Angouri et al. (2009), an awareness of radical contingency in social relations allows for a richer understanding of how culture informs business practices and management styles. Through an appreciation of the performative aspect of cultural identity, international managers are more able to adopt a critical stance that appreciates the dynamic nature of communication in different environments. The ultimate outcome is not merely to contribute further academic debate into cross-cultural communication but also to equip practitioners with the toolkits with which to thrive in complex global environments.

Definition of Cross-Cultural Communication

Deciphering the dynamics of human communication across various cultures is a complicated situation, particularly in international management. The center of cross-cultural communication involves appreciating how context impacts both verbal and non-verbal communication between individuals from diverse cultures. High-context cultures, where there is indirect communication and situational cues, are starkly contrasted with low-context cultures that opt for directness and openness when sharing information. This variation can result in misunderstandings if not managed properly. Since international business interactions are nurtured on teamwork and cooperation, recognizing these communication patterns becomes crucial for creating an inclusive environment that appreciates varied perspectives and fosters productive dialogue. Furthermore, the obstacles hindering successful cross-cultural communication are multileveled and need to be attended to consciously. Challenges like language variances, cultural differences in social norms, and perception disparities of authority can be barriers in open communication among multinational teams (Figure 4.1).

Figure 4.1. Understanding the dynamics of human interaction across cross-cultural communication.

Source: https://www.languagesunlimited.com/wp-content/uploads/2023/03/373477-PBEEAE-983-e1679562992562.jpg.

For instance, a company's failure to fund language translation strategies may lock out non-native speakers and restrict their participation in central discussion. This deficiency not only damages the potential for innovation but also fuels tensions between teams. This challenge is evident through the argument for working knowledge of language translation in crisis communication, which strongly illustrates the significance of good communication during the critical moments of collective work (Federici et al., 2019). Through actively acknowledging and dismantling these barriers, organizations are able to create a better sense of cohesion within the workplace. The theoretical understanding of identity, difference, and conflict in cross-cultural context enriches our understanding of communication in global management. Leaving behind the essentialist understanding of culture, it becomes necessary to locate the contingent and dynamic character of cultural contacts. It is this perspective that draws attention to the imperative of navigating complexity in cross-cultural settings, where individuals resort to forming their own identities either in terms of fit or conflict with dominant narratives of the corporate structure. Using a critical lens to appreciate cross-cultural differences makes it possible for leaders to create more compassionate and attuned organizational cultures that create opportunities for effective collaboration. With a post-structural approach to cultural encounters, the companies become more capable of fostering dialogue that is responsive to diversity, hence contributing towards greater operational effectiveness on the international scene (Angouri et al., 2009). With this kind of approach, not just is the communication enriched, but the organizational culture also becomes sensitive to the evolving requirements of international business.

Importance of Communication in International Management

Effective management globally requires a sensitive understanding of verbal as well as non-verbal communication styles, which can differ significantly across cultures. While some cultures practice direct, open communication, known as low-context communication, others prefer to communicate indirectly, implying in accordance with high-context cultures. These differences can lead to misunderstandings as messages can be interpreted differently than intended. For instance, in a high-context culture, the employment of non-verbal cues and subtleties of context are most essential in conveying meaning.

Thus, international managers must learn the art of navigating these variations and establish an environment where everyone within a team feels appreciated and recognized. This sensitivity does not only increase interpersonal relations but forms the basis for successful collaboration in various cultural settings and ultimately influences organizational performance in the global setting. Cross-cultural communication barriers may come in numerous formats, and awareness of these barriers is the international manager's ticket. Cross-cultural communication may be hindered by variation in language, say, and its flow restriction and misinterpretation may be interpreted as instigating conflict or diminished morale on the team. Other than language, cross-cultural misunderstanding of values, norms, and beliefs can make matters even more complicated. For example, practices deemed as respectful in a culture are discovered to be deemed rude in another, such as evading direct conflict or the significance of eye contact. By understanding such barriers, managers can implement steps towards increasing intercultural competency within their workforce. Training and promoting cultural awareness encourages a diversified setting, hence strengthening overall lines of communication and allowing for more effective teamwork across borders. The significance of congruence of leader and societal values is revealed when one considers the international manager's function in communication. Research has indicated that when leaders communicate in ways that are aligned with the cultural values of employees, they can create a sense of belongingness and commitment among employees. This congruence of individual leaders' cultural orientation and societal values facilitates easier interactions and ensures mutual respect. Therefore, effective communication styles in culturally diverse contexts not only foster team integration but serve as the foundation of long-term relationship development in international partnerships. As international contexts continue to shift—through the globalization of markets and internationalization of workforces—the demand for managers to become culturally aware in the approach to communication will continue to escalate. The ongoing building up of successful intercultural communication skills is therefore an organizational goal attainment priority in the globalized world, once again affirming the inherent relationship between international management and successful communication.

4.1. VERBAL COMMUNICATION STYLES

Communication is imperative in international management, particularly in verbal communication among cultures. The distinction between high-context and low-context communication is directly related to how messages are constructed and interpreted.

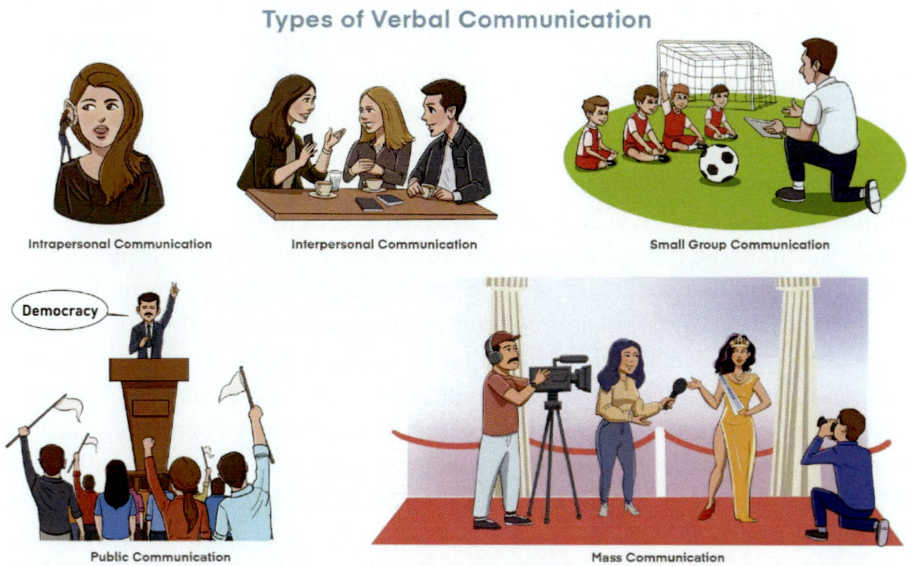

Figure 4.2. Types of verbal communication style.

Source: https://www.communicationtheory.org/wp-content/uploads/2022/05/types-of-verbal-communication.webp.

High-context societies such as those in Japan and most Arab nations rely heavily on the environment around them, facial expressions, and unexpressed messages. Low-context cultures like in Germany and the United States place high emphasis on verbal communication where clarity and directness are most appreciated. The difference can result in misunderstanding and communication breakdowns unless managed with a lot of caution in international business settings. The managers need to know these styles so that they can communicate effectively with various teams and clients across cultures, facilitate working relationships, and bridge potential gaps due to varying expectations of verbal interactions. The importance of verbal communication styles extends beyond the realm of differences in languages; it also plays a significant role in influencing interpersonal relationships in multicultural environments. Managers and leaders need to realign their communication patterns to suit the cultural climates of their teams since mismatches result in decreased morale and productivity. Studies highlight that leaders must strive for congruence between their own communication styles and the cultural values of societies they operate in, further enhancing leader-society value congruence (Mustafa et al., 2015) (Figure 4.2).

This consistency is vital in building rapport and trust, such fundamental aspects of effective international management leadership. A knowledge of verbal communication styles subtleties thus helps managers communicate better with their staff, creating a participative environment where everyone is given attention and respect. However, efficient cross-cultural communication is often sabotaged by varying verbal communication styles, which can impede collaboration and projects. Misperceptions, due to varying cultural assumptions about communication, can lead to conflict and frustration. For instance, directness and no-nonsense approach favored in low-context cultures might be perceived as rude or offensive in high-context cultures where greater emphasis is put on indirectness and subtlety. Moreover, cross-national management requires not only an awareness of verbal style of communication but also of hidden cultural values that guide such styles (Schadewitz et al., 2009). This multi-faceted awareness enables managers to defuse possible miscommunications and more effectively navigate the complexities of multicultural environments. Through the improvement of verbal skills, world managers can develop a culture of clarity and respect that is vital to driving organizational success in a globalized business scenario.

4.1.1. Differences in Language and Dialects

Language is a vital bearer of cultural identity and communication that surfaces in numerous forms and dialects mirroring the richness of human life. In global management, becoming familiar with the variations between languages and their dialectical forms is an imperative for cross-cultural communication. For example, dialects typically consist of distinctive expressive features which provide a potential for miscommunications when cross-linguistic interaction occurs. In such languages as Javanese, native dialects like Banyumasan have distinctive conversational implicatures that are fundamental to grasping underlying meaning in a conversation. These differences underscore the importance of contextuality, in that a seemingly straightforward utterance might be dense with implications governed by local custom and tradition (Hadiati et al., 2012). Therefore, international managers must develop a culture-sensitized comprehension of these differences to minimize the chances of miscommunication. Effective communication is more than mere words; it is an advanced integration of verbal and non-verbal signals conditioned by culture (Figure 4.3).

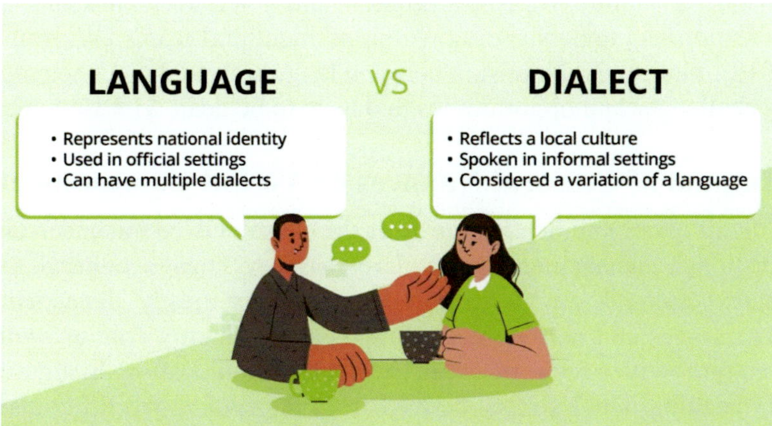

Figure 4.3. Understanding linguistic variations in language vs dialect.

Source: https://bayan-tech.com/wp-content/uploads/2024/11/02-What-Is-a-Dialect-1024x538.webp.

In high-context cultures, such as in Japanese or Arab cultures, subtlety of communication is context, body language, and indirectness. This is very much at odds with low-context cultures, where messages are clear and reliant upon overt verbal communication, which is typical in much Western communication. As cross-cultural communication becomes more common, it is now increasingly necessary for managers to appreciate these differences in an effort to build effective relationships across cultures. The mix of language and dialects, with the associated non-verbal cues, may lead to productive cooperation or sophisticated communication barriers on the basis of the sensitivity and flexibility of the actors (Widyaningrum et al., 2012). It is therefore essential to facilitate an inclusive communication context that considers these diverse styles. The bilingualism and multilingualism dynamics also make the situation of language and dialect diversity more complicated in cross-cultural communication. The rise in international schools and double-language education has been followed by a skyrocketing population of children who speak foreign languages. While the trend is good for world unification, it poses danger to indigenous languages and dialects at the same time. As the image of dwindling indigenous speakers in a majority of communities shows, linguistic heritage must be attended to equally. The loss of vernacular languages not only jeopardizes genuine cultural perspectives but also risks the expansion of communicative diversity necessary for effective global collaboration. For international managers, a requirement of the appreciation and recognition of majority as well as minority languages can generate a culture of respectfulness and tolerance, enriching overall communication and understanding within multicultural teams (Widyaningrum et al., 2012). Thus, the relationship between language and dialect heterogeneity presents challenges and opportunities that have to be dealt with strategically.

4.1.2. Impact of Cultural Nuances on Verbal Communication

The subtleties of communication are often the cause of deep misunderstandings in international management, particularly as they engage cultural settings. High-context cultures, in which communication is mostly dependent upon implicit messages and non-verbal communication, sharply contrast with low-context cultures with a focus on explicit verbal communication. In high-context cultures, meaning is not simply derived from the spoken word but also from context, such as relationships and shared history (Eaves et al., 2013). Low-context cultures, on the other hand, favor the use of clarity and directness and, therefore, a potential source of tension when individuals who come from such different backgrounds are engaged in conversation.

It is essential for managers to realize such differences so that they can foster effective communication among diverse groups of people because assumptions based on one's own culture can prove to be hindrances and prevent collaboration in the modern globalized corporate world. Cultural diversity impacts not only variations in style of communication but even the manner of perceiving and interpreting verbal communications. This process is particularly evident while addressing power distance problems—a process that describes how weaker society members acquiesce to more dominant members. With cultures with high power distance, the communication can be formal and subtle, while with low power distance cultures, interactions are straightforward and egalitarian (Keys et al., 2012). Such variations can lead to misinterpretation, which subsequently leads to conflicts or confusion when interactions occur across cultures. It is such a manager who fails to value such nuances who may inadvertently alienate employees, stifle imagination, or lose valuable insights. This would mean that dealing with verbal communication in cross-cultural settings calls for high sensitivity to the underlying structures which govern interaction among employees. To benefit fully from the challenges posed by cross-cultural communication, global managers need to develop culturally competent strategies. This involves not only understanding patterns of verbal communication but also being attuned to likely communication barriers that can arise while communicating. Communication barriers such as variance in languages, varied cultural references, and varied expectations can prevent successful dialogue (Eaves et al., 2013). Managers must thus embark on an adaptive communication approach, remaining open to learning while hoping to bridge these gaps in communication. Adding feedback mechanisms and creating a culture in which employees are comfortable giving their opinions can improve communication effectiveness. By carefully traversing such cultural subtleties, managers are able to establish trust and encourage a more diverse environment, leading ultimately to better teamwork and increased organizational performance in a global setting.

4.1.3. Strategies for Effective Verbal Communication

In the context of global management, an understanding of the nuances of verbal communication is paramount, particularly keeping in mind the variance in communicative practices among cultures. Variations in communication style are generally based on variations in cultural backgrounds, where direct or indirect verbalization may differ. For instance, low-context cultures such as the United States and Germany appreciate explicit verbal communication, where explicitness and directness are much appreciated. Conversely, cultures like Japan and Saudi Arabia have faith in implicit communication, and stress non-verbal communication and common knowledge. This divergence will lead to misunderstandings if not approached with sensitivity. Effective communication thus calls for sensitivity towards such styles so that managers can adjust their messages and communicate more effectively with global teams, and eventually establish a culture that fosters cooperation and respect. Plugging the potential gaps in good cross-cultural communication is crucial in building understanding among global teams. Gaps might be differences in languages, where proficiency levels can prevent clarity and misunderstanding. Differences in cultures' expectations of politeness and formality may also exist; a simple question in one culture may be considered impolite in another, and tension is created. Thus, implementing ways to fill gaps is necessary (Figure 4.4).

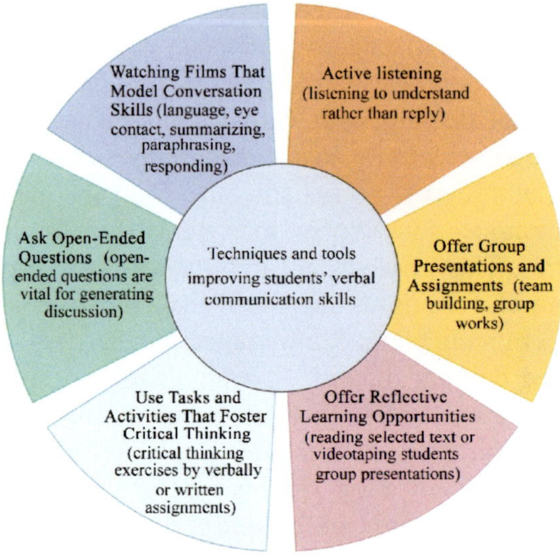

Figure 4.4. Understanding the nuances of verbal communication.

Source: https://www.researchgate.net/publication/349186884/figure/fig1/AS:989983452192772@1613041856764/Techniques-and-tools-for-improving-students-verbal-communication-skills.png.

For example, using plain language, accompanied by culturally applicable illustrations, can ease understanding. A stress on patience and empathy in the approach to clarifying misunderstandings can also tighten interpersonal bonds. By creating a supportive environment where group members have confidence in raising issues, organizations can establish a better communicative climate, permitting more fruitful interactions and creative solution-finding. Besides, integrating intercultural competence training is important in developing effective verbal communication methods in multinational corporations. Training can be designed towards being sensitive to different communication patterns, where the workers are encouraged to develop adaptive behavior during communicative interactions between cultures. Improving competence in active listening, asking inquiring questions for meaning clarification, and providing constructive criticisms may enable managers and their subordinates to overcome difficult communicative contexts. For example, in leadership scenarios where distant multicultural teams need to be managed, such as digital tools and platforms that enable asynchronous communication, becomes imperative to ensure clarity. As exemplified in cross-cultural leadership research, effective management is characterized by sensitivity and adaptability to culture, which underscores the application of certain verbal strategies aimed at constructing successful international collaborations (Makhmudova, 2025). Last but not least, a commitment to ongoing improvement of communication skills not only benefits individual members of the team but also enhances organizational performance overall (Boonmatun et al., 2025).

4.2. NON-VERBAL COMMUNICATION STYLES

In the intricate sphere of cross-cultural interactions, non-verbal communication styles are significant indicators of underlying cultural norms and values. These styles include a broad set of behaviors such as facial expressions, gestures, and posture that have the tendency to be ingrained deeply in culture. For instance, in Japan and the majority of Middle Eastern nations that are high-context cultures, non-verbal communication will be more powerful than verbal communication, because harmony and embeddedness will carry a great deal of importance. In contrast, the low-context cultures of the United States or Germany place a stronger emphasis on direct verbal communication, where gestures will be supplementary rather than dominant.

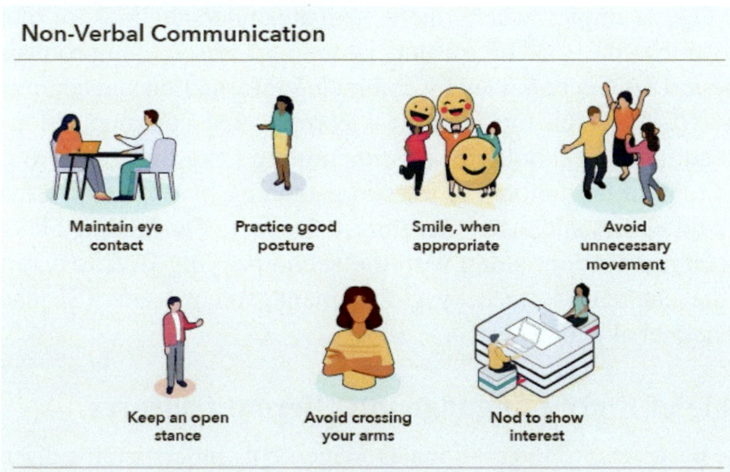

Figure 4.5. The intricate landscape of non-verbal communication styles.

Source: https://www.hubspot.com/hs-fs/hubfs/Core%20Blog%20-%20Service_V3_Non-Verbal%20Communication.jpg?width=1300&name=Core%20Blog%20-%20Service_V3_Non-Verbal%20Communication.jpg.

Understandings of these differences are important to global managers who seek to create healthy team dynamics and minimize misunderstandings, particularly in pluralistic settings where cultural nuances potentially create huge misreadings of intention and meaning. Beyond mere expressions, the integration of communication styles and context also extends its influence to organizational leadership and team dynamics. Leaders have to observe the non-verbal communications along with the words in order to handle the complexities of communication in multicultural environments. As noted by the research, congruence between leader values and social values can significantly affect modes of communication and self-construal among team members (Figure 4.5).

By knowing how cultures decode non-verbal cues, managers are well placed to tailor their leadership styles to meet the expectations set by their multi-cultural teams and, in the process, foster an atmosphere that is conducive to teamwork and productivity. Failure to do so can result in conflicting expectations, which can influence decision-making processes and team cohesion, especially in situations where members are from multi-cultural backgrounds. In considering the inhibitors to effective cross-cultural communication, it is apparent that non-verbal communications are the determinants of bringing together and separating team members. Cultural diversity issues encountered by studies in global teams uncover that while decision-making can be optimized, communication becomes complex. For example, where there are misunderstandings of non-verbal communications, the risk of misunderstandings arises, compromising team effectiveness. This can be solved by embracing information and communication technology (ICT) which facilitates less complicated communication in spite of diverse cultures. Technologies for functioning have the ability to close the gap brought about by non-verbal misunderstanding by providing a systematic framework for communication. Therefore, a deeper understanding of non-verbal forms of communication, along with the accompanying ICT, is paramount to handling the challenges faced by global management teams (Shachaf et al., 2008; Mustafa et al., 2015).

4.2.1. Role of Body Language in Different Cultures

Amidst the intricacies of international management, understanding discreet non-verbal communication becomes crucial since these often dictate interpersonal interactions' efficacy. Body language, such as gestures, stance, eye contact, and facial expressions, constitutes a significant cultural context indicator that affects perception and relationships. For instance, in Japan and other Middle Eastern high-context cultures, nonverbal communication is highly valued and often employed to convey feelings and intentions that are tacitly held by the participants. Low-context cultures like the United States and Northern Europe may overemphasize overt verbal communication and generate varied interpretations of the same body language signals. This deviation brings to the fore the likelihood of cross-cultural miscommunications, particularly when individuals from diverse cultural groups interact in cross-cultural business settings. Cross-cultural communication is typically confronted by problems where body language does not translate across cultures. Implications are particularly important in cases where international managers handle multicultural teams. For instance, as was observed in the case of a study on Norway's oil business, Norwegian employees are direct in their communication, which in some instances is perceived as rude for individuals who come from more indirect communication cultures (Figure 4.6).

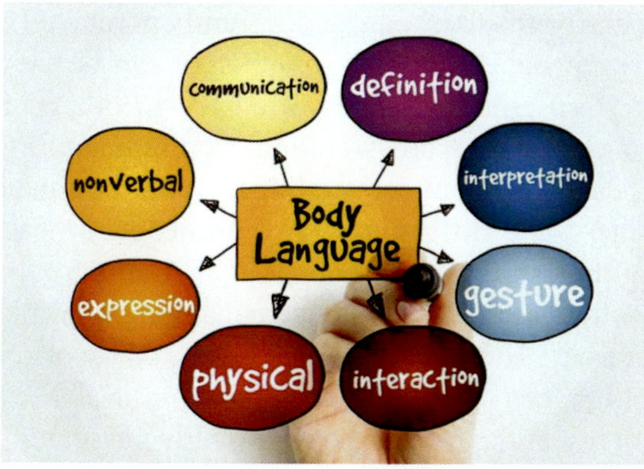

Figure 4.6. The intricate landscape of international management body language.

Source: https://www.shutterstock.com/image-photo/body-language-mind-map-marker-600nw-2402492549.jpg.

Besides, the distant body attitude that is typical for Norwegians can get misinterpreted by non-Norwegian employees who might struggle to decode these signs. Such relationships can cause delays in decision making and hinder effective strategy implementation, thereby emphasizing the importance of managers possessing an advanced understanding of how body language finds itself within more pervasive cultural situations (Strand et al., 2017). Overcoming these barriers must be addressed through an organized attempt, particularly bridging the interpretation gap of different body language cultural norms. Sensitivity training programs that enhance awareness of non-verbal communications can equip international managers with the ability required to effectively manage these intricacies. Research has shown that adding body language training to cross-cultural training can enable leaders to become proficient in comprehending and interpreting their own non-verbal signals and interpreting others.' Fostering an environment in which body language is openly talked about can provide an opportunity to neutralize opportunities for miscommunication and build a trust-enhancing atmosphere, particularly in cultures that focus on relationship building rather than legal contract establishment. Striving for ensuring global teams possess such information will ultimately result in more effective working relationships across diverse cultural landscapes (Busa' et al., 2015).

4.2.2. Variations in Gestures and Their Meanings

Communication heavily incorporates the mixing of verbal and non-verbal components, influencing the mode of message delivery across cultures. Non-verbal cues, particularly gestures, can be differently perceived depending on the cultural context. For instance, the thumbs-up sign can be viewed as a gesture of approval in Western cultures but as offensive in others. Such a disparity highlights the complexities of cross-cultural communication, how variations in gestures can lead to misunderstandings. With companies increasingly globalized in business, the differences are significant to note in international management. Highlighting the differences of non-verbal communication encourages harmonious interactions, hence enhancing workplace relationships and overall productivity. It is therefore imperative that world business leaders build cultural intelligence (CQ), the term referred to in the revised framework employed by recent research, in order to successfully navigate such complexities and improve communication programs in multi-culture environments (Todd et al., 2012). Since company strategies are often debated by multiple cultures, variations in communication styles manifest as important variables that can determine business outcomes. High-context cultures, such as in the majority of Asian countries, rely heavily on the environmental context, including non-verbal communication like body language, tone, and facial expressions. High-context cultures, in contrast, typically typical in North America and Western Europe, emphasize concise verbal communications with less reliance on non-verbal communications. This is a reflection of the fact that body language can be a focal instrument of communication in some cultures while functioning in the background in others. Thus, international managers must adapt their communication styles to the specific cultural context in a bid to facilitate successful interactions. Being responsive in this manner not only minimizes potential miscommunications but also strengthens collaboration between multicultural teams and becomes supportive, with positive implications for the attainment of international business enterprises and international business cohesion (Todd et al., 2012). Barriers to cross-cultural communication also come into existence through misinterpretation of body language and failure to recognize cultural undertones. These barriers can interfere with global team performance and obstruct organizational objectives. Misinterpretations caused by varying meaningful gestures can lead team members to experience conflict or tension, eventually affecting morale and productivity. Managers should devise techniques that are sensitive to culture in order to bridge these barriers. Cultural awareness and competence training programs can equip employees with the tools to effectively manage such problems. By fostering respect and openness, organizations can develop a setting that values diversity. As a result, appreciation and recognition of gesture differences not only enhance interpersonal communications but also tighten team performance, which enhances overall success in the global economy (Dyne et al., 2012).

4.2.3. Importance of eye Contact and Personal Space

In the intricate world of international management, one needs to understand the subtleties of communication. One such subtlety is non-verbal communication like eye contact and personal space, which has a strong impact on cross-cultural communication. Eye contact can be a significant indicator of participation and commitment, but its interpretation could vary significantly across cultures. In some cultures, direct gaze is a sign of confidence and interest, but in other cultures it may be experienced as intrusive or disrespectful. This divergence points to the significance of context in culture in shaping norms for communication. With businesses now operating internationally, leaders are required to comprehend these variations in order to avoid misunderstandings that could hinder cooperation and trust in culturally diverse teams. To realize these nuances is most important to creating successful relationships in today's global business environment. The concept of personal space complicates cross-cultural communication even further. Cultures vary in their expectations for how intimate they should be with one another during a communication, and miscommunication and discomfort occur when the boundary is not respected. High-context cultures, for example, may favor close physical proximity as a sign of warmth and familiarity, while low-context cultures may value personal space and respond to increased distancing in social behavior. These differences can compromise fluid communication if not managed. Individuals with high awareness of these cultural tendencies are then in a stronger position to manage discussions and negotiations, making a conducive climate for cooperation. This understanding can lead to more productive dialogue, eventually enhancing team cohesion and organizational performance in a multicultural setting. Additionally, the coexistence of eye contact and body space demonstrates a hidden cultural framework that shapes verbal and non-verbal patterns of communication. Cultures tend to place varying values on communication, typically classified in the broader terms of high-context and low-context communications. In working with these various styles, international managers must learn and respect the host country's conventions for eye contact and physical proximity. As proposed by existing literature, becoming culturally competent can assist in building improved relationships and trust in multicultural teams, thus bridging barriers in intercultural interactions (Thanaraj et al., 2016). Effective management of these communication dynamics allows organizations to leverage the strengths of their global workforce, enhancing overall performance in a multicultural work environment. Awareness and response to these cultural differences can be an impetus for success in international management.

4.3. HIGH-CONTEXT VS. LOW-CONTEXT CULTURES

The intricate dynamics of communication in international management are often based on theoretical high-context and low-context culture paradigms. High-context cultures, generally characterized by an emphasis on shared experience, subtle messages, and non-verbal communications, generally foster interpersonal relationship and community.

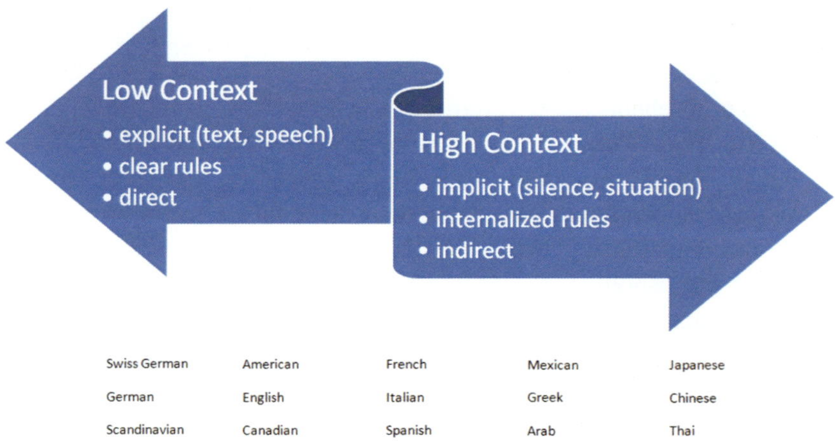

Figure 4.7. Conceptual frameworks of high-context and low-context cultures.

Source: https://langsolinc.com/wp-content/uploads/2019/05/HC-LC.png.

Low-context cultures, on the other hand, value verbal communication in which directness and specificity are central. This difference illustrates how cultural background can determine expectations of communication, ranging from how one negotiates to how an international team operates. For instance, high-context managers, who are typical in Asian cultures, may find silence or a blunt reply meaningful, but their low-context colleagues, which are typical in

Western cultures, would view this as evasiveness or indifference. It is crucial that these nuances are grasped by global managers aiming to design efficient communication strategies and foster cooperation (Zografi, 2025). Moreover, the comprehension of the impact of high-context and low-context communication can assist organizations in overcoming barriers in successful cross-cultural cooperation. In high-context societies, people have a tendency to come before some job roles or formal titles and thus confuse pyramid hierarchies found in low-context cultures (Figure 4.7).

These disparities lead to conflict in global negotiations or group interactions because the parties end up misinterpreting each other's intentions or commitments. The intercultural skill for dealing with such disparities goes beyond knowledge and involves adapting the communication style to suit different cultural demands and setting up a welcoming place where everyone feels valued. With increasing world interdependence, it is essential for organizations to develop such skills to flourish in today's multicultural market (Lincke et al., 2025). Lastly, the meeting of high-context and low-context communication models points towards ongoing cultural sensitivity education and intercultural competencies building within organizations. Managers are tasked with filling these cultural gaps that typically include a deep understanding of the staff backgrounds to create fruitful interactions. By implementing training programs focusing on the development of communication skills in relation to the high-context and low-context model, organizations are able to enable their employees to cope with these difficult interactions in a professional manner. Improved intercultural communication skill not only builds better relationships between different teams but also results in the success of international management policies overall. This integrated approach facilitates enhanced work environment equilibrium and productivity toward organizational goals within a more globalized economy (Zografi, 2025).

4.3.1. Characteristics of High-Context Cultures

The communication patterns of high-context cultures have a significant effect on business interpersonal relationships. In these cultures, non-verbal aspects of communication—tone of voice, body language, and hints from the context—are often accountable for the bulk of the message communicated. Such a focus on the non-verbal aspects means that reading between the lines is crucial, as literal word statements often fail to convey the complete meaning. Thus, high-context managers must possess extremely good observational skill and emotional intelligence to be able to manage complex social realities effectively. As it is really the case that relationship-oriented significance creates strong trust among colleagues, the capability of reading between lines takes center stage in having effective discussions and negotiations in cross-cultural management environments. Effective cross-cultural management relies on such relational dynamics underlying high-context interactions. Further, high-context cultures tend to favor indirect communication, which can be challenging for individuals accustomed to low-context environments. While there are deviations from cultures where both clarity and explicitness are valued, high-context communication allows for room for ambiguity since messages are stacked in cultural references as well as common knowledge. Such implicitness requires managers to listen intently but also develop relationships over time in order to grasp. Interpersonal rapport has the potential to decrease significantly the likelihood of misinterpretations, allowing managers to reach a level of understanding that might otherwise be impossible (Figure 4.8).

Figure 4.8. High context culture marketing.

Source: https://www.mbaskool.com/2019_images/stories/may_images/high-context-culture.jpg.

As indicated in previous studies, cultural context and communication patterns synergy is key to guaranteeing individual and societal values' congruence, creating an enabling environment for successful cross-cultural management practices (Mustafa et al., 2015). Synergy between cultural values and high-context communication practices also testifies to the necessity of developing cross-cultural leadership competencies. For international managers, comprehension of the influence of high-context traits in the workplace dynamics can enhance their performance in multicultural environments. The emergence of Turkey as one of the premier emerging markets, for example, implies it is essential to appreciate the intricacy of high-context relationships to encourage collaboration between Turkish and American professionals. A combined approach to studying dimensions of culture derived from classical theories such as Hofstedes categorizations illustrates the manner in which high-context orientations require subtle communication tactics. With intentional application of such knowledge, managers can establish more harmonious coexistence and communication plans that are effective across cultures to ultimately realize healthy working environments as well as improved organizational performance (Halub et al., 2017).

4.3.2. Characteristics of Low-Context Cultures

Within global management, it is necessary to understand the cultural dissimilarities in communication. Low-context cultures typically engage in direct verbal communication, whereby words convey most of the message that is meant to be communicated. Businesses that operate within low-context cultures, such as the United States and Germany, typically engage in simple and clear language with less reliance on non-verbal communication. This directness has a functional value in the sense that messages are delivered consistently across diversified audiences. With leaders in such environments engaging with members of various backgrounds, they must understand that all cultures might not welcome this demand for direct communication. This awareness is thus still needed in building an appreciation of the role played by low-context orientations in shaping intra- and inter-organizational communication, facilitating transactions in multinational environments. The high communication efficiency of such cultures is due to their formalized processes of communicating information. High transparency typifies such cultures so that documentation and instructions can be easily followed with every aspect laid down clearly. This feature enables the creation of cultures in which responsibility and the definition of roles are very important because individuals are expected to trust words rather than contextually derived meanings. Consequently, opportunities of miscommunication arise when communicators from low-context cultures interact with high-context counterparts because where non-verbal signals play a key role in the transmission of messages. Gaining sensitivity to such differences is most crucial for international managers aiming at forming warm and effective relationships. The interplay between cultural contexts also points to the imperative for adaptive communication styles that are responsive to various expectations and practices among all participants, ultimately enhancing cross-cultural effectiveness. Additionally, the impacts of low-context communication extend beyond mere information exchange; they have relational implications for team dynamics as well. In environments prioritizing efficiency and task-oriented interactions, participants will be inclined to place results above interpersonal relationship, which accordingly creates impressions of impersonal relationships. But this attribute also tends to bring along a problem-solving culture, where direct issue-solving is valued. Research shows that leaders' harmony with societal values can enhance communication as an effective means since low-context trait leaders are more effective in providing clear communication within such organizations (Mustafa et al., 2015). With international managers confronting the issues of cross-cultural communication, they have to reconcile the directness of low-context styles with the richer and more elaborate forms of high-context cultures, culminating in a more accommodative organizational culture (Fitó Bertran et al., 2018).

4.3.3. Implications for International Business Communication

Effective cross-border business communication is more about appreciating the nuances inherent in various cultures. Once companies expand to global levels, the impossibility of uni-dimensional communication becomes apparent. Not only do the cultures differ in oral communication but also in the non-verbal cues, which can generate miscommunicated meaning in case they are not explained adequately. For instance, high-context cultures, prevalent in regions such as Asia, are often subtle in message and body language and thus might struggle with low-context cultures, prevalent in the majority of Western nations, where directness is prevalent. These disparities are likely to create misunderstandings, which have implications for negotiations and the formation of partnerships. Discovery of such differences is significant in forming communication mechanisms that are flexible in dealing with divergent cultural structures, thereby optimizing overall performance in cross-cultural business settings. As businesses stretch for worldwide interaction, the cultural dynamics of perspectives keep on complicating international communication. Cultures vary significantly with respect to prioritizing relationship maintenance and task accomplishment and then influencing management styles and decision-making. In the context of hierarchical systems prevalent in Vietnam, the value of authority might influence communication patterns and assumptions. In societies like Finland where there is higher egalitarianism, collaborative approaches thrive. Understanding these cultural differences allows global managers to create a more welcoming space for communication, ultimately resulting in improved team relations and outcomes. Extensions of these differences extend beyond individual relationships; they determine the very framework in which companies operate across cultures. To navigate all of this requires adopting specialized approaches for communication that are based on cultural awareness and sensitivity. The message of cultural differences in communication puts a premium on cross-cultural skills programs. Training programs such as collaborative projects between institutions from different countries, which were researched in a study by Bain et al. (2016), are essential learning experiences.

Not only do these training programs provide students with hands-on skills, but they also encourage empathy towards differing perspectives, something critical for future international business leaders. By integrating cultural training into business courses, educational institutions can better prepare students to tackle the challenges of operating in multicultural environments. Additionally, what one learns about the consequences of differences between cultures, as seen in Dang et al. (2024), speaks to the necessity for adaptive management strategies. This educational focus on cultural awareness can lead to more successful international endeavors and long-term partnerships, stressing the greatest importance of effective cross-cultural communication in international management.

4.4. BARRIERS TO EFFECTIVE CROSS-CULTURAL COMMUNICATION

In global management, it is essential to appreciate the nuances of verbal and non-verbal communication styles in order to facilitate effective cross-cultural relationships. Discrepancies between these styles often lead to misunderstanding and conflict.

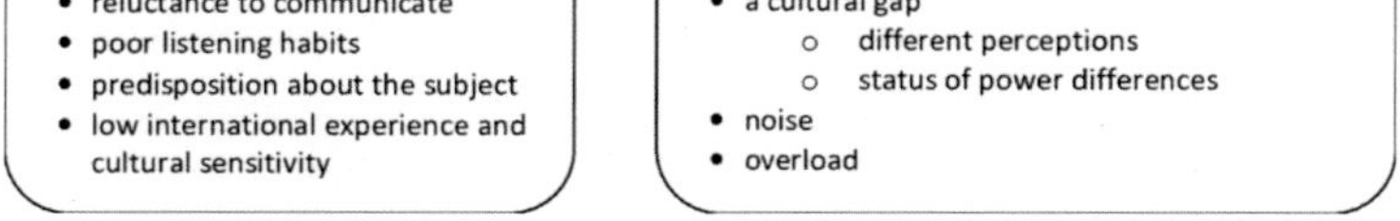

Figure 4.9. Potential barriers to effective cross-cultural communication.

Source: https://www.researchgate.net/profile/Marta-Szeluga-Romanska/publication/340931541/figure/fig1/AS:884527144632320@1587899113331/Potential-Barriers-to-Effective-Cross-cultural-Communication.png.

For instance, high-context cultures such as in most Asian societies heavily rely on inferred messages as well as environmental information. Low-context cultures such as in Western societies, on the other hand, favor explicit verbal messages. This gap is a challenge in that low-context people may misinterpret the subtlety employed by their high-context peers. Failing to comprehend these differing styles can be a hurdle to teamwork and lead to inadvertent faux pas, ultimately disrupting the efficacy of international partnerships and bargains. Moreover, the challenge of successfully negotiating language diversity contributes to the barriers of communication across cultures. Language ability is more than vocabulary; it encompasses idiomatic expressions and cultural references. This is particularly crucial in workplace settings where clear and precise communication is paramount. The need for interpreter services or advocacy then becomes apparent as organizations try to bridge these language gaps (Figure 4.9).

For example, studies emphasized the importance of interpreter services in ensuring equal access to healthcare among diverse populations effectively proving that interpreter services are important not only in the health field but also in business settings where client consultations vary greatly in language backgrounds (Clay et al., 2005). Proper resources can significantly enhance the effectiveness of communication when eliminating language barriers. The coming together of culturally competent behaviors manifests itself as a notable variable in eradicating obstacles to effective cross-cultural communication. Such an awareness is of utmost value in global management, whereby the ability to navigate various cultural landscapes is capable of guaranteeing the success of a business endeavor. Studies show that culturally aware practices establish an environment conducive to free flow of communication, thereby eradicating miscommunication. As has been put forward by research on the healthcare sector, the creation of culturally sensitive communication systems not only remedies inequalities but also promotes equitable ground for interaction (Keys et al., 2012). By starting training and awareness programs that emphasize cultural sensitivity, organizations can broaden channels of communication, leading to improved collaboration and stronger relationships within diverse collectives.

4.4.1. Language Barriers and Misunderstandings

Effective international management communication is fraught with traps, and the majority of these are caused by language variations and miscommunication. The greatest challenges are largely brought about by communication styles through words and non-words that are likely to vary from culture to culture. For instance, high-context cultures that are likely to contain a lot of implicit information and non-words are likely to have misunderstandings when communicating with low-context cultures that facilitate explicitness and directness. The variations between these styles can be the cause of not only confusion but also unintentional offense, and it is thus paramount that international managers learn about these variations. Emphasized by research, the ability to recognize and appreciate variations in culture, as explicated in Thanaraj et al. (2016), is crucial in conflict minimization and effective interpersonal relations in multicultural business environments. Also, language differences do not only occur through vocabulary and grammar differences but through the different meanings attributed to words and phrases between cultures. Misunderstandings tend to become exaggerated where there are dialects or regional colloquialism involved, which tends to veil the intended meaning. This is particularly true in global management, where members of a team or customers may employ a commonly used lingua franca such as English but yet experience huge challenges in conveying complex thoughts. Intercultural competence, as in Antal et al. (2025), not only necessitates the ability to communicate across such barriers, but also sensing and negotiating the underlying cultural dynamics (Figure 4.10).

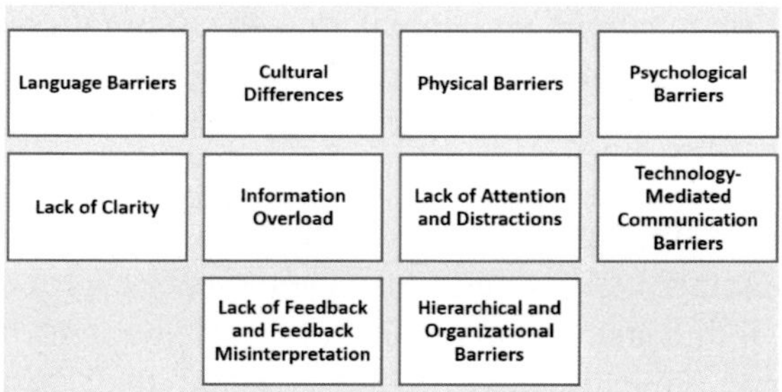

Figure 4.10. Barrier to communication of international management.

Source: https://i0.wp.com/www.managementnote.com/wp-content/uploads/2023/07/Barrier-to-communication.jpg?resize=624%2C319&ssl=1.

Through these skills, managers can effectively turn potential communication problems into learning opportunities, enhancing their overall professional and social relationships in multicultural environments. In international business activities, understanding the relationship between language and culture is necessary for successful management strategies. Language differences can lead to misunderstanding and tension, and in most situations, hinder negotiation activities or collaboration efforts. When the employees are diverse in terms of cultures, miscommunication may arise due to differences in interpretations of silence, tone, and body language—facts that are very volatile across cultures. Thus, a keen awareness of such differences is what can streamline the workings. By equipping the employees with training programs in intercultural communication, the employees can be made self-assured with the ability to deal with such sophistication, as indicated by research in Thanaraj et al. (2016). Finally, such initiatives not only facilitate collaboration but also improve a company's reputation in the global marketplace by encouraging respectful and effective communication in multicultures.

4.4.2. Stereotypes and Cultural Biases

Communication is a multifaceted process influenced by numerous variables, including personal and cultural background stereotypes. High-context cultures, for example, those prevailing in the majority of Asian societies, rely significantly on non-verbal cues and the context in close proximity for meaning, leading to a less obvious style of communication. Conversely, low-context cultures, prevalent in Western environments, focus on open verbal expression. This difference can result in misunderstandings, where low-context members will accuse high-context members of being evasive or vague. The stereotypes about such communication styles reinforce the misunderstandings by causing misinterpretation of meaning and intent due to assumptions about cultural behavior. It is essential in international management because it makes for more effective communication and conflict avoidance that is based on assumptions about culture.

The impact of stereotypes in cross-cultural communication goes beyond mere misunderstanding; it also affects management policies and team harmony. Foreign students, for instance, who participate in programs such as the Erasmus exchange program, typically have concerns about their respective cultural origins and how other people may perceive them due to their origin. As is noted in a study on Turkish students, fears regarding misconceptions related to Turkey as a Muslim and Third World nation can cause immense concern for their future global experience (Aktas et al., 2011). Such biases can hamper the ability to form genuine relationships and establish effective teamwork within multicultural settings. When international managers encounter such stereotypes, it is critically imperative to build a culture that ensures open communication and intercultural understanding, thereby minimizing the role of cultural prejudices on performance and cooperation. To respond most effectively to the challenges presented by stereotypes and cultural prejudice, organizations must become proactive in managing diversity.

Accepting the reality that diversity improves the workplace and stimulates creativity, managers have to work towards establishing an inclusive workplace that respects differences (Dhiman et al., 2019). This entails that there need to be active steps in examining internal biases that undermine efforts towards diversity. Moreover, organizations should sponsor training programs that help employees navigate the multiple cultures and communication patterns that are present within their teams. These programs can facilitate individuals to identify their biases and develop skills to engage productively with individuals of diverse backgrounds. Finally, fighting stereotypes and cultural biases not only improves communication but also improves organizational resilience and adaptability in the global market.

4.4.3. Differences in Communication Styles and Expectations

An understanding of how communication takes place in varied cultural settings is a requirement for international management. For instance, cultural definitions of verbal and non-verbal communication can be quite different. For instance, in countries like Finland, where directness and explicitness of communications are valued, there is very little room for ambiguity. Conversely, Vietnamese in high-context cultures such as Vietnam would communicate more by implication and gestures rather than direct talk. Such a difference may lead to misunderstanding when Finnish managers misinterpret Vietnamese indirectness as vacillation or lack of commitment. The interaction between these two styles highlights that international managers must adapt their communication style. These nuances can be identified and take advantage of more productive relationships, coordination of cross-cultural teams, and ultimately improved business outcomes and an improved working environment (Dang et al., 2024). High-context and low-context communication approaches also make a difference when it comes to behavior and expectations in cross-cultural interactions. High-context cultures place strong stress on relational dynamics, context knowledge, and nonverbal communication, which has a tendency to lead to more implicit communication approaches. On the other hand, low-context cultures prioritize direct expression and factual transmission and place value on overt verbal language. This contrast could be a stumbling block when individuals of different cultural backgrounds are placed in the same group. As an illustration, a Vietnamese employee could be highly reliant on non-verbal cues and context to navigate, while a Finnish manager could be expecting loud declarations in order to understand the complexities of a project. These discrepancies can generate frustration on both sides, making the effectiveness of cross-cultural collaboration difficult. Therefore, an awareness of the discrepancies is highly significant in framing strategies for bridging communication gaps and aligning expectations accordingly (Mustafa et al., 2015). These discrepancies in expectations and styles of communication can shape barriers to effective cross-cultural communication, making it a significant issue in international management. Cultural misunderstandings can lead to conflicts and poor productivity in multicultural teams. For example, direct questioning by a Finnish leader may be perceived as confrontational or disrespectful by Vietnamese staff, and rapport and trust will be lost. Moreover, varying time-related attitudes can further exacerbate misunderstandings because different cultures believe in different aspects of communication and team collaboration. It is essential that global managers develop cultural intelligence in the form of not just knowledge but also sensitivity to different modes and expectations of communication. In developing training sessions addressing such cultural differences, organizations can reduce barriers in intercommunication among team members, leading to a setting where everyone feels valued and valued (Dang et al., 2024).

4.5. STRATEGIES FOR OVERCOMING COMMUNICATION BARRIERS

Understanding the intricacies of verbal and non-verbal communication is crucial in addressing barriers in cross-cultural management contexts. Different cultures, in turn, have distinct patterns of communication that significantly influence interactions in international teams. For instance, high-context cultures such as those in the majority of Asia are highly reliant on implicit messages and non-verbal cues.

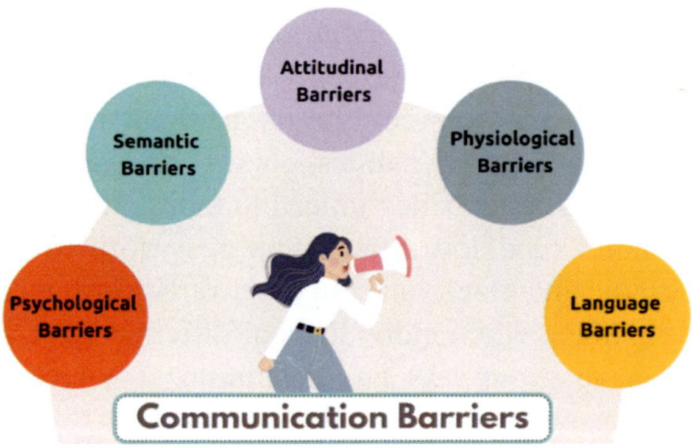

Figure 4.11. Diverse cultures often possess distinct communication barrier.

Source: https://www.risely.me/wp-content/uploads/2023/07/Risely-Featured-Image-Deeksha-39-1024x576.png.

Conversely, low-context cultures such as those in the United States and Germany emphasize explicit and clear communication. Misunderstandings may occur when the team members are not aware of these differences and, hence, resort to potential conflict or misunderstanding. Organizations can mitigate these problems by incorporating training modules into the program that introduce employees to various communication styles, evoking empathy and adaptability in communications. Enhancing the skills of workers to handle these nuances ultimately creates an inclusive culture that is imperative to effective collaboration in global markets, thereby mitigating the threats of miscommunication (Amos et al., 2011). Utilizing an understanding of communication styles, firms also have to devise strategies for bridging the gap caused by language differences in foreign settings. Language skills are generally the biggest hinderance in cross-cultural communications, with miscommunications occurring as a result of varying levels of fluency. To ensure this, organizations can employ multilingual staff or offer language courses so that communication efficacy is easy to promote (Figure 4.11).

In addition, the application of plain language—using simplified expressions for straightforward ones—can diminish confusion and so improve clarity in heterogeneous groups. Active listening capabilities and the asking of feedback are equally important to check understanding and ensure that all members are on equal footing. When language is made accessible and clear, companies can build an atmosphere of inclusion, whose outcome is much less likely to be disagreement and much more likely to be increased international cooperations (Thanaraj et al., 2016). In addition to spoken content, non-verbal communication also plays an important role in the way messages are interpreted and received within different cultures. Body language, personal space, and eye contact might all vary enormously in the values placed on them. Thus, maintaining eye contact may demonstrate confidence and focus within some cultures but be disrespectful or overly aggressive in others. To minimize these risks, global managers should provide intercultural training emphasizing the importance of non-verbal behaviors in different cultures. Such training must include not only the identification of these differences but also practical steps to adjust one's own non-verbal behavior. By developing sensitivity and awareness of the nuances of non-verbal communication, organizations can enhance their overall effectiveness and interpersonal relationships within a diverse workforce and therefore make collaboration and interaction simpler (Amos et al., 2011).

4.5.1. Cultural Awareness and Sensitivity Training

Communication in the context of an international business is often based on how a person can adjust to various cultural dynamics. Communication with other cultures demands familiarity with verbal as well as non-verbal communication styles that tend to be much different from culture to culture. High-context cultures, for example, are greatly reliant on implicit communication and shared perception, whereas low-context cultures usually accommodate explicit and direct communication. Cultural awareness training and cultural sensitivity train international managers to navigate these intricate layers of communication effectively. By instilling appreciation for different styles, companies can minimize miscommunication and enhance collaboration across cultural divides. Cultural awareness training is not an abstract exercise; instead, it is part of organizational effectiveness in a multicultural setup where a single misstep in communication can lead to severe operations setbacks. Cross-cultural communication barriers are normally grounded in conceptual and practical difficulties. Cultural awareness training will dismantle such barriers by highlighting the fundamental differences between cultures, including time, context, and authority attitudes. Sensitivity training also provides managers with techniques for dealing with such differences positively. Due to increasing organizations in the world, cultural intelligence turns into the most valuable necessity as observed through several cases indicating the risks of disregarding this training (Figure 4.12).

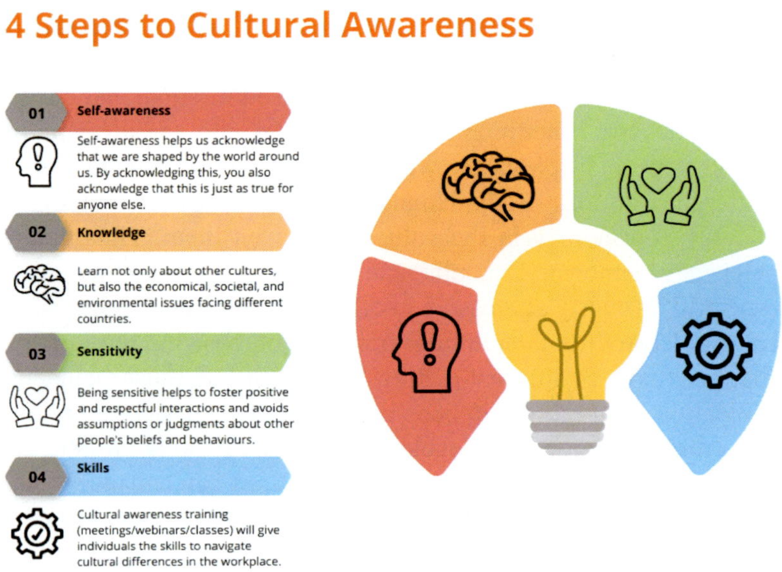

Figure 4.12. Cultural sensitivity in international employment.

Source: https://global.gibsonwatts.com/wp-content/uploads/2023/06/cultural-awareness-1.png.

For instance, failed alliances typically are the result of an inability to see through cultural sensitivities that drive business practices. As literature puts it, cultural intelligence building is at the heart of the success of global interactions because it allows workers to effectively manage cultural challenges and develop innovative solutions from alternative sources (Marcotte et al., 2019). The use of large-scale cultural awareness and sensitivity training programs can yield rich rewards in managing globally. These assignments promote mutual respect and accommodation, offering a framework for successful intercultural relations. Specifically, such training programs enable such open discourses concerning cultural differences that employees are able to express concerns and exchange experiences. Through this interaction, not only is greater understanding created, but trust among the members is also built. Furthermore, with organizations becoming increasingly global in operations, building cultural competency aligns with broader strategic goals. Companies that emphasize this training enhance their communication process, leading to more effective partnerships and collaborations within the global marketplace. Resolving the complexities of communication through targeted training not only minimizes risks but also creates an organizational culture with a diversity appreciation—a signature of modern international business (Federici et al., 2019).

4.5.2. Use of Technology in Bridging Communication Gaps

As there is a more globalized world, the complexities of verbal and non-verbal communication across cultures bring high challenges to international management. High-context cultures, in which extensive reliance is made on implicit messages and non-verbal cues, find it difficult to comprehend communication methods employed by low-context cultures that rely extensively on explicit, direct communication. Such a disparity can lead to misunderstandings that hinder effective cooperation. Therefore, technology plays a key role in bridging these gaps, providing a platform for clear communication regardless of cultural frameworks. Technology such as video conferencing and instant messaging not only allows for real-time dialogue but also facial expressions, which can be quite beneficial when working with teams based in high-context cultures. Therefore, technology can facilitate a better comprehension, and hence open the door for successful cross-cultural communication and prevent potential miscommunications. Moreover, the relationship between business and IT departments of organizations has been influenced predominantly by communication technologies. Often, these departments are proved to lack coordination with one another because of ineffective exchanges concerning strategic alignment and infrastructure needs. To replace these gaps, technological advancements can help ease communication through a shared platform of collaboration to facilitate better mutual understanding and operational effectiveness. For instance, the use of project management software and collaborative applications allows for instant updates and feedback, which can help harmonize business and IT strategies better. By embracing such systems, organizations can overcome traditional boundaries and thrust a shared vision to enable cross-cultural teams in enhancing performance in global management environments (Al-Karaghouli et al., 2005). Additionally, stakeholder needs are a central aspect of effective communication during system development but are overshadowed by errors due to breakdown in communications. The process of requirements gathering necessitates a definitive methodology and an inner understanding of multicultural thinking, as stakeholders representing diverse groups can express their requirements differently in terms of communication. Technology in this context is a significant enabler, offering frameworks that facilitate the systematic structuring and analysis of stakeholder input. For example, collaborative web-based tools can ensure that multitudes of diverse contributors' input are captured and made traceable, minimizing miscommunication. This technologically mediated mediation underscores the significance of effective communication, particularly in cross-cultural environments, where delicacy about special issues of communication is crucial. The use of technologically based models can result in ultimately better accuracy of requirements elicitation, opening doors for effective project attainment (Al-Rawas et al., 2003).

4.5.3. Building Relationships and Trust Across Cultures

Effective international management relies on strong communication, especially in the development of relationships and trust among cultures. Sensitization to verbal and non-verbal communications' nuances is important because they may greatly vary between cultures. High-context societies, prevalent in East Asia, depend to a significant degree on implied meaning and subtle cues, often amplifying the meaning of non-verbal cues such as body language and eye contact. Low-context cultures, typical of most Western societies, emphasize explicit verbal communication where clarity and directness are vital. Misunderstandings are likely to surface where these different styles intersect, and this may pose potential hurdles in building trust-based relationships. These nuances require higher sensitivity to culture for all parties engaged in international business to provide an environment supportive of respect and understanding for one another. Trust-building efforts depend largely on cultural knowledge. As highlighted by global sourcing of IT services research, the need to fit trust into specific cultural contexts cannot be overemphasized. The study notes that in contexts such as China, where concepts of guanxi (relation) and mianzi (face) play an influential part in determining interpersonal relations, there is a necessity of cultural awareness as a prerequisite to establishing trust. Lacking the cultural awareness, relationship construction attempts will collapse because people would inadvertently violate contextual norms of what could be considered trustworthiness. This renders the construction of cultural competencies not only enhance interpersonal relationships but also facilitate easier knowledge sharing—a critical element towards successful cross-border cooperation. Organizations and agencies should integrate cultural sensitivity in their systems of work to minimize misunderstandings and enhance cooperation in international settings, as this research outcome illustrates. Regular training and facilities can also address gaps in cross-cultural communication. Materials developed through the eChina-UK program are an excellent illustration of such facilities. These books offer useful insights and models for dealing with the nuances of cross-national partnerships, with a general emphasis placed on intercultural effectiveness. They identify the need for proactive approaches that overcome the differences in communication style, cultural values, and expectations that are naturally associated with international ventures. By giving people and organizations the tools to manage diversity—national, regional, or institutional—stakeholders are able to maximize their collaborative work. Such readiness not only contributes to smoother interactions but also fosters an environment of trust, eventually positioning organizations for greater success in the area of international management (Ewington et al., 2009).

4.6. CASE STUDIES IN CROSS-CULTURAL COMMUNICATION

Understanding communication styles is critical in addressing the complexity of cross-cultural interaction due to the fact that communication styles are important determinants of business results. Communication in high-context cultures such as Japan and the majority of Arab states depends greatly on context, body language, and relational dynamic among parties. In contrast, low-context cultures such as Germany and the United States employ clear verbal communication in which obviousness and honesty are emphasized. The difference speaks to the aspects of possible misunderstanding; the American may perceive a Japanese colleague's indirectness as evasive or unprofessional, while the latter can perceive the formers directness as too blunt or disrespectful. Such variations can be sources of barriers that can impede cross-cultural communication in global management, where some sensitivity and flexibility towards different communicative habits is required (Marcotte et al., 2019). Building cultural intelligence is also crucial in such cases, allowing managers to read and deal with various styles effectively. Blocking effective cross-cultural communication can contribute significantly to hindering organizational performance by causing costly misunderstandings and lessened cooperation. Typical barriers include disparities in language, diversities in norms, and preconceived views that distort one's own perceptions. For instance, a Western-Eastern business deal between companies can break down due to inconsistency in attitudes towards time, whereby punctuality is a crucial factor in the West, and in the East, relationship development becomes essential. This divergence may cause frustration and suspicion, and collaboration will be affected (Bormann et al., 2001). In surmounting these barriers, global managers need to build an atmosphere of open communication, where members feel free to voice concerns and make things clear. Besides avoiding the danger of miscommunication, it promotes an atmosphere of respectfulness and inclusiveness, which reinforces the structure of the organization in multicultural environments. Cross-cultural communication case studies provide valuable lessons on how international management problems may be overcome with successful strategies. These cases typically illustrate real-life circumstances in which miscommunication led to economic loss or relationship breakdown, and thus highlight the importance of cultural intelligence in averting such misadventures. Analysis of successful alliances provides firms with lessons to affirm the importance of creating cultural awareness in their employees. Recommendations may include implementing cross-cultural training programs, promoting various work teams, and instituting policies that embrace inclusive practices. For instance, organizations benefit by intentionally seating employees of various cultures side by side to promote understanding and empathy, leading to enhanced performance (Marcotte et al., 2019). Thus, case studies are a valuable asset to organizations that desire to thrive in an increasingly globalized marketplace, giving them the tools they require to navigate complex cultural landscapes.

4.6.1. Successful International Management Examples

As the world continues to globalize, how different types of communication interact has been the most important aspect in international management. One great example can be noted in companies that handle the dynamics between high-context and low-context cultures efficiently. High-context cultures such as Japan or China are more inclined towards non-verbal communication and context, whereas low-context cultures such as the United States and Germany are more direct and simple. Firms that recognize these differences in communication style have found ways of modifying their management practice, developing a culture where workers are made to feel valued and heard. This does not only solidify interpersonal relationships but also minimizes the danger of misunderstandings due to misinterpretation. Consequently, cultural sensitivity as part of management planning is the secret to effective international business since it provides the foundation for effective collaboration in different cultural settings. Further, successful international management demands the removal of barriers to cross-cultural communication. For instance, language differences have a tendency to act as an obstacle to practitioners, and the utilization of translators or bilingual employees is necessary to bridge the communication gap. Companies that invest in language courses and cultural awareness workshops can enhance their operational efficiency within global markets considerably. This is a proactive measure against miscommunications, which otherwise could mean financial losses or reputational damage. IKEA is a firm that exemplifies this practice, with culturally sensitive marketing policies and ensuring that employees are equipped with the appropriate tools for cross-cultural communications. By focusing on breakdown of communication barriers and cross-cultural intelligence, such organizations optimize their performance towards creating harmony for various groups, ultimately resulting in success at a global scale (Marcotte et al., 2019). Finally, an understanding of the dynamics that govern international management is incomplete without the acknowledgement of the power that diversity exerts in forming creative solutions. To this end, investments in workplace diversity are a key resource. For instance, institutions embracing official diversity training programs not only enhance employees' best abilities but also create a setting in which each voice matters and is heard. Such a practice supports new thinking that emerges from varied inputs, leading to improved problem-solving capabilities and innovative outputs. The Workplace Diversity Network, for example, provides a range of resources that can support diversity practitioners in their job, reflective of growing awareness that diverse teams will lead to greater performance outcomes. As the globe is opened up by companies seeking international markets, the ability to capitalize on cultural differences as strengths becomes an imperative, further supporting the argument that effective international management relies on the ability to communicate across cultures (Bormann et al., 2001).

4.6.2. Lessons Learned from Communication Failures

In cross-cultural management, communication dynamics are essential in order to avoid misunderstandings based on cultural differences. High-context and low-context communication styles heavily determine how messages are received between cultures. In high-context cultures like Japan and most Middle Eastern countries, the context of a conversation tends to matter more than the actual words used. Conversely, low-context cultures such as Germany and the United States rely heavily on explicit verbal communication. This could lead to significant misinterpretations; what would constitute a firm directive in a low-context culture would only be perceived as a request in a high-context culture. Experiences obtained from such failures in communication highlight the importance of cultural sensitivity and adaptability when interacting across cultures, reinforcing the necessity of adjusting communication plans to the culture in a way to achieve clarity of communication as well as avoid conflicts. Also, non-verbal communication plays a crucial part in cross-cultural communication as it occasionally conveys meanings that are diametrically different from culture to culture. Posture, facial expression, and social distance preferences can have varied meanings based on cultures. For instance, direct stares may express confidence and honesty in some cultures and insolence or hostility in others. These variations must be recognized and understood for effective communication in international management. Misunderstandings regarding these non-verbal behaviors can cause strained relationships and unsuccessful negotiations (Figure 4.13).

Figure 4.13. Communication failures highlight the necessity of cultural sensitivity.

Source: https://image.marriage.com/advice/wp-content/uploads/2018/11/12-Communication-Failures-That-Cause-Even-the-Strongest-Marriage-to-Fail.jpg.

The behavior of business organizations navigating these cultural nuances in this respect highlights the need for large-scale training programs that equip employees with the capability to read and respond to verbal and non-verbal communication accordingly. Besides this, language differences also create a problem in the field of international communication. All these issues highlight the importance of clarity and the need to validate understanding for people from diverse linguistic backgrounds. Information and Communication Technology (ICT) introduction into multinationals is a pragmatic solution to such obstacles in that it allows for increased cooperation amid differences in languages. The venture, as noted in Chang et al. (2015), emphasizes the significant contribution of technology in closing gaps in communication while also underlining the significance of cultural competency. Additionally, reflective practice on failed communications can lead to the opening of doors for improved methods, and an environment of constant learning and adaptation. Ultimately, breaking down and identifying these complicated obstacles has the potential to significantly enhance communication effectiveness and business success in international management environments.

4.6.3. Analysis of Cultural Adaptation in Global Teams

In global teams, effective communication relies upon a sophisticated understanding of the various verbal and non-verbal ways of communicating found in different cultures. There are high-context cultures, as one would normally find in Asian cultures, that rely heavily on context and underlying cues when and where they occur, to convey meaning. This contrasts starkly with low-context cultures found in Western cultures, where communications are explicit and direct. When groups move beyond these cultural structures, miscommunication may happen, against which cooperation and productivity are lost. For instance, a low-context member may perceive a high-context communicator as evasive or indirect, which brings frustration and perplexity. The implications of such differences demand global teams to acquire a deeper insight into patterns of cultural communication to counteract conflict and produce an enabling environment for collaboration and success (Reid et al., 2009; Bemelmans et al., 2025). The constraint to successful cross-cultural communication is another significant issue that organizations face. Such barriers are typically derived from stereotypes, ethnocentrism, and linguistic differences, which can deter the flow of information. Stereotypes generate preconceptions that govern behavior and expectations, generally leading to biases which distort interactions between various groups. Ethnocentrism, the notion that one's culture is superior, may cause a lack of appreciation for other viewpoints. Additionally, language variations not just encompass words but also the shades of meaning put into phrases and words each culture employs. It is thus crucial that these challenges are overcome with cultural sensitivity and awareness training by organizations striving to promote communication and establish better global partnerships (Reid et al., 2009; Bemelmans et al., 2025). In pursuing cultural adaptation within international teams, the development of intercultural competence emerges as a critical component. Intercultural competence entails a series of skills and attributes such as self-knowledge, culture knowledge, and flexible communication styles. The team members ought to be encouraged to reflect on their own cultural assumptions and simultaneously work hard to acquire and appreciate the diverse cultural orientations of others. The literature emphasizes that competencies of being open to try new things and effective communication strategies play an essential role in establishing strong relationships across cultures. As more organizations engage in international partnerships, the creation of these abilities not only allows for stronger interpersonal connections but also helps with improved team functioning and innovative problem-solving. If harnessed effectively, intercultural competence can be the foundation for transforming global teams into cohesive units capable of managing complex cultural landscapes (Reid et al., 2009; Bemelmans et al., 2025).

SUMMARY

The nature of cross-cultural communication reveals the intricacies involved in international management to lie beyond mere language difference. Other factors, such as high-context and low-context style of culture, come into play crucially in how messages are communicated and decoded across cultures. High-context cultures prefer implicit communication, with much said through context and non-verbal cues, compared to the employment of explicit and direct communication in low-context cultures. This information is most essential to global managers that aim to foster effective working relationships among diverse teams. Knowing these differences in communication styles, firms can lower miscommunications and enable smoother interactions, increasing overall productivity and morale. Obstacles of effective communication most often stem from different cultural models that control individuals' perceptions and interpretation. Misalignment between high-context and low-context communication styles may produce miscommunication, frustration, and conflict, ultimately hindering organizational goals. International management firms should actively address these challenges by way of training programs and sensitivity programs, equipping staff with the survival strategies for navigating culturally sophisticated interactions. Furthermore, through the application of effective communication skills, such as active listening and empathy, there will be a more embracing environment welcoming diverse perspective. These programs not only encourage cooperative cooperation but also contribute significantly towards the achievement of organizational success in a global market. Last but not least, for effective international management, excellent knowledge of cross-cultural communication patterns is crucial. According to studies, it is possible that there are variations in human resource practices, although differences may often be overstated given cultural diversity, as discussed in Van de Voorde et al. (2007). Instead, focus should be put on the underlying institutional frameworks that organize communication practices. In addition, the role of language translation cannot be disregarded in crisis communication; its role is increasingly better appreciated by scholars and practitioners, based on (Federici et al., 2019). By encouraging an open culture of communication and cultural awareness, companies can not only break down barriers but also leverage the diverse strengths of their multinational employees and create more innovative and competitive business solutions.

In cross-cultural management, understanding the levels of communication is crucial in order to perform better in cross-cultural environments. Most of the debate is about verbal and non-verbal types of communication, which are quite dissimilar across cultures. For instance, while clear verbal communication is most sought after in low-context cultures, high-context cultures rely almost entirely on non-verbal cues and contextual knowledge. This variation can lead to mis-communication if not perceived, with individuals from low-context environments misinterpreting high-context nuances of communication. Secondly, being capable of dealing with such variation enhances inter-personal relations and supports successful team work within multi-cultural groups, a critical ability in global business processes. Recognizing these differences enables managers to adjust their own communication style accordingly, ultimately enhancing a better working environment. The importance of differentiating high-context and low-context cultures cannot be overestimated in international management. High-context cultures, typically characterized by more implicit, subtle communication styles, require a degree of familiarity and shared understanding that is challenging for people from low-context cultures. Low-context cultures, in contrast, prioritize explicit verbal communication that permits more direct interaction. The available literature points out that such differences can lead to barriers in communication, which further can lead to conflicts or misunderstandings preventing organizational success. As it has been pointed out by recent research, individuals empowered with cultural intelligence are better placed to bridge such barriers, eventually leading to greater cooperation between multicultural teams. By grasping the underlying dimensions of these modes of communication, managers can map out methods that allow bridging and organizational effectiveness. Lastly, the analysis of barriers to effective cross-cultural communication points out many challenges that globally operating organizations face. The obstacles are likely to stem from cultural misunderstandings, linguistic variation, and conceptions of time and space being different. Misunderstandings will lead to mistrust and decreased morale among teams, impacting productivity directly. Evidence shows that people's perceptions regarding communication efficacy also change depending on their cultural environment and past experiences, further complicating the process in multicultural settings. For example, students in various European cultural contexts have indicated a diverse appreciation for certain managerial competencies fostered through collaborative exercises, showing that these perceptions largely dictate their learning experiences (Fitó et al., 2018). Overcoming these barriers involves not only training but a willingness to establish an ethnically diverse work environment where open communication is encouraged. By giving priority to effective cross-cultural communication, firms can overcome such barriers and facilitate greater cooperation in global management activities.

REFERENCES

1. Aktas, G., & Brown, L. (2011). Fear of the unknown: A pre-departure qualitative study of Turkish international students. https://core.ac.uk/download/4898311.pdf (accessed on 24th September 2025).
2. Al-Karaghouli, A., Burn, J., Carr, M., Coughlan, J., Curry, E., Dewett, T., et al. (2005). Seeing the big PICTURE: A framework for improving the communication of requirements within the Business-IT relationship. https://core.ac.uk/download/333170.pdf (accessed on 24th September 2025).
3. Al-Rawas, A., Beirne, M., Bellotti, V., Beyer, H., Boland, R., Bostrum, R., Button, G., et al. (2003). Communication issues in requirements elicitation: A content analysis of stakeholder experiences. https://core.ac.uk/download/333160.pdf (accessed on 24th September 2025).
4. Amos, M., & Jacobs, N. (2011). NanoInfoBio: A case-study in interdisciplinary research. http://arxiv.org/abs/1211.5508 (accessed on 24th September 2025).
5. Angouri, J., & Glynos, J. (2009). Managing cultural diversity in the multinational corporate workplace: Solution or symptom? https://core.ac.uk/download/9341781.pdf (accessed on 24th September 2025).
6. Antal, A. B., & Friedman, V. (2025). Negotiating reality as an approach to intercultural competence. https://core.ac.uk/download/pdf/6653866.pdf (accessed on 24th September 2025).
7. Bain, J. D., Biggs, J., Blessinger, P., Boje, D., Bovée, C., Gillispie, M. D., Henderson, J. K., et al. (2016). Reaching across continents: Engaging students through virtual collaborations. https://core.ac.uk/download/77594277.pdf (accessed on 24th September 2025).
8. Bemelmans, T. M. B., Ulijn, J. M., & Vogel, D. (2025). ICT study implications for human interaction and culture: Intro to a special issue. https://core.ac.uk/download/pdf/6501262.pdf (accessed on 24th September 2025).
9. Boonmatun, S., & Huttyayavilaiphan, R. (2025). Intercultural communication in the temple: Challenges and strategies for Thai monks using English to share Buddhist teachings. World Journal of English Language. https://www.semanticscholar.org/paper/42c068feec09fa2b4a40785d06a2d5b494651745 (accessed on 24th September 2025).
10. Bormann, T., Brooks-Cooper, C., Farley, J., Fuerstenau, M., et al. (2001). Resources for workplace diversity: An annotated practitioner guide to information. https://core.ac.uk/download/5127328.pdf (accessed on 24th September 2025).

11. Busa,' M. G. (2015). Teaching learners to communicate effectively in the L2: Integrating body language in the students' syllabus. https://core.ac.uk/download/53526787.pdf (accessed on 24th September 2025).
12. Chang, Z., Krug, D., Mike, B., Smulders, M., et al. (2015). Integrating ICT in Kenyan secondary schools: An exploratory case study of a professional development program. https://core.ac.uk/download/55843865.pdf (accessed on 24th September 2025).
13. Clay, D., Gumber, A., Johnson, M. R. D., et al. (2005). An overview of the research evidence on ethnicity and communication in healthcare. https://core.ac.uk/download/105291.pdf (accessed on 24th September 2025).
14. Dang, V. (2024). A comparative analysis of starting a business in Finland and Vietnam–Case study: Sorento Korso and Moon Coffee. https://core.ac.uk/download/638721482.pdf (accessed on 24th September 2025).
15. Dhiman, S. K., Kumar, V., & Modi, S. (2019). Celebrating diversity through spirituality in the workplace: Transforming organizations holistically. https://core.ac.uk/download/216809948.pdf (accessed on 24th September 2025).
16. Eaves, S., & Walton, J. (2013). A multi-layered approach to surfacing and analyzing organizational narratives: Increasing representational authenticity. https://core.ac.uk/download/18407762.pdf (accessed on 24th September 2025).
17. Ewington, N., Reid, S., Spencer-Oatey, H., Stadler, S., et al. (2009). The Global People tool book: Managing the life cycle of intercultural partnerships. https://core.ac.uk/download/46446.pdf (accessed on 24th September 2025).
18. Federici, F., & O'Brien, S. (2019). Crisis translation: Considering language needs in multilingual disaster settings. https://core.ac.uk/download/294759802.pdf (accessed on 24th September 2025).
19. Fitó Bertran, M. À., Hernández Lara, A. B., & Serradell-López, E. (2018). Do business games foster skills? A cross-cultural study from learners' views. https://core.ac.uk/download/157812216.pdf (accessed on 24th September 2025).
20. Freeberg, T. M., Dunbar, R. I. M., & Ord, T. J. (2012). Social complexity as a proximate and ultimate factor in communicative complexity. Philosophical Transactions of the Royal Society B: Biological Sciences, 367, 1785–1801. https://doi.org/10.1098/rstb.2011.0213 (accessed on 24th September 2025).
21. Hadiati, C. (2012). The characteristics of Banyumasan conversational implicatures. https://core.ac.uk/download/84726423.pdf (accessed on 24th September 2025).

22. Halub, H., Sauber, A., & Stück, J. (2017). The Turk and the Yankee: A cross-cultural comparison between Turkish and American managers. https://core.ac.uk/download/84885650.pdf (accessed on 24th September 2025).
23. Heaton, L. (1998). Preserving communication context: Virtual workspace and interpersonal space in Japanese CSCW. https://core.ac.uk/download/pdf/12237589.pdf (accessed on 24th September 2025).
24. Keys, T. R. (2012). Behaviors that eliminate health disparities for racial and ethnic minorities: A narrative systematic review. https://core.ac.uk/download/56703666.pdf (accessed on 24th September 2025).
25. Lincke, A., Ulijn, J. M., & Wynstra, J. Y. F. (2025). The effect of Dutch and German cultures on negotiation strategy: Comparing operations and innovation management in the supply chain. https://core.ac.uk/download/pdf/6501211.pdf (accessed on 24th September 2025).
26. Makhmudova, A. (2025). Cross-cultural leadership and remote team management in international business. Successes and Achievements in Science. https://www.semanticscholar.org/paper/bf04bcb2a510fe13b71837148394e19deed61e6e (accessed on 24th September 2025).
27. Marcotte, D., Rustambekov, E., & Trendowski, J. (2019). Importance of cultural intelligence: Cross-cultural examination and analysis. https://core.ac.uk/download/231818803.pdf (accessed on 24th September 2025).
28. Menkel-Meadow, C. (2003). Correspondences and contradictions in international and domestic conflict resolution: Lessons from general theory and varied contexts. https://core.ac.uk/download/70373725.pdf (accessed on 24th September 2025).
29. Mustafa, G. (2015). The emergence of leader-society value congruence: A cross-cultural perspective. https://core.ac.uk/download/144552158.pdf (accessed on 24th September 2025).
30. Rai, A., De Jong, B. A., Wegner, D. M., Feeny, D., Carmel, E., Schoorman, F. D., Trompenaars, F., et al. (2011). Contextual factors, knowledge processes and performance in global sourcing of IT services: An investigation in China. https://core.ac.uk/download/19784800.pdf (accessed on 24th September 2025).
31. Reid, S., Spencer-Oatey, H., & Stadler, S. (2009). The Global People landscaping study: Intercultural effectiveness in global education partnerships. https://core.ac.uk/download/46447.pdf (accessed on 24th September 2025).

32. Schadewitz, N. (2009). Innovative collaborative design in international interaction design summer schools. https://core.ac.uk/download/256120.pdf (accessed on 24th September 2025).
33. Shachaf, P. (2008). Cultural diversity and information and communication technology impacts on global virtual teams: An exploratory study. https://core.ac.uk/download/11887687.pdf (accessed on 24th September 2025).
34. Strand, S. (2017). International managers in Norway: Cross-cultural challenges in the Norwegian context. https://core.ac.uk/download/249952884.pdf (accessed on 24th September 2025).
35. Thanaraj, A. (2016). Internationalizing education: Evaluating the growth of intercultural communication and competency in students through an international negotiation project using an online law office. https://core.ac.uk/download/43757997.pdf (accessed on 24th September 2025).
36. Van de Voorde, K., & Wright, P. M. (2007). Multi-level issues in international HRM: Mean differences, explained variance, and moderated relationships. https://core.ac.uk/download/5121553.pdf (accessed on 24th September 2025).
37. Van Dyne, L., Ang, S., Ng, K. Y., Rockstuhl, T., Tan, M., & Koh, C. (2012). Sub-dimensions of the four-factor model of cultural intelligence: Expanding the conceptualization and measurement of cultural intelligence. Social and Personality Psychology Compass, 6, 295–313. https://doi.org/10.1111/j.1751-9004.2012.00429.x (accessed on 24th September 2025).
38. Widyaningrum, A. (2012). Preserving and maintaining native tongue through cultural exposure. https://core.ac.uk/download/84727450.pdf (accessed on 24th September 2025).
39. Zografi, M. (2025). Relevance of intercultural communication for human resources management. https://core.ac.uk/download/pdf/6312382.pdf (accessed on 24th September 2025).

Chapter 5

Leadership Across Cultures in International Management

Contents

INTRODUCTION

With the increasingly globalized nature of the world, the practice of international management demands a nuanced understanding of leadership across cultures. Leadership theories that gain popularity within one environment are not necessarily transferable to another due to varying expectations and values between cultures. Transformational leadership, for instance, which is postulated to inspire and motivate others through a shared vision, may find strong foothold in certain collectivist cultures founded on cooperation and community. On the other hand, transactional leadership that emphasizes formalized rewards and tasks tends to be more suited to individualistic cultures that strongly emphasize personal achievement and autonomy. This divergence underscores the necessity of considering culture when practicing global leadership theories because it directly impacts organizational performance and worker satisfaction in diverse workplaces. A leadership expectations review reveals that cultural values significantly impact perceptions and evaluation of leaders worldwide. This is evident in studies conducted on Australian and Malaysian middle managers; evaluations of the female managers revealed a radical difference typical of the prevailing beliefs and attitudes in each country, particularly regarding gender leadership roles (Jogulu et al., 2008). In Malaysia, societal expectations can get in the way of women's capacity to lead as proficiently as their Australian counterparts, observing that success in leadership highly rests on adhering to cultural expectations. Such measures demonstrate the importance of recognizing how local contexts influence leadership expectations so a culturally sensitive approach to international management practice is needed to make leaders effective across different contexts. To be able to comprehend the differences in leadership across the globe, it is significant to study different cultural orientations and how they influence the behaviors of leaders. Research shows that paternalistic leadership, for instance, is more effective in collectivist societies like Turkey where loyalty and trust in hierarchical relations are values compared to individualistic settings like the Netherlands (Born et al., 2012). Contrarily, strong empowering leadership styles with their encouragement of autonomy would be more likely to flourish in cultures that are embracing individualism. This difference captures the richness of complexity in global leadership practices and how leaders must adapt their own styles to fit the cultural fabric of their groups. As corporations expand internationally, embracing this cultural sensitivity will be critical towards achieving effective management and enhancing overall organizational performance across various global settings.

Definition of Leadership in a Global Context

Global leadership demands that the leader is familiar with various theories underlying practices across cultures. Global leadership theories such as transformational and transactional leadership provide models by which leaders can cope with the complexity of global management. Transformational leadership that includes inspiring and motivating the followers for superior levels of performance is usually accepted where the culture values innovation and joint success. Conversely, transactional leadership, with its emphasis on fixed forms and rewards for performance, is attractive in cultures that have well-defined hierarchies and an emphasis on compliance. In most cases, an effective global leader has to adapt these theories in a way that they can sit in harmony with local values and organizational objectives, always remaining effective and yet sensitive to local norms. Local cultural variations exert significant influence on leadership expectations, defining how leaders are viewed and their capacity to realize their vision. In individualistic cultures, such as in the United States, leaders are generally expected to be assertive and risk-taking in orientation, compared to collectivistic cultures, such as in Japan, where group harmony and consensus take precedence. Such variant expectations necessitate that leaders cultivate cultural intelligence so that they can make their leadership style fit the intricate web of cultural imperatives confronting them (Figure 5.1).

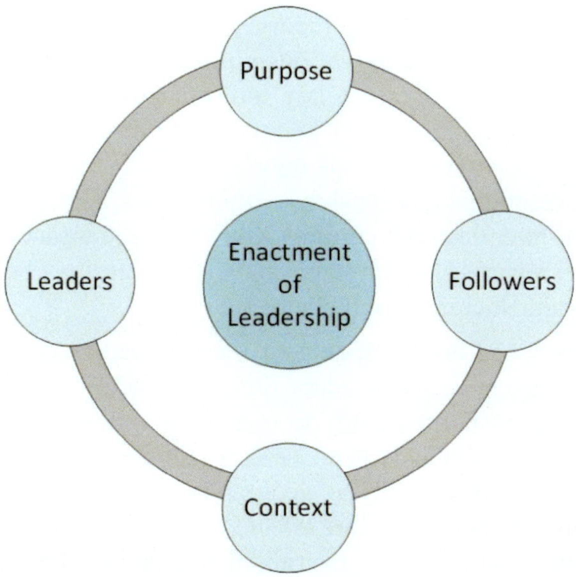

Figure 5.1. Adaptability of leadership.

Source: https://warwick.ac.uk/fac/cross_fac/globalpeople2/companies/gpatwork/globalleadership/leadership_multiplex.jpg.

This kind of flexibility is crucial as it not only promises respect and trust among various teams but also enhances overall productivity and performance in international operations. Being aware of these cultural differences helps in formulating leadership plans that are reconcilable with indigenous practices and beliefs, thereby promising ease of interaction in foreign environments. The varied dynamics of transformational and transactional leadership also have interesting implications in an international context. While transformational leadership seeks to inspire change and innovation, it will be perhaps less so in cultures where stability and order are given priority. Transactional styles, on the other hand, may falter in cultures that prioritize or require more visionary and innovative forms of leadership. The key to global leaders is knowing when to apply each style, blending them as the situation calls for. Also, as McKenzie et al. (2008) surmises, senior managers in international contexts do face competing demands that call for a balance leadership philosophy. Leaders must consider not only individual and organizational outcomes but corporate and social responsibilities in the global economy, hence a multifaceted leadership model that is responsive and culturally sensitive.

Importance of Understanding Cultural Differences in Leadership

In international business, varying theories of leadership emerge as central models that guide leaders across various cultural environments. The theories are critical to understand because they indicate how cultural underpinnings affect managerial assumptions and behavior. For instance, transformational leadership is often associated with the development of a vision that is shared by all and initiating emotional relationships within groups, something which can be highly functional in collectivist cultures. Conversely, transactional leadership, which focuses on reward-based systems and clear rules, may be more effective in cultures that value hierarchy and obedience.

Building a nuanced understanding of these varied leadership approaches makes global managers ready to adapt their approaches based on situational requirements and local norms, ready to manage the multifaceted dynamics of teams that comprise individuals from several cultures (Marcotte et al., 2019). Leadership needs vary immensely by geographic locale, and the characteristics that are needed in leaders to thrive are affected. Leaders, for instance, are bred in some Asian cultures to be humble, restrained, and involved in decision-making because these are highly valued locally as respect for hierarchy and harmony. In contrast, Western cultures might demand assertive and independent decision-making with strong value placed on leaders who inspire through independent charisma and self-directed authority. Understanding such expectations allows leaders to modify their approach and actions to conform to prevailing cultural standards, creating trust and respect among their subordinates. Leadership adaptability is especially crucial in multinational enterprises, where local traditions and practices can be the determinant of success and failure (N/A, 2016). Differences in transactional and transformational leadership are not only theoretical, but have direct practical uses within cross-cultural environments. Transformational leadership with an emphasis on motivation and alignment of purpose for individual and organizational goals can be particularly beneficial in cultures that emphasize collective achievement and employee autonomy. Transactional leadership can benefit organizations in situations where there are heavy bureaucratic systems and strict adherence to pre-existing procedures is necessary. Leaders who are aware of these strategies are capable of handling cultural complexities with ease, enabling smooth operations and successful communications within multicultural teams. Developing sensitive awareness of cultural diversity in leadership thus becomes more than intellectual exercise but a condition for developing responsive and agile management styles in any international setting (Marcotte et al., 2019).

5.1. GLOBAL LEADERSHIP THEORIES

The uncovering of global leadership theories generally reveals differential expectations and actions across cultures. For instance, in collectivistic cultures where collective harmony is paramount, leaders may be expected to be more participative in style with a focus on consensus and building relationship.

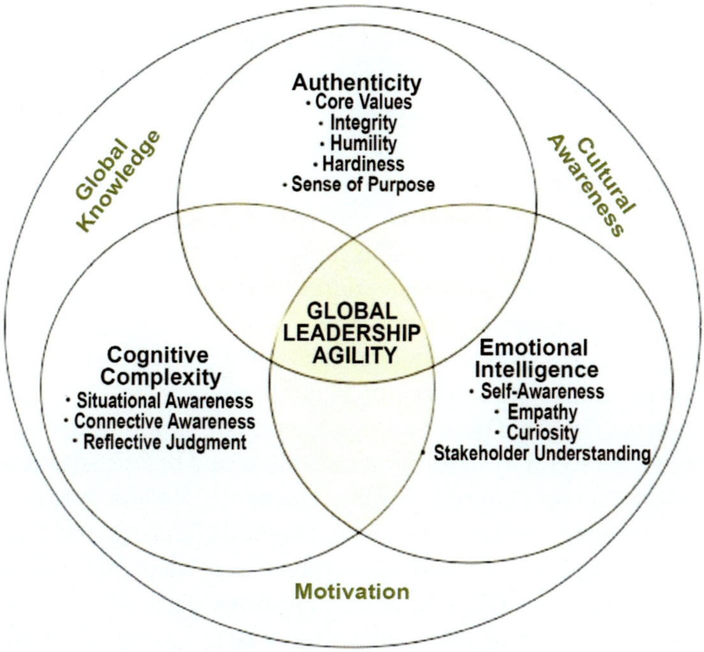

Figure 5.2. Global leadership agility model.

Source: https://lauramccracken.wordpress.com/wp-content/uploads/2009/09/model.jpg?w=768&h=695.

Conversely, in individualistic societies, a concern for autonomy and personal achievement may lead to a demand for a more directive style of leadership.

This cultural difference influences the practice and understanding of leadership everywhere. What the studies on middle managers in Australia and Malaysia indicate is this: Malaysian women leaders failed not because the women themselves were flawed but because cultural gender beliefs about gender roles (Jogulu et al., 2008). Australian women leaders, by way of contrast, performed better, showing the necessity to frame theories of leadership in their own culture (Jogulu et al., 2008). Thus, cultural norms are fundamental to learning in order to exercise effective international management leadership. Within the context of global leadership models, transformational and transactional forms of leadership rank as fundamental concepts that ought to be examined. Transformational leaders are said to inspire and energize their subordinates to exceed expectations, focusing on change and vision. Such a style is likely to suit cultures that encourage creativity and risk-taking. On the other hand, transactional leadership is more about setting clear structures, rewards, and sanctions, appealing to stability- and predictability-oriented cultures (Figure 5.2).

The preference of one style over the other often is rooted in cultural dimensions, such as uncertainty avoidance and power distance. For instance, high power distance cultures can opt for transactional leaders who demand hierarchical structures, while those with less power distance can use transformational leaders who promote team effort and empowerment and demonstrate that the effectiveness of leadership styles can differ significantly between cultures (Li et al., 2017). The impact of leadership behaviors on the attitudes and health of followers also addresses the cross-cultural applicability of global leadership theories. For instance, in contexts such as China, where avoiding conflict is part of interpersonal relationships, research has established that leaders who employ this behavior benefit subordinates' ratings of justice and trust (Li et al., 2017). These findings are an attestation to the necessity for adaptive leadership styles to allow for local values and beliefs so that leaders not only succeed but remain culturally aware. Therefore, leaders in foreign settings must remain extremely sensitive to such cultural differences and their nuances so that there can be fostered a leadership model that is adaptable, responsive, and sensitive to the dynamics of diverse cultural settings. This awareness eventually enriches global leadership practice, providing a space where all employees can develop.

5.1.1. Overview of Major Global Leadership Theories

When looking at the theory of leadership around the world, it is evident that factors in the environment in different parts of the world contribute significantly to shaping expectations and practice of leaders. Cultural influences deeply impact the way people view leaders, and varying expectations arise under varying circumstances. For instance, leaders in collectivistic cultures such as China are likely to be expected to remain harmonious and non-confrontational, as indicated by studies which have revealed that avoidance behavior on the part of leaders can positively influence followers' sense of justice as well as emotional well-being (Li et al., 2017). Leadership in more individualistic cultures such as the United States is, however, frequently synonymous with assertiveness and decisiveness. Understanding of these dimensions of culture is necessary to international managers since they must adapt their leadership styles to mesh with the values and expectations that exist in various areas to achieve effective cooperation and engagement (Figure 5.3).

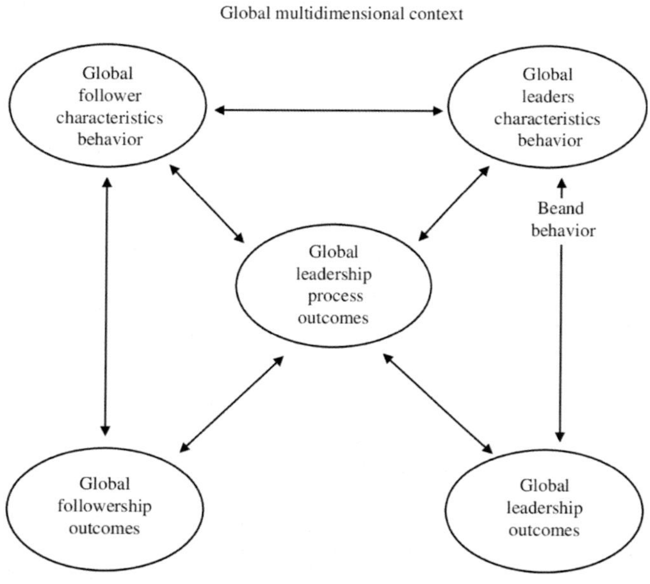

Figure 5.3. Global leadership model.

Source: https://www.researchgate.net/profile/Yulia-Tolstikov-Mast/publication/306035796/figure/fig2/AS:663204162203649@1535131602532/Global-Leadership-Model.png.

The differences between transformational and transactional leadership are yet another sophistication level in international leadership theories. Transformational leadership, with its act of inspiring and motivating others, will most probably be more influential in societies where they value long-term relationships and personal development. Transactional leadership, founded on the reward for performance exchange, can perform more effectively in a setting where well-structured hierarchies exist and where short-term results take preeminence. Research highlights that cultural context can be a determining factor in mediating the way in which these leadership styles are evaluated and applied within different contexts. Examples include leaders who are female in Malaysia being examined differently from their Australian counterparts, in accordance with more general assumptions in the culture about gender roles and effective leadership (Jogulu et al., 2008). This highlights the importance of global managers cultivating an informed appreciation of these theories within diverse cultural contexts. Besides, leadership performance complexities are also advanced further by gender-culture interactions in leadership measurement. Leadership is interpreted differently according to culture and societal desires, yet ultimately resulting in leadership practice across nations. Female leadership, for instance, may be confronted with resistance in gender-normative cultures since these can suppress the recognition of their effectiveness. This is illustrated in studies that reveal Malaysian women managers found it difficult to gain credibility compared to their Australian counterparts, with cultural assumptions playing a substantial role in making such judgments (Jogulu et al., 2008). These findings are crucial to the development of inclusive leadership practices mindful of cultural values and yet seeking equity within international organizations. Emphasizing an awareness of these diverse perspectives fosters an environment in which effective leadership is more likely to thrive across cultures within global management.

5.1.2. Comparison of Western and Eastern Leadership Models

In global management today, leadership theories have evolved to accommodate the complexities of local cultural expectations. Scholars contend that leadership is not merely an international phenomenon but is greatly conditioned by situational factors like culture and values. For instance, Western leadership frameworks often focus on personalism, creativity, and results-oriented approaches, which view transformational leadership as a means to energize followers and bring about change. Conversely, however, Eastern leadership approaches, particularly in Confucian-conditioned cultures, prioritize the building of relationships, harmony, and collectivism, to a transactional approach that prioritizes stability and respect for order hierarchy. This difference reflects more fundamental cultural structures, whereby success is as much a function of the ability to maintain relational processes as of ultimate outcome, where showing respect to authority is paramount (Reid et al., 2009). These findings are an indicator of the need for leaders to acquire intercultural competence as a strict prerequisite in order to thrive in a multicultural global world. Furthermore, Western and Eastern societies have expectations concerning leadership roles that vary significantly, influencing international cooperation strategies of managers. In Western societies, leaders will be visionary pro-actives who can drive organizations forward through proposing aggressive strategies and single-performance criteria. This is quite contrary to what is anticipated in the East, where leaders should construct environments of stability and common good, oftentimes employing collective decision-making structures. The value placed on consensus in Eastern leadership reflects the cultural premium on sharedness and harmony, signifying societal values. This provides a leadership dynamic where the authority of the leader is usually less confrontational but solidly established on mutual respect and interdependence (Halub et al., 2017). Hence, understanding these local norms can make cross-cultural management more effective and improve the leader-follower dynamic in global contexts. When a global dichotomy between transformational and transactional leadership is considered, it is evident that their success hinges upon context of culture. Transformational leadership, where leaders inspire and encourage followers to pursue a shared vision, gains more traction in Western contexts where individual achievement and innovation are promoted. In comparison, transactional leadership that emphasizes rule-based operations and exchange-based relationships fares better in stability- and hierarchy-embracing Eastern societies. Although the transactional leaders may not possess the same charisma or inspiration that transfigures their transformational counterparts, they are worth their salt for their ability to provide order and stability in organizational contexts within cultures that value group cohesion and hierarchy. Therefore, a wise manager will be able to recognize when to apply each style, tailoring their leadership style according to the cultural norms and values existing within the varied organizational environments, thereby creating the foundation for fruitful international collaboration (Reid et al., 2009).

5.1.3. The Role of Cultural Intelligence in Effective Leadership

In the present-day reality of global management, one has to comprehend the theories of global leadership in a more nuanced sense with the contemporary era of high-speed globalization and technological advancement. Leadership theories such as transformational leadership and transactional leadership happen in different forms in different cultures, making cultural intelligence an essential skill for a leader. For instance, transformational leadership, which is directed towards inspiration and revolution, would be a suitable fit in cultures with a powerful collectivist orientation and long-term relationship perspective, such as in the majority of Asian cultures. Transactional leadership, with its structured tasks and rewards, would suit cultures with a short-term goal orientation and a focus on individual success, such as in North America. It is therefore imperative for leaders to be able to vary their style of leadership according to the cultural setting of their teams, to optimize their performance across varied situations and enhance motivation and dedication among staff globally, as identified through studies of leadership dynamics in various cultural environments (Lim, 2022). Leadership expectations vary dramatically across regions and are strongly influenced by core cultural norms and values. To illustrate, in high-context cultures like Japan or France, leaders are more likely to be asked to embody a more paternalistic leadership, blending authority with human touch, as this encourages followers to be trusting and committed. On the other hand, low-context cultures like the United States or Germany are more likely to embrace open communications, directness, and an egalitarian approach to leadership, where results and efficiency often become the focus. Thus, cultural smart leaders can navigate such expectations with greater ease, bending their leadership to create better relationships with their staffs. Knowledge of these differences within regions not only enhances people-to-people relations in international settings but also guarantees organizational success by aligning leadership initiatives with the employees' cultural setting, thereby increasing overall efficiency (Margaret et al., 2018). Furthermore, the contrast between transformational and transactional leadership applies particularly when contrasting how effective they are in multi-cultural environments. Transformational leadership fosters environments that are innovative, creative, and highly motivating of employees, which are relevant to organizations operating in the fast-paced global market. Transactional leadership, however, focuses on systematic processes and reward systems as a means to establish stability and order within the environments that may require strict rules. However, the effectiveness of either style is contingent on leaders' cultural intelligence. Those who have the ability to recognize when to apply a transformational as opposed to a transactional style are better placed to deal with the diverse needs of their staff. This strategic flexibility is imperative in today's globally connected world, where cultural awareness not only enhances personal and group performance but can also allow an organization to be flexible when reacting to worldwide issues and opportunities (Lim, 2022).

5.2. LEADERSHIP EXPECTATIONS IN DIFFERENT REGIONS

In an era of increasing globalization, the leadership environment is strongly influenced by cultural variables and varying expectations based on geographic areas. Proper appreciation of the differences becomes essential in global management, where leaders have the responsibility to react to diverse beliefs and practices that shape their organizations. For instance, while Western countries may focus on transformational leadership—whereby inspiring and motivating employees towards collective goals and innovativeness—Eastern countries may be inclined towards a transactional style based on clearly defined roles, duties, and hierarchical structures. These diverging paradigms point to the importance of adapting leadership styles according to regional expectations, which can significantly impact organizational performance and employee satisfaction in an international context. Different areas of the world have different leadership expectations that are based on their socio-economic environment, history, and culture. For example, in collectivist cultures, such as the majority of the nations in Asia, the expectation is that leaders should be modest and emphasize group harmony, thus fostering the type of atmosphere that promotes collaboration (Figure 5.4).

Figure 5.4. Leadership essentials for managers.

Source: https://blogger.googleusercontent.com/img/b/R29vZ2xl/AVvXsEhcOV-8l7VReinySucq38Vw7cuhJb_PRYJFPtepbsDkKviOAGJAI7wCFWQVF3DiRp-g5ttua7ub-ySbTXn0Nw0pb_mUCIe-O7IyB00pDNTxjNWf44dkILoswcsbdKdP-GNnDGdoaOix1lXKbD/w640-h480/Leadership+essentials.jpeg.

Alternatively, in individualist societies, like in America, leaders have to be assertive, innovative, and achievement-oriented. Such conflicting expectations compel international leaders to blend different styles of leadership in a way to attract local workers while preserving the organization's big picture and intentions. Hence, cultural intelligence-accepting managers and independently made efforts to comprehend cultural differences can induce a series of open-minded environments that foster higher levels of participation and commitment among the workforce. Making a comparison between the transformational and transactional leadership paradox, it is evident that success of each of these approaches can be widely variable depending on the culture context. For instance, transformational leadership will flourish in situations of open communication and broad visions, which prevail in Western organizations. Conversely, where order and stability are most important, transactional leadership can optimize productivity and efficiency well-suited to the expectations of followers well-accustomed to authority. This contrast underlines the fact that single-style leadership is not effective; leaders must not only shift their strategies as per cultural customs but also blend elements of both transformational and transactional leadership styles in order to be successful in multicultural global settings. Lastly, achieving such nuances allows leaders to create a highly sensitive approach and build better and adaptive teams across global divides.

5.2.1. Leadership Styles Prevalent in North America

The leadership environment in North America draws on a rich combination of cultural values and prevailing leadership theories in the world. In particular, the continent is biased towards transformational leadership, which is characterized by an orientation towards vision, inspiration, and motivation. This leadership approach not only seeks to increase the performance of individuals but also seeks to develop a sound organizational culture. North American transformational leaders' success is in a cultural inclination towards innovation and autonomy, which motivates employees to come forward with ideas and contribute actively to organizational transformation.

The leaders create an environment where collaboration and communication are appreciated, fitting the pervasive culture of empowerment and inclusion in North American workplaces. These characteristics help leaders respond to the demands emerging from the fast-changing business environment at the international level, and they assist in building resilience and dynamism in their teams. Transactional leadership, however, overpowers structured environments where clear instructions and outcomes are sought. Leadership is premised on a reward-and-punishment system where the workers are rewarded for meeting specific objectives while being held accountable for failure. North American organizations are inclined to utilize this approach in situations calling for operational efficiency and compliance, where specific standards serve to maintain standards and improve performance (Figure 5.5).

While transactional leadership is somewhat less flexible than its transformational counterpart, it does find application in those situations calling for accountability and maintenance-level management. As a combination of these two styles is required for leaders to navigate the complexities of mixed work cultures, the fact of the matter is that both the transformational and the transactional style will be employed effectively depending on situational pressures and organizational objectives. Moreover, leadership theories across the world highlight the importance of sensitivity towards regional styles of leadership across various regions, e.g., North America.

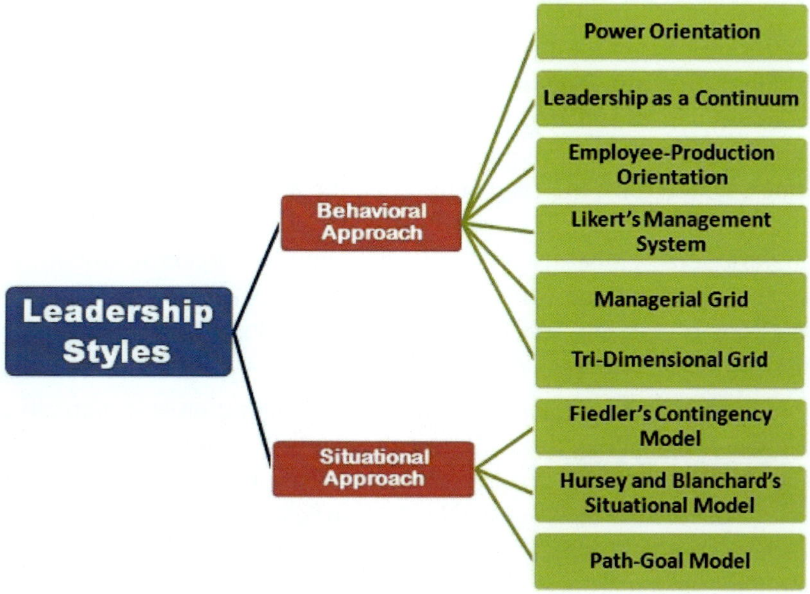

Figure 5.5. Understanding the balance of leadership styles.

Source: https://indiafreenotes.com/wp-content/uploads/2020/03/Leadership-Styles.jpg.

Leadership behavior expectations in varying environments are framed by cultural dimensions including power distance, individualism-collectivism, and uncertainty avoidance. For instance, while North American leaders may enjoy a low power distance and emphasis on individual contribution, most Asian leaders will be more collectivist and hierarchical. This reflects how global managers should be adaptable in their leadership style based on cultural values and norms. The dynamic nature of work environments demands constant sensitivity to such varied expectations so that leaders can implement the most appropriate steps while developing effective team dynamics geographically. Such flexibility is all the more important in today's more globalized and interconnected business environment, further underlining the importance of cultural competence in the practice of leadership.

5.2.2. Leadership Expectations in Asia

The Asian leadership expectation matrix is informed by a diverse array of economic, social, and cultural drivers that are far different from Western models. Expectations about leadership practice are typically informed by collectivist ideologies prevalent across the majority of Asian cultures, where harmony, group consensus, and respect for the hierarchy are the concerns. As a result, Asian leaders are typically expected to be more paternalistic and caring, placing the interests of their subordinates above all else while channeling group energies into the firm. This is a long way from Western models that seek to glorify individualism and assertiveness as leadership traits. Thus, moving across these cultural sensitivities requires a deep understanding of native traditions and values, which form the essence of effective leadership in the region within the rapidly connected world economy (Yogesh et al., 2020). Aside from these cultural variations, global leadership theory supposes a central role in shaping the manner leaders are perceived and must function worldwide. The contrasts between transformational and transactional leadership also indicate the varied anticipations that Asian leaders have.

Transformational leadership's emphasis on inspiration and motivation can easily fit into the collectivist nature of most Asian societies in which leaders are conceived as visionaries who inspire dedication and loyalty among their followers. Conversely, transactional leadership based on exchanges and tangible rewards has been faulted in Asian contexts as being superficial in establishing trust and long-term relations. Such conflicting expectations raise the imperative for leaders to be accommodating, using a combination style that mixes the strengths of the two models in consideration of the complex nature of diversified Asian markets (Ullah et al., 2019). As the world business environment gets increasingly connected, it is essential for international managers to understand and implement proper leadership expectations in Asia.

The focus on building relationships, respect for each other, and a longer-term perspective of leadership tends to go beyond just transactional relationships. Furthermore, the blending of transformational and transactional dimensions paves the way for a more adaptive leadership approach well equipped to navigate the numerous challenges occasioned by the regions constantly shifting economic landscape. With the development of cultural intelligence and empathy, leaders may build a collaborative culture that not only meets local needs but also fosters long-term success within Asias intricate markets. This adaptability is one of many trends in global management where being unable to learn and conform to regional leadership requirements can lead to stagnation or market entry failure (Yogesh et al., 2020).

5.2.3. Differences in Leadership Approaches in Europe

European leadership styles present a rich fabric of cultural complexities and organizational requirements which defy a one-size-fits-all solution. Countries across the continent possess variations determined by their histories, social systems, as well as regional conventions. Northern European countries, for instance, generally stress egalitarian leadership and participative leadership styles, whereas Southern European countries tend to exhibit a propensity towards hierarchical organization with a bias towards equating leadership with command structures. The interaction of these cultural dimensions leads us to accept that effective leadership cannot be separated from specific societal values prevalent in each region. Therefore, an understanding of these differences is essential for global managers who want to navigate the complicated terrain of Europe and employ diverse leadership styles to their best potential, with maximum organizational performance and worker satisfaction. The backdrop of global leadership theories also renders the problem of good leadership in Europe more difficult to understand. Various theoretical frameworks, such as transformational and transactional leadership, resonate to greater or lesser extents across international borders. Transformational leadership, the capability of leaders to inspire and encourage employees towards a shared vision, could potentially have fertile ground in innovation and flexibility-oriented cultures, prevalent in the Nordic countries. Conversely, transactional leadership founded on standard operating procedures and reward structures is more aligned with the structured and traditional Southern European cultures that define business success. This distinction calls for a consideration of leadership expectations, hence affecting international management practices that must be tailored to resonate with the existing local paradigms. These evolving expectations impact deeply upon the leadership role of spearheading organizational change in the diverse European context. In addition to the identification of these theoretical paradigms, identification of the role of senior managers in shaping leadership practice within European institutions is necessary. The increasing focus on internationalization and sustainable development is in line with a need for leaders to reconcile institutional values with market forces, as highlighted by authors in leadership literature (McKenzie et al., 2008). Here, the ability of leaders to be both transformational and transactional allows them to navigate between competing demands smoothly, and they are able to create an innovative climate as well as stability. Leadership sophistication in multicultural European cultures stresses the need for adaptable management styles. Top managers, therefore, need to be well-versed in developing flexibility in their leadership, demonstrating profound commitment to corporate and social responsibilities while leading change (Fisk et al., 2013).

5.3. TRANSFORMATIONAL LEADERSHIP

The landscape of leadership theories is dynamic, mirroring the nature of global business scenarios and the multi-cultural context in which organizations need to operate. Among them, transformational leadership has emerged as a vital method, particularly in international management, as it emphasizes mobilizing and enlisting followers beyond their self-interests for the betterment of the organization. This type of leadership generates a culture of trust and commitment that performs quite effectively in multicultural contexts. As organizations expand globally, leaders must recognize differences in expectations and perceptions of transformational leadership across regions. For instance, while Western societies will readily embrace and value charismatic leaders who create innovation and change, other cultures may prioritize stability and authority, generating other visions of what contributes to effective leadership (Jogulu et al., 2008). When comparing transformational and transactional leadership, it is critical to consider how these styles manifest in varying cultural settings. Transformational leadership is characterized by its ability to motivate followers to stretch towards shared visions, while transactional leadership depends on contingent rewards and performance management. This is reflected most in Malaysia and Australia, where gender perceptions and cultural values influence judgments of managerial effectiveness. Studies show that cultural nuances give rise to divergent expectations, as indicated through the evaluation of female managers across cultures (Figure 5.6).

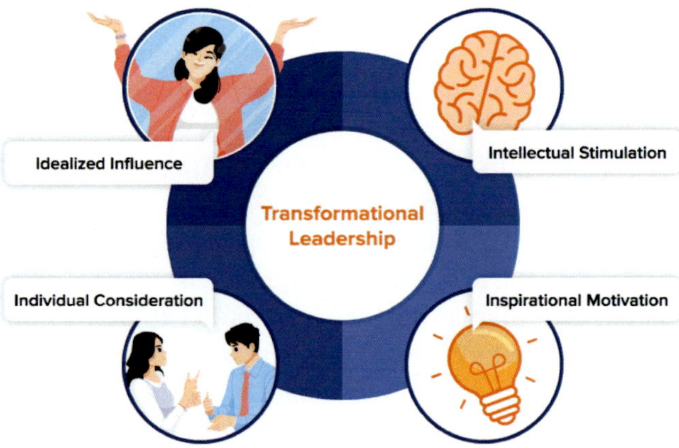

Figure 5.6. Transformational leadership to bring a positive change.

Source: https://factohr-1a56a.kxcdn.com/wp-content/themes/factohr-theme/images/glossary/transformational-leadership/Transformational-Leadership.png.

For instance, in Malaysia, cultural beliefs may discourage the recognition of transformational leadership traits of women managers than decidedly contrasting perceptions in Australia where the same traits may be readily adopted (Li et al., 2017). It is, thus, important to comprehend such cultural factors for multinational corporations intending to implement successful models of leadership. Moreover, the understanding of leadership expectations is deeply integrated with the cultural identity of a nation and, in turn, affects the manner in which leaders control their groups. The utility of cultural dimensions like individualism and collectivism also affects the implementation of transformational leadership in various parts of the world. While in collectivist societies leaders would be asked to assume more nurturing and supportive roles which are empathetic to transformational values to better followers' emotional well-being and perceived workplace justice. For example, it has been demonstrated in China that Chinese leaders who exhibit conflict avoidance—typically associated with transformational leadership—are able to establish trust as well as increase followers' emotional well-being (Li et al., 2017). This indicates the intricate relationship between cultural values and leadership styles, highlighting the need for leaders to cultivate adaptive approaches that are culturally oriented and to develop collective objectives in overseas settings.

5.3.1. Definition and Characteristics of Transformational Leadership

In global leadership theory discourse, transformational leadership is a paradigm that encapsulates the energizing interpersonal relations between leaders and followers. Committed to energizing and stimulating individuals above their own self-interests for the common good, such leadership motivates radical organizational change and development. Transformational leaders are characterized by their ability to establish a driving vision, develop an inclination towards innovation, and develop a sense of teamwork. In contrast to transactional leadership, which is primarily concerned with exchange and reward for performance, transformational leadership seeks to elevate the commitment and hopes of followers, engendering a perception of common purpose and group achievement. Transformational leadership is particularly effective in multicultural settings, where leaders must come to terms with variations in values and expectations and combine their approach to leadership with the cultural sensitivity that exists within different regions of the world. An examination of leadership assumptions illustrates the profound effect of cultural environment on leadership behavior and style. In regions such as Western Europe and North America, transformational leadership is commonly associated with democratic values, whereby leaders are expected to engage their employees, encourage diversity, and promote individual development. Conversely, however, in collectivistic cultures such as those in Asia, leadership will most likely be of a more hierarchical style with a focus on harmony and avoiding conflict (Figure 5.7).

Figure 5.7. Characteristics of transformational leadership.

Source: https://www.simplypsychology.org/wp-content/uploads/Transformational-Leadership.jpeg.

Researchers have suggested that transformational leadership can cater to these diverse expectations, and in different cultures, work. For instance, in Chinese firms, leaders who employ avoidance strategies can generate feelings of justice and trust within their followers, demonstrating that transformational practice and culturally-based leadership behavior co-exist, as discussed in Li et al. (2017). The difference between transformational and transactional leadership is critical within the field of international management. While transactional leadership is founded upon a reward-based system of transactions, it is unenthusiastic and fails to create long-term organizational loyalty. Transformational leadership, by contrast, not only encourages the development of the individual but also alters organizational culture through the encouragement of innovation and proactive challenge response. Organizational culture literature identifies this dynamic factor, with leaders needing the ability to transform and modify their behaviors in accordance with the evolving cultural environment within their organizations (Indu, 2025). Thus, studying definitions and features of transformational leadership becomes essential for leaders operating in multicultural global settings, as they strive to master the art of leading across cultures and matching practice to varied expectations.

5.3.2. Impact of Transformational Leadership on Organizational Culture

Leadership styles reflect significant differences in different cultures, primarily influenced by domestic values and expectations. With regard to transformational leadership, this style—characterized by inspiring and motivating workers—is typically considered a better method of creating adaptive organizational culture. This is particularly relevant in multicultural foreign settings where leaders are required to bridge cultural gaps. For instance, while transformational leadership might thrive in more collectivist cultures through team cohesion and collective vision, transactional leadership focusing on structure and reward might suit individualistic cultures that prioritize personal achievement. The ability to meet these conflicting expectations requires leaders to exercise a flexible style of leadership, with significant implications for organizational culture and performance across international companies. A close look at particular cultural environments establishes the manner in which transformational leadership is able to revolutionize organizational culture by embedding it in indigenous values. In Malaysia, for instance, deeply rooted cultural perceptions could influence the perception of women as leaders, who would be perceived as less effective even when able (Jogulu et al., 2008). This serves to underscore the significance of sensitivity and flexibility in leadership approaches. Transformational leaders can create inclusive organizational culture by recognizing and respecting local traditions while, at the same time, challenging assumptions traditional. In contrast, in Australia, where there is a stronger tradition of gender equality in organizational systems, transformational leadership can empower innovation as well as collaboration with few cultural constraints. An understanding of these cultural sensitivities enables global leaders to evolve practices that build strong organizational cultures in multi-cultural settings, not only guaranteeing the success of operations but also worker welfare. Further, the interaction between transformational leadership and organizational culture is also illustrated by how conflict within a leader's team is handled. In such societies as China, leaders utilizing avoidance mechanisms can create a climate of trust and emotional well-being among their subordinates, hence enhancing the transformational leadership style (Li et al., 2017). This illustrates how strong leadership transcends mere transactional relationships, initiating transformative changes within organizations. Leaders whose style is adapted to the cultural context not only amplify the level of acceptance for transformational practices but also foster openness and respect for each other. Therefore, the impact of transformational leadership on organizational culture relies ultimately on a sound appreciation for, and sensitivity to, the specific cultural dynamics that prevail in different parts of the world.

5.3.3. Examples of Transformational Leaders in a Global Context

The worldwide leadership context is greatly influenced by variations in local expectations and norms, in turn influencing the perception of leaders and how they operate within their immediate environments. The difference usually results in a split between transformational and transactional leadership styles, which are fashioned for the needs of the local environment. For instance, whereas transformational leaders, who engage and motivate their groups to a shared vision, are respected in the majority of Western settings for their innovative approaches, transactional leaders, who prioritize clear structures and pay, may be more popular in top-down oriented cultures such as those found in Asia. Being aware of these geographic variations is essential to leaders as they navigate through different organizational models. Their ability to bend their leadership style to accommodate mutual understanding with cultural sensitivities best depicts the complexities of cross-border team management and thus underscores the place of cultural intelligence in global leadership. Transformational leadership is marked by its emphasis on inspiring followers beyond self-interest for the greater good, which can generate more enthusiasm across cultures. Leaders like Nelson Mandela and Mahatma Gandhi are always quoted as model transformational leaders whose ability to mobilize the masses toward gigantic social change speaks volumes about the power of this style. Conversely, there are some regions of the globe that like to apply the transactional style, whereby the focus is on the exchange between leader and follower, scripted in terms of expectations and rewards. This is usually observed in business where compliance with scripted procedures and formalized relationships are paramount. As businesses increasingly venture into multicultural spaces, their leaders must navigate the differences between expectations effectively by applying a combination of transformational inspirational strategies with transactional managerial approaches to thrive across the globe. Examining the leadership role within countries that possess disparate cultural systems reveals the finesse of successful international management leadership. As an example, in cultures with high power distance, like Chinese culture, evidence indicates that leaders who employ conflict avoidance as a tactic can improve their followers' sense of justice, trust, and emotional well-being, as observed in studies highlighting the favorable consequences of such an action in these environments (Li et al., 2017). On the contrary, in environments with low power distance where empowering leadership with its well-established effectiveness in fostering psychological empowerment and self-leadership was demonstrated to dominate by research conducted in Rwanda as well as the United States (Rahschulte et al., 2018). These examples highlight the potential for change that can be found with leaders who can adapt their style within specific cultural contexts and also recognize the performance-enhancing nature of having a culturally sensitive leadership in creating success within transnational organizations.

5.4. TRANSACTIONAL LEADERSHIP

In global leadership theory, transactional leadership has been hailed for its methodical management approach across different cultures. The leadership style is centered on a clear-cut system of reward and punishment, which can be particularly effective when there are clear rules and measurable outcomes. For instance, in some Asian cultures, such as China, transactional leaders can strive for behaviors such as conflict avoidance, which have been proven to enhance perceptions of justice and trust by followers.

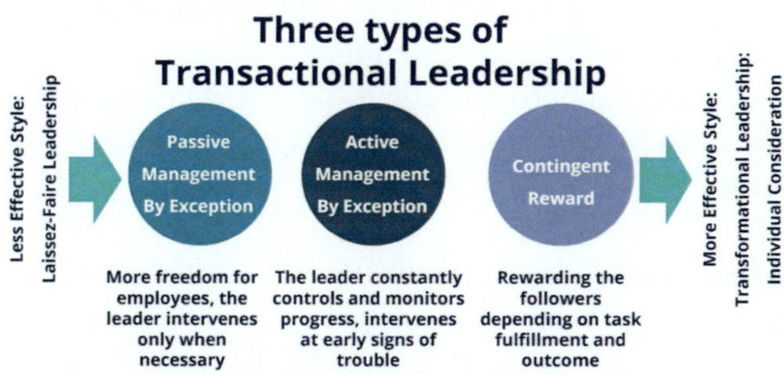

Figure 5.8. The components of transactional leadership.

Source: https://www.leadershipahoy.com/wp-content/uploads/2020/05/Three-types-of-transactional-leadership-2048x1033.jpg.

Consequently, transactional leadership theory is able to construct stability in organizations found in cultures where harmony as well as a group-oriented strategy is of importance, demonstrating the means by which leadership styles are constructed to support cultural norms and expectations within cross-cultural management contexts. In dramatic contrast to transformational leadership, which seeks to inspire and stimulate followers above their individual self-interests for the common good, transactional leadership is based on a more concrete exchange. Transformational leaders are likely to emphasize vision and emotional relating, promoting innovation and personal development in their followers. Transactional leaders might be more controlling in contexts where organizational dedication is sustained by formal behavioral expectations and traditional hierarchies (Figure 5.8).

Studies have shown that in sub-Saharan Africa, transactional leadership factors seemed to have little correlation with leadership effectiveness when moderated by organizational commitment, reflecting the cultural dynamics affecting leadership perception across various regions (Fadare et al., 2018). This situational context unveils that transactional leadership may be effective in obtaining instant compliance but its long-term effectiveness may depend on local cultural dynamics. As multinational companies confront the intricacies of cross-cultural management, recognizing the intermingling of transactional and transformational leadership approaches grows more critical. In collectivist cultures, where individualism is deemphasized, the transactional approach could become the preferred choice, protecting task-oriented workers and providing incentives for their work. One of the best examples lies with senior leaders in big Chinese firms, where conflict avoidance can be equally well-served by transactional incentives alongside its positive impact on worker wellbeing and trust (Li et al., 2017). Thus, it is essential that global managers acknowledge how the differences in culture influence the expectations and outcomes of leadership in international viewpoints. By meshing these disparate styles, leaders can cultivate a culture that respects cultural values yet drives organizational success.

5.4.1. Definition and Characteristics of Transactional Leadership

The complexity of leadership relations in global management often calls for an enhanced understanding of various leadership styles. Transactional leadership is a such type that is based on formal interactions and exchange between subordinates and leaders. It is characterized by separation of roles and function, where the performance of subordinates is rewarded or punished. The predictability inherent in transactional leadership can similarly be highly effective in uncertainty avoidance cultures, where rigid rules provide the sense of security. Thus, organizations operating in such environments may identify with transactional forms of leadership that are well-suited to such cultural expectations, fostering the compliance requirements and stability in goal attainment within the organization. Conversely, transactional leadership is oftentimes contrasted with transformational leadership, where change and inspiration are preferred to compliance. Based on the cultural context, leaders have to balance between these styles to meet some expectations. Whereas western worlds, for instance, would accept transformational leadership—a style that enhances motivation and performance through the power of inspiration—other regions in the world might accept the security of transactional habits. Such divergence highlights the relevance of cultural models in determining leadership preferences and outcomes. From studies, the effectiveness of leadership could be highly dependent on such cultural differences that indicate the relevance of variability in management styles with different settings (Jogulu et al., 2008). Underpinning within these is the recognition that leadership expectations may differ significantly according to cultural values and norms. In contexts such as Malaysia, for instance, female managers' leadership effectiveness has been established to be highly determined by gender role beliefs in the culture (Jogulu et al., 2006). This discovery raises serious questions about transactional leadership in multicultural environments. A leaders transactional style being at variance with the cultural context in which they are operating can hinder the effectiveness of their leadership approach. Therefore, it is necessary for international managers to have a deep understanding of transactional leadership, complemented with cultural awareness, in order to be able to move through the complexities of leadership across many cultures effectively such that their policies are both culturally correct and pragmatically viable in achieving organizational success.

5.4.2. Effectiveness of Transactional Leadership in Various Cultures

With globalization rushing over the globe, cultural appreciation of various styles of leadership in relation to different cultures is becoming increasingly important. Leadership theories must adapt to the differences in cultures, particularly when transactional leadership—characterized by formal duties, rewards, and obedience—comes into play. For example, cultures like East Asia are collectivist and hierarchical in nature, which could adequately provide for the transactional leadership approaches that emphasize order and authority. Conversely, individualistic cultures such as North America may favor transformational leadership types which emphasize innovation and personal development. This divide illustrates how leadership efficacy may differ significantly according to the culture in which it operates, pointing to the need for certain leadership approaches in international management. In evaluating the transactional leadership effectiveness across diverse cultures, it should be kept in mind that leadership expectations should also be considered. For instance, as when there is high power distance in some cultures like in Malaysia, then the transactional leaders are rated more effective due to respect for hierarchical organizations. In contrast, in cultures like Australia, where egalitarianism dominates, transactional methods might also be viewed as too formalized or boring. Peer opinions comment on such a dynamic; research indicates Malaysian women leaders are assessed based on cultural standards that confine their perceived effectiveness in transactional roles, compared to Australians, for whom more egalitarian views prevail (Jogulu et al., 2008). Such types of cultural matrices remind us of the variation of leadership expectations and effectiveness, reminding us of the significance of contextual intelligence in leadership practices. Furthermore, the distinction between transformational and transactional leadership necessarily affects conceptions of effectiveness in diverse contexts. Whereas transactional leadership is interested in performance and compliance in the context of reward-and-punishment systems, transformational leadership inspires in the context of vision and inspiration. Research indicates that transformational leadership is likely to be associated with greater effectiveness in cultures where emotional bonding and individual growth are placed high on the agenda. However, transactional leadership is effective in bringing discipline and order in more formalized environments. The nuanced interaction of these types of leadership with cultural environments indicates that while transactional leadership may work effectively in specific situations, it may not be able to appeal universally, as evidenced by divergent women's managerial competency frames in different cultures (Jogulu et al., 2006). This intricacy calls for continued probing of leadership effectiveness as it converges with cultural worldviews in global management.

5.4.3. Case Studies of Transactional Leadership in International Firms

In the intricate practice of global management, interaction of leadership styles is essential to understand organizational behavior. Particularly, transactional leadership, which emphasizes formal work and rewards, has looked different in varying cultural environments. For instance, in East Asia, where collectivism prevails, transactional leaders can thrive by encouraging group objectives and sustaining obedience of established procedure. In these types of cultural environments, explicit articulation of expectations and behavioral control through incentives will be capable of building harmony and effectiveness in teams. This is unlike Western cultures, in which leaders can prefer to select among a charismatic mode of leadership, which differs from the transactional form, but stresses the need for tailoring leadership styles to changing environments. Moreover, economic stability and business culture differences around the world shape leadership expectations, where a contextualized transactional leadership is required. Where there is political instability or economic instability, transactional leaders can provide the stability and predictability that organizations seek. By employing demarcativity in defining roles and extrinsic motivation, leadership can establish a culture of compliance and control, which in most cases is required for an uncertain environment. This is particularly evident for corporations in emerging nations, where transactional leadership can fill gaps in weaker organizational systems. The ensuing frameworks from transactional leadership can then be locally tuned to respect local business customs and social norms, aligning global functions with local specifics while still pursuing corporate-level goals. The difference between transformational and transactional leadership worldwide underscores other intricacies in leadership expectations. Transformational leadership, focusing on inspirational and motivational employees, is quite the opposite of the goal-centered style of transactional leadership. However, the two coexist in organizations as complementary frameworks, particularly in multinational organizations that operate in diverse cultural contexts. For instance, research shows that managers in environments that emphasize autonomy and self-agency may adopt a transformational approach to stimulate innovation with transactional control, serving the purpose of regulation (Edward et al., 2017). Understanding of the situational use of both types of leadership is essential as it enables international firms to cross challenging-to-navigate cultures and align their strategies in harmony with the psychological requirements of their employees and thus enhance performance and well-being in general (Amy et al., 2009).

5.5.CROSS-CULTURALLEADERSHIPCHALLENGES

The landscape of leadership in global management is multifaceted by design, as leadership behaviors are anticipated differently in diverse cultures. Transformational and transactional leadership theories illustrate the variation in managerial attitude and value between regions. Transformational leadership, with inspiration and change at the core, could be more intriguing in collectivist cultures where group solidarity is valued. On the other hand, transactional leadership, premised on formal rewards and punishments, tends to fit more comfortably in individualistic cultures that emphasize personal success and responsibility. This imbalance challenges international leaders to balance different expectations and adjust their leadership styles in a way that ensures integration and convergence across multicultural teams. As highlighted in multicultural team studies, managers must be made globally competent so that they are able to handle such differences and their strategies mesh with team culture and local conventions of leadership (Nishii et al., 2007). Cross-cultural communication has never been more critical, especially in fostering global management leadership in multinational companies (Figure 5.9).

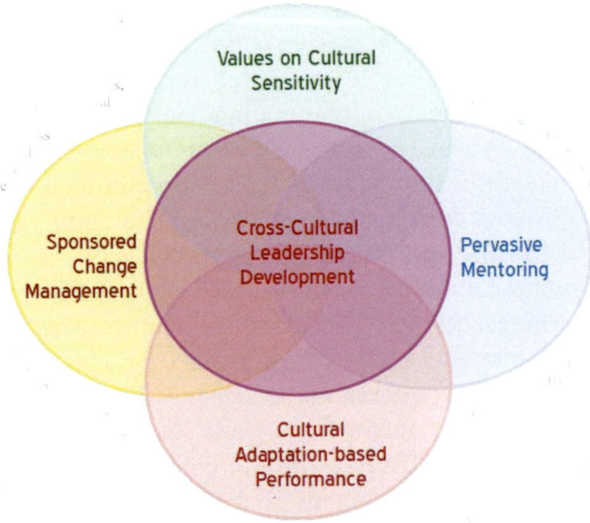

Figure 5.9. Cross-cultural leadership development.

Source: https://bmkltsly13vb.compat.objectstorage.ap-mumbai-1.oraclecloud.com/cdn.dailymirror.lk/media/images/MB-_4(13).jpg.

In regions where indirect communication is the norm, as in most of Asia, leaders must be masterful at reading between lines and decoding subtle cues. This is an altogether different world from direct and assertive communication, such as exists in most regions of North America. Accordingly, leaders must reconcile such forms of communication with the necessity to be forceful and consistent within diverse groups of teammates. It is critical for leaders to gain deep understanding of such cultural nuances in a bid to avoid miscommunications that would negatively affect team performance. Effective leaders are well aware that adapting communication style not only enhances relational relationships but also places their style of leadership in the cultural context of their teams and therefore fostering a united and collaborative environment (Eyong et al., 2016). In addition, an integrated framework for global diversity is essential to managing cross-cultural leadership effectively. Despite growing research in multicultural teams and global competence, more frameworks are needed that integrate instruction on how leaders can successfully navigate cultural diversity in the organization. If frameworks are not implemented, it will become more challenging for global leaders to build inclusive environments that respect and leverage diverse perspectives. Organizations that fail to acknowledge and adopt the cultural dimensions of leadership risk decreasing employee engagement and team performance. Theoretical and applied models endeavoring to fill these dimensions can therefore significantly empower leaders as they work to deal with global diversity. Through identification and application of these models, leaders are in a better position to enhance employees' cultural competence and receive the successful integration of various leadership styles among their staff (Nishii et al., 2007).

5.5.1. Communication Barriers in International Management

Effective global management communication process is highly influenced by the diverse cultural settings in which global leaders operate. Leadership theories, particularly in a global context, need to understand how cultural diversity influences what is known about management and authority. For instance, leaders operating in collectivist cultures can emphasize group consensus and coherence while leaders operating in individualistic cultures will emphasize assertiveness and individual achievement. Thus, global leaders must be effective in negotiating such expectations since, in the absence of local norms, misalignment can yield deep-seated communication obstacles. These obstacles do not just manifest in style but also in interpretation of messages as a respectful tone in one culture could be perceived as passive or unassertive in another culture and thus make intercultural collaboration difficult (Apelehin et al., 2025). In addition, the cultural aspect of the influence of leadership cannot be overstated in that it dictates the fundamental principles upon which communication activities are based. Transformational leadership, where the goal is to inspire and motivate members above immediate self-interests, can have strong resonance in harmony- and productivity-oriented cultures (Figure 5.10).

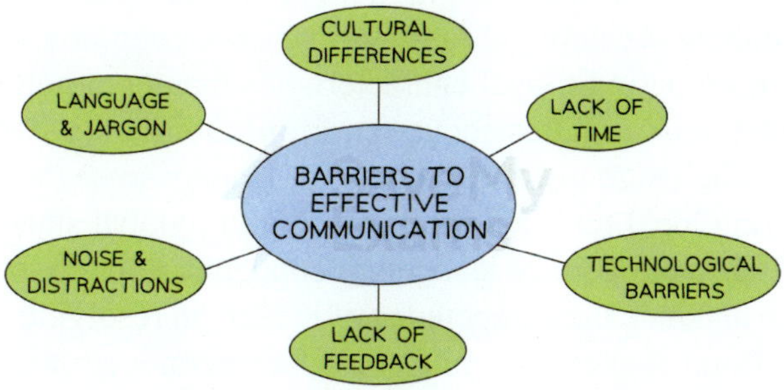

Figure 5.10. The barrier of effective communication in international management.

Source: https://cdn.savemyexams.com/uploads/2024/03/barriers-to-effective-communication-cie-igcse-business-rn.png.

Conversely, in transactional cultures, the focus on clear expectations and codified rewards can facilitate improved communication but of less emotional intensity that is required to tie teams together. While leaders are adapting their styles to meet varied expectations in different cultures, they end up confronting communication obstacles arising from divergent interpretations of motivation and management (Salamanina et al., 2025). A leader's achievement hinges on his/her ability to identify and respond to these distinctions, which have immediate implications for the function of bridging cross-cultural distances. Furthermore, communication challenges in global management are augmented by the far-reaching shift toward virtual teamwork and remote collaboration. As companies span borders geographically, leaders increasingly rely on digital media to reach culturally mixed teams. However, these platforms have a tendency to weaken the subtlety inherent in direct contact, which leads to miscommunication and potential conflict. In the absence of non-verbal cues, leaders need to develop highly sophisticated systems to maintain clarity and cohesiveness in their communication. Emphasizing adaptability and cross-cultural skills, leaders need to adopt pioneering digital communication tools while establishing a culture that is inclusive in nature and encourages members with dissimilar cultural backgrounds to express themselves freely. Thus, efficient communication barrier management is central to effective leadership in every global environment (Salamanina et al., 2025).

5.5.2. Navigating Ethical Dilemmas Across Cultures

Global theories of leadership inform our understanding of how leaders should go about handling ethical issues in various cultural environments. Different parts of the world have varying expectations and values that influence leadership style and ethical decision-making practices. For example, individualism and accountability dictate Western cultures, setting up a condition where decisions are influenced more by individual characteristics than common values. On the other hand, collectivist cultures focus more on community welfare and may present a unique challenge to ethical issues for leaders since they might be torn between respecting local traditions and maintaining global standards of ethics. The incorporation of indigenous leadership concepts, as cited in Abiodun et al. (2011), serves to enhance the competence of leaders in resolving such dilemmas by uniting the cultural nuances that guide acceptable conduct and ethical behavior in different parts. The distinction between transformational and transactional leadership merely makes it more difficult to maneuver ethical challenges across cultures. Transformational leadership, founded on vision and inspiration, most often thrives in an environment that supports open communication and group decision-making. This allows leaders to sustain an ethical sensitivity culture, which resonates with the propositions in Fu et al. (2015). Transactional leadership, founded on a more directive and hierarchical style of leadership, most often sustains unethical behavior where obedience to authority takes priority over morality. Managers who manage globally must therefore evaluate which leadership style will most effectively foster ethical business practices in multicultural settings and balance empowerment's benefits with requirements for compliance and control. Cultural diversity within the workplace evinces the subtlety of ethical leadership as leaders work with conflicting values, perceptions, and expectations. The meeting of different backgrounds can release ethical dilemmas that are not easily solvable under traditional models of choice. Since Abiodun et al. (2011) could expound, workers often find them facing conflicts between organizational ethics and self-interest more broadly, exerting a pressure that can break down integrity. By adopting ethical models, such as those presented by Shapiro and Stefkovich in Fu et al. (2015), bosses are better positioned to solve such dilemmas. The lenses of justice, critique, care, and profession provide good counsel in ethical leadership decision-making that enables leaders to synthesize diverse visions and build a corporate culture that holds integrity dear in order to align individual behavior with shared ethical standards in the context of globalization.

5.5.3. Adapting Leadership Styles to Diverse Teams

Since the global business environment is so varied and complex, leadership theories in the past have had to adapt to meet the infinite expectations of international teams. Take, for instance, some areas that emphasize collectivism and prefer leadership styles that make use of group harmony and consensus decision-making. Individualist cultures may, however, require assertive and decisive leaders. These distinctions matter; setting aside leadership styles to conform to cultural tastes can significantly raise the performance of global teams. Transformational leadership, in its focus on inspiring and encouraging subordinates, will be appreciated in cultures that support change and innovation. Transactional leadership, founded on well-defined structures and incentives, could be more effective in the domains with a focus on hierarchy and stability. These elements not only create stronger relationships within subordinates but also drive group performance towards the long term, thus furthering organizational success (Reid et al., 2009). Examining the transformational-transactional paradigm also sheds some light on how these practices manifest differently across cultures. Empirical research does exist to indicate that transformational leadership is most likely connected to more employee involvement and satisfaction, particularly where high value is placed on personal development and empowerment. Such leadership promotes transparent communication and creative problem-solving, which can be really handy in culturally diverse teams where ideas from different backgrounds give birth to richer decision-making. Transactional leadership, on the other hand, thrives in environments that require efficiency, order, and predictability and is best suited to cultures that highly value formal duties and roles. The most crucial concern for leaders of multi-regional contexts is to realize when and how to utilize these styles in a manner that optimizes their effectiveness, thereby achieving a balanced style of leadership that will resonate across cultures (Shachaf et al., 2008). Further, virtual and multicultural team functioning demands an advanced understanding of leadership adaptiveness. With increasing organizations embracing technology-based cross-border teamwork, leaders ought to be expert users of communication platforms to engender an environment of inclusivity and comprehending through diverse team members. The application of information and communication technology (ICT) plays a crucial role in bridging cultural differences by improving decision-making as well as averting the downfalls of poor communication. For instance, tools such as teleconferencing and collaborative online workspace can facilitate more equitable participation across teams, fostering the sense of belonging between varied cultural populations. These technological resources not only facilitate the support of varied leadership styles but also allow leaders to modify their style, thus enhancing team performance and teamwork in a global environment (Shachaf et al., 2008).

5.6. THE ROLE OF TECHNOLOGY IN GLOBAL LEADERSHIP

In global management, the convergence of leadership and technology has played a significant role in shaping various global leadership theories. As international organizations extend themselves across national boundaries, their leaders must navigate diverse cultural sensitivities as they employ technology to communicate and collaborate with each other. Specifically, it is notable that the deployment of virtual teams has made it obligatory for organizations to change from autocratic leadership styles towards more participative styles centered on connection and inclusion. Technology facilitates the exchange of ideas between cultures, which transformational leaders require in order to inspire and motivate teams. The ability to utilize communications platforms ensures that leaders can modify their style according to regional norms, thus enhancing their ability to create shared visions within the team. Flexibility showcases the need for an understanding of technology as a fundamental leadership skill in the fast-evolving business world today (Johnson et al., 2010). The expectations of leadership vary significantly from region to region based on cultural values and attitudes. Leaders are expected to hold certain characteristics that are in line with traditional ways and values locally; for instance, in collectivistic cultures, group harmony-focused leaders and collective success-oriented leaders are appreciated. In more individualistic societies, transformational leaders who advocate individual growth and autonomy can be more effective (Figure 5.11).

Figure 5.11. The interplay between technology and leadership.

Source: https://archive.opengovasia.com/wp-content/uploads/2024/11/Article-Sam_Ind-Nov-25-main.jpg.

These cross-cultural differences also shape the leadership styles, such that models transactional in nature, which rely on rewards and punishments, may dominate power distance cultures. This difference highlights the importance of the culturally intelligent global leader, the ability further enhanced by technology to give immediate feedback on regional practice and expectation. With these results included in their leadership practices, managers are more capable of dealing with global settings (Boudreau et al., 2002). In distinguishing the differences between transformational and transactional leadership at the international level, technology is a critical component for encouraging innovative team involvement strategies. Transformational leaders use technological means to create environments that foster creativity and collaboration, as through the use of collaborative technologies that remove geographical constraints. Transactional leaders, on the other hand, may use technology to monitor and reward performance in a more formalized manner, in keeping with their focus on clear goals and measurable outcomes. But with organizations needing flexibility and quick realignment according to marketplace changes, the line between transformational and transactional leadership is lost. Leaders skilled at blending both approaches are able to traverse varied team relationships and cultural realities, and technological literacy is essential when orchestrating global initiatives. Thus, the role of technology in shaping leadership patterns cannot be overstated, since it ultimately influences the capacity for leadership in multi-cultural landscapes (Johnson et al., 2010).

5.6.1. Influence of Digital Communication on Leadership Practices

The revolutionary landscape of electronic communication has profoundly changed the expectations and roles of leaders in the worlds' contexts. This revolution requires one to be highly conversant with various global leadership theories, which highlight that effective leadership is often contingent upon the cultural dynamics. For instance, while North American leaders will lean towards a participative and individualistic style of leadership, their collectivist counterparts in cultures such as East Asia may rely more on consensus and harmony. Virtual channels enable leaders to bridge geographical distance, exchanging ideas and best practices that resonate with various cultural demands. In addition, while navigating these complexities, leaders must be adept at harnessing the exploitation of digital communication tools to facilitate interactions and collaboration among multicultural teams. Such adaptability is essential in creating inclusive environments where all participants feel valued and empowered to construct organizational goals. The convergence of digital communication and leadership practice has also highlighted the distinction between transformational and transactional leadership styles at an international scale. Transformational leadership that involves sharing inspiration and vision is now able to harness digital spaces to address larger audiences and create a feeling of community and common purpose between scattered teams.

This porosity allows transformational leaders to pursue an international outlook, enhancing their authority in global contexts. Transactional leadership, which depends on formalized work and reward-performance, finds that set hierarchical units are increasingly being replaced by online communication platforms. These tools may be employed to clarify matters and accelerate feedback loops, but can also have the possibility of undermining interpersonal connections. Leaders therefore have to strike a balance between the transactional aspect of their profession and the need for genuine relationships established via quality digital relations so that members are not alienated while seeking efficiency via technology. The emergence of digital communication also highlights the need for leaders to continuously adapt their methods in response to the pressures of the globalized economy. One pragmatic approach is that leadership practices are not homogeneous; instead, they have to be done in response to the cultural sensitivities of a given region or team. For example, institutions operating under guidelines established by institutions like Northwestern University's Global

Vision for 2020 emphasize the development of a culture of global understanding and local consciousness, reflecting an understanding that a literal imposition of digital strategy will not suit all settings equally well (N/A, 2016). This flexibility is added to by the evolving training requirements in the workplace, where the demand for leaders with technical and behavioral skills is paramount (Kanabar et al., 2018). Hence, leaders must use digital communication as a tool not only of efficiency, but of establishing meaningful connections and developing their organizational culture in a multicultural setting.

5.6.2. Virtual Leadership and Its Challenges

Global management intricacies require leaders to have a deep understanding of complex leadership theories. Global leadership theories, ranging from transformational to transactional approaches, recognize various expectations in various cultures. For instance, transformational leadership, which emphasizes motivating and inspiring followers, may be greatly valued in collectivist cultures where cooperation and group harmony are prized. Conversely, transactional leadership, in which a focus on reward and punishment is used, might have more value in individualistic cultures where individual achievement is so noted. With teams increasingly going virtual, these different expectations of culture complicate leadership dynamics, generating a need for leaders to be able to adapt their leadership styles to fit a variety of different cultural settings. The challenge, therefore, lies not just in the establishment of the appropriate leadership type, but also in fostering an inclusive environment that transcends cultural boundaries.

Virtual leadership entails special challenges driven by a lack of direct face-to-face interaction and reliance on technology aids for communication. Exceptional leaders must fill the gaps created by geographical distances through technology to communicate with diverse global teams. These managers must also possess expertise in the management of the nuances of cross-cultural communication, as variations in communication style and cultural values can create misunderstandings. Cross-cultural competencies development for managers, particularly in a virtual environment, is thus a crucial component of international management. This training should involve elements such as active listening, empathy, and adaptability so that managers can facilitate effective interactions among their team members. Notably, innovative programs, as highlighted in previous studies, have demonstrated remarkable improvement in developing intercultural competence and teamwork abilities among the learners of virtual exchanges (Christina et al., 2024). Moreover, the push for virtual team collaboration often reveals underlying problems in team dynamics that need to be addressed in order to develop effective leadership. Shared issues such as imbalance in task commitment, time management, and maintaining interest may influence team performance within virtual contexts. Evidence from biology education programs shows that there are signs that systematic structures and increased scaffolding are determinants that generate shared leadership and teamwork (Vesala-Varttala et al., 2023). Leaders must play an active role in implementing measures that enhance collaboration and hold team members accountable to one another. By establishing clear expectations and using digital tools that facilitate collaboration, virtual leaders are able to maximize productivity and engagement. Ultimately, addressing these issues is key to creating a robust leadership model that can manage virtual teams in heterogeneous cultures in global management contexts.

5.6.3. Technology as a Tool for Fostering Cross-Cultural Collaboration

The age of the internet has irreversibly transformed the nature of world leadership by making it possible for more complex interactions among cultures. Leaders must navigate diverse expectations defined by local cultural assumptions. For instance, in collectivistic cultures, leadership can be conceived as a mode of relational interdependence, in which harmony among group members and coming to common ground are emphasized. Individualist cultures, conversely, may necessitate charismatic visionary leadership that inspires and drives results. Proper application of technology facilitates such flexibility through the ability to adjust their communication and participation patterns in terms of cultural context.

Technology is thus a critical tool for facilitating such understanding of diversified models of leadership, enabling platforms through which leaders can effectively communicate and interact constructively across geographical boundaries (Lim, 2022). This dynamic is crucial in world management, where leaders must internalize knowledge of such multi-faceted cultures and yet keep holding on to the general organizational mission. In the emerging literature on global leadership, transformational and transactional leadership are seen as blueprints that may vary in acceptance and effect across cultures. Transformational leadership, that uses inspiration and stimulation through vision and emotional connection, will perform better in relationship- and community-based cultures. Transactional leadership with its reliance on structure, reward, and punishment may resonate with regions that emphasize efficiency and effectiveness-biased behaviors. The usage of technology allows leaders to navigate these preferences and antipathies more effectively, allowing for tailored management styles that resonate with heterogeneous teams (Figure 5.12).

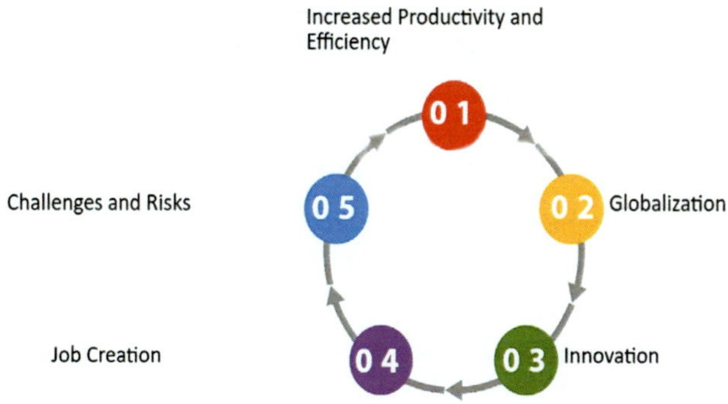

Figure 5.12. The role of technology in global business expansion.

Source: https://fastercapital.co/i/Understanding-Global-Economies-through-the-Lens-of-Reuters--The-Role-of-Technology-in-Global-Economic-Growth.webp.

For example, collaborative platforms and tools foster transformational leadership traits such as participation and inspiration while adapting to transactional actions by setting measurable performance objectives. Thus, technology not only bridges cultural divides but also encourages a hybrid style of leadership under which transactional and transformational styles of leadership exist together and thrive (Mensah, 2019). The role of technology as a catalyst for cross-cultural collaboration cannot be overstressed. It assists in dismantling language and distance barriers along with foster more equal participation in multicultural teams. Video conferencing technology, shared online workspaces, and instant messaging software enables real-time collaboration, fostering a sense of belonging in even dispersed teams. Technology can also provide rich data analytics that guide leaders on how to better understand and appreciate regional communication cultures as well as decision-making processes. Through the incorporation of these technology tools in their leadership strategies, leaders can create inclusive environments in which different voices are not just accepted but actively sought. This strategic deployment of technology in leadership across cultures develops organizational responsiveness and agility, positioning companies to thrive in the expanding interconnected global economy (Lim, 2022).

SUMMARY

As companies continue to diversify their operations across international borders, the importance of quality leadership continues to become increasingly fundamental. Theories of global leadership, including transformational and transactional leadership, are frameworks that can be used to help leaders manage the intricacies of managing internationally. Transformational leadership, through its emphasis on engaging and motivating employees to transcend self-interest for the organization, will most resonate in collectivist cultures where collective harmony and shared goals are most cherished. Transactional leadership, being framed around structure, rewards, and compliance, will be best suited to cultures that revere hierarchy and power distance. Understandings of these theories assist leaders in conceptualizing their plans on the basis of the cultures of regions where they are operating, ultimately resulting in a more productive and encouraged workforce. Leadership expectations can significantly vary across different regions as a function of cultural values, norms, and histories. When individualism prevails in regions such as North America, leaders are likely to develop personal initiative and innovation in their team members. In contrast, in collectivistic cultures, common in Asia, leadership is expected to uphold societal norms and prioritize group solidarity over individual achievement. This difference in expectation underscores the value placed on leaders being culturally responsive and competent because ignoring to honor such differences can lead to miscommunication and decreased employee morale. By embracing the nuances of culture, leaders can cultivate a climate that tolerates but also leverages divergent perspectives in enriching global organizational performance. The transformational-transactional leadership paradigm also further complicates the international management stage. Transformational leadership encourages a visionary approach to leading that is capable of sparking innovation and transformation, but transactional leadership is more likely to dominate in formal environments where clear expectations and rewards become paramount. Empowering leadership has been identified as playing a pivotal role in psychological empowerment of employees in the global landscape, with comparative studies examining Rwandan and American leadership styles (Rahschulte et al., 2018). Adaptability of leadership style and familiarity with cultural dimensions of power distance and individualism vs. collectivism have been identified as pivotal factors in employee empowerment and attainment of organizational success in the global environment. Therefore, global management executives must maintain the vibrant relationship between these leadership mindsets and cultural expectations to drive sustainable development in diverse markets.

A leadership study across cultures introduces that various global leadership theories play a very important part in how leaders engage their teams in various settings. For instance, the GLOBE (Global Leadership and Organizational Behavior Effectiveness) study identifies cultural dimensions that contextualize leadership behaviors and expectations from varying regions. It identifies inherent traits, such as the need for participative leadership in Nordic countries compared to authoritarian forms of leadership that are widely favored across some cultures in Asia. Identifying these variations enables leaders to shape their style in accordance with cultural norms, thereby demonstrating that great leadership is not fixed but context-dependent and framed by local conventions and mores. This cultural adaptability is crucial to forging productive organizational relationships, increasing team integration, and ultimately maximizing organizational performance in an era of globalization. Different regions have varying expectations of leadership behaviors, typically established in light of historical, societal, and economic factors. North American and Western European leadership are frequently characterized by its emphasis on innovation, self-management, and personal performance. Conversely, in collectivist cultures, such as most Asian cultures, leaders are expected to focus on consensus and harmony in the group. Such a cultural difference indicates that there can be no one leadership style that can work everywhere; rather, leaders must acquire knowledge of regional differences so that they can lead effectively. This knowledge of the cultural expectations serves not only to facilitate effective team management but also builds trust and loyalty among members of the team, resulting in organizational success in the long run. Understanding these diverse leadership expectations is therefore very important for any organization in an international environment. The distinction between transformational and transactional leadership introduces a level of sophistication in international management. Transformational leadership, which activates and motivates followers to a shared vision, is typically viewed positively by most cultures and is associated with fostering change and innovation. Transactional leadership, which focuses on maintaining the usual flow of procedures, employs penalty and reward as an obedience tool. An awareness of both leaderships' strengths and weaknesses is paramount, as both will be effective to some extent depending on the culture. For instance, transformational leaders will prosper more in cultures that place greater importance on cooperation and collective achievement, while transactional leaders will prosper in cultures that place more emphasis on structure and stability. A sophisticated knowledge of these leadership dynamics will be capable of enabling global managers to modify their strategies and collaborate with a diverse range of people efficiently, correlating leadership style with cultural expectations for maximum results.

REFERENCES

1. Abiodun, A. J., & Oyeniyi, O. (2011). Ethical dilemmas in management: An African perspective. https://core.ac.uk/download/18295013.pdf (accessed on 24th September 2025).
2. Apelehin, A. A., Imohiosen, C., Ajuluchukwu, P., Abutu, D. E., Udeh, C. A., & Iguma, D. R. (2025). Transforming organizational and educational cultures: Developing global leadership and building inclusive workplaces through innovative HR and educational practices. *International Journal of Multidisciplinary Research and Growth Evaluation.* https://www.semanticscholar.org/paper/bbdeef0735d22a495b61defefaca007d3b303762 (accessed on 24th September 2025).
3. Bormann, T., Brooks-Cooper, C., Farley, J., Fuerstenau, M., et al. (2001). Resources for workplace diversity: An annotated practitioner guide to information. https://core.ac.uk/download/5127328.pdf (accessed on 24th September 2025).
4. Born, M. P., Cem-Ersoy, N., Derous, E., van der Molen, H. T., et al. (2012). The effect of cultural orientation and leadership style on self- versus other-oriented organizational citizenship behavior in Turkey and the Netherlands. https://core.ac.uk/download/55806965.pdf (accessed on 24th September 2025).
5. Boudreau, J. W., Dowling, P. J., & Ramstad, P. M. (2002). Global talent ship: Toward a decision science connecting talent to global strategic success. https://core.ac.uk/download/5131512.pdf (accessed on 24th September 2025).
6. Campagna, C. D., Searles, M. P., Suser, J. L., Omar, R. M. K., Bugaigis, H., Muftah, K., Mansur, H., et al. (2024). Bridging cultures to defeat COVID-19: An innovative virtual exchange program in global medical education. https://www.semanticscholar.org/paper/12f038b2b22282c545ee52d31b2be2701a718f27 (accessed on 24th September 2025).
7. Deci, E. L., Olafsen, A. H., & Ryan, R. M. (2017). Self-determination theory in work organizations: The state of a science. *Annual Review of Organizational Psychology and Organizational Behavior, 4*, 19–43. https://doi.org/10.1146/annurev-orgpsych-032516-113108 (accessed on 24th September 2025).
8. Dolan, S. M. (2004). Executive compensation eligibility in global businesses: A global banding approach. https://core.ac.uk/download/5121925.pdf (accessed on 24th September 2025).

9. Dwivedi, Y. K., Ismagilova, E., Hughes, D. L., Carlson, J., Filieri, R., Jacobson, J., Jain, V., et al. (2020). Setting the future of digital and social media marketing research: Perspectives and research propositions. International Journal of Information Management, 59, 102168–102168. https://doi.org/10.1016/j.ijinfomgt.2020.102168 (accessed on 24th September 2025).
10. Eyong, J. E. (2016). Indigenous African leadership: Key differences from Anglo-centric thinking and writings. https://core.ac.uk/download/287585828.pdf (accessed on 24th September 2025).
11. Fadare, S. (2018). Leadership styles and effectiveness among Sub-Saharan African employees. https://core.ac.uk/download/216808917.pdf (accessed on 24th September 2025).
12. Fisk, A., & Gunn, V. (2013). Considering teaching excellence in higher education: 2007–2013: A literature review since the CHERI report 2007. https://core.ac.uk/download/16460312.pdf (accessed on 24th September 2025).
13. Ford, D. L., & Whaley, G. L. (2012). Examining collegiality and social justice in academia and the private sector: An exploratory SYMLOG analysis. https://core.ac.uk/download/70426054.pdf (accessed on 24th September 2025).
14. Fu, I. P. (2015). Favoritism: Ethical dilemmas viewed through multiple paradigms. https://core.ac.uk/download/144551980.pdf (accessed on 24th September 2025).
15. Halub, H., Sauber, A., & Stück, J. (2017). The Turk and the Yankee: A cross-cultural comparison between Turkish and American managers. https://core.ac.uk/download/84885650.pdf (accessed on 24th September 2025).
16. Hillman, A. J., Withers, M. C., & Collins, B. J. (2009). Resource dependence theory: A review. *Journal of Management, 35*, 1404–1427. https://doi.org/10.1177/0149206309343469 (accessed on 24th September 2025).
17. Jogulu, U. D., & Wood, G. J. (2006). Malaysian and Australian male and female middle managers: A cross-cultural comparison of workplace attitudes, aspirations for promotion, and self-rated leadership styles. http://hdl.handle.net/10536/DRO/DU:30020923 (accessed on 24th September 2025).
18. Johnson, K. (2010). Virtual leadership: Required competencies for effective leaders. https://core.ac.uk/download/219377043.pdf (accessed on 24th September 2025).

19. Kanabar, V., Messikomer, C., & Thomas, A. (2018). Enhancing project-related behavioral competence in education. https://open.bu.edu/bitstream/2144/29016/1/Enhancing%20Project-Related%20Behavioral%20Competence%20in%20Education.pdf (accessed on 24th September 2025).
20. Kruk, M. E., Gage, A., Arsenault, C., Jordan, K., Leslie, H. H., Roder-DeWan, S., Adeyi, O., et al. (2018). High-quality health systems in the Sustainable Development Goals era: Time for a revolution. The Lancet Global Health, 6, e1196–e1252. https://doi.org/10.1016/s2214-109x(18)30386-3 (accessed on 24th September 2025).
21. Li, M., & Yang, I. (2017). Can absent leadership be positive in team conflicts? An examination of leaders' avoidance behavior in China. https://core.ac.uk/download/151161261.pdf (accessed on 24th September 2025).
22. Lim, W. M. (2022). Ushering a new era of Global Business and Organizational Excellence: Taking a leaf out of recent trends in the new normal. Global Business and Organizational Excellence, 41, 5–13. https://doi.org/10.1002/joe.22163 (accessed on 24th September 2025).
23. Lyons, K., Christopoulos, A., & Brock, T. (2020). Sustainable pharmacy education in the time of COVID-19. American Journal of Pharmaceutical Education, 84, ajpe8088–ajpe8088. https://doi.org/10.5688/ajpe8088 (accessed on 24th September 2025).
24. Marcotte, D., Rustambekov, E., & Trendowski, J. (2019). Importance of cultural intelligence: Cross-cultural examination and analysis. https://core.ac.uk/download/231818803.pdf (accessed on 24th September 2025).
25. McKenzie, A., & Shiel, C. (2008). The global university: The role of senior managers. https://core.ac.uk/download/75202.pdf (accessed on 24th September 2025).
26. Mensah, J. (2019). Sustainable development: Meaning, history, principles, pillars, and implications for human action: Literature review. *Cogent Social Sciences, 5.* https://doi.org/10.1080/23311886.2019.1653531 (accessed on 24th September 2025).
27. Nishii, L. H., & Özbilgin, M. F. (2007). Global diversity management: Towards a conceptual framework. https://core.ac.uk/download/219376625.pdf (accessed on 24th September 2025).
28. Rahschulte, T., & Thomas, D. (2018). The moderating effects of power distance and individualism/collectivism on empowering leadership, psychological empowerment, and self-leadership in international development organizations. https://digitalcommons.georgefox.edu/

cgi/viewcontent.cgi?article=1098&context=gfsb (accessed on 24th September 2025).

29. Rao, I. (2025). The behavioral equivalence of organizational culture. https://core.ac.uk/download/pdf/6443708.pdf (accessed on 24th September 2025).
30. Reid, S., Spencer-Oatey, H., & Stadler, S. (2009). The Global People landscaping study: Intercultural effectiveness in global education partnerships. https://core.ac.uk/download/46447.pdf (accessed on 24th September 2025).
31. Salamanina, S., & Meshko, N. (2025). Strategies for managing remote teams in international enterprises. International Journal of Psychology and Strategic Communication. https://www.semanticscholar.org/paper/47b7bd0aab191a1950f570845bc06e6ade22f506 (accessed on 24th September 2025).
32. Shachaf, P. (2008). Cultural diversity and information and communication technology impacts on global virtual teams: An exploratory study. https://core.ac.uk/download/11887687.pdf (accessed on 24th September 2025).
33. Ullah, K., Lill, I., & Witt, E. (2019). An overview of BIM adoption in the construction industry: Benefits and barriers. *Emerald Reach Proceedings Series*. https://doi.org/10.1108/s2516-285320190000002052 (accessed on 24th September 2025).
34. Vesala-Varttala, T., & Morgado, M. (2023). Teachers' perceptions on international online teamwork and how it can be improved. Education and New Developments 2023–Volume 2. https://www.semanticscholar.org/paper/ec4a16aaddc592ba49ce3e0adf012cf5b79d2796 (accessed on 24th September 2025).

Chapter 6

Organizational and Strategic Behavior

Contents

INTRODUCTION

The ever-evolving global business context requires organizations to adopt new strategies that enhance their effectiveness and competitiveness. As companies expand internationally, they face a plethora of challenges that compel them to rethink traditional management practices and organizational forms. The synergistic relationship between organizational behavior and strategic decision-making is crucial in addressing the complexities of multicultural, economic, and legal environments. This essay discusses organizational and strategic behavior in global management, highlighting the significance of the understanding of various frameworks such as centralization v. decentralization that play a significant role in determining how multinational firms operate globally. By discussing such dynamics, it is possible to learn about how these organizational arrangements influence strategic behavior and eventually determine the success of a firm on the world map (Martin et al., 2017). Global strategic action typically characterizes the requirement for flexibility and adaptability to the market idiosyncrasies of the host country. Multinational corporations (MNCs) historically are caught between maintaining a single corporate strategy and being able to tailor their strategies for regional differences. That conflict is then followed by the decision between centralized decision-making, which ensures consistency, and decentralized models that leave local managers free to enable quick decision-making. Furthermore, having an understanding of the matrix structures and virtual organizations that most firms employ can provide insight needed in reconciling resources and abilities with strategic objectives. These forms of organizational structures not only influence the information flow but also define how firms co-operate and compete in different global places (Shankar et al., 2012). With companies navigating at the intersection of behavior and strategy in international management, cross-border collaboration and cultural intelligence cannot be overstressed. The intricacies of cross-cultural relations compel firms to continuously reinvent their management methods, challenging leaders to be open and pliable in their responses. Commitment of workers, motivation, and communication become crucial ingredients of successful international strategies. In addition, the essay will highlight how varied organizational behaviors impact growth tendencies and competitive advantage in varying global environments. By paying attention to the dynamics between organizational types and strategic programs, one can realize how firms may achieve their quest for world market leadership with the ongoing challenges posed by globalization.

Importance of Organizational Behavior in Global Context

In order to survive in an global business environment, one needs a sophisticated understanding of principles of organizational behavior, particularly on how the principles influence strategic decisions across different contexts. As organizations expand overseas, flexibility is a key requirement, as seen through the nuances in reconciling reliability and flexibility, and most significantly, in partnerships. Joint ventures, for instance, require organizations to maintain themselves in a position of being extremely responsive to competitive uncertainty while being contained within structured controls that prevent opportunism and complacency. The shifting expectations resulting from cultural differences only compound the complexity of striking this balance, which requires good communication and establishing trust. Thus, learning organizational behavior enables businesses to maximize their global operations by being able to coordinate and innovate with adherence to local habits and customs, ultimately resulting in performance within strategic partnerships within multicultural markets. Ethical organizational behavior also plays a vital role in global management. Businesses that operate globally must manage several ethical practices and cultural norms, which might significantly differ from the ethics and expectations of the home country. Building ethical leadership is a imperative methodology, not only to compliance with worldwide requirements but also to organizational integrity. Empirical evidence reveals that accountability and moral ability have a positive impact on ethical leadership across industries and geographies. By training leaders on self-monitoring behaviors and moral development, organizations can enhance their ethical structure, a key filter to sustain trust continuity in multinationals. This focus on ethical leadership may be a source of competitive advantage for organizations, as they build effective relationships and reputations in global markets that are crucial for long-term success. Furthermore, the structure of the multinational business organization has a far-reaching effect on organizational behavior and strategic performance. Centralization-decentralization choices, and the utilization of matrix or virtual organizational structures, have an impact on how effectively an organization can operate across geographic boundaries. Centralized configurations have the ability to encourage consistency in decision-making and compliance with policy, particularly within sectors where conformity and compliance are essential. Decentralization, as opposed to centralization, allows for local responsiveness, which allows regional managers to make decisions specific to their markets, enhancing competitive advantage. The hybrid strategies embodied by matrix configurations have the ability to capitalize on both efficiency and local responsiveness, but at the same time can also introduce complexity into management dynamics. Understanding these structural implications allows companies to coordinate their strategies with the multi-dimensional needs of global management in a way that results in increased performance outcomes within a global setting.

Overview of Strategic Behavior in Multinational Firms

In the complex landscape of international management, various strategic behaviors emerge as multinational firms navigate diverse markets. One critical aspect involves the choice between centralization and decentralization, which significantly influences decision-making processes and operational efficiency. Centralization entails consolidating authority at the corporate level, allowing for uniformity and coherence in strategies across subsidiaries. Decentralization, on the other hand, makes it possible for local subsidiaries to make decisions more appropriate to a specific regional environment and enhance responsiveness to consumer wants and market forces. This management divide is a firm's general approach to operating its business, ultimately determining its flexibility, competitiveness, and ability to innovate in the global marketplace. Multinational corporations (MNCs) must strategically evaluate these organizational models while they proceed to pursue global ends, weighing control and local knowledge in order to reach optimal performance. Moreover, the organizational model adopted by multinational corporations also has a major impact on their strategic behavior. The majority of MNCs are currently trending towards matrix organizations and virtual organizations since these can facilitate flexibility and coordination over distance. Under a matrix structure, teams consist of different functional departments and geographic locations, facilitating cross-functional coordination and knowledge sharing. This structure allows businesses to act more rapidly in response to changing global markets and competition. Or, virtual organizations use information technologies to form loosely connected networks of experts that collaborate without the overhead of an antiquated office. This promotes creativity and can save significant costs. However, such complex structures also pose issues such as complexities in communications and potential conflicts regarding power that have to be addressed by MNCs for strategic fit. Multinational firms' strategic moves also capture broader organizational concerns such as managing cultural diversity and adapting to various regulatory environments. It is imperative for MNCs that aim to build a strong presence in foreign markets to have knowledge of local cultures and regulatory environments. Such firms tend to use tailored approaches that resonate with local stakeholders but are still aligned with their international ambitions. Latest research suggests that there is a necessity for aligning strategies to the corresponding local contexts of subsidiaries, supporting the two tensions between local responsiveness and global standardization. The dualism can be particularly challenging as it requires careful handling of subtleties in cross-border activities. Against this background, literature on multinational companies tells us that effective organizational strategies must marry firm centralized control with adaptive local flexibility, summarizing the essence of effective management in the dynamically changing global business landscape (Kang et al., 2020; Alarik et al., 2025).

6.1. TYPES OF INTERNATIONAL FIRMS

One key component in global management is the recognition of different kinds of firms that cross international boundaries. Multinational corporations (MNCs) are likely the most well-known, where they set up subsidiaries in a number of countries but still have substantial control from the home country. This centralization allows them to be consistent in brand and operating measures across their international branches. However, its success may depend on local responsiveness to market demand because excessively centralized decision-making could hinder the adaptation to local preferences. Operational success of MNCs often depends on effective strategic human resource management practices that coordinate employee behavior and capabilities with firm objectives, subsequently affecting their competitive advantage in diversified markets (Boudreau et al., 2002). On the other hand, multinational companies emphasize standardization and efficiency and are likely to adopt a centralized structure to ensure standardized operations. The companies gain economies of scale through uniform products offered worldwide, which will considerably lower costs. While such a strategy can enhance profitability, it is likely to overlook the regional market variations, leading to missing the opportunity to exploit growth and market penetration (Figure 6.1).

Figure 6.1. A crucial element in international business to understanding the various types of firms that operate across borders.

Source: https://indiafreenotes.com/wp-content/uploads/2020/04/topic-3-1.png.

Transnational firms try to resolve this conflict by integrating the best of global efficiency and local responsiveness. Matrix structures are employed that encourage cross-functional working with a view to generate innovation and responsiveness to effectively manage the complexity of foreign environments (Boudreau et al., 2002). This strategic move facilitates a culture in which knowledge moves easily across boundaries, augmenting the firm's overall ability to adapt and thrive. The growth of virtual organizations makes it even more challenging to navigate the international firm scenario, as digital development allows companies to operate independent of geographical boundaries. Such companies are likely to be anchored in decentralized networks that enable them to effectively access global pools of talent and resources. Decentralization leads to a collaborative environment where knowledge-sharing is the most important consideration, which aligns with the general trend in organizational behavior. The writer's strategic relevance derives from the fact that they have the potential to create responsiveness and flexibility in an increasingly rapidly changing world market, thereby increasing organizational resilience. As organizations continue to evolve due to technological innovation, understanding the implications of various international firm types is essential to optimize the formulation of management strategies to take advantage of the strength of each model (Snell et al., 1997).

6.1.1. Characteristics of Multinational Firms

The complexity of functioning in multiple countries necessitates a unique organizational structure commonly found in multinational corporations. These organizations typically apply various ways of balancing global integration and local responsiveness. Among the most important features of the majority of multinational corporations (MNCs) is how they structure decision-making. Centralization offers uniform strategic guidance and allocation of resources but could hinder local market reaction. Conversely, decentralization gives the subsidiaries room to come up with strategy adjustments based on regionized market settings, thus driving innovation and customer satisfaction. Getting the balance correct is key since this dictates the general performance of an MNC's global strategy. For instance, firms can adopt hybrid frameworks that tap into elements from both centralization and decentralization so that they are able to leverage the efficiencies of global presence as well as react to local needs (Kang et al., 2020). A further distinguishing characteristic of multinational corporations is their structural complexity, as a rule presented in matrix or virtual organizational forms. Matrix configurations enable MNCs to combine functional and product-based structures and provide greater flexibility when coordinating projects within different regions and departments. This enables companies to allocate resources in a flexible manner and respond to market changes more aggressively (Figure 6.2).

Conversely, virtual organization development marks increasing reliance on computer technologies to manage geographically dispersed teams. Virtual companies leverage sophisticated communication networks to coordinate international operations efficiently, moving beyond traditional distance and time limitations. This transformation reflects the fluid nature of multinational operations in today's globalized economy, where flexibility and creativity are required to sustain competitive advantage. Their tactical efficacy is underpinned by the ability to handle diverse units (Alarik et al., 2025). Finally, multinational organizations are likely to have distinctive cultural and operational dynamics that are crucial to organizational culture.

Figure 6.2. Role and characteristics of multinational corporations.

Source: https://library.fiveable.me/_next/image?url=https%3A%2F%2Fstorage.googleapis.com%2Fstatic.prod.fiveable.me%2Fsearch-images%252F%2522Global_presence_of_multinational_corporations_centralized_management_diverse_products_compliance_and_risk_management_systems%2522-FourGlobalBusinessStrategies2.png&w=640&q=75.

These firms must deal with diverse cultural environments, regulatory situations, and customer attitudes in the countries where they are based. As a result, MNCs are likely to concentrate on cross-cultural management and global leadership development in creating an adaptable workforce that can effectively manage these complexities. Through training sessions and diversity programs, these organizations aim to create a diverse organizational culture that promotes employee motivation and cooperation across the borders. Additionally, knowledge of local markets is included in strategy developments that will attract regional customers and stakeholders. By creating a nuanced grasp of cultural diversity, multinational firms are able to enhance their global performance while driving innovation unique to each market (Kang et al., 2020).

6.1.2. Global Firms and Their Operational Strategies

Evolution of multinational corporations has necessitated a sophisticated navigating of several operational strategies, which are often established by the specific organizational structure utilized by a firm. Multinational corporations, for instance, have a focus on local responsiveness and often prefer a decentralized framework that allows regional subsidiaries to tailor products to domestic markets. By contrast, multinational firms pursue a balance between worldwide efficiency and local responsiveness, usually taking on a matrix form with the ability to simultaneously emphasize decentralized operation and centralized control. Such an organizational form can increase flexibility as it enables firms to reallocate resources and strategies with response to exigent market needs while facilitating collaboration among a variety of different business units. Ultimately, the strategic choice between decentralization and centralization has a significant influence on the operational effectiveness of multinational companies and thereby their competitiveness in diverse markets. The complexity of operating strategies in multinational companies also spans the level of partnership and cooperation, more so in product-service offerings. A majority of producers are gradually but progressively experiencing the advantages of developing a product-service system that enhances their competitive edge. Through partnerships with expert providers of services, companies can harness external knowledge-based assets in order to develop and enhance service offerings, thereby enhancing performance outcomes. Evidence from research points out that successful servitization, while being industry-specific, flourishes in settings where manufacturers partner on specific business services but hold core competencies within. This sophisticated approach optimizes operational performance so that organizations may choose to outsource value-added activities such as maintenance or logistics support and focus on high-level planning and product design internally. Strategic partnering with specialist players is thus at the heart of effective maneuvering within the complex global business environment. Apart from structural and cooperative dynamics, the role of a well-crafted marketing strategy simply cannot be marginalized in the operational strategies of international corporations. Successful marketing plans, like the orchestration of a symphony, involve a syncretic blending of creativity and analytical abilities. Marketing managers must develop and implement plans to attract different customer segments in different geographies while, simultaneously, fulfilling the firm's overall objectives. Also, successful marketing strategy implementation is contingent upon the strategic coordination of various business activities, which requires a dynamic marketing-mix suited for competitive contexts. By creating good internal communication and a clearly defined knowledge of consumer needs, global firms are able to enhance market performance. Thus, evidence from literature suggests that firms prioritizing customer-oriented strategies have a better prospect of delivering good performance in highly competitive settings in favor of establishing adaptive marketing frameworks.

6.1.3. Transnational Firms and Their Hybrid Approaches

Organizational dynamics within transnational firms finally set their international management strategy. These firms possess a multiple environment that need to be centralized as well as decentralized in order to form hybrid strategies that enable them to exploit local knowledge but remain coherently global. Through the application of matrix structures, these organizations are able to effectively handle diffuse operations in different countries to enable agility as well as responsiveness in local markets while not compromising against corporate targets. This balance can be particularly crucial in sectors where local tastes have significant impacts on consumers and where it is critical for transnational corporations to adapt while simultaneously imposing standardized processes across their operation. The strategic advantages of such hybrid arrangements are noteworthy, providing firms with the adaptability they require to respond to worldwide issues while optimizing the utilization of resource allocation in a big pool of operations (Doherty et al., 2012).

Moreover, the role played by SHRM in transnational firms cannot be overemphasized, especially concerning how such firms leverage human capital as a means of ensuring maximum competitive advantage. As firms strive to internationalize and localize their HR practices, the issue of strategic groups consequently arises as a model to scan their practices. HR managers' participation in the creation of managerial assets is a demonstration of the strategic relevance of human capital in global operations, particularly in the hospitality industry where leadership efficacies directly relate to service quality and consumer satisfaction. Hence, understanding the opportunities and constraints offered by strategic groups gives insightful information regarding the SHRM dynamics, thereby driving international firms further towards operational excellence across cultures (Cieri et al., 1998). Secondly, the integration of strategic international human resource management (SIHRM) within the general strategic frameworks of transnational corporations signifies a trend towards a more advanced understanding of organizational behavior. As SIHRM becomes a prominent feature in international management, it generates questions regarding the adequacy of existing theory and practice in being sensitive to cross-border operations' intricacies. The development of the transparent typologies and common terminology in SIHRM makes theory construction easier and also serves as an educational tool for prospective managers who are about to be working in the sophisticated field of international business. In understanding the need for new theoretical study and bridging current gaps in the research, transnational firms will be able to employ their human assets efficiently and develop innovative and trend-oriented strategies (Cieri et al., 1998).

6.2. ORGANIZATIONAL STRUCTURES IN INTERNATIONAL MANAGEMENT

Managing the complexities of international markets necessitates that organizations adopt appropriate structures, which can be significantly different depending on their strategic function and operational requirements. In international management, organizations can be classified into various forms of business, such as multinational, global, transnational, and international firms, each having distinct organizational structure approaches. Multinational companies typically centralize control at the corporate level while allocating a high degree of autonomy to subsidiaries to modify practices to fit regional contexts. Global corporations, on the other hand, seek a uniform form, realizing efficiency through centralized authority.

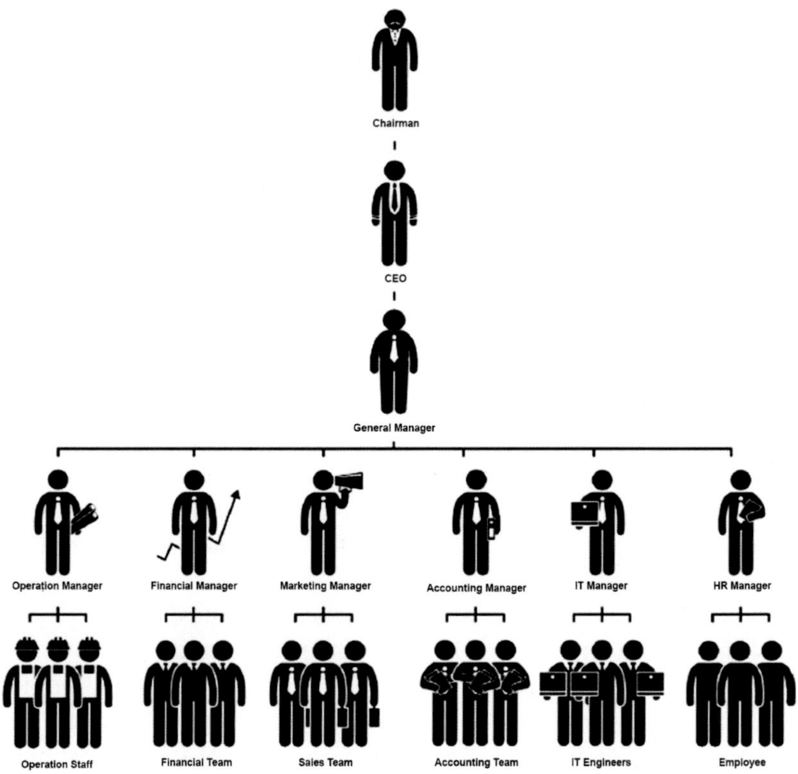

Figure 6.3. Diversity of organizational structure considerations.

Source: https://www.tutorialspoint.com/international_business_management/images/organizational_structures.jpg.

This distinction in organizational form reflects distinctions in strategic focus and cultural issues, which are vital to deciding how companies leverage knowledge and realize competitive advantage. Effective handling of these characteristics enables organizations to effectively navigate the sophisticated landscape of international business and forms a key building block towards their success and endurance. The conundrum of centralization versus decentralization is key in determining how effectively an international organization can operate across various markets. Systems of centralization have the potential to promote homogeneity and effective decision-making; however, they are found to be inadequate in supporting the specific needs of varying regional markets. In contrast, decentralized structures allow local managers to be flexible and responsive in an increasingly fluid competitive landscape (Figure 6.3).

This flexibility is of vital importance to organizations, particularly in the instance of international joint ventures, where partners must balance dependability against flexibility, a fact underscored by Parkhes assertion that strong adaptation necessitates achieving a delicate balance between the twin virtues of reliability and flexibility (Barden et al., 2000). Lastly, choosing the right route towards centralization vs. decentralization can greatly influence an organization's ability to use local know-how and chase competitive excellence in an increasingly integrated world. Matrix organization and virtual organization are new techniques of adapting to challenges facing globally operating companies. Matrix organization is a structure that blends functional and product divisions in an effort to be capable of assigning resources that react to both global and local demands. This structure enhances cross-functional contact and communication, bridging the knowledge gap among independent units of the organization. In virtual firms, spatial distances break down, employing technology as a facilitator of contact among varying teams that are distributed across different locations. As highlighted by the analysis of knowledge indicators within organizations, the understanding of the stock and flow of knowledge, as well as the creation of enabling procedures, becomes increasingly important (Boudreau et al., 2002). These organizational frameworks allow companies to react to rapidly changing environments and leverage intellectual capital, which is imperative for maintaining competitive positioning in the intricate global management landscape.

6.2.1. Centralization vs. Decentralization in Decision-Making

In global operations, companies must walk carefully in structure decisions that will inform their strategic action. Centralization will ensure homogeneity and standardization of procedures, a well-defined framework that can enhance efficiency in branches. In centralization, the most important decisions are started by high-level management, which can lead to quicker decision-making and consistent policy application. But in this way, innovation and responsiveness are stifled, particularly in unstable environments where regional chiefs have critical information regarding local markets. Therefore, the organizations are required to balance the need for consistency against the demand for local adaptation, a challenge that is commonly experienced by multinational corporations. Literature shows that efficient centralization may be beneficial to firms that desire standardized products in numerous various markets but would be a hindrance to competitiveness if local responsiveness is a key necessity (Glock et al., 2025). Decentralization enables firms to provide authority to regional or operation managers, promoting more responsive and dynamic decision-making, while empowering local leaders can assist corporations in adapting their strategies more appropriately to suit the diverse needs of global markets. This design enhances the capacity for innovation and can speed up tactical responses to shifting local demands. Decentralization, as recognized in recent research, does have its weaknesses, i.e., the risk of unequal practices and delayed cross-unit communication. Decision structures within multinational companies must therefore be carefully balanced. Where tax differentials are considerable, decentralized decision systems can be more profitable, and hence an argument does exist for tailor-made approaches closely related to host country tax conditions and company facts (Schjelderup et al., 2025). Ultimately, centralization/decentralization balance relies on broader organizational priorities and the industry environment within which a firm operates. Large and complex organizations, such as transnationals, tend to combine elements of both strategies and adopt hybrid solutions—a matrix organization with centralized control and decentralized application can provide the flexibility required. This combination enables firms not only to standardize parts of their operations but also to utilize local knowledge for competitive advantage in a global setting. To be able to navigate, organizations must develop a sophisticated awareness of the internal strengths and weaknesses and the external market realities in order to establish decision-making models that facilitate both efficiency and flexibility in international management (Glock et al., 2025).

6.2.2. Matrix Structures and Their Applications

With contemporary organizational design, flexibility and responsiveness are accorded more prominence, especially for multinational and transnational corporations with activities across many markets. The traditional hierarchical systems are found wanting in addressing the challenges of managing cross-functional and geographically dispersed teams. Matrix structures have emerged as a innovative response that facilitate centralization of decision making and decentralization of mundane activities. Such alignments allow firms to seize global efficiencies while simultaneously addressing local responsiveness, thus establishing the perfect model of strategic behavior for international management. This dualism not only promotes clearer communication but also allows companies to draw upon diverse pools of talent within their operations, establishing a culture of collaboration and shared objectives. Matrix structures' use also brings its implications into inter-organizational dynamics, particularly in the case of inter-firm alliances and other larger networks (Figure 6.4).

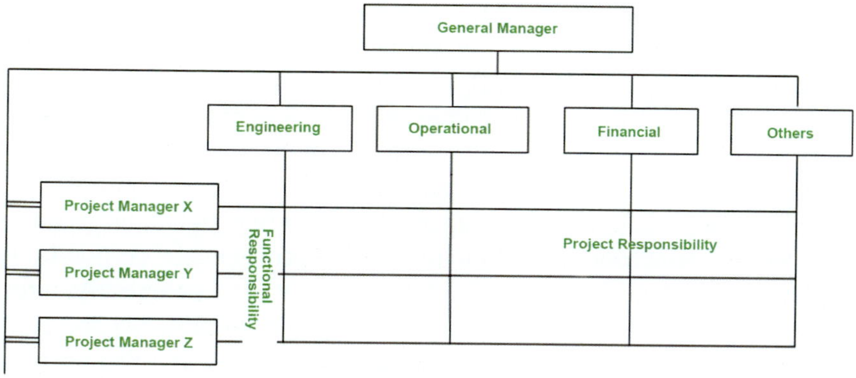

Figure 6.4. The dynamics of matrix structures and their flexibility.

Source: https://media.geeksforgeeks.org/wp-content/uploads/20211220190047/matrixdrawio.png.

Firms that adopt matrix structures can enhance their dynamic capabilities through facilitating interdependencies within various organizational units. This is even more evident when considering how varying sets of dynamic capabilities are triggered within various structures. Research has indicated that firms can utilize their sensing and seizing capabilities differently across inter-organization settings, thereby maximizing innovation performance (Petricevic et al., 2019). This strategy is important, as it focuses on the necessity of tailored strategic solutions that suit particular alliances or larger cooperation frameworks, ultimately leading to enhanced competitive capabilities in dynamic industries. In addition, the integration of matrix structures and persistent organizational approaches enhances the applicability of organizational and strategic behavior in global management. By situating business processes within a culture and product matrix, businesses are able to develop nuanced understanding of their operation systems, bringing attention to the multi-aspect decision-making scenarios such as whether to adopt local or global strategy for their sales organizations

(Boudreau et al., 2002). Not only does this analytical foundation facilitate the identification of such key talent pools but also human resource investment that is strategic in nature. Hence, leaders can concentrate their focus on those most likely to make the greatest contribution toward organizational success, thereby driving performance in an expanding connected global marketplace.

6.2.3. Virtual Organizations and Their Impact on Global Operations

Virtual organizations have radically transformed the worldwide operating environment, leading to a paradigm shift in multinational and international business firms' business style. By facilitating teamwork via geographic remoteness, these organizations leverage technology in order to construct teams with no geographical limitations. The decentralization vs. centralization question is particularly timely in this connection, given the fact that corporations are faced with the task of aggregating dispersed teams while maintaining corporate control. Virtual organizations, often in matrix form, enable corporations to respond to market demands promptly and efficiently use resources. As a result, the ability of firms to respond to shifting regulatory environments and cultural niceties has improved, with potential for increased agility and responsiveness overseas. In addition, virtual frameworks have profound implications for research and development (R&D) in small and medium-sized businesses (SMEs). These types of firms, generally with limited resources, can take advantage of virtual R&D teams so that they can innovate and develop new products with speed and low cost. As indicated in the literature, virtual R&D collaborative dynamics are still in their developmental stages, particularly for SMEs, which are currently broadly viewed as being world economic growth drivers (Ahmed et al., 2010). Through the establishment of an open collaborative platform, virtual R&D teams can rationalize new product development, thereby improving competitiveness within an unpredictable world economy. This trend highlights the necessity for advanced managerial solutions that aim to integrate virtual capabilities into organizational forms. Last but not least, although the advantages of virtual organizations are immense, they do come with problems. Chief among these is the need for a good technological framework and capable management practices to guarantee communication and synergy in dispersed teams. Earlier research emphasized that creating a virtual R&D infrastructure, particularly within SMEs, is a formidable engineering task and requires careful planning from the part of the top management (Ahmed et al., 2009). Overcoming these challenges is a highest priority for organizations aiming to reach their global potential through virtual collaboration. By focusing on virtual team dynamics and structure, organizations can tap their entire potential, hence leading to enhanced performance in international operations as well as sustained competitive advantage in the ever-evolving global market.

6.3. CULTURAL CONSIDERATIONS IN INTERNATIONAL MANAGEMENT

When handling the complexity of managing across the globe, companies must strategically chart the host countries' cultural spheres to effectively operate. A key point to bear in mind is understanding various cultural dimensions influencing employee conduct and expectations. For multinationals, understanding the diversity of individualism versus collectivism can break or make team unity and project success. In addition, orientations towards authority, uncertainty avoidance, and time orientation may significantly affect managerial practices to necessitate a tailored style of motivation and leadership. Since (Antila et al., 2012) emphasized, heightened sensitivity to such differences between cultures enhances organizational change capacity, which is critical to designing strategies and practices on the basis of local expectations while aligning global operational objectives. This responsive interaction of strategic management and cultural awareness informs the foundations upon which organizations build sustainable competitive advantage in local markets. Furthermore, the organizational structure adopted by internationalizing companies plays a pivotal part in handling cultural challenges successfully. Centralized structures can provide ease of decision-making, but through the expense of forfeiting the responsiveness necessary in heterogenous cultural contexts wherein local sensitivities dominate (Figure 6.5).

Figure 6.5. The Role of culture in international businesses.

Source: https://cdn.prod.website-files.com/6476d5da6421f487199abe68/64ed97bd6b74f784b53cd2b8_p19LLp3vWX5xs3KF4KUpQlSzENj0Ur-nOIDlsi7Ion-qUf58UllDmY0tbRWUZOdJpY2HYck-NuL4uLVL0etV8rqNLpP8uNlSXKRmyD-hhmCraGvAp9dfnj6P3RM3OUml9CqS_oByIsxFWiSt3SXbszg2k.png.

In contrast, decentralized approaches empower local managers to innovate strategies that are relevant to local customs so that there can be increased participation and a deeper trusting relationship with stakeholders. This is in agreement with the sustainable management concepts articulated in Gonzalez et al. (2010), which foreground the role of integrating social and cultural insights into corporate strategy. By promoting a culture of sustainability that values local wisdom and is inclusive, organizations are able to enhance their operational efficiency and reinforce their corporate reputation in an increasingly interdependent global environment. Finally, integration of cultural considerations into strategic management frameworks must be committed to on an ongoing basis to developing a business culture that values diversity as organizational strength. Firms must develop a culture in which employees are made to feel important and encouraged to contribute their diverse perspectives. To this end, an ethical code that guides choice-making must be developed, as well as fostered trust and transparency among stakeholders. Organizational design that supports vertical and horizontal communication, as observed in Gonzalez et al. (2010), plays a vital role in the facilitation of worker involvement and risk-taking. By aligning cultural efforts with the overall strategy, organizations reinforce not only internal dynamics but also their ability to respond to increasing global issues. This approach eventually leads to sustainable long-term economic returns, building a strong and adaptable organization well placed to cope with the complexities of international management.

6.3.1. Understanding Cross-Cultural Communication

Effective communication across cultures is imperative in the new globalized business world, where greater numbers of organizations operate within multi-cultural global environments. As multinational, global, transnational, and international firms seek to take advantage of the differences of cultural contexts, so too they find chances and challenges arising out of the interactions. Understanding the subtleties of cross-cultural communication can influence organizational and strategic behavior in a way that firms can avoid possible misunderstandings arising due to different cultural perspectives. Differences in language, non-verbal communications, and contextual undertones significantly influence what and how project members differing in background are communicating. Thus, business organizations must devise tough strategies addressing these complexities and build a culture of inclusiveness and flexibility in team dynamics. One of the key areas to facilitate greater cross-cultural communication is to grasp the institutional contexts where communication styles and practices are shaped by various countries. It is stated by Van de Voorde et al. (2007) that while there is a realization of variation in human resource practices across different cultural settings, the nature of such differences and their implications may be overstated sometimes. Quite possibly, differences in communication may not be as much about the difference between cultures as about variations in institutions that affect organizational behavior. This perspective highlights that multinational companies must not only adapt their communications activities to specific cultural contexts but also position themselves in the broader institutional networks that govern employee relations and expectations. To this effect, leaders should set cultural intelligence as a core competency in strategic planning so that all levels of the organization are ready to continue productive dialogue amidst pluralistic cultural settings. Further, the congruence between leadership values and societal expectations about culture is also a key consideration in effective cross-cultural communication. According to Mustafa et al. (2015), understanding how leaders' cultural orientations are congruent with values of societies in which they work is essential in establishing effective communication and organizational harmony. Sensitive leaders to these dynamics are more successful in navigating the nuances of cross-cultural interactions and are able to alter their methods of communication to establish cooperation. Training programs that heighten cultural awareness and flexibility are used by organizations to prepare their leaders with closing gaps between differing cultural perspectives. Ultimately, this alignment in value and communication enables organizations to utilize the potential of their diverse labor force toward enhanced overall performance and an innovation culture for international management success.

6.3.2. The Role of Cultural Intelligence in Leadership

With companies navigating the complexities of worldwide landscapes, cultural intelligence becomes increasingly vital. Transnational and multinational company leaders must comprehend and appreciate the complex aspects of cultures that define their employees' dynamics and performance potential. Understanding these is important not just for the sake of inclusivity but also to fill the gap of collaboration across borders. Unless managers are culturally intelligent, they will inadvertently help foster misunderstandings or conflicts that can undermine strategic initiatives. Organizations with cultural intelligence focus are able to leverage multiple perspectives, thus making it simpler for them to face challenges with adaptability and creativity. This shift not only supports good decision-making but also aligns with the overall goal of building high trust and high commitment workplace cultures within multinational organizations, more imperative to the work of cultural intelligence in leadership environments (Marcotte et al., 2019). Furthermore, the role of cultural intelligence goes beyond difference awareness; it encompasses the capacity to adapt leadership styles to address various cultural environments. For global management, this adaptability is crucial. Executives with the ability to recognize and implement locally appropriate strategies are more likely to succeed in decentralized organizational structures where decision authority is dispersed among disparate regions. Such managers not only build trust but foster a culture of respect for diversity of contribution so that the organization is poised to meet local market needs while remaining faithful to worldwide objectives (Figure 6.6).

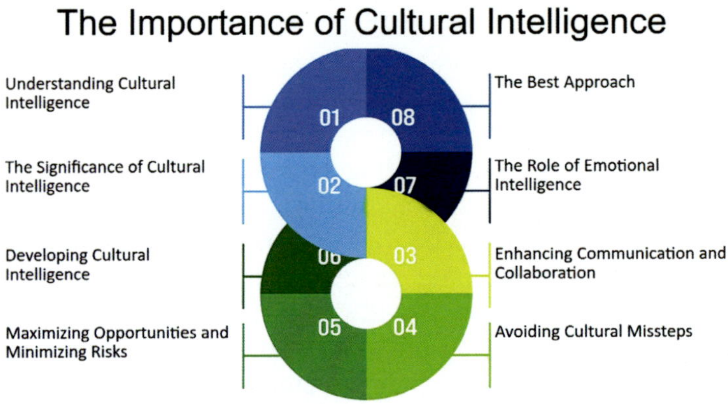

Figure 6.6. Importance of cultural intelligence in leadership.

Source: https://fastercapital.co/i/Cultural-intelligence--Unlocking-the-Power-of-Cultural-Understanding--The-Importance-of-Cultural-Intelligence.webp.

As organizations develop their strategic reactions to advanced environments, leaders possessing expertise in cultural intelligence are better able to maneuver issues of matrix structures and distributed teams with greater facility, thus setting them up for long-term achievement (Caldwell et al., 2017). In addition to boosting operational effectiveness, cultural intelligence plays a central role in shaping organizational culture. Such leaders have a significant contribution to make in designing systems, processes, and practices that are appealing to the diverse workforce. Such alignment creates shared vision, which makes it simple for organizations to fulfill their purpose. As organizations keep developing and increasing their global outreach, the emphasis on human resource professionals increases; they must align HRM practices with culturally astute leadership. This fusion is at the heart of building a high-commitment and engagement culture, which fosters a sense of belonging among a diverse workforce. Focusing on cultural intelligence enables organizations not only to take advantage of the assets of a diverse workforce but also creates a robust platform for collaboration and innovation, hence driving their strategy (Caldwell et al., 2017).

6.3.3. Adapting Organizational Behavior to Local Cultures

The interplay between organizational behavior and the local cultures is essential for multinational companies seeking to achieve effective management within geographically dispersed areas. With globalization, companies find themselves handling other paradigms of culture that impact workers' behaviors, decision-making, and overall workplace environment. In certain cases, for instance, while centralization can ensure easier decision-making, it can contradict the dominance of autonomy and empowerment within the local culture. Local culture adaptation must be done selectively and on a combination of the global strategies with local practices, reminding managers of glocalization significance. As Clegg et al. (2025) argues, the blending allows firms to have high levels of global integration while still embracing the localized nuances that are vital for effective operations. Ultimately, organizational behavior must evolve to fit cultural intricacies that have direct impacts on management practices and employee engagement. Successful adjustment to the local cultures involves not only awareness but also embracement of the unique values and social norms existing in different locations. For multinationals, this means developing and exercising intercultural competence among their leadership and employees. As Antal et al. (2025) articulates it, intercultural competence includes the ability to value and utilize cultural differences as tools for learning and for solving problems. In the real world, this entails training programs that equip workers with the skills to handle cross-cultural communications and build trust within heterogeneous teams. Secondly, adapting organizational culture to fit regional cultures also has the promise of enhancing teamwork, which is an important consideration in fostering a harmonious working atmosphere. Hence, businesses have the obligation to concentrate on building a workforce effective in engaging diverse cultural settings, ultimately culminating in fostering innovation and teamwork globally. The strategic institutionalization of local culture into organizational practices could be very rewarding for competitive markets. Multinationals prefer to pilot decentralized matrix designs that provide flexibility within local markets and synchronization with global commands. This design not only provides local managers with the power to make timely decisions with regional cultural sensitivities but also helps to establish a strong organizational structure. It helps organizations remain sensitive to local customers' preferences and needs, facilitating successful market interaction. Incorporating local culture in organizational behavior by pooling varied perceptions, businesses are able to leverage diverse inputs for improved strategic decision-making. Realizing that seamless adaptation is an ongoing process rather than a discrete one-time modification, organizations must constantly adjust their practices to suit the evolving cultural landscapes within which they operate.

6.4. STRATEGIC PLANNING IN INTERNATIONAL CONTEXTS

The dynamic management paradigm of the globe calls for a subtle approach to strategic planning that is adaptable enough to reflect the dynamics of competition across different cultural and regulatory environments. Firms must balance centralizing and decentralizing, especially in determining decision-making guidelines that suit global objectives as well as meet local market demands. It is challenging for multinational corporations to create an organizational structure that allows for free information flow and responsiveness. Matrix firms and virtual companies are typically found to be best options, which enable firms to leverage resources across borders effectively. However, strategic planning within such settings demands a fundamental understanding of complexities involved in leadership practice that not only affect internal dynamics but also facilitate adaptability in varied external settings (Adams et al., 2010). Thus, embedding local leadership knowledge within general strategic frameworks can help organizations compete successfully on the international platform. As companies move abroad, the tension between global integration and local responsiveness is even more emphasized (Figure 6.7).

Figure 6.7. The dynamic of international management necessitates approach to strategic planning.

Source: https://saylordotorg.github.io/text_international-business/section_14/6d9b318d2663b0805b1fd1268ddd738f.jpg.

For newer thought, the success of multinationals (MNEs) hinges predominantly on whether or not they frame their strategies to fit global mandates versus local quirks. Strategic fit, in its framing in international human resource management, compels firms to conceive relative flexibility within the local environment as a core variable influencing managerial decision-making. This pragmatism allows MNEs to experiment with their internal processes, establishing an environment for innovation and coordinating local practices with corporate-wide strategies. Balancing these tensions is necessary for organizations to leverage their global footprint while being relevant and competitive in independent markets (Bloom et al., 2000). Strategic planning then needs to capture the mandate of a responsive strategy that aligns such diversified pressures, ultimately resulting in sustainable success. Leadership at the global level also calls for critical examination of the manner organizational actors interact with each other trans-territorially. Strategic planning is not simply a question of formulating a vision; it calls for integration of various leadership approaches and practices that communicate well in different clusters or networks. Structuration theory sheds light on the complexities of leadership dynamics in such contexts, positing that regional innovation systems must be tackled with profound knowledge of leadership that considers the ambivalence of individuals who may not want to be led. Cultivating an organizational culture of mutual leadership can assist in bridging such problems, fostering collaboration and innovation in the clusters. By positioning leadership activities strategically in this manner, firms are more apt to tap into local knowledge and ability and thus enhance their ability to achieve long-term strategic targets. With this, the leadership discussion must evolve to aid adaptive and context-aware approaches to global strategic planning (Adams et al., 2010).

6.4.1. Importance of Market Analysis and Research

Market research and analysis are critical for multinational enterprises (MNEs) that need to effectively enter the complexities of international markets. The dynamic nature of globalization necessitates companies to continuously assess the shifting market scenario, consumer behavior, and competitor dynamics. By undertaking comprehensive market studies, firms are able to discover hidden opportunities or imminent threats that will influence their strategic decision-making. This forward-looking process allows MNEs to adjust their products and marketing strategy accordingly, thereby synchronizing with local consumer behavior and expectation. In addition, what is learned from this analysis can be utilized to determine organizational structure, whether decentralization or centralization is applied, to facilitate strategic adaptation to local market requirements and maximize competitive achievement in varying international environments. In addition to facilitating well-informed decision-making, market analysis also facilitates foreign expansion risk management. MNEs must take into account variations in market conditions, regulatory environment, and culture likely to influence their operations outside home countries. As articulated in the triple bottom line (TBL) theory in Fauzi et al. (2013), companies must monitor financial, social, and environmental performance in geographically dispersed environments (Figure 6.8).

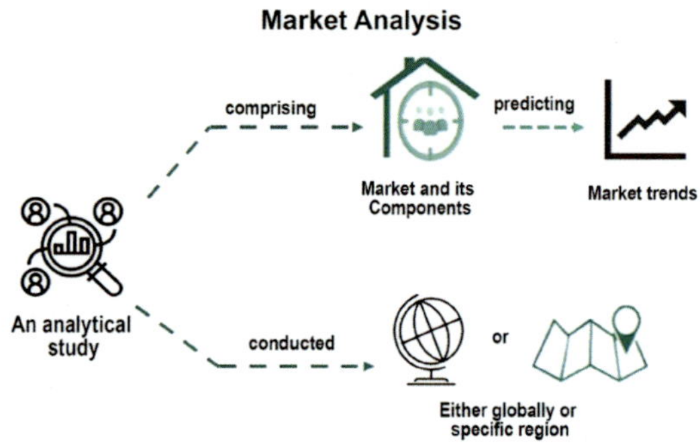

Figure 6.8. The dynamic nature of market analysis.

Source: https://wallstreetmojo-files.s3.ap-south-1.amazonaws.com/2023/02/Market-Analysis.jpg.

Adopting this holistic approach enables business firms to appreciate the interconnectedness of such determinants and align their purposes with the greater aspirations of society, thereby optimizing overall sustainability. Through rigorous market research, MNEs are able to view how these determinants interact and transform one another, allowing them to navigate likely setbacks and capitalize on synergy opportunities strategically. Continuous market studies are also a foundation for innovation and strategic fit within MNEs. Identification of varied needs in target markets is crucial to the tailoring of goods and services that resonate with consumers in different areas. As outlined in the discoveries reported in Bloom et al. (2000), the relationship between globalization and local forces is the basis of managerial decisions, and identification of this relationship is crucial for planning. Through prioritizing market research, businesses are able to promote a culture of experimental pragmatism, whereby managers test hypotheses of market viability and adjust in accordance with consumer responses. This iterative improvement not only enhances product development but also the establishment of appropriate matrix structures or virtual organizations so that all levels of the company react to shifting market forces.

6.4.2. Competitive Strategies for Global Markets

In order to survive the complexities of international markets, businesses are required to adopt various competitive strategies that suit their organizational forms. Multinational, global, transnational, and international firms utilize distinct approaches to conduct businesses across nations. Multinational companies tend to customize their products and marketing approaches according to local preferences, with a focus on decentralization to facilitate regional managers. Conversely, multinational firms attempt to standardize products to facilitate cost efficiencies, thus creating a more centralized configuration. Transnational firms, on the other hand, complicate these divisions since they seek to capitalize on local responsiveness as well as global integration. It is an intriguing terrain that demonstrates how organizational behavior has become inextricably linked with competitive strategies, so that corporations must constantly analyze their structural choices in order to enhance performance in global markets. One of the most important areas of global competitive strategy is a consciousness of how centralized and decentralized power bases affect decision-making and responsiveness.

Centralized organizations may have homogeneous strategies that make operations simpler but may be out of touch with local market variations. Decentralized structures may be able to facilitate flexibility and tailored responses to different customer preferences but may not be able to hold together a single corporate identity. As firms formulate their strategy, matrix arrangements and virtual organizations are becoming increasingly common to balance the advantages of centralized control with local responsiveness. This shift reflects the demand for strategic alignment to achieve competitive advantage, particularly as firms deal with cultural, regulatory, and operating complexities in numerous regions. The wine sector in Portugal exemplifies the need for nuanced competitive strategies informed by a firm's resource capabilities and environmental factors. By analyzing the competitive landscape using models like PEST and Porter's Five Forces, companies can identify crucial strategic guidelines for international expansion. In the wine industry, research has highlighted how businesses must leverage their own resources while adhering to the constantly shifting market propelled by global trends and consumer preferences. This is also what various studies have found to be the case, where robust international orientation is a determinant of export performance. As pointed out by recent research, market dynamism and innovative capacity are some of the drivers that serve as moderators in steering this relationship to a preferred direction, eventually determining competitive strategies that organizations must adopt in order to sustain themselves in the global marketplace environment (Escandón et al., 2017; Sousa et al., 2012).

6.4.3. Risk Management in International Operations

The complexities associated with transnational operations necessitate a good organizational framework for risk management, which remains one of the biggest challenges for transnational and multinational firms. They are likely to be confronted with a series of issues, from geopolitical tensions to differences in regulation, and market volatilities that threaten their operational efficacy. A centralized solution to risk management allows for a universal strategy that can be utilized in various settings, while decentralization offers regional managers the flexibility to respond to regional risks quickly. By compromising between these two approaches, firms optimize their potential to avoid risk while fostering quick decision-making. Moreover, having a matrix organization will enable better communication and collaboration between different departments, thus further supporting the firms ability to sense forthcoming disruptions (Koufteros et al., 2015). Responsiveness and flexibility are crucial needs for organizations that seek to be able to survive in the international market. Since the process involves expanding operations internationally, integration of advanced technology becomes core in the prevention of expected risks. Management control systems, particularly in industries like hospitality, place emphasis on the need to leverage contextual variables like culture, technology, and strategy in constructing such systems. Empirical evidence indicates that sophisticated management control systems are strongly related to contextual variables; firms must adopt an inclusive awareness of local variables while constructing operations in overseas countries (Fauzi et al., 2013). In harmonizing technological abilities with strategic goals, companies are able to leverage data analytics and real-time tracking systems that not only reduce risks but also maximize overall performance. Such an anticipatory strategy enables companies to foresee changes in the environment, in tandem with those changes that are normal within global operations, so that they can continue to be resilient as well as competitive. Moreover, the application of relational governance is significant in international operations risk management. Since organizations deal with various stakeholders like suppliers, customers, and regulatory bodies, fostering strategic relationships can serve as a protection against danger. A healthy relational framework induces trust and coordination that are vital in handling uncertainties of international operations. By emphasizing mutual communication and shared objectives, organizations are able to form a more holistic operations plan that targets not just financial risk but also reputational and operational risk. This holistic approach to risk management understands that creating an interlocking network of strategic alliances deepens the firms resilience so that it is better positioned to deal with rapid changes in global market conditions (Koufteros et al., 2015; Fauzi et al., 2013).

6.5. LEADERSHIP STYLES IN INTERNATIONAL MANAGEMENT

The international management leadership challenges underscore the necessity for leaders to improvise their strategies in order to fit multidisciplinary cultures and organizational levels. Such improvisation is particularly true among multinational companies, where styles of leadership are compelled to manage differences in business practices and cultural norms in various geographies. Empowering leadership, for instance, becomes a necessary paradigm that effectively mobilizes teams composed of multidisciplinary backgrounds. Research indicates that empowering leadership does not only generate psychological empowerment among employees but also enhances self-leadership abilities, particularly in divergent cultural environments, such as Rwanda and America. The power of distance in these environments further supports the necessity for situational leadership approaches, where hierarchies may be subject to different limitations and possibilities for employee engagement (Figure 6.9).

Figure 6.9. The complexities of leadership style within international management.

Source: https://cdn.corporatefinanceinstitute.com/assets/leadership-styles.png.

Consequently, leaders must understand these dynamics in order to create cooperative and effective work cultures in cross-border businesses (Rahschulte et al., 2018). As another dimension outside of the cultural context of leadership, the structural configuration of multinational corporations largely determines the efficacy of various forms of leadership. More specifically, the decision between decentralization and centralization is pivotal. Centralized designs can be aided by standardized strategic direction, but can choke local innovation and sensitivity to the local cultural environment. Decentralized designs permit local managers to exercise more suitable leadership styles that are sensitive to their own particular cultural contexts. The autonomy is not only inspiring leadership styles that acknowledge motivation and empowerment but also improves a culture of accountability. For instance, managers who embrace altruistic models—seeing themselves as agents of employees' welfare—may foster a prosocial organization with high collective performance and decentralization sustainability (Vieweg et al., 2018). Furthermore, growing matrix structures and virtual organizations bring another complexity aspect to international leadership. In such structures, leaders must frequently deal with multiple lines of reporting, suggesting a well-evolved understanding of organizational as well as local culture. The evolving dynamics of such organizations demand a flexible leadership style that could bend according to circumstance and make-up of the team. Virtual organization leaders, in particular, must face the challenge of establishing team cohesion and cooperation in the absence of proximity. With the deployment of technology and open communication channels, leaders can create a sense of belonging and shared purpose among their dispersed global teams. In this regard, adopting an inclusive and empathetic leadership style becomes critical where leaders are not only executives but also mentors and facilitators of collaboration that transcend the limits of traditional organizational structures, impacting overall strategic action in global management settings (Rahschulte et al., 2018).

6.5.1. Transformational Leadership in Multinational Firms

Amidst the diverse surroundings that multinational companies find themselves within, leadership plays an important role in determining organizational performance. Transformational leadership, emphasizing inspiring and motivating employees towards shared visions, is particularly well-suited for such diverse settings. Such leaders will be more likely to practice open communication and facilitate employee participation, enabling more organic organizational development. This flexibility is most important in multinational settings where there are varied work habits and cultural mores. Furthermore, drawing from empirical evidence, transformational leadership positively influences not only the morale of teams but also the overall well-being of the organization, thereby making the organization more resilient to external pressures (Gandolfi, 2025). By maintaining the health and wellbeing of their followers, such leaders can optimize performance across various levels of a multinational corporation, generating sustained competitive advantage. Organizational behavior within multinational corporations directly influences how well their leadership practices work. Transformational leaders particularly can bring the key organizational values that direct the behavior of employees across geographies. Research has demonstrated that the fundamental principles that govern the activities of a company significantly affect how employees and teams in the company act and react (Figure 6.10).

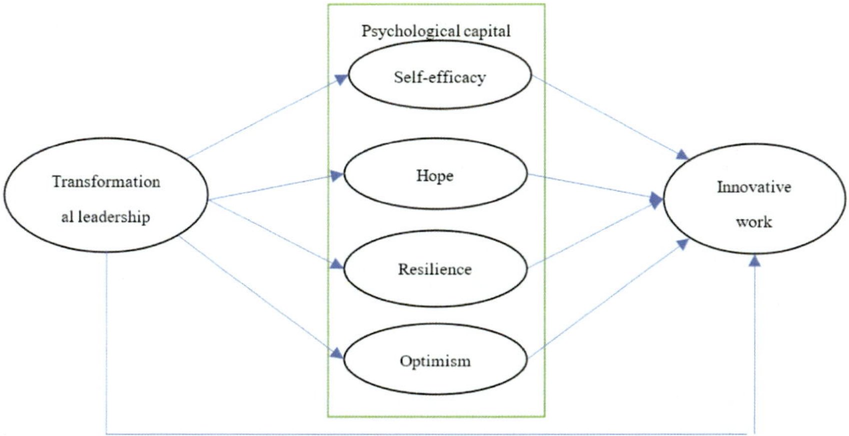

Figure 6.10. The role of transformational leadership in developing innovative work behaviors.

Source: https://www.mdpi.com/sustainability/sustainability-15-01267/article_deploy/html/images/sustainability-15-01267-g001.png.

Particularly in decentralization contexts where local offices possess high levels of autonomy, this core values guide decision-making and establish the organizational culture (Androniceanu, 2025). By offering a robust set of values that are significant to local cultures but also address world challenges, transformational leaders can create a cohesive organizational identity that facilitates collaboration and innovation across boundaries. The integration of transformational leadership into a multinational corporation's framework facilitates increased dynamic strategic action, particularly in balancing centralization and decentralization.

The matrix structures that the majority of international companies subscribe to make the process possible since they accommodate two-way reporting relationships, which facilitate enhanced communication and better coordination of resources. Transformational leaders are central connectors in this framework, which promotes all units to work towards a single vision while observing local diversities. This ability to balance central direction and local action requires a subtle understanding of varied market demands and employee motivations. Transformational leadership, thus, not merely elevates operational performance but also forges an environment of innovation, which is essential to handling the complexities of global management in the contemporary competitive environment.

6.5.2. Transactional Leadership and Its Effectiveness

Through the complexity of international management, organizations are frequently challenged to respond to various leadership styles in a way that effectively empowers different groups. Transactional leadership, characterized by its focus on systematic tasks, rewards, and observation of performance, can be a useful model for multinational and transnational organizations. Creating stability and predictability in high-stress conditions by setting clear expectations and rewarding conformity, this style of leadership can be an effective framework in multinational and transnational organizations. In a transactional leadership framework, the emphasis on immediate results and operating efficiency rings especially true in cultures that place an emphasis on compliance and hierarchies, allowing organizations to be in charge but still leveraging global markets. Transactional leadership is effective in this instance if organizations are consolidating decision-making activities, thus promoting a uniform approach across various branches in various geographic locations. But the challenges of bridging a transition towards a more adaptive form of leadership become apparent in looking at the effect on employee empowerment and engagement across cultures. While transactional leadership may be useful in the short term, it would lack the emotional commitment and intrinsic motivation necessary for long-term commitment and innovation. Empowerment was seen to play a mediating role in the impact of a number of leadership approaches on organizational commitment, suggesting that reliance solely on transactional approaches may crush potential (Ismail et al., 2025). As multinational organizations work to grasp the intricacies of decentralized operations and matrix management, the limitations of transactional leadership may be limiting their ability to leverage the full potential of employees, particularly in multicultural settings. In an attempt to effectively deal with the emerging environment of global management, organizations must realize the significance of adopting leadership styles that embrace differences at the cultural and individual level. Empowering leadership, for example, has been found to have far-reaching positive effects on psychological empowerment and self-leadership, activating employees' internal motivations and instilling a badge of autonomy (Rahschulte et al., 2018). Unlike transactional styles, in which individual development is a secondary concern to trigger results, empowering leadership is more aligned with collectivist cultures' values, with an encouragement of a supporting culture even in high-power distance societies.

Consequently, given the growth of businesses across global markets, strategic injection of empowering leadership behaviors will not only enhance employee morale but also allow organizations to remain sensitive to culture, ultimately ensuring sustainable growth and efficacy in global markets.

6.5.3. Situational Leadership in Diverse Environments

With a more interconnected global world, organizations face both challenges and opportunities with a workforce diversity. Diversity in culture, values, and perspectives can significantly influence leadership styles. Multinational and international company leaders must cope with situational approaches to leadership that are adaptable across contexts and individual needs. Adaptability plays a key role in building positive interpersonal relations and a good team working environment. By situationally adjusting their leadership styles, managers can create team cohesion and performance, with workforce motivations in alignment with organizational goals. Notably, high organizational performance is linked with successful management of diversity, but this only occurs with reflective thought and respect for various contributions within teams (Karma et al., 2025). Hence, it is critical for leaders who are seeking strategic success within global management to understand the situational interdependency of leadership and employee diversity (Figure 6.11).

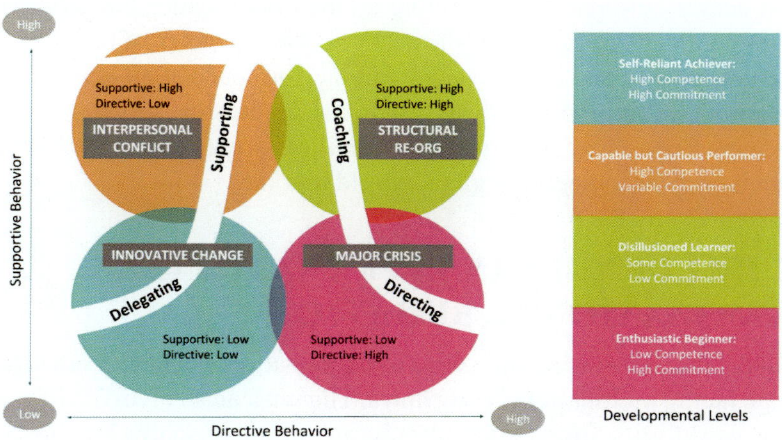

Figure 6.11. Situational leadership and workforce diversity in international management.

Source: https://guntergroup.com/wp-content/uploads/2019/10/Situational-Leadership-2-1.png.

Moreover, situational leadership needs to have a keen awareness of cultural intelligence that is a vital component to navigate multicultural environments. Cultural intelligence helps leaders appreciate and understand various customs and practices of different cultures and also directly determines their effectiveness as leaders. Leaders need to shift their styles based on the unique dynamics of people from other backgrounds in multicultural teams. This tailored approach not only enables resolution of conflict but also enhances global competency for employees. According to studies, diversity management in teams has become one of the top areas of research, with the contention that leaders must learn the ability to build inclusiveness in their organizations (Nishii et al., 2007). Therefore, successful leaders who utilize cultural intelligence are able to establish settings in which multiple worldviews can coexist, ultimately facilitating greater strategic returns in international business operations. Incorporating these concepts into organizational policy is highly advantageous for both employees and leaders. Implementing matrix and virtual organization structures permits greater flexibility in communication and collaboration across geographical space, making it easier for leaders to practice situational leadership on an increased scale. Centralizing certain strategic decisions and decentralizing others makes room for sensitivity to local market needs, thus an appropriate balance of global integration and adaptation. Such strategic flexibility is also essential in addressing mixed employee needs and expectations that might be material across cultures. Implementing a situational leadership model in such organizational designs facilitates the best possible guidance of teams by leaders through complexity and change, achieving performance at all levels within the organization. Lastly, the blend of situational leadership and robust diversity management makes way for a robust and resilient organizational culture needed to thrive in todays competitive global world market.

6.6. CHALLENGES IN INTERNATIONAL ORGANIZATIONAL BEHAVIOR

Globalizing the dynamic relationships of organizational behavior is a significant challenge facing multinational companies. The intricacies involved in managing different workforces from different cultural settings usually lead to conflicts and misunderstanding, particularly when integrating workers of different backgrounds. For instance, multinational companies must fine-tune the balancing between centralization and decentralization to create a healthy organizational structure. A hub-and-spoke decision-making approach might propel processes and insure consistency in corporate strategy but disconnect regional managers who better understand local intricacies. Decentralization, in contrast, empowers regional leaders to respond better to unique market dynamics but can result in isolated corporate objectives. Creating harmony among these structures requires subtle awareness of cultural forces and therefore the decision-making process for international managers who desire strategic consensus and organizational cohesion to be a challenge. Organizational behavior and structure have a strong bearing on the functionality of global firms. The utilization of matrix and virtual organizational forms has gained popularity in the dynamic global business arena, but these forms are fraught with built-in complications. Matrix structures, where functional and project-based approaches are combined, can lead to confusion and uncertainty regarding reporting relationships and accountability. There is potential for employees to face conflicting priorities from dual managers, which may decrease productivity and morale. Similarly, virtual organizations, where technology is used to link geographically dispersed teams, can add to issues related to trust, communication, and teamwork (Figure 6.12).

Figure 6.12. Challenges and opportunities of organizational behavior.

Source: https://www.theknowledgeacademy.com/_files/images/Challenges_and_Opportunities_of_Organisational_Behaviour_6.png.

Ensuring team members align with organizational goals is critical but requires robust communication processes and tools. With increasing openness of organizations towards such unorthodox structures, understanding their impact on employee behavior and organizational performance is crucial in addressing challenges posed in global settings. A thorough analysis of talent management across global organizations poses more challenges driven by varying cultural needs and practices. The progressive principle of Talentship, as advocated by Boudreau and Ramstad, emphasizes a human resource management-talent development-sustainable organizational success strategic linking (Boudreau et al., 2003). It addresses the aspirations of organizations aiming to capture and retain the best talent in competitive global environments. Challenges to implementation can encompass conflicting perceptions of leadership and talent across societies. In addition, the integration of sustainability into talent management, while visionary in character, would require a mindset change that might not be uniform across and embraced universally. Realizing the unique challenges that face global businesses, such as the need for constant adjustment and alignment of talent actions with overall corporate aims, becomes more critical for leaders in today's complex global landscape (Mohanty et al., 2007).

6.6.1. Managing Diversity and Inclusion

As the economy becomes more globalized, businesses are compelled to navigate the challenges that come with having a global workforce. The existence of multinational and transnational businesses highlights the significance of strategies for managing diversity and inclusivity. The success of a company also depends not merely on how it can survive in markets but on how it can leverage the different mindsets and experiences of its employees. This emphasis on diversity works to underscore the importance of adopting inclusive practices, which can facilitate innovative solutions and enhance decision-making. The integration of a diversified workforce unlocks access to a more vibrant company culture, again enhancing employee satisfaction and retention. An innovative approach towards managing diversity allows businesses to build cultures where differences are appreciated, leading to improved overall performance and global competitive advantage. Effective diversity and inclusion management needs profound knowledge of organizational design. Decentralization versus centralization often decides how diversity programs are implemented in different levels of an enterprise. Decentralized design could offer greater flexibility and immediate response to local cultural idiosyncrasies, which can lead to a culture of inclusion unique to regional needs. Then again, centralized approaches may struggle to deal with the unique challenges posed by diverse employees, particularly in global settings where a single policy may alienate certain groups. A matrix can strike a balance between cooperation across departments and preserving that diversity and inclusion efforts are supplementary to the firm's strategic goals. Knowledge of the implications of these frameworks is critical for implementing successful diversity management in line with international business objectives. Research attention has increasingly come to be directed towards the theory of inclusion as core to organizational diversity management. Studies confirm that the creation of inclusive environments not only facilitates a diverse workforce, but also enhances organizational effectiveness overall. The inclusion literature provides various areas of emphasis, from leadership to organizational practice and climate, and all of which are part of a better comprehension of what is happening. Through stitching these pieces together, firms can develop models for inclusion that are attuned to challenges within and outside the firm. It is an integrated understanding that must be brought to bear in order to produce an inclusive workplace that will ultimately pay returns in terms of better innovation and flexibility in global management. As organizations continue to grapple with the complexities of multidisciplinary settings, maximizing the performance of all staff through tailored inclusion plans will continue to be an essential aspect of organizational strategic behavior in the future (Dimitratos et al., 2017; Cleveland et al., 2018).

6.6.2. Navigating Legal and Ethical Issues

In contemporary global management, businesses must navigate the treacherous landscape of legal and moral problems that arise in a diverse array of work environments. Multinational firms often deal with distinct legal frameworks, regulatory frameworks, and cultural protocols in the markets where they operate. This renders compliance an ongoing endeavor which greatly influences strategic action and firm performance. Therefore, familiarity with local law, say employment law or environmental law, is not an issue of legal compliance alone, but a strategic necessity that can enhance a firms reputation and market standing. By harmonizing activities with legal needs and ethical standards, organizations can establish trust and credibility with stakeholders, which is instrumental to success in the long run in international markets. Also, the ethical issue at times transcends law, and organizations have to also weigh their policies and practices against more general moral imperatives. A decentralized system can enable the establishment of a more responsive organization culture whereby the local managers are empowered to make decisions in accordance with local beliefs and corporate values. This is in line with the belief that relationship-building is a must in international management. As stated, "beyond rules, procedures, and manuals lie relationships," highlighting the importance of empathy in creating an organizational purpose (Holt et al., 2017). Hence, ethical problems may necessitate that organizational forms be reconsidered, particularly in matrix or virtual organizations, where various perspectives can lead to more ethical decision-making processes and construct one global strategy. Accurate navigation of such legal and ethical frameworks further supports an organization's adherence to accountability and transparency. For instance, in the not-for-profit sector, some organizations voluntarily disclose more than is required by statute, an attitude which demonstrates a stakeholder relations and ethical transparency commitment (Donleavy et al., 2014). This kind of strategic move maximizes their legitimacy and stakeholder trust, illustrating the advantages of proactive disclosures. At the global management level, these practices may be pivotal in building organizational culture based on ethical integrity. By investing in practices that are more than mere compliance, organizations can build a competitive advantage founded on their credibility for governance and ultimately gain long-term organizational success in the global market.

6.6.3. Addressing Communication Barriers Across Borders

Communication is vital for international companies in the pursuit to navigate the complex nature of global management. Central to this challenge is the recognition of communication barriers as a force that can successfully inhibit organizational performance and strategic action. As companies venture into cross-border operations, cultural and linguistic differences emerge as critical issues in communication processes. These issues necessitate that organizations adopt creativity measures to integrate diverse groups of employees towards congruence.

Figure 6.13. The transition of communication practices in multinational firms.

Source: https://thegoodista.com/wp-content/uploads/2015/02/Communication-Barriers.jpg.

Through the incorporation of communication practices that recognize and accept cultural subtleties, businesses are able to include people and further improve collaborative efforts. In addition, reviewing the performance of communication measurement and evaluation programs, as noted in Anderson et al. (2018), illustrates how aligning communication with organizational goals strategically can foster overall effectiveness internationally. Consequently, surmounting such impediments not only enhances daily communication but also forms a central determinant of long-term organizational success. The culturalization of communication norms within multinationals tends to encounter resistance as a result of deep-seated underlying local traditions and issues concerning change. As illustrated from the findings presented in Vlachoutsicos et al. (1999), stakeholders tend to be concerned with loss of employment security, control, and status in the event of organizational change (Figure 6.13).

Thus, strategic focus on such internal hindrances is required for effective cross-border communication. Local culture values must be considered and an effort should be made to implement the existing frameworks of managerial behavior in order to make more effective application of communication strategies. Thus, global corporations can create an environment that will facilitate trust building and collaboration among employees, thereby reducing resistance to change. This approach facilitates the application of the superior practices of local customs and moving to new market-based management practices more smoothly, resulting in better communication. In dealing with the complexities of global business, decentralization of communications planning can facilitate easier adaptability to change and flexibility. This approach allows for local managers and local teams to be empowered and for a culture to be developed where communications are attuned to regional sensitivities and contexts. Decentralizing a company creates a culture of responsibility where decisions are taken with empowered authority, thus facilitating quicker responses to local market trends. Additionally, effective networks of communication are essential under a matrix organization where teams across geographies must collaborate seamlessly. Through promoting a harmonized structure of communication in organizational setups such as these, companies are in a position to overcome obstacles highlighted in previous debates regarding transitional issues. Lastly, building communications practices through consideration of the importance of centralization or decentralization can pave the way to strategic agility and improved performance in a global competitive context.

SUMMARY

In contemporary global management, organizations are faced with complex issues that call for a refined understanding of strategic action and organizational form. Companies that fall under the categories of multinational, global, transnational, or international must effectively operate across several markets as well as cultural environments. Effectiveness in these companies relies on their ability to bridge their strategic objectives with operational frameworks, such as centralization and decentralization. Centralized schemes can promote consistency and efficient decision-making but squelch local responsiveness.

Decentralization, on the other hand, supports greater flexibility to local markets but creates coordination issues. It is therefore crucial for businesses attempting to optimize their global competitive advantage to establish the right balance between these strategies. This dynamic tension between structure and strategy is most prominent for global organizations attempting to achieve organizational excellence. Further, the intricacies of virtual organizations and matrix structures emphasize the fluidity of global management. Matrix structures facilitate collaboration among geographic locations and functions and support adaptability and sensitivity to host country environments. However, these structures induce ambiguity of role and responsibility and promote potential conflict. Virtual organizations, on the other hand, use technology to create effective channels of interaction regardless of geographical distances. This approach not only enhances operational efficiency but also fosters innovation from interdependencies among heterogeneous groups. Over-reliance on technology may still prove difficult in maintaining organizational culture and harmony. By strategic evaluation of these forms of organizations, international management practitioners can develop plans that build on strengths while counteracting built-in disadvantages. In conclusion, effective management of organizational and strategic conduct in the global environment requires a wide knowledge of different operating environments and their implications. The integration of economic and management knowledge enables organizations to handle the complexities of global environments more effectively and with greater efficiency. As cited, the convergence of these disciplines not only assists in finding solutions to issues related to resource distribution and market power but also facilitates better managerial decision-making. Utilizing the ideas obtained from these interdisciplinary studies, managers are able to create innovative solutions to enhance organizational performance and thus facilitate sustainable growth. Thus, embracing a holistic approach that considers both the nuances of strategy and organizational behavior norms is crucial to succeed in the discipline of international management (John et al., 2020; N/A, 2020).

The complexities that are associated with organizational designs have a significant influence on strategic behavior in the context of international management. Different firm types such as multinational, global, transnational, and international firms exhibit differential organizational design and management of staff. These structures suggest centralization or decentralization levels, which have the potential to decide decision-making processes and operational efficiency. For instance, decentralized firms are prevalent in multinational corporations that have the ability to respond rapidly to local market demands, whereas global firms may prefer centralization for maintaining control and monitoring uniformity by region. Such flexibility is crucial for companies seeking success in competitive global economies, thus placing a premium on strategic congruence between organizational structure and international operating modalities. Enduring the forces of global markets requires firms to employ innovative organizational designs, such as matrix organizations and virtual organizations. Matrix organizations assist in ensuring flexibility and cooperation through the ability of workers to report to two or more managers, hence enhancing cross-functional collaboration that is essential in a global environment. Alternatively, virtual organizations enable firms to reach beyond geographic boundaries of talent, hence leveraging resources and reducing operating costs. Such structures become more vital as they allow companies to quickly respond to market trends and technological developments, leading to a more responsive reaction to global competition. The organizational structure, thus, not only affects operational efficiency but also determines the way companies react strategically to external pressures. Talent management and knowledge measurement integration becomes a central theme in developing strategic behavior in international organizations. As the future of Human Resource Management unfolds, the Talentship notion brings focus on the imperative for a disciplined approach in leveraging human resources as is found in finance and marketing decision sciences (Boudreau et al., 2002). In addition, calling knowledge and intellectual capital most valuable assets brings to light the significance of strong knowledge management processes that drive organizational and individual performance. By focusing on knowledge metrics in organizations and teams, leaders are able to unlock talent pools essential to maintaining competitive advantage (Boudreau et al., 2002). This convergence of strategic behavior knowledge and resource management serves to underscore the importance of matching organizational capabilities to global challenges, thereby achieving long-term success in international management.

REFERENCES

1. Adams, R., Alvesson, M., Antonelli, C., Asheim, B., Balkundi, P., Barden, J., Barley, S., et al. (2010). A silent cry for leadership: Organizing for leading (in) clusters. https://core.ac.uk/download/9030719.pdf (accessed on 24th September 2025).
2. Ahmed, S., Ale Ebrahim, N., & Taha, Z. (2009). Virtual R&D teams in small and medium enterprises: A literature review. https://core.ac.uk/download/pdf/332902.pdf (accessed on 24th September 2025).
3. Ahmed, S., Ale Ebrahim, N., & Taha, Z. (2010). SMEs; Virtual research and development (R&D) teams and new product development: A literature review. https://core.ac.uk/download/pdf/107707.pdf (accessed on 24th September 2025).
4. Alarik, B. (2025). From M-form to N-form: The structure of multinational corporations. https://core.ac.uk/download/pdf/7281164.pdf (accessed on 24th September 2025).
5. Anderson, F. W., Gilkerson, N., Likely, F., Swenson, R., et al. (2018). Insights from industry leaders: A maturity model for strengthening communication measurement and evaluation. https://core.ac.uk/download/231843468.pdf (accessed on 24th September 2025).
6. Androniceanu, A. (2025). Organizational behavior in the knowledge-based society: Practical research in the Romanian business environment. https://core.ac.uk/download/pdf/6538836.pdf (accessed on 24th September 2025).
7. Antal, A. B., & Friedman, V. (2025). Negotiating reality as an approach to intercultural competence. https://core.ac.uk/download/pdf/6653866.pdf (accessed on 24th September 2025).
8. Antila, E., Armenakis, A., Aycan, Z., Bach, S., Barney, J., Becker, B., Bowen, D., et al. (2012). HRM, organizational capacity for change, and performance: A global perspective. https://core.ac.uk/download/30634792.pdf (accessed on 24th September 2025).
9. Barden, J. Q., Doanh, L. D., & Lyles, M. A. (2000). Trust, organizational controls, knowledge acquisition from the foreign parents, and performance in Vietnamese international joint ventures. http://www.wdi.umich.edu/files/Publications/WorkingPapers/wp329.pdf (accessed on 24th September 2025).
10. Bloom, M., Milkovich, G. T., & Mitra, A. (2000). Toward a model of international compensation and rewards: Learning from how managers respond to variations in local host contexts. https://core.ac.uk/download/5131305.pdf (accessed on 24th September 2025).

11. Botin Gonzalez, J. A., & de Palacios, M. (2010). Sustainable management: A strategic challenge for a global minerals and metals industry. http://oa.upm.es/7603/ (accessed on 24th September 2025).
12. Boudreau, J. W. (2002). Strategic knowledge measurement and management. https://core.ac.uk/download/5118424.pdf (accessed on 24th September 2025).
13. Boudreau, J. W., & Ramstad, P. M. (2002). Strategic HRM measurement in the 21st century: From justifying HR to strategic talent leadership. https://core.ac.uk/download/5131515.pdf (accessed on 24th September 2025).
14. Bustinza, O., Lafuente González, E. M., Rabetino, R., Vaillant, Y., et al. (2019). Make-or-buy configurational approaches in product-service ecosystems and performance. https://core.ac.uk/download/187768760.pdf (accessed on 24th September 2025).
15. Caldwell, C. (2017). Understanding kindness–A moral duty of human resource leaders. https://core.ac.uk/download/144553716.pdf (accessed on 24th September 2025).
16. Castelli, P. A., & Ghanem, K. A. (2019). Accountability and moral competence promote ethical leadership. https://core.ac.uk/download/216809967.pdf (accessed on 24th September 2025).
17. Clegg, S. R., da Cunha, J. V., & Cunha, M. P. e. (2025). Structuring for glocalization: The minimal network. https://core.ac.uk/download/pdf/6776120.pdf (accessed on 24th September 2025).
18. Cleveland, J. N., Sanchez, D., & Shore, L. (2018). Inclusive workplaces: A review and model. https://core.ac.uk/download/288817598.pdf (accessed on 24th September 2025).
19. De Cieri, H., Cox, J. W., & Fenwick, M. (1998). Representing strategic international human resource management: Is the map the territory? https://core.ac.uk/download/5124432.pdf (accessed on 24th September 2025).
20. Dimitratos, P., Kuivalainen, O., & Reuber, A. R. (2017). Beyond categorization: New directions for theory development about entrepreneurial internationalization. https://core.ac.uk/download/77601465.pdf (accessed on 24th September 2025).
21. Doherty, L., Gannon, J., & Roper, A. (2012). The role of strategic groups in understanding strategic human resource management. https://core.ac.uk/download/46597458.pdf (accessed on 24th September 2025).
22. Donleavy, G., & Ghoorah-Hurrychurn, U. (2014). Third sector accounting and accountability in Australia: Anything but a level playing field. https://

core.ac.uk/download/pdf/30672758.pdf (accessed on 24th September 2025).

23. Dykes, B. J., Ferrier, W. J., Hughes-Morgan, M., Kolev, K., et al. (2019). Organizational speed as a dynamic capability: Toward a holistic perspective. https://core.ac.uk/download/231843485.pdf (accessed on 24th September 2025).
24. Escandón Barbosa, D. M., Hernández Espallardo, M., Rodríguez, A., Rondán Cataluña, F. J., et al. (2017). International orientation and export performance: Exploring the moderating effect of innovative capacity, market dynamism, and a favorable business environment. https://core.ac.uk/download/161253997.pdf (accessed on 24th September 2025).
25. Fauzi, H. (2013). The performance implications of fit among environment, strategy, structure, control system and social performance. https://core.ac.uk/download/12345566.pdf (accessed on 24th September 2025).
26. Gandolfi, F. (2025). The impact of leadership on health–A preliminary discussion. https://core.ac.uk/download/pdf/6314806.pdf (accessed on 24th September 2025).
27. Gannon, M. J., & Newman, K. L. (2017). The Blackwell Handbook of Cross-Cultural Management. Wiley eBooks. https://doi.org/10.1002/9781405164030 (accessed on 24th September 2025).
28. Glock, C., & Hochrein, S. (2025). Purchasing organization and design: A literature review. https://core.ac.uk/download/pdf/6783738.pdf (accessed on 24th September 2025).
29. Holt, S., Hu, J., Marques, J., Wood, G., et al. (2017). Cultivating empathy: New perspectives on educating business leaders. https://core.ac.uk/download/144553128.pdf (accessed on 24th September 2025).
30. Ismail, A., & Yusuf, M. H. (2025). The relationship between transformational leadership, empowerment and organizational commitment: A mediating model testing. https://core.ac.uk/download/pdf/6273901.pdf (accessed on 24th September 2025).
31. Kang, Y., Liu, Y., Mi, L., Shao, J., et al. (2020). Strategic asset seeking and innovation performance: The role of innovation capabilities and host country institutions. https://core.ac.uk/download/322968499.pdf (accessed on 24th September 2025).
32. Karma, K., & Vedina, R. (2025). Cultural intelligence as a prism between workforce diversity and performance in a modern organization. https://core.ac.uk/download/pdf/6314774.pdf (accessed on 24th September 2025).

33. Koufteros, X., Dabic, M., Gonzalez-Loureiro, M., Saenz, M. J., & Kiessling, T. (2015). Supply chain management as the key to a firm's strategy in the global marketplace. https://core.ac.uk/download/30650361.pdf (accessed on 24th September 2025).
34. Lewis, J. L., Stricklin, W. D., & Schroeder, B. L. (2020). Economics and management. https://doi.org/10.31483/a-166 (accessed on 24th September 2025).
35. Marcotte, D., Rustambekov, E., & Trendowski, J. (2019). Importance of cultural intelligence: Cross-cultural examination and analysis. https://core.ac.uk/download/231818803.pdf (accessed on 24th September 2025).
36. Mohanty, J., & Brown, L. D. (2007). Civil society legitimacy and accountability: Issues and challenges. https://core.ac.uk/download/71340791.pdf (accessed on 24th September 2025).
37. Mustafa, G. (2015). The emergence of leader-society value congruence: A cross-cultural perspective. https://core.ac.uk/download/144552158.pdf (accessed on 24th September 2025).
38. Nishii, L. H., & Özbilgin, M. F. (2007). Global diversity management: Towards a conceptual framework. https://core.ac.uk/download/219376625.pdf (accessed on 24th September 2025).
39. Petricevic, O., & Verbeke, A. (2019). Unbundling dynamic capabilities for inter-organizational collaboration. https://core.ac.uk/download/323052643.pdf (accessed on 24th September 2025).
40. Rahschulte, T., & Thomas, D. (2018). The moderating effects of power distance and individualism/collectivism on empowering leadership, psychological empowerment, and self-leadership in international development organizations. https://digitalcommons.georgefox.edu/cgi/viewcontent.cgi?article=1098&context=gfsb (accessed on 24th September 2025).
41. Rajagopal. (2025). Orchestration of the marketing strategy under competitive dynamics. https://core.ac.uk/download/pdf/6262521.pdf (accessed on 24th September 2025).
42. Schjelderup, G., Raimondos-Møller, P., & Nielsen, S. B. (2025). Centralized vs. de-centralized multinationals and taxes. https://core.ac.uk/download/pdf/6634263.pdf (accessed on 24th September 2025).
43. Shankar, V., & Carpenter, G. S. (2012). Handbook of Marketing Strategy. Edward Elgar Publishing eBooks. https://doi.org/10.4337/9781781005224 (accessed on 24th September 2025).
44. Snell, S. A., & Wright, P. M. (1997). Toward a unifying framework for exploring fit and flexibility in strategic human resource management.

https://core.ac.uk/download/5132398.pdf (accessed on 24th September 2025).

45. Sousa, A., & Vivas, C. (2012). Internationalization strategies of companies in the wine industry in Portugal–Context, forms of action and performance. https://core.ac.uk/download/62455439.pdf (accessed on 24th September 2025).
46. Van de Voorde, K., & Wright, P. M. (2007). Multi-level issues in international HRM: Mean differences, explained variance, and moderated relationships. https://core.ac.uk/download/5121553.pdf (accessed on 24th September 2025).
47. Vieweg, J. C. (2018). Prosocial behaviors: Their motivations and impacts on organizational culture. https://core.ac.uk/download/216808919.pdf (accessed on 24th September 2025).
48. Vlachoutsicos, C. (1999). Internal barriers in the transition of enterprises from central plan to market. http://www.wdi.umich.edu/files/Publications/WorkingPapers/wp248.pdf (accessed on 24th September 2025).

Chapter 7

Decision-Making in International Management

Contents

INTRODUCTION

In global management, decision-making is part of the complex balancing act between rationality and intuition that is greatly conditioned by cultural realities. The rational process tends to emphasize systematic approaches and evidence-based analysis, whereby managers are able to analyze alternatives and possibilities systematically. Intuitive decision-making is founded on instincts and personal experience, and this tends to come up with quick answers in volatile situations. The co-existence of the two paradigms reflects the necessity for managers to modify their decision-making styles, balancing analysis and intuition. Since global managers must operate in several cultures, it is essential to understand how these styles work out under varying circumstances. Research shows that rational decision-making will prevail in more individualistic cultures while intuitive approaches will be predominant in collectivist cultures, thus the need to possess an advanced understanding of such determinants in global settings (Marsh et al., 2025). Perception of risk is also crucial in shaping decision-making across cultures. The manner in which cultures perceive risk can lead to highly different reactions from managers, affecting strategic decisions in global settings. For instance, highly uncertainty-avoidant cultures may prefer very detailed risk analysis and long planning, whereas cautiously avoiding risks in decision-making. On the contrary, low uncertainty-avoidant cultures may be relatively risk tolerant and tend to be more opportunistic and adaptive in management. Such differing perspectives can have a significant impact on overseas businesses operating abroad as they must navigate various local perceptions of risk in their decision-making. An understanding of these cultural dimensions will enable international managers to fashion their strategies appropriately, allowing for effective decision-making in multicultural environments (Marsh et al., 2025). Apart from individual decision-making patterns, the group decision dynamics within multicultural teams present another layer of complexity in managing globally. The combination of viewpoints can generate innovation and creativity but may give rise to conflicts and misunderstandings unless managed effectively. Successful global managers must build a culture that encourages open communication and collaboration so that team members will be able to share their ideas and experiences. Encouraging diversity and respecting diverse viewpoints actually enhances decision-making outcomes by taking advantage of the strength of a multicultural team. By proper handling of these group dynamics and harnessing the unique talents of each member, managers can achieve decisions that are holistic and wise and comprise a multitude of cultural frames and thus ensure global market success.

Definition of Decision-Making in the Context of International Management

In the dynamic world of international management, the subtlety of decision-making is underscored through the conflict between rational and intuitive paradigms. Rational decision-making through systematic analysis and evidence-driven conclusions is juxtaposed with intuitive decision-making through intuitions and impressions based on cultural settings. International managers must navigate these paradigms skillfully and recognize the realization that excess reliance on either could lead to suboptimal decisions. For instance, in group harmony-oriented societies, intuitive processes would be more highly attuned within group functioning to facilitate group consensus-derived outcomes. Where the linear mind is prioritized, however, a rational process might give better attention and precision to decision-making. Thus, the balance between these methods is key to international managers' success, as they work to optimize each approach's strengths to thrive in different international markets. Risk perception is a critical element that significantly contributes to international management decision-making because of the differential nature of uncertainty attitudes between cultures. Different cultures have different perceptions of risk, where some view it as a challenge to development and others view it as a threat (Figure 7.1).

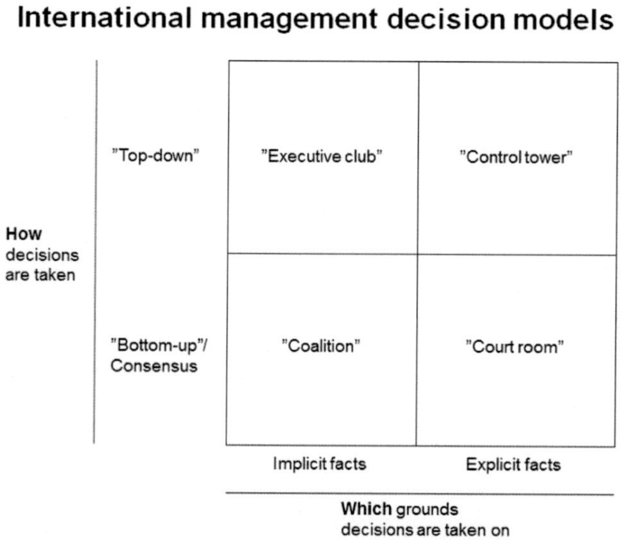

Figure 7.1. The intricacies of decision-model for international management.

Source: https://oleto.com/media/1307/makedecisions.jpg.

This divergence necessitates the need for managers to make a comprehensive review of the dimensions of culture that affect the assessment of risk within their respective teams. With the application of ideas both locally and internationally, managers are able to make decisions that consider these differences in terms of how risk is tolerated. The blending of different perspectives in the evaluation of risks can thus enhance the effectiveness of decisions, allowing for richer knowledge of market forces and operating circumstances for areas. Such sharp awareness helps multinational companies position their strategies appropriately and establish competitive advantages within diverse environments. International management through group decision-making has a tendency to absorb the problems presented by cultural diversity within groups. Collaborative teams demand sensitivity to diverse communication styles, conflict resolution styles, and decision-making processes that are culturally present. Through the creation of an inclusive climate, leaders can tap into the rich collection of understandings generated from a multicultural team and improve the overall decision-making process. For instance, applying methodically devised instruments like decision maps, as outlined in Chakhar et al. (2005), helps team members notice shared objectives and personal interests, facilitating negotiation and concertation among stakeholders. Such instruments promote effective communication and exchange, ensuring every voice is heard and considered. Last but not least, by embracing diversity strengths, managers are able to solidify their decision-making methods, leading to innovative solutions that enhance a firm's fortunes in global markets.

Importance of Effective Decision-Making in Global Business

While one is skilled through the complexity of global business, efficient decision-making is a key skill that can make or break an organization's ultimate triumph. It becomes particularly clear in viewing different decision-making models, such as rational versus intuitive models. Rational decision-making, based on systematic analysis and evaluation of data, is generally preferred within orderly settings but can fail in changing and uncertain situations where instinct, stemming from experience and intuition, can provide a more adaptive reaction. The pairing of both techniques, however, allows managers to mold themselves to fit changing situations in order to be able to make decisions on the basis of facts as well as deep local environment knowledge, ultimately resulting in a stronger organizational strategy. International management is greatly dependent upon the use of both mechanisms, for it means that decisions with astronomically high stakes need to be made, affecting market position and business performance. Risk perception is another key factor that plays a significant role in influencing decision-making within cross-cultural business settings. The concept of risk may vary significantly across cultures, and this has a bearing on the manner in which organizations formulate their strategic plans. Uncertainty-avoidant cultures, for instance, may be highly risk-sensitive and exhibit more cautious decision-making approaches. Risk-taking cultures, on the other hand, may pursue more innovative approaches, viewing uncertainty as a means of growth. Thus, it is imperative for managers who are responsible for making decisions that comply with the organizations values and the desired expectations of the diverse constituents. Communication and cultural competency are vital here since they facilitate leaders to create decisions that resonate across different cultural environments, create collaboration as well as alignment between global teams (Marcotte et al., 2019). International organization member heterogeneity tends to naturally impact group decision-making processes. The heterogeneity in groups can enrich discussions by offering innovative ideas and well-balanced decisions. However, the same heterogeneity is also a source of issues like miscommunication and conflict because of diverging backgrounds. To manage these issues, managers must rise above them by fostering an environment where every member's contribution is valued while establishing definite decision-making processes that result in consensus. It is essential to create shared visions among employees, particularly in matrix organizations that require collaboration by function and geographically. Employing the value of diversity in group decision-making, corporations will be able to construct more responsive strategies, leading eventually to improved performance in the g`lobal market. The application of models that combine strategy with talent management can continue to empower global leaders to develop good teams, stretching for greatest leverage into international pools of talent (Boudreau et al., 2002).

7.1. RATIONAL VS. INTUITIVE APPROACHES

Global management decision-making necessitates the advanced understanding of how rational and intuitive approaches function in practice. Rational decision-making is characterized by controlled consideration, such as the gathering of information, assessment of options, and a conscious choice arrived at through reasoning. The model functions optimally in cases of extensive information and much at stake since it allows managers to minimize risks through the use of measurable evidence. On the other hand, intuitive decision-making is heuristically or instinctively based, and although these can be helpful in uncertain or time-constrained situations, they will not likely be optimal. As managers navigate dynamic global markets, having the capacity to switch between these modes of decision-making can contribute to their strategic power by allowing both deliberative analysis and speed in responding to unexpected crises. Understanding differences in risk perception across cultures is crucial in deciding whether to apply a rational or intuitive approach. Cultures differ in how they tolerate ambiguity, which influences decision-making styles considerably. For instance, uncertainty-avoidant cultures tend to favor systematic, rational approaches, appreciating extensive data analysis to minimize perceived risk. Conversely, spontaneous decisions in low uncertainty avoidance countries are perhaps more likely to be tolerated, allowing individuals to make decisions based on intuition or feeling. That this cultural variation is of paramount significance in international management means that respect and adaptation of such distinctions can create decisions that are more effective. Cultural intelligence can develop in leaders, allowing them to blend decision styles, being rational when appropriate and relying on intuition when necessary, to become better leaders in a multicultural context. Group decision-making for international management also has other difficulties when rational and intuitive approaches clash. Multicultural teams are likely to bring variety in the form of experiences and frames of reference that add depth to the discussion but generate conflict when the members revert to their own favorite decision style. Logical thinking could dominate in discussions aimed at producing data-driven results, while intuitive thinking could emerge where creative and quick thinking is critical. It is necessary for managers to establish a setting where the voices of all are heard in order to benefit from their capabilities. Facilitation can make a useful contribution to ensuring a balance between making decisions that are not just data-driven but also consider the nuances of human experience and intuition. By implementing both the rational and intuitive methods in group settings, groups can make more holistic and sound decisions that reflect the spirit of the international business environment.

7.1.1. Explanation of Rational Decision-Making Processes

In choice making, managers oscillate between making choices rationally and intuitively in global management situations. Rational choice making entails a procedure of orderly examination of information, and only those choices backed by empirical data and logical reasoning are carried out. This approach is especially significant when dealing with complex cross-cultural dynamics because different cultural contexts can influence perceptions of risk, and therefore the same information can be perceived differently. It is critical to integrate rational planning practices such as strategic planning so that decisions are suitably informed and justifiable in diverse cultural contexts. Thus, by adopting a rational process, decision-makers are better able to manage cultural subtleties while basing their decisions on tangible information, thus enhancing strategic-decision quality in a more globalized environment (Desmidt et al., 2018). Enhancing the process of making rational decisions in international management calls for organizations to focus more on effective information sharing within decision-making teams. This is particularly the case when decision-making in groups from multicultural backgrounds is at hand, where conflicting opinions result in a more well-rounded perception of potential risks and rewards. Through procedural justice in decision-making, organizations can foster team members to contribute voluntarily, therefore improving collective decision-making. Formal information exchange not only lowers risks arising from uncertainty but also increases the foundation on which strategic decisions are made (Figure 7.2).

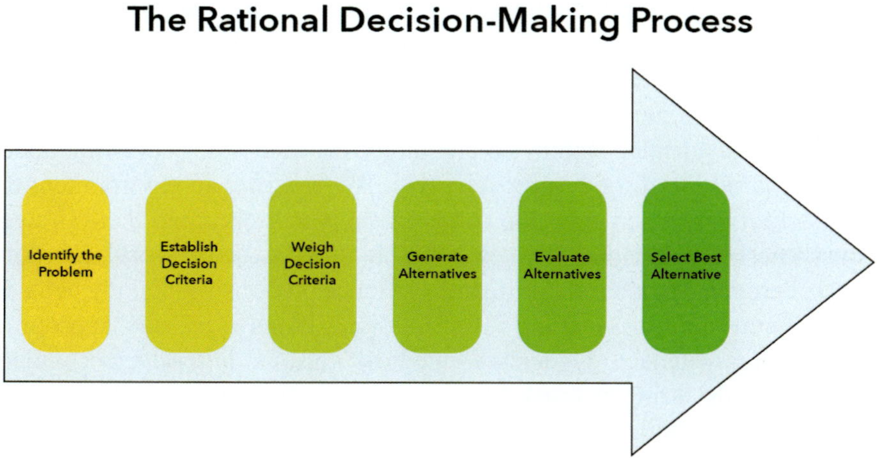

Figure 7.2. The complication of rational decision-making processes.

Source: https://s3-us-west-2.amazonaws.com/courses-images/wp-content/uploads/sites/1972/2017/07/03203825/RationalDecisionMaking.png.

As has been observed in studies that highlight the significance of information processing theory, decision quality is enhanced when systematically gathered information is used, making rational processes a critical part of international management effectiveness (Desmidt et al., 2018). Moreover, the typical global environment involving information technology imposes additional levels of complexity and risk on the decision-making process. As technology is changing so rapidly, managers must cultivate insights supporting breakthrough applications amidst uncertainties in the marketplace. Utilizing innovative decision-making methods, such as discrete choice analysis, assists managers in making decisions on a behaviorally robust foundation. Rigor in methods is offered to enable more relative importance estimates and greater ability to control confounding variables. In the context of international management, such advanced decision-making mechanisms allow institutions to not only reduce uncertainty but also create effective service strategies in line with organizational goals and respond favorably to international market forces.

7.1.2. Overview of Intuitive Decision-Making and its Relevance

Global management decision-making will show a balancing act between intuitive and rational decision-making. Managers in ambiguous and changeable environments may find that sole reliance on data-driven decision-making causes them to lose out on opportunities or experience delays. Intuitive decision-making with its reliance on emotional intelligence and speedy judgments becomes an adjunct to more traditional rational-based approaches. This blending is particularly useful in comprehending cross-cultural relations dynamics, where local nuance and context are lost to an analytical framework. Empirical studies show that the best leaders achieve a blending of such styles by drawing upon a situational variation of their approach style. By fostering an environment that combines rationality and intuition, organizations can optimize their strategic responsiveness and adaptability, essential in the fast-pace world of global business. Perceived risk has a significant influence on decision-making behavior across different cultures, making intuitive dispositions especially appropriate in certain circumstances. Understanding how various cultural environments shape individuals' attitudes toward uncertainty can lead to improved collective decision-making in global teams (Figure 7.3).

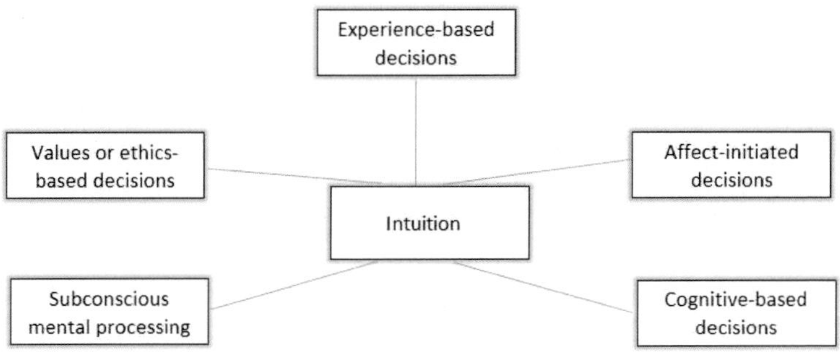

Figure 7.3. Intuitive decision-making.

Source: https://www.researchgate.net/profile/Sevinj-Omarli-2/publication/314262104/figure/fig3/AS:469246284177413@1488888440891/ntuitive-decision-making.png.

For example, more ambiguity-tolerant cultures may tend to utilize intuition, while cultures favoring systematic strategies will apply rational analysis. Embedding these cultural elements in strategic systems can produce improved results as teams handle complex global issues. Making decisions based on intuition could not only decrease risks but also allow leaders to step in in due time. This is particularly significant in low-data or unreliable accurate data environments, where decision-makers have no choice but to make decisions based on intuition where there are no definitive analytics (Baesens et al., 2020). Multicultural global group decision-making can greatly benefit from an understanding of intuitive decision-making. When faced with tough decisions, groups whose members are composed of people of various cultural backgrounds can employ their collective intuition to come up with innovative solutions. But the issue comes in balancing the opposing styles of decision-making, as some people might like intuitive leaps and others demand systematic thinking. Building a structure that respects intuitive input but ensures that rational thinking is at the center is essential. This can allow the building of a synergistic atmosphere where conflicting views are blended into cohesive strategies. Through appreciation of the power of the limitations of rational methods, organizations can better effectively access the potential of intuition, enabling the teams to effectively manage complexities as well as generate strategic insights that drive international success (de Freitas et al., 2016).

7.1.3. Comparison of the Effectiveness of Both Approaches in International Contexts

Decision-making styles, in international management, play a pivotal role in organizational performance. The rational approach, characterized by methodical investigation and logical reasoning, offers a methodical approach to establishing likely actions from empirical data. This style is highly effective where homogeneity of cultural risk perceptions is present, since it offers uniformity in the assessment of outcomes and mitigation of uncertainties. However, when used in broad cultural contexts, the vulnerabilities of rationality make themselves known as cultural variations underpin individual risk and opportunity perception. Notably, the integration of intuitive approaches, underpinned by gut feeling and experience, has a tendency to seem more effective where there is ambiguity or accelerated change, allowing leaders to stay ahead of complexities present in global contexts. Consequently, while both approaches are useful, their applicability is more prone to be context-dependent in cultural diversity and situational need. Risk perception's interaction with decision-making further complicates rational versus intuitive approaches on the global stage. Collectivist cultures are more risk-averse, having a tendency towards being conservative in decision-making, tending towards rationality. On the contrary, cultures that support individualism can be risk-taking, and in such cultures, intuition can be a more feasible route to decision-making. Thus, international managers who struggle with these opposing viewpoints find that they must adopt a flexible approach combining rational analysis with intuition. Understanding how cultural dimensions affect individual and group behavior in decision-making is essential for successful leadership of diverse teams. Such comprehension makes a more robust decision-making process because managers strive to balance the realities of multi-cultural environments with adapting their approaches to fit local conditions and different mindsets.

In addition, the dynamics of group decision-making also require a cautious evaluation of both approaches in a global environment. Those groups that have members with diverse cultural backgrounds can introduce more innovative ideas through multiple views but struggle to reach agreement. The rational approach is weakened by the other concepts and approaches that team members put forward, especially when operating in high-context cultures with indirect communications. Under these circumstances, intuitive approaches provide quicker decision-making by using more collaboration and the capacity to access emotional intelligence among team members. This conflict suggests the utilization of a hybrid approach that uses both rational and intuitive approaches as a model that can enhance efficacy in various teams. By integrating various decision-making approaches, managers can capitalize on the strengths of their teams, founded on cultural diversity, ultimately optimizing organizational performance and flexibility in the global economy today.

7.2. RISK PERCEPTION ACROSS CULTURES

In making decisions, the balance between rationality and intuition is very applicable in observing risk perception across cultures. Cultural structures influence people's propensities to take risk, and this can determine if they apply rational analytical methods or intuitive responses in domains of uncertainty. For instance, some societies are centered on collective decision-making, which can lead to being more risk-averse in evaluating risks.

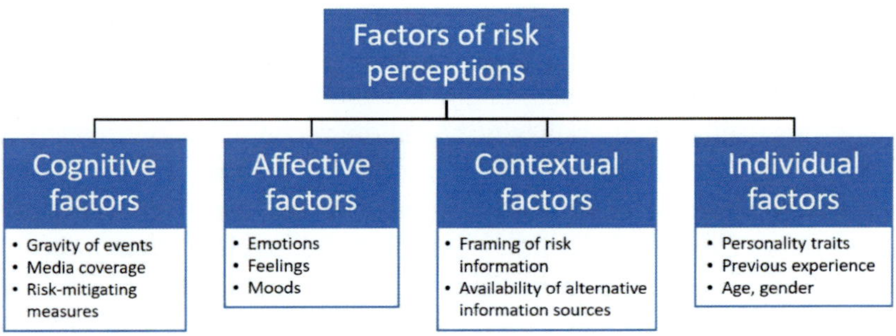

Figure 7.4. Factors of risk perceptions.

Source: https://upload.wikimedia.org/wikipedia/commons/c/cb/Factors_of_risk_perceptions._Adapted_from_Godovykh_et_al._%282021%29.jpg.

On the contrary, other cultures tend to follow a more individualistic pattern that favors fast, instinctual choices that may be short of necessary risk scrutiny.

Such information is instrumental to managing globally because it allows leaders to tailor their strategies and support systems in accordance with culture and expectations so as to optimize decision effectiveness. As the results on cross-cultural differences in risk perception indicate, a certain decision context may be the difference in managerial outcomes. Empirical evidence confirms that learning environments and experiential educational activities shape students' perceptions of risk and management approaches. To illustrate, comparison of management students in five European countries revealed considerable differences in how they evaluated such traits as decision-making and leadership when compared in business simulations. This indicates that managerial risks and decision-making choices depend on the cultural background in which one is trained (Figure 7.4).

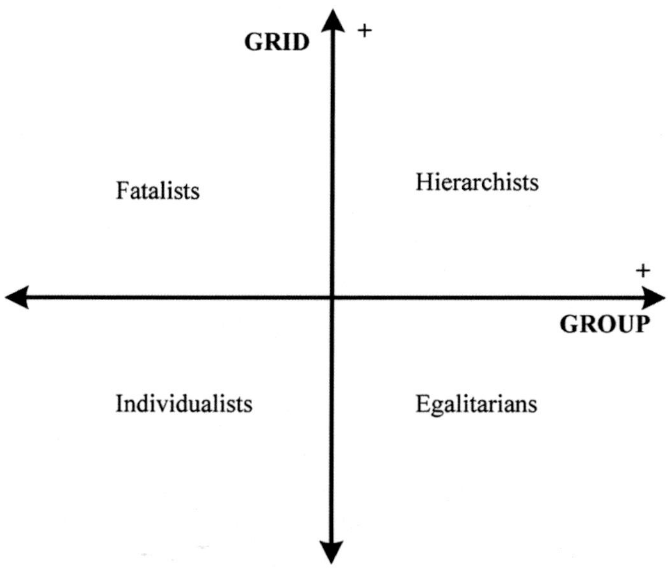

Figure 7.5. The cultural theory of risk model based on Thompson and Wildavsky.

Source: https://www.researchgate.net/publication/347852664/figure/fig1/AS:11431281172852940@1688664709722/The-cultural-theory-of-risk-model-based-on-Thompson-and-Wildavsky-1990.png.

Therefore, global managers must consider these dimensions of culture in order to effectively develop and expand managerial abilities in multicultural teams and maintain decision-making appropriate for the varying perceptions of risk therein in multinational environments (Fitó et al., 2018). Cultural tendencies also add on to the trade-off between reward and risk, making it more complex by highlighting the complexities of group decision-making across global environments. For example, research has indicated Australian students tend to choose riskier options than their German counterparts, who display a more calculated sense of risk and reward balance. The difference suggests that Australian decision-makers might prioritize the excitement of uncertainty from risky options over other considerations, whereas Germans take painstaking considerations of consequences. These cultural distinctions must be realized in business models because they can have a major impact on team dynamics and the general effectiveness of decision-making processes in cross-cultural management contexts. Ultimately, eliminating these distinctions in risk perception can enhance decision-making frameworks and enable improved cooperation among culturally diverse teams (Vogt et al., 2025) (Figure 7.5).

7.2.1. Cultural Differences in Risk Assessment and Management

In the contemporary global economy, an understanding of the nuances of culturally heterogeneous group decision-making has become increasingly important. Various paradigms of risk assessment often stand as a surrogate for underlying cultural values, defining how groups perceive and respond to uncertainty. Collectivist cultures, for instance, may perceive risk through a consensual process, where intuitive choice prevails with a consonance bias towards group goals. Conversely, individualist cultures are more inclined to a rational approach, with extensive use of quantitative data and personal responsibility in making decisions. This divergence emphasizes the necessity for organizations to make management strategies conform to various perceptions of risk so that they can align their strategy in spite of cultural differences that influence group behavior and leads to different outcomes in global environments. The varying perceptions of risk across cultures significantly influence organizational behavior and management practices. Research has shown that the effectiveness of methods like business games in cultivating management skills such as decision-making and leadership is generally cross-cultural dependent. As a survey of management students from different nations of Europe revealed, significant variation was found between the educational systems and cultural backgrounds in regard to the emphasis on specific skills. For example, collectivist learners may be less focused on planning and theoretical abstract knowledge, highlighting their demands for experiential learning environments encouraging collective experience and teamwork. Such findings highlight the need for international managers to customize training and development efforts based on the cultural expectations and learning preferences of their employees, resulting in increased overall motivation and mastery of skills (Fitó et al., 2018). Furthermore, awareness of the various interdependencies and stakeholder interests involved in risk management is essential for sound international decision-making. The establishment and implementation of biosafety systems, for instance, requires a refined awareness of the various ways in which cultural settings impact stakeholder interests. An oversimplified strategy that fails to acknowledge such differences may not only omit major players but also jeopardize policy advancement. A progressive and context-aware approach incorporating the voices and visions of all stakeholders raises prospects for successful biosafety realization. It fosters co-operation among stakeholders by integrating scientific analysis with local cultural values, thus maximizing the deployment of resources and guaranteeing maximum prospects for success in international management environments (Makinde et al., 2012). This strategic adaptability is imperative in an attempt to understand complexities of the global markets and synchronize the risk management strategies in culturally diverse environments.

7.2.2. Impact of Cultural Values on Decision-Making Styles

The interplay of different cultural backgrounds has a wide impact on the manner in which individuals approach decision-making, notably rational and intuitive processes. Rational is prevalent in rationality-oriented cultures, whose decision-making is analytical and systematic in nature and, by implication, reliant on data and objective measures for appraisals. Intuitive practices prevail in collectivist cultures that prioritize emotions and social feelings. This divergence shows that managers must change their decision patterns to align with the culture values of their teams, establishing the potential for successful communication in multicultures. This requirement is augmented by the fact that decision-making approaches in multinational corporations are likely to symbolize typical trends of culture, which can be required outright labeling within organizational frameworks to improve cooperative efforts and evolve more diverse management practices, especially in regions where the prevailing cultural norms considerably diverge from the managerial pool (Saeed et al., 2002). Risk perception also varies profoundly between cultures and influences decision-making in international management scenarios. For instance, high uncertainty avoidance cultures will typically have a tendency to eschew risk through meticulous analysis and contingency planning. Uncertainty-accepting cultures may see risk as an essential component of innovation and opportunity. This variation can be crucial to international managers since it requires the unconscious understanding of home country risk attitudes while entering new markets. Managerial decision-making on the basis of the presumption that individual risk tolerance is applicable everywhere, thus, can lead to actual pitfalls, even miscalculations or missed opportunities. Understanding risk perception as deeply rooted in culture can enhance decision-making interventions and allow leaders to modify meaningful strategies to suit local stakeholders (Jogulu et al., 2008). Decision-making processes at the group level in multi-cultural contexts generally reveal the complexities of cultural influences on interactions. Interactions within multicultural groups tend to shift between consensus-based processes through collaborative endeavors and directive processes based on hierarchical demands, depending on prevailing cultural norms. For instance, individualist cultures may have a high regard for assertiveness and personal accountability, while collectivist cultures emphasize consensus and harmony. This diversity calls for international managers to have a sense of the different decision-making styles prevalent in their teams. Additionally, leaders must employ methods that encourage participation but remain attuned to the cultural values of those involved, creating an accommodative space where more perspectives are valued. These discussions play a critical role in developing good teamwork as they enable teams to harness the various thinking and sound judgment in decision-making (Saeed et al., 2002).

7.2.3. Case Studies Illustrating Varying Risk Perceptions in International Firms

In international management, decision-making under uncertainty compels firms to navigate through a quite complicated ensemble of cultural and contextual issues. Case studies most often discover that perception of risk is hardly an innate feature but is shaped by considerable cultural influences. For instance, research indicates that firms operating in highly uncertainty avoiding societies may be more analytical and rational in their decision-making process, often dwelling on careful market research as well as risk analysis. Firms operating in low uncertainty avoidance societies may be inclined to make intuitive decisions based on experience and intuition in their strategic decisions. These differences create the necessity for multinational firms to optimize decision models to reflect culture's underlying risk perceptions in target markets because these perceptions have the ability to boost or hinder performance in international markets (Perk et al., 2012).

Examining group decision dynamics within cross-cultural groups also demonstrates how various risk perceptions can lead to different results. Case studies show that multicultural teams will have a range of risk assessment methodologies based on the background of their members, which will elicit creative solutions but also generate conflict. In particular, firms that are engaged in alliances or joint ventures can find variations in cultural values influencing risk perception and communication. For example, a Japanese firm may approach risk with caution and require agreement, while an American peer would opt for expediency in decisions and assertiveness. This kind of difference can result in procedural inefficiencies or differences in strategy unless they are properly managed. Understanding and blending these different styles is crucial for international firms that are looking for unified decision-making styles in culturally dissimilar environments (Farole et al., 2011). The implications of differential risk perceptions extend much farther than strategic planning; they actually shape organizational behavior and the international risk appetite of global business companies. Firms that effectively analyze and integrate the various risk perceptions of their global employees stand a better chance of seeing opportunities and keeping potential hazards at bay. Importantly, firms that employ robust communication and cultivate inclusive environments can harness differences between cultures to enhance the quality of decision-making. In this way, they not only achieve mastery of the complexities involved in operating on an international scale but also improve their competitiveness. Adopting multiple perceptions of risk as a strategic resource is thus an essential shift in strategy by international firms to decision-making in an increasingly interdependent world to react in more nuanced and effective manners to global challenges (Perk et al., 2012; Farole et al., 2011).

7.3. GROUP DECISION-MAKING IN DIVERSE ENVIRONMENTS

In global management, the complexity of group decision-making is again heightened when put within the backdrop of multi-cultural environments. The dynamic exchange of varied visions from varied cultures demands breaking away from that typically paradigmatic rationalistic approach to decision-making trending in homogenous groups. In multi-cultural teams, where all employ a different world view, it could be suggested that purely analytical decision-making will overlook important details, thereby the lower overall effectiveness of the group. By having integrative conversations that call upon the unique knowledge of every member, organizations can access the collective genius of heterogeneous groups. Not only does this approach encourage creative solutions but it also encourages a feeling of belonging, which is instrumental in enhancing inclusion in the workplace. Demand for an inclusivity model of diversity is supported by readings that highlight the importance of diverse focal points such as organizational behaviors and work group processes (Cleveland et al., 2018). Risk perception is inherently shaped by cultural contexts, which in turn influence the manner groups evaluate uncertainty while making decisions. In inclusive teams, members will possess varying risk appetites, which are largely determined by their cultural contexts (Figure 7.6).

Figure 7.6. The complexity of group decision-making.

Source: https://cloudinary.hbs.edu/hbsit/image/upload/s--tZZQtah4--/f_auto,c_fill,h_375,w_750,/v20200101/DDA1D55F4B271983B2EF55DA835ECD16.jpg.

This difference can lead to a better consideration of possible threats and advantages, and thus to greater consideration and eventually better decision-making results. However, these differences can also present huge challenges, most notably in unifying group members towards a common goal. Proper management of these diverse risk perceptions entails establishing open lines of communication and respect among members of the team, in such a way that every member's perspective is heard and valued. Since diverse environments support higher participation and performance outcomes, leaders must prioritize approaches supporting understanding across various teams, aligning them toward shared goals and fostering collaborative work on cultural fronts (Lipinski et al., 2009). Further, the speed with which strategic decision is made in diverse groups is important, especially when dealing with rapidly evolving global markets. As organizations navigate tough environments, the ability to respond quickly will typically rely on sound decision-making processes capable of managing multiple cultural orientations. This means employing responsive methods that strike a balance between collegial input and adherence to timely implementation. Provided the right tools and structures are given to groups for quick decision-making, groups can succeed at balancing the time costs traditionally associated with consensus generation in diverse teams. Lastly, developing an environment conducive to timely and intelligent decision-making based on collective wisdom not only optimizes organizational resilience but also sets enterprises up to thrive in uncertainty in global management practices (Lipinski et al., 2009).

7.3.1. Benefits of Group Decision-Making in Multicultural Teams

The collaboration between rational and intuitive decision-making styles reveals vast benefits when applied to multicultural teams. Diversely recruited members from various cultures bring different cognitive schemata to decision-making, which affects the way they make decisions. Diversity in decision-making produces more rigorous probing of solution options because each member's contribution is a unique thought process that supplements group thinking. Besides, the combination of rational and intuitive methods can strengthen decisions since the team members learn to balance logical thinking and intuitive wisdom. Not only does this kind of interaction encourage creativity, but overall consideration of the risks as well, eventually offering higher efficiency in international management situations. As risk perception varies widely across cultures, group decision-making among multicultural teams gains considerable impact. The multicultural team is likely to behave differently in terms of risk, balancing caution with boldness based on their cultural background and experiences. For instance, some cultures may value consensus and risk aversion, while others will be more likely to take risk as innovation. This conflict of views can stimulate rigorous discussion of risk management, whereby groups are in a position to devise strategies that align with different cultural expectations and market conditions. This collective deliberation enhances the capability of the groups to confront complexities, with fewer mistakes but more potential for growth in global markets. Besides this, the application of information and communication technology (ICT) plays a crucial role in facilitating quality decision-making in multicultural teams. With modern organizations relying more and more on virtual locations, adopting digital communication technologies can balance the shortcomings of cultural diversity. Cutting-edge technologies such as e-mail, teleconferencing, and virtual meeting rooms ease intercultural communication by providing level playing fields where every voice is heard. In addition to introducing inclusivity, this collaboration enables team members to overcome communication gaps caused by their differences. Research has also discovered that cultural diversity can impede face-to-face communication but ICT makes significant contributions towards the effectiveness of decision-making by providing environments favorable to teamwork, hence bolstering the strengths of diverse inputs in team settings (Shachaf et al., 2008).

7.3.2. Challenges Faced in Group Decision-Making Across Cultures

In the context of international management, conflicting decision-making styles are the major issues when team members of mixed cultural orientations come together. Cultures lean towards dissimilar styles with some focusing more on rational, analytical decision-making and others favoring intuitive, experiential decision-making. Such a disparity leads to conflict within teams, as team members do not appreciate other perspectives or methods. Consequently, this incompatibility can lead to the failure of collaborative work and therefore create misunderstandings and conflict. Such conflict is itself best illustrated in the Pardee Center Task Force studies, which show the importance of understanding different kinds of decision-making styles to address complex issues faced by international teams (Bachofen et al., 2012). Through the establishment of a working environment that fosters cultural adaptability and sensitivity, organizations are able to circumvent such conflict and thereby maximize the effectiveness and unity of groups involved in decision-making. Risk perception, inextricably interwoven with cultural context, is a part of group decision-making processes. For instance, cultures that have high uncertainty avoidance will perceive risks differently than cultures that accept ambiguity (Figure 7.7).

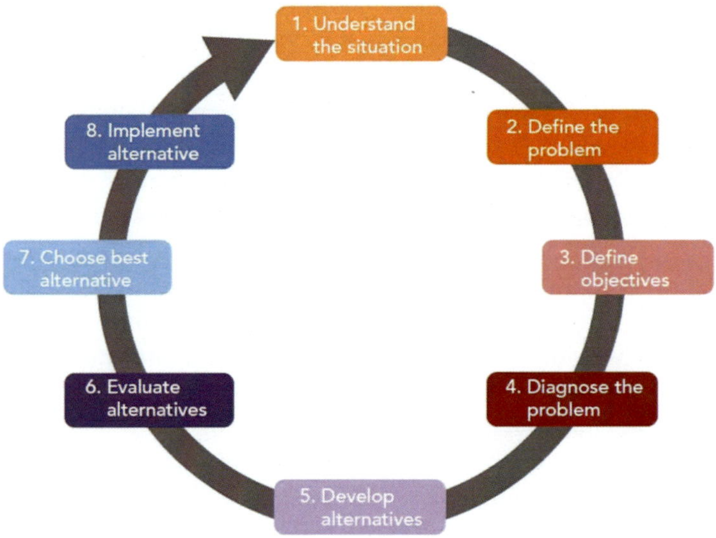

Figure 7.7. Group vs. individual decision-making in various cultures.

Source: https://library.fiveable.me/_next/image?url=https%3A%2F%2Fstorage.googleapis.com%2Fstatic.prod.fiveable.me%2Fsearch-images%252F%2522Group_vs_individual_decision-making_characteristics_processes_cross-cultural_management_diverse_perspectives_accountability_groupthink_social_loafing%2522-DecisionMakingProcess-1024x788.jpg&w=828&q=75.

This differential risk tolerance has the potential to create a polarized group culture in which the decisions become contentious and lengthy. In multicultural teams, various members may prioritize managing risk higher than innovations; hence, striking a balance that is representative of each party's perspective may be challenging. Qualitative research findings also highlight that global and local perspectives in global teams can result in status rivalry as well as creative debate if managed prudently (Haas et al., 2003). Firms that actively foster a shared perception of risk across cultures have the capability not just to enhance decisions but also to bring about a sense of togetherness in their teams, resulting in better outcomes. Moreover, the effectiveness of group decision-making largely depends on the cultural context in which such decisions are made. In the case of global management teams, cultural norms governing authority, communication, and agreement-making significantly influence how decisions are reached. Relational cues and indirect communication may heavily rely on high-context cultures, while low-context cultures typically depend on direct and explicit messages. These contrasting styles can potentially lead to miscommunication and irritation among team members, complicating decision-making. These cultural differences need to be understood by managers to facilitate effective communication and the convergence of strengths in multicultural teams. The ability to cope with such subtleties actually determines the success of the decisions taken, not merely the immediate outcome but also the long-run sustainability of organizational strategies in today's global business scenario.

7.3.3. Strategies for Effective Group Decision-Making in International Settings

The complexity in global settings calls for comprehension of diverse styles of decision-making. Rational decision-making, involving systematic examination and formalized procedures, is vastly different from intuitive decision-making, which relies on gut feelings and experience. In multicultural settings, decision-makers should realize that individuals with different backgrounds may tend to favor one over the other. The difference may determine group dynamics, leading either to conflict or synergy. For instance, while rational approaches might resonate with fact-oriented cultures, intuitive practices would resonate better with those who appreciate interpersonal relationships in decision-making. Leadership that is able to balance these practices along with accepting rational and intuitive inputs is required to ensure a balanced approach that does not negate diversity. Such perception is particularly important in international management, where recognition of multiple risk perceptions held by different cultures can inherently decide the results of decisions, calling for a flexible approach (Adam et al., 2015). Communication is the pillar of quality decision-making in multicultural group compositions. The intricate and multifaceted nature of group dynamics in international contexts can generate misperceptions, especially when participants are exposed to different cultural norms. Encouraging open discussion not only reduces the risk of conflict but also increases the depth of the decision-making process by combining multiple viewpoints. Good leaders ought to develop a setting that allows all voices to be heard, being inclusive and collaborative. This spirit of collaboration is vital in recognizing different risk perceptions across cultures, which can really affect group decisions. When individuals are appreciated and their respective unique thoughts are included in the decision-making process, it leads to more balanced, sound results. These practices emphasize the importance of sensitivity to culture and flexibility by group leaders in global management initiatives (Anderson et al., 2009). Furthermore, the use of technology can have a huge impact on enhancing the success of group decision-making in global contexts. Technologies such as team collaboration platforms enable simultaneous communication and collaborative sharing of documents, bridging geographical differences typical in cross-cultural interactions. The technologies provide a more level-playing field discussion environment where contribution is enabled by members irrespective of location or time zone. Furthermore, virtual environments enable the integration of decision-making simulations, such as emotional control measures critical to handling group dynamics, as identified in a research on financial traders (Adam et al., 2015). These technologies not only accelerate the process of decision-making but also generate a sense of ownership among team members. Finally, the marriage of the utilization of technological solutions with the traditional approach to cultural sensitiveness and frank communication gives a good basis for effective and powerful decision-making in global management.

7.4. THE ROLE OF TECHNOLOGY IN DECISION-MAKING

The rapidly changing context of international management requires a thoughtful examination of the technology's role in mediating decision-making. As organizations are becoming more reliant on advanced data analytics, managers are compelled to balance rational and intuitive types of decision-making. While data insights promote a systemic examination that can reveal subtle patterns, intuition remains essential where response speed matters. Here, technology is a double-edged sword: it elevates rational judgments to new heights but also the risk of overpowering subtle perception that intuition offers. Therefore, decision-makers have to cultivate a sensitive awareness of when to seek analytical prowess and when to depend on intuition, finding a balanced strategy that entwines the two. Cultural differences hold far-reaching implications in risk perception in the course of decision-making, particularly in cross-national settings. Technological advances making possible real-time communication and information exchange have the potential to join or even expand such cultural gaps. For instance, cultures understand risk differently; they are some of them conservative and others risk-tolerant. Utilizing technology in the presentation of germane information can facilitate enhanced mutual understanding among team members, allowing more informed joint decision-making. However, this is rendered difficult by the occurrence of information overload, where group decision-makers are unable to extract significant insight from a deluge of information (Figure 7.8).

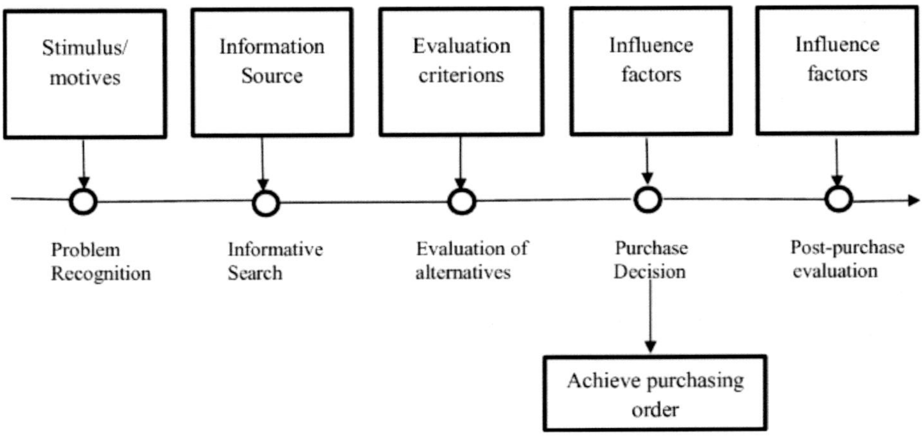

Figure 7.8. The dynamic landscape of international management necessitates a deliberate examination of how technology mediates the decision -making process.

Source: https://media.springernature.com/lw685/springer-static/image/chp%3A10.1007%2F978-981-16-0282-5_1/MediaObjects/508007_1_En_1_Fig2_HTML.png.

As a result, ensuring that technology becomes a collaborator in such cultural bridging is vital to effective international management practice. In multicultural group environments, the role of technology extends beyond mere communication establishment; it actually drives collective decision-making activities. Using decision-support tools and collaboration tools, technology not only facilitates interactions but also determines what emerges from group discussion. The implementation of technology which encourages anonymous feedback can potentially minimize social biases and encourage participation by all members regardless of their hierarchical rank. Also, as businesses engage in cross-cultural collaboration, an important awareness of how differently positioned cultural settings affect group dynamics arises. Disjointed information and divergent communication styles pose challenges to decision-making. In order to overcome these challenges, it is necessary to reform how technologies are applied in models of decision-making so that they contribute meaningfully to the structuring of integrated teams with the same objective of achieving organizational goals (Coltman et al., 2009; Badii et al., 2003).

7.4.1. Influence of Data Analytics on Decision-Making Processes

The use of analytics in decision-making radically changes the operations of organizations, particularly in international management situations. Rational or intuitive decisions for decision-makers heavily rely on empirical data gained through analytics. Rational decision-making emphasizes logical reasoning and sequential analysis, relying heavily on quantitative data to guide decisions. Intuitive decision-making applies personal knowledge and experience, which may not be empirical. Using data analytics gives the more structured environment in which decisions are made from concrete evidence, rendering intuitive decisions irreparable risks. Shifting to data-driven culture not only enhances the effectiveness of decisions but also aligns with the fast and ever-evolving state of global markets, where predictive analytics is able to provide insights into trends and potential pitfalls. The cultural view of risk also has a significant impact on the part that data analytics will play in advising decision-making. Risk has different meanings across cultures, and this may influence data insights being accepted and correctly interpreted. There may be a desire for a more cautious, analytics-based approach in some cultures, where analytics is viewed as a necessary tool for resisting uncertainty. Conversely, more risk-tolerant cultures will rely less on fact and more on intuition. With the embracing of a complete appreciation of such cultural variance, decision-makers can tailor their analytical methods to accommodate the values and expectations of their international stakeholders. So, data analytics bridges over cultural difference through having a sound theoretical foundation for understanding risk from diverse perspectives and making decision-making more agreeable. Decision-making collaboration in multicultural teams is significantly enhanced with the strategic use of data analytics. Group decision-making, particularly in international management, involves bringing together various viewpoints and expertise and ultimately results in more balanced outcomes. Data analytics serves as a shared language, providing an objective metric that can bring together opposing views and permit informed discussion. By providing easy-to-understand, graphical presentations of information, groups of individuals are able to use analytics collectively as a group, dispelling communication and decision-style-based cultural barriers. Data-driven methods encourage transparency and responsibility throughout the group through the creation of an open atmosphere where decisions are made via informed, group input. As highlighted in supply chain evaluation and strategic planning in geopolitically volatile regions, for instance, Azerbaijan's geopolitical location between Europe and Asia (Jafari, 2024), applying analytics increases the effectiveness of operations while accepting complexity inherent in global markets, ultimately increasing decision-making efficiency.

7.4.2. Use of Communication Tools in Facilitating International Decisions

In global management, sophisticated decision-making dynamics typically necessitate resort to high-level communication devices that transcend boundaries. Such devices not only make it possible to exchange information, but also facilitate the harmonization of discordant ideas, which take place in multinational environments.

Figure 7.9. Communication tools inside of distributed and interconnected enterprise to communicate and collaborate.

Source: https://www.researchgate.net/profile/N-Kryvinska/publication/221617598/figure/fig1/AS:671538139369490@1537118577835/Communication-Tools-Inside-of-Distributed-and-Interconnected-Enterprise-to-Communicate.png.

For instance, when companies move into joint ventures across cultures, not only can the linguistic difference create misunderstandings but also differing decision-making styles, whether rational or intuitive. A sound communication base that is technology-driven enables all concerned to become part of the discussion with the respective cultural settings bringing to bear a more comprehensive decision-making process and, in turn, business objectives. By using technologies such as video conferencing, collaborative sites, and social media, organizations can foster greater awareness and establish trust among members and then lay the groundwork for greater success in global operations. Less applicable is the recognition of risk perception differences across cultures and how it affects global decision-making. Cultural origins have a profound influence on risk perception and management, necessitating communication approaches that are sensitized to differences and responsive to them. For example, whereas a risk-averse culture may be how some conduct business decisions, others may thrive in ambiguity, with risk being viewed as a spur to innovation (Figure 7.9).

Communication mediums can be utilized to bridge such gaps to enable groups to collaborate on risk analysis and strategy formulation. This ensures that all voices are heard, enabling collective decision-making to thrive in an open environment. Incorporating cultural sensitivity into communication platforms not only enhances the intelligibility of arguments but also enhances organizational resilience through the construction of an imminent shared perception of risks involved, thus enabling informed decision-making in a global setting. The role of communication tools in group decision-making in multicultural environments cannot be exaggerated. Effective communication is important in making sure that the various points of view are given respect and included in the decision-making process. Communication tools such as collaborative modeling, as presented in recent studies, are rich bases of understanding of group dynamics, enabling stakeholders to view and model various situations in real-time. This evaluation approach, often supplemented by web tools, encourages partnership, particularly in situations that are riddled with uncertainty and complexity. Specifically, Companion Modelling-type approaches have been successful in brokering debate among actors who have diverse interests, as evidenced by the case put forward by this study. By facilitating communication among stakeholders in designed simulations, communication tools improve conflict management capabilities of teams and conclude with more democratic and well-informed decision-making processes showing commitment to shared objectives within the global sphere (Acikalin et al., 2009; Dumrongrojwatthana et al., 2010).

7.4.3. Ethical Considerations in Technology-Driven Decision-Making

In today's world of global management, the movement between rational and intuitive decision-making propensities most often leads to significant consequential ethical problems when technology plays a central role. Rational decision-making is apt to concentrate on the consideration of information and methodical techniques, which could eliminate the ethical aspects of decisions. Intuitive decision-making is based on intuition, which introduces subjectivity and could lead to ethical failure if accompanied by no strong moral structure. Technology is both an enabler and a challenge in this sense as it presents substantial volumes of data while simultaneously distorting human perception of risk and reward. Leaders therefore must navigate the intricacy of these strategies and incorporate ethical viewpoints to strike a balance between technological advances and ethical responsibility in decision-making. Ethical considerations also vary immensely when taking into account risk perception from various cultures. What one culture finds an acceptable risk may be found intolerable by another, complicating decision-making even in multinational settings. Technical developments can enhance such variations to render a one-size-fits-all approach to making decisions unsuitable. For instance, genetic modification technologies may be extremely controversial in some countries and widely accepted in others. Accordingly, global managers must adopt a holistic understanding of the multilevel cultural world and the ethical dimensions of their technological choice. By being proactive to collaborate with diverse stakeholders in listening to their perspectives on risk, managers are able to develop an inclusive workplace that not only enhances the quality of decisions but also strengthens relationships with local communities and stakeholders (Makinde et al., 2012). In addition, effective group decision-making across diverse contexts demands a reflective integration of technology solutions and ethics. As organizations increasingly rely on collaborative software and data analysis, group processes can be maximized or negatively impacted by technology mediation. With multicultural groups, the possibility of misunderstanding and miscommunication is higher, necessitating an ethical code of behavior that maximizes inclusiveness and respect for all members. Incorporating ethical values into decision-making helps to foster trust and cooperation, which are fundamental to goal accomplishment in diversified settings. Further, emphasizing ethical conduct encourages stakeholders to contribute their individual perspectives without apprehension of exclusion, thus enhancing the decision product. Hence, embracing ethical culture together with the appropriate application of technology can lead to sustainable management outcomes aligned with the long-term interests of all the stakeholders (Gonzalez et al., 2010).

7.5. THE IMPACT OF GLOBALIZATION ON DECISION-MAKING

The diversity embedded in the contemporary global management context requires a harmonious approach to decision-making. As operations spread across borders, managers are likely to be confronted with varying cultural demands and traditions that shape beliefs and actions. This comes vividly evident in variations between rational and intuitive forms of decision-making with an enormous variation across cultures. Logical approaches, typically favored in Western cultures, value systematic reasoning and results based on facts, whereas intuitive decisions based on experience and instinct could be more prevalent in extremely uncertainty-avoidant cultures. Hence, an awareness of how different cultures decide can assist managers in creating strategies appealing to local parties and resulting in more successful global operations. Added to this, risk perception associated with globalization presents additional challenges for decision-makers. Various cultural backgrounds influence the way organizations view risk, shaping investment choices through to operating policy. For instance, increased risk acceptance in certain cultures promotes innovation and active market penetration, while others require conservatism and stability (Figure 7.10).

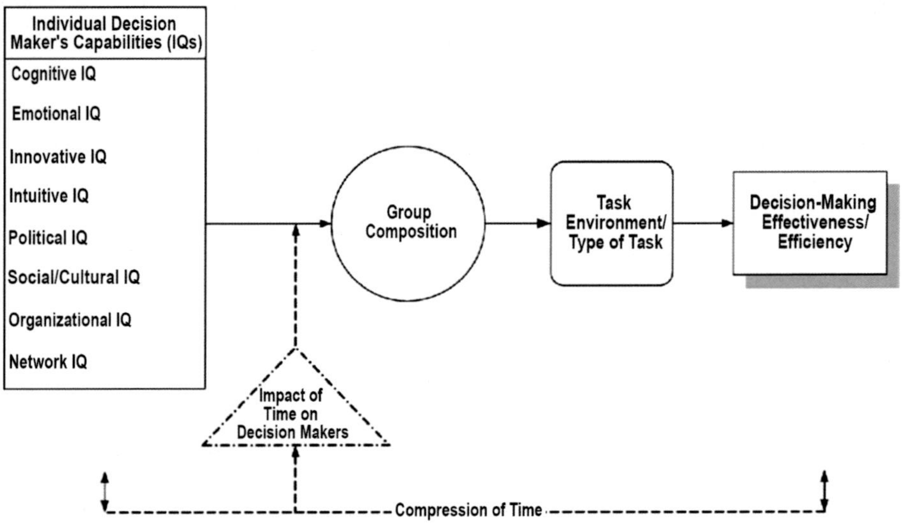

Figure 7.10. Global decision-making model.

Source: https://www.researchgate.net/profile/Ron_Fisher2/publication/44708246/figure/fig2/AS:468506052435968@1488711955245/Global-decision-making-model.png.

This difference not only affects individual decision-making processes but also group behavior in multinational teams, wherein varied risk assessments can lead to discord or indecision. Hence, understanding and working through these differences is crucial to achieving cooperation and to making decisions informed by a whole picture view of the international market environment.

The group decision-making dynamic is also strongly impacted by globalization because groups become more multicultural. This diversity can promote innovation and creativity through bringing together differing points of view, but can also make it more difficult to form a consensus. Bringing together differing points of view normally requires facilitated communication with everyone being heard, particularly on the question of balance between assertiveness and cooperativeness in negotiations. Successful managers must, as such, establish a culture that supports these diversities and promotes a shared vision. As demonstrated in studies, integrating some of the cross-cultural insights can lead to framing solutions that prioritize being innovative as well as culturally relevant and therefore add value to overall organizational performance across globalized challenges (Andronikou et al., 2013; Alács et al., 2009).

7.5.1. How Globalization Influences Managerial Decisions

Globalization has also reorganized the context in which managerial decisions are made, introducing a whole array of variables that affect rational and intuitive approaches employed by managers.

Figure 7.11. Many knowledge-related, people-focused factors influence globalization opportunities and challenges-and the society ability to succeed and individual people's ability to thrive.

Source: https://www.researchgate.net/profile/Karl-Martin-Wiig/publication/220610478/figure/fig8/AS:668488561606665@1536391501819/Many-knowledge-related-people-focused-factors-influence-globalisation-opportunities-and.ppm.

As companies expand operations across boundaries, they encounter various markets that possess varying consumer demands and regulatory environments. This compels managers to lean toward more analytical decision-making based on data and empirical observation, particularly when rational approaches are favored. However, in cultures where intuition is valued, decision-making may favor gut or experiential intelligence, and therefore a combination of styles with potential to profoundly impact organizational practices. Interplay between these styles calls for a sensitive understanding of local contexts, since this determines the manner in which decisions are made in cross-cultural environments, and therefore determines a firms global competitiveness and capacity to innovate. Besides, globalization demands a delicate understanding of risk perception across various cultures, which will in turn influence managerial decision-making. Cross-cultural perceptions of risk can have a significant influence on decision-making, from aggressive market entry strategies to more conservative operational policies (Figure 7.11).

Managers must work with these dynamics so that their policies are aligned with what is locally perceived and expected. For instance, some cultures may pride themselves on risk aversion, making managers less aggressive in orientation, while others prize risk-taking as an opportunity for innovation. The ability to quantify these cultural differences is essential to effectively make decisions that promote operational success in multicultural markets since failure to account for these differences results in strategic misalignments and operational failures. Finally, group decision-making across multicultural settings has additional challenges and opportunities instigated by globalization. The integration of diverse perceptions can enrich the decision-making process, as managers are drawing from a wider pool of ideas and understanding. The diversity, nonetheless, generates communication and agreement-building challenges, leading to disagreements or miscommunications. Managers must ensure an open environment in which every member's input is valued while crossing likely cultural clashes that arise from dissimilar communication styles. Effective use of information and communication technology can create cooperation and bridge decision-making distances since the axis points at the management of foreign economic activity by means of information systems (Noha, 2025). Hence, such dynamics need to be realized by managers who want to harvest diversity effectively in an effort to support general decision-making around the world.

7.5.2. The Role of International Regulations and Policies

In global management, decision-making problems are aggravated by the interaction of multiple rules and policies in a number of jurisdictions. While operating the global market, familiarity with the regulatory frameworks takes on a critical function in aiding compliance and strategic advantage. International rules have a tendency to establish minimum operating parameters, dictating managerial choices on the matter of risk perception and resource allocation. For instance, managers have to balance conformance to local rules and global guidelines, thereby developing a necessity for every manager to be familiar with both sides thoroughly. This two-faceted model of decision-making develops an environment within which leaders are not only supposed to rely on analytical thinking but also synthesize intuitive judgments, keeping in view various settings of cultures as well as the situational nature of stakeholder requirements. Also, worldwide regulations have a critical impact on the way risk is perceived and managed in multicultural settings. Each culture possesses distinct perceptions regarding risk, which can impact group decision-making. As international managers encounter diverse styles of perceiving risk, it becomes essential to create a context of cultural sensitivity. For example, whereas some communities will choose to proceed with caution, others will not shy away from exploring uncertainty for opportunities. By the inclusion of global regulatory standards and native cultural factors, decision-making instruments can be improved. This two-way focus not only assists in avoiding potential slip-ups but also ensures harmony among culturally diverse teams, which opens the way toward more robust and better-informed managerial decisions. In addition, international standards have the effect of establishing a model of enabling marginalized groups in decision-making, hence making management practices more inclusive. By virtue of initiatives towards gender equality in land acquisition processes, policy reforms can provide channels through which voiceless stakeholders can communicate their concerns and interests effectively. These reforms highlight the necessity of integrating womens participatory rights in management decision-making on resource allocation, such as in various countries plagued by the impacts of commercialization and land acquisition conflicts (Celine et al., 2016). Whenever organizations prioritize inclusive regulatory practice, they establish an environment for enhanced decision-making and people's participation. Similarly, the development of integrated frameworks, such as the Estuarine Planning Support System (EPSS), illustrates how integrating policies under one umbrella in harmony with ecological and economic needs offers a systematic solution for resolving complex management scenarios (Barnard et al., 2015). By recognizing international regulations as the backbone of the practice of inclusivity, organizations are able to design more sustainable and balanced solutions within the globalized world.

7.5.3. Adaptation of Decision-Making Strategies in a Globalized Market

In the rapidly changing global management world, it is necessary to understand the nuanced dynamics of rational and intuitive styles of decision-making.

Different cultural settings have different tendencies towards these styles, and these can play a pivotal role in business strategy. Rational decision-making goes with official analysis and systematic approach, typically in Western corporate culture. In contrast, intuitive decision-making assumes center stage in cultures that focus on relational knowledge and experience-based wisdom, characteristic of most Eastern cultures.

This differentiation mandates worldwide managers to synchronize their strategies with the local cultures' decision-making patterns. By embracing an integrative process that unites rational analysis with intuitive sense-making, managers can optimize organizational and decision-making effectiveness across different markets while responding to values embedded within different cultures. Cultural perceptions of risk lay the basis for the development of decision-making strategies at a global level. Across diverse cultural settings, the assessment of risk and its management may dramatically vary, determining organizational reactions to ambiguity. For example, highly uncertainty-avoiding cultures can be supportive of cautious decision-making strategies with great emphasis on thorough analysis of data and on risk-reducing strategies. In contrast, cultures that feel at ease with uncertainty can promote adventurous decision-making by enabling teams to take calculated risks for the sake of innovation. As a result, managers operating internationally need to develop an intimate knowledge of such differences in cultures regarding risk perception.

Thus, they are in a position to structure their models for decision-making so that they not only embrace but take advantage of such differences and build a robust and flexible organizational culture that can handle the challenges of an internationalized market. Successful group decision-making across diverse environments relies on appropriate combining of diverse ideas and information. Diverse groups offer a high level of diverse ideas, which can enhance creativity and lead to improved solutions. But managing dynamics in such multicultural groups calls for a tailored approach to decision-making that recognizes and capitalizes on differences.

Global managers must create inclusive environments that promote free flow of communication and collaboration, in which everyone is heard and treated with respect. Practices such as structured brainstorming and consensus can facilitate equal and equitable participation by team members of multicultural backgrounds. Aligning itself with shared goals and shared responsibility also enables transcending cultural barriers, leading to more informed and innovative decision-making. In this way, the use of decision-making techniques in global management proves to be not just a necessity, but an asset for strategy in dealing with globalizations complexity.

7.6. LEADERSHIP STYLES AND THEIR INFLUENCE ON DECISION-MAKING

In global management, the dynamic between decision-making processes and styles of leadership can't be overlooked. Leaders are not only tasked with guiding their subordinates but also with shaping the culture of decision-making within their organizations. Leadership styles, such as authoritative and democratic, convey quite different messages about decision-making processes. For instance, authoritarian leaders will immediately, from the top down, decide, which can prove helpful in high-pressure situations, while democratic leaders encourage consensus-based decision-making habits that can optimize stakeholder acceptance and moral commitment.

Figure 7.12. Leadership styles dynamics for multinational organizations.

Source: https://d8it4huxumps7.cloudfront.net/uploads/images/66699133c4d14_leadership_styles.jpg?d=2000x2000.

Understanding these dynamics is essential for multinational corporations operating in various cultural settings with varied decision-making norms and practices. The effectiveness of the style of a leader typically hinges on his or her ability to adapt the style to suit the cultural context, establishing a harmonious environment for effective cooperation and decision-making. Cross-cultural management introduces additional dimensions of complexity to decision-making, particularly with regard to how risks are perceived. There are various approaches to risk in different cultures, and they are capable of significantly influencing decision-making and execution. In high uncertainty avoidance cultures, leaders tend to prefer formal decision-making procedures and risk avoidance mechanisms, as noted in many crisis management situations (Gaju, 2025) (Figure 7.12).

On the contrary, low uncertainty avoidance cultures would like risk-taking and flexibility in deciding what to do. The disparity helps to emphasize that cultural intelligence must be cultivated by leaders so that they can appreciate various perceptions of risk and decision-making. By adopting a modest interpretation of these cultural differences, leaders will be able to adjust their style to successfully overcome the complexities of decision-making within a globalized scenario, thus enhancing their organizations adaptability and responsiveness in the face of uncertainty. Secondly, group decision-making in multicultural settings calls for extensive consideration of leadership styles. In multinational teams, where points of view, experiences, and backgrounds vary widely, leaders must be democratic yet authoritative in demeanor to strike the right balance between support and involvement. Research has proven that democratic leadership, wherein process is through participation, stands a better chance of leading to successful outcomes in the classroom setting through empowering group members, facilitating cooperation, and improving instruction quality (Rafiq-Uz-Zaman et al., 2025). Conversely, in situations that require immediate decision-making, the authoritarian style can accelerate processes. The leaders who can ride between these styles by actively engaging different team members in the process of decision-making are in a position to harness the collective intelligence of their teams. Ultimately, the best leaders can sense the specific requirements of unique situations and adjust their styles to enhance group unity and create effective outcomes in global management.

7.6.1. Overview of Different Leadership Styles in International Management

In the context of global management, the interaction between various styles of leadership is crucial in influencing decision-making structures. Leaders engaged in a rational style would place greater emphasis on factual-based decision-making, assigning weightage to empirical facts and rationality to arrive at conclusions. This style would normally be functional within frameworks placing value on structure and predictability, allowing managers to define predictable outcomes based on systematic analysis. On the other hand, intuitive leaders will make decisions depending on their experience and intuition, reflecting a less controlled and more flexible type. This blend of rationality and intuition calls for a degree of adaptability by leaders in adjusting to the cultural context in which they work, demanding a leadership approach that acquires an awareness of diversity in international markets and stakeholders' values (Harrison et al., 2011). Cultural dimensions also play a crucial role in establishing the risk perception of leaders and, consequently, affecting their decision-making. Cultural values and norms condition different cultures and their resulting attitudes towards uncertainty and risk-taking. For instance, those societies that have a high uncertainty avoidance index are likely to have more formalized decision-making processes for risk avoidance, while those that adopt a lenient approach are likely to have more impulsive and permissive leadership styles. This divergence underscores the need for building up cultural intelligence in leaders so that they can calibrate their leadership behavior to align with their global teams' risk perceptions. Understanding these cultural dynamics can enable an inclusive climate where decision-makers feel comfortable sharing their views, eventually leading to a more inclusive leadership and decision-making model across contexts (Mustafa et al., 2015). International group decision-making also reflects the impact of leadership style on managerial ability. Leaders of multicultural groups will need to handle dissimilar ways and modes of communication derived from individuals who have come from various cultures. A focus on participative leadership can enhance group cohesion by encouraging input from all, particularly in settings where collectivist culture prevails. Conversely, in an individualistic society, a transformational style of leadership may be more desirable because it encourages members of the team to take ownership and develop innovative thoughts. By adapting their leadership style to fit the dynamics of the groups culture, leaders are able to create a synergistic environment that optimizes the quality of decisions output. Creating the type of environment requires leaders not only to embrace cross-cultural differences but also to embrace them, reframing their approach to creating cooperation and knowledge-based choices in global management (Harrison et al., 2011).

7.6.2. The Relationship Between Leadership and Decision-Making Effectiveness

The interface between decision competence and leadership styles gains prominence in global management. Leaders must be capable of adapting decision-making methods to various group dynamics and individual perceptions in multicultural environments. Rational decision-making processes, relying on systematic analysis, tend to be complemented with intuitive processes drawing on the experience and intuition of the leaders. This duality is particularly pertinent when operating in the complicated field of global business, where leaders are faced by multifaceted challenges and opportunities. Successful leaders not only gather and analyze relevant data but also create a culture that encourages creativity and collaboration. Research has shown that the integration of logical reasoning with intuitive awareness could generate more efficient decision-making outcomes, as leaders use various insights and an open-communication culture that complements critical thinking and creativity in team members (Siregar et al., 2025). Furthermore, the relationship between decision-making efficiency and perceived risk is also very disparate across cultures. Global leaders must realize that milieus in cultures vary in affecting the manner in which teams assess and respond to risks, in turn influencing their patterns of decision-making. For instance, while individualistic societies prefer careful risk-taking, consensus-based societies prefer being risk-averse. These variations highlight the importance of cultural intelligence, as an understanding of these nuances allows leaders to modify their constructs of decision-making as a function of the same (Figure 7.13).

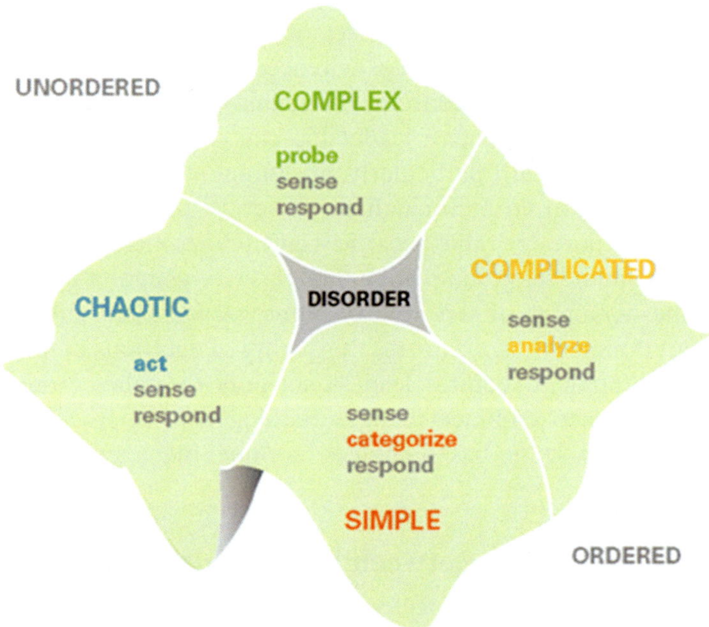

Figure 7.13. Effectiveness of leadership decision-making in complex systems.

Source: https://www.mdpi.com/systems/systems-08-00005/article_deploy/html/images/systems-08-00005-g001.png.

Effective decision-making internationally therefore requires not only that the risk tolerance of the leader themselves be understood, but that they are also skilled at navigating and coping with the diverse perceptions of risk among their groups. By encouraging open discussion of risk and decision-making, leaders can maximize the effectiveness of their strategy and resulting outcomes

(Hermawan et al., 2025). Group decision-making as a core component of leadership success becomes all the more pertinent in multicultural teams. Group environments call for an understanding of how members from various backgrounds add value to the decision. Leaders own a best role in the facilitation of such meetings, striking a balance between being assertive and inclusive in order to enable all voices to be heard. Effective leaders draw the best from several perspectives, reducing conflict and promoting respect within the team. The application of structured decision-making aids can also introduce coherence and consistency into group discussion, improving group output. By employing creative problem-solving techniques and drawing lessons from the members' profound experiences, leaders can significantly improve the quality of their decision-making processes, ultimately leading to more innovative solutions and enhanced organizational performance around the world.

7.6.3. Case Examples of Leadership Impact on International Decisions

In the intricate realm of international decision-making, leadership shown by leaders in positions of authority considerably influences decisions, be they rational or intuitive. The understanding of the situational complexities of one's environment by a leader can have an influence on the course of international negotiations and alliances. For instance, executives who like structure in decision-making will utilize data and analytical processes to direct their decisions such that they align with global best practices and company objectives. Those who favor intuitive orientations, by contrast, tend to center on personal experience and intuition and consequently may end up creating riskier choices. This decision-making duality can result in conflicting fates for global relations, hence suggesting the imperative of leaders adapting their strategies based on the cultural context and working relations of the specific decision. Cross-cultural perception of risk further complicates the leadership landscape in international affairs. Leaders must navigate through a range of risk analyses that vary quite significantly across cultures and impact joint ventures and alliances. For example, a risk-taking culture leader will embrace bolder global setups, while another from a risk-averse culture will prefer stability and caution. This difference in the way risks are perceived also affects not just decision-making processes but the trust that exists between global players. Leaders must embrace a culturally adaptive leadership style, leveraging their understanding of different perceptions of risks to foster cooperation and decrease conflict. By doing this, they can cope with the complexities that come with international management and find better outcomes for their organizations. Additionally, group decision-making across cultures places high emphasis on the impact of leadership on global decisions. Effective leaders of multicultural teams must create a sense of cohesion in which various voices receive attention and are included in the decision-making process. These settings flourish in democratic styles of leadership that allow for active participation, as they differ from more autocratic styles that may suppress creativity and challenge group strength. For instance, studies show that leadership styles combining inclusiveness with systematic guidance can enhance group performance and job satisfaction in international teams (Adjei et al., 2019). When leaders recognize and leverage the abilities of global group members, they create solid bases for strategic decision-making that resonates beyond borders. This strategic inclusiveness not only enhances decision value but also enhances relationships among global stakeholders, leading to sustainable organizational performance and resilience.

SUMMARY

The dynamic nature of the global management context demands a delicate approach to decision-making in various contexts. As organizations operate increasingly in multicultural environments, the line between rational and intuitive approaches to decision-making becomes a critical influencer. Rational decision-making, which entails a systematic analysis of information and outcomes, yields a systematic process helpful for predictable contexts. Conversely, intuitive decision-making will lean on instincts based on cultural awareness and social contexts. International management leaders will need to tread carefully and harmonize these approaches while aiming to harmonize methods to accommodate the diverse team dynamics and with consideration of the risks associated with both methods. Ultimately, creating harmony among these methods will be key to facilitating beneficial decision-making process in global organizations. In risk perception, one should note that cultural settings play a significant role in risk evaluation and regulation in international decision-making. Cultures exhibit varying levels of risk tolerance, and this, in turn, affects organizational goals and outcomes. For instance, some cultures tend to be conservative, risk-avoiding approaches, while others will be optimistic with an eye to discovering novel opportunities in spite of prevailing uncertainties. Such cultural complexity demands consideration by international managers of their group's risk attitude, since alignment of attitude is important to avoid conflicts or lose opportunities. Therefore, constructing a whole picture of such cultural risk profiles is imperative for making informed decisions, nexintegrate various global management scenarios. The group decision-making dynamics in multicultural environments further add to the need for great management globally. Given that teams may comprise individuals of multiple cultures, consensus-making can be a difficult yet rewarding experience. Different communication habits, decision-making options, and ways of solving disagreements can significantly affect the behavior of groups. As organizational behavior research has emphasized, group performance and cohesion can be enhanced through the development of open environments that value each member's voice while respecting the variety of perspectives. Through the application of consensus-building methods and the recognition of the importance of being culturally aware, improved decision-making can be achieved. Thus, capitalizing on the strengths of diversity in teams is not only necessary for organizational performance but also a vital aspect of effective leadership strategies in global management, as reflected in ongoing debates among concerned research communities, such as at recent conferences that focused on creative strategies for global collaboration and decision-making in organizations (Main et al., 2016; Driessen et al., 2009).

In international management, decision-making is often influenced by the interplay between rational and intuitive approaches. While rational decision-making is marked by systematic analysis and reasoning, intuitive approaches are based on experience and intuition. The two often come to a more clear display within complex situations, where there is uncertainty and pressure of time. The decision-making process is also made more challenging because of cultural differences, which can change perception and effect on preferences between doing one versus the other. Global managers need to have an understanding of these differences because it will enable them to make their strategies fit the culture, resulting in improved decision-making outcomes. The critical analysis of these two approaches brings to fore the significance of flexibility enabling a framework of decision-making with a blend of rational analysis as well as intuitive judgments within various cultural environments. Further, risk perception differs greatly among cultures, and hence affect managerial decisions while operating internationally. High uncertainty avoidance cultures are more cautious and like thorough analysis and decision-making by consensus, while low uncertainty avoidance cultures are more risk-friendly and like accepting decisions more quickly. The difference in risk appetite requires global managers to become culturally competent, whereby they recognize and adapt to varying risk appetites when they work with global teams. For instance, a risk-averse manager would always be more inclined towards cautious analysis and heaps of data gathering before acting, while in a risk-taking culture, speedy decision-making would be rewarded. An acute awareness of such cultural factors provides international managers with greater resilience to address complex decision-making contexts, foster cooperation, and enhance the global management practices' effectiveness. The dynamics of group decision-making in multicultural environments is another key aspect of international management. The authority of cultural origin to affect the interaction among groups can lead to varying decision-making processes that define a team's function and productivity. In multicultural teams, individuals will have varying perceptions based on their individual cultural backgrounds, which will contribute richer discussions but also potential misunderstandings. The role of managers is to foster a culture that includes everyone's voice and tolerates varying views. This means not only promoting open communication but also adopting approaches that allow for effective collaboration among diverse culture members. Combining strategies that facilitate bridging such differences can enhance the quality of decisions made, improve team cohesion, and lead to innovative solutions tailored for global markets. Thus, addressing the complexity of decision-making in a group within an international context remains vital in achieving effective management outcomes.

REFERENCES

1. Acikalin, U., Goulding, J. S., Isikdag, U., et al. (2009). Construction informatics in Turkey: Strategic role of ICT and future research directions. https://core.ac.uk/download/1666747.pdf (accessed on 24th September 2025).
2. Adam, M., Clough, G., Conole, G., et al. (2015). A game-based approach to improve traders' decision-making. https://core.ac.uk/download/30475169.pdf (accessed on 24th September 2025).
3. Adjei, A., & Aruzie, R. S. (2019). The impact of leadership styles on teaching and learning outcomes: A case study of selected senior high schools in the Nkronza districts of Brong Ahafo Region in Ghana. https://core.ac.uk/download/287611643.pdf (accessed on 24th September 2025).
4. Alács, P., Hideg, É., Kiss, E., et al. (2009). Futures studies in the interactive society. https://core.ac.uk/download/11854405.pdf (accessed on 24th September 2025).
5. Aldina Correia, & Ribeiro, D. (2025). Longitudinal features extraction in international logistics performance index. *WSEAS Transactions on Business and Economics*. https://www.semanticscholar.org/paper/4b6332a24f68c1ccfe909ff7afd9dd3d69d375f5 (accessed on 24th September 2025).
6. Allan, R., Clarke, M., Jeffrey, P., et al. (2013). The impact of regulation, ownership and business culture on managing corporate risk within the water industry. https://core.ac.uk/download/74409703.pdf (accessed on 24th September 2025).
7. Anderson, R. M., Dickinson, K. L., Fowler, V. G., et al. (2009). Using decision analysis to improve malaria control policy making. https://core.ac.uk/download/62565298.pdf (accessed on 24th September 2025).
8. Andronikou, A., Archontides, M., Barkey, D., Bastin, G., Beirman, D., Bianchi, C., Boukas, et al. (2013). Impacts of the global economic crisis on Cyprus tourism and policy responses. https://core.ac.uk/download/29018464.pdf (accessed on 24th September 2025).
9. Bachofen, C., Fortugno, N., Goentzel, J., et al. (2012). Games for a new climate: Experiencing the complexity of future risks. https://open.bu.edu/bitstream/2144/22902/1/Games-for-a-New-Climate-TF-Nov2012.pdf (accessed on 24th September 2025).
10. Bäcklund, J., & Werr, A. (2025). The construction of global management consulting–A study of consultancies' web presentations. https://core.ac.uk/download/pdf/7281372.pdf (accessed on 24th September 2025).

11. Badii, A., & Sharif, A. M. (2003). Integrating information and knowledge for enterprise innovation. https://core.ac.uk/download/335039.pdf (accessed on 24th September 2025).
12. Baesens, B., Berrevoets, J., Verbeke, W., et al. (2020). Autoencoders for strategic decision support. http://arxiv.org/abs/2005.01075 (accessed on 24th September 2025).
13. Barnard, S., Boyes, S. J., Elliott, M., et al. (2015). Integrating management tools and concepts to develop an estuarine planning support system: A case study of the Humber Estuary, Eastern England. https://core.ac.uk/download/151157186.pdf (accessed on 24th September 2025).
14. Botin Gonzalez, J. A., & de Palacios, M. (2010). Sustainable management: A strategic challenge for a global minerals and metals industry. http://oa.upm.es/7603/ (accessed on 24th September 2025).
15. Boudreau, J. W., Dowling, P. J., & Ramstad, P. M. (2002). Global talent ship: Toward a decision science connecting talent to global strategic success. https://core.ac.uk/download/5131512.pdf (accessed on 24th September 2025).
16. Chakhar, S., Mousseau, V., Pusceddu, C., et al. (2005). Decision map for spatial decision making in urban planning. https://core.ac.uk/download/29589016.pdf (accessed on 24th September 2025).
17. Cheney, H., Willetts, J., Ovington, K., & Winterford, K. (2025). Working in decentralized service systems: Challenges and choices for the Australian aid program. https://core.ac.uk/download/pdf/30672623.pdf (accessed on 24th September 2025).
18. Childs, S., & McLeod, J. (2013). A strategic approach to making sense of the "wicked" problem of ERM. https://core.ac.uk/download/17298788.pdf (accessed on 24th September 2025).
19. Cleveland, J. N., Sanchez, D., & Shore, L. (2018). Inclusive workplaces: A review and model. https://core.ac.uk/download/288817598.pdf (accessed on 24th September 2025).
20. Coltman, T., Keating, B. W., & Richard, P. J. (2009). Designing IS service strategy: An information acceleration approach. https://core.ac.uk/download/12033426.pdf (accessed on 24th September 2025).
21. de Freitas, H. M. R., Lacerda, F. M., & Martens, C. D. P. (2016). A project portfolio management model adapted to non-profit organizations. https://core.ac.uk/download/213631182.pdf (accessed on 24th September 2025).
22. Desmidt, S., & George, B. (2018). Strategic-decision quality in public organizations: An information processing perspective. https://core.ac.uk/download/55854234.pdf (accessed on 24th September 2025).

23. Driessen, P. P. J., van Nieuwaal, K., Spit, T. J. M., et al. (2009). A state of the art of governance literature on adaptation to climate change: Towards a research agenda. https://core.ac.uk/download/pdf/29253490.pdf (accessed on 24th September 2025).

24. Dumrongrojwatthana, P., & Trébuil, G. (2010). Negotiating the forest–farmland interface in northern Thailand with companion modelling. http://agritrop.cirad.fr/555388/1/document_555388.pdf (accessed on 24th September 2025).

25. Farole, T., & Akinci, G. (2011). Special Economic Zones. The World Bank eBooks. https://doi.org/10.1596/978-0-8213-8763-4 (accessed on 24th September 2025).

26. Fitó Bertran, M. À., Hernández Lara, A. B., & Serradell-Lopez, E. (2018). Do business games foster skills? A cross-cultural study from learners' views. https://core.ac.uk/download/157812216.pdf (accessed on 24th September 2025).

27. Gaju, A. (2025). Uncertainty avoidance and crisis management: Theoretical insights into cultural dynamics in navigating crises. *Proceedings of the International Conference on Applied Research in Business, Management and Economics.* https://www.semanticscholar.org/paper/0a1714bd4a15ca439424dfc2f01a1a8b7d2ab24a (accessed on 24th September 2025).

28. Haas, M. R. (2003). Cosmopolitans and locals: Status rivalries, deference, and knowledge in international teams. https://core.ac.uk/download/5129158.pdf (accessed on 24th September 2025).

29. Harrison, P., & Roomi, M. A. (2011). Entrepreneurial leadership: What is it and how should it be taught? https://core.ac.uk/download/29819519.pdf (accessed on 24th September 2025).

30. Hermawan, A., Alwi, M., & Alhamdan, L. S. (2025). Strategy to decision making effectiveness through strengthening digital leadership, creativity, knowledge management and organizational support. *International Journal of Multidisciplinary Research and Growth Evaluation.* https://www.semanticscholar.org/paper/805d459735d99839819ad25003ea80a4075eb14c (accessed on 24th September 2025).

31. Hodgkinson, A., Kowalczyk, J., Markey, R., et al. (2025). Gender, part-time employment and employee participation in the workplace: Comparing Australia and the European Union. https://core.ac.uk/download/pdf/7141964.pdf (accessed on 24th September 2025).

32. Jafari, N. (2024). Toward an analytical technique for evaluating alternative East-West supply chain routes through Azerbaijan. 2024 3rd International Conference on Problems of Logistics, Management and Operation in the

East-West Transport Corridor (PLMO). https://www.semanticscholar.org/paper/c1997003f80b54aa8742b751de2d0de34ad29050 (accessed on 24th September 2025).

33. Jogulu, U. D., & Wood, G. J. (2008). A cross-cultural study into peer evaluations of women's leadership effectiveness. http://hdl.handle.net/10536/DRO/DU:30017687 (accessed on 24th September 2025).
34. Kanabar, V., Messikomer, C., & Thomas, A. (2018). Enhancing project-related behavioral competence in education. https://open.bu.edu/bitstream/2144/29016/1/Enhancing%20Project-Related%20Behavioral%20Competence%20in%20Education.pdf (accessed on 24th September 2025).
35. Lipinski, J., & Potter, J. A. (2009). Key factors for hastening the strategic issue diagnosis process: A within-organizational model. https://core.ac.uk/download/12116410.pdf (accessed on 24th September 2025).
36. Lomas, R. (2024). AI-driven FinTech solutions for financial inclusion: A study on MSME sector empowerment. 2024 1st International Conference on Advances in Computing, Communication and Networking (ICAC2N). https://www.semanticscholar.org/paper/49b6182e82284b2b42882d8c641b1784b0aaced9 (accessed on 24th September 2025).
37. Main, C., & Shaw, W. (2016). Employer policies and practices to manage and prevent disability: Conclusion to the special issue. https://core.ac.uk/download/76978402.pdf (accessed on 24th September 2025).
38. Makinde, D., & Mugwagwa, J. (2012). Governance of biotechnology in Africa: The challenge of reconciling interdependencies and differences. https://core.ac.uk/download/9543525.pdf (accessed on 24th September 2025).
39. Marcotte, D., Rustambekov, E., & Trendowski, J. (2019). Importance of cultural intelligence: Cross-cultural examination and analysis. https://core.ac.uk/download/231818803.pdf (accessed on 24th September 2025).
40. Marsh, T. L., Wahl, T. I., & Zhao, Z. (2025). Invasive species management: Foot-and-mouth disease in the U.S. beef industry. https://core.ac.uk/download/pdf/7055920.pdf (accessed on 24th September 2025).
41. Mustafa, G. (2015). The emergence of leader-society value congruence: A cross-cultural perspective. https://core.ac.uk/download/144552158.pdf (accessed on 24th September 2025).
42. N/A. (2012). Resilient livelihoods and food security in coastal aquatic agricultural systems: Investing in transformational change. https://core.ac.uk/download/11024818.pdf (accessed on 24th September 2025).

43. Nishii, L. H., & Özbilgin, M. F. (2007). Global diversity management: Towards a conceptual framework. https://core.ac.uk/download/219376625.pdf (accessed on 24th September 2025).

44. Noha, O. (2025). The essence and importance of information and communication support in the management of enterprises' foreign economic activity. Economics. Finances. Law. https://www.semanticscholar.org/paper/993462eed53d9519d40cdf5483852d8197493443 (accessed on 24th September 2025).

45. Perk, J., De Backer, G., Gohlke, H., Graham, I., Reiner, Ž., Verschuren, M., Albus, C., et al. (2012). European guidelines on cardiovascular disease prevention in clinical practice (version 2012): The Fifth Joint Task Force of the European Society of Cardiology and other societies on cardiovascular disease prevention in clinical practice (constituted by representatives of nine societies and by invited experts). European Heart Journal, 33, 1635–1701. https://doi.org/10.1093/eurheartj/ehs092 (accessed on 24th September 2025).

46. Rafiq-uz-Zaman, M., Bano, S., & Naveed, Y. (2025). Comparative analysis of authoritative and democratic leadership styles and their impact on school management effectiveness. Inverse Journal of Social Sciences. https://www.semanticscholar.org/paper/e1eb0b23f9244bf05b2894a2dee1b932961e4fa8 (accessed on 24th September 2025).

47. Saeed, M., & Sohail, M. S. (2002). Cross-cultural perspectives of decision-making and control in multinational corporations operating in ASEAN. https://core.ac.uk/download/12116281.pdf (accessed on 24th September 2025).

48. Salcedo-La Viña, C., & Morarji, M. (2016). Making women's voices count in community decision-making on land investments. https://core.ac.uk/download/71338675.pdf (accessed on 24th September 2025).

49. Shachaf, P. (2008). Cultural diversity and information and communication technology impacts on global virtual teams: An exploratory study. https://core.ac.uk/download/11887687.pdf (accessed on 24th September 2025).

50. Siregar, U. R., & Hermawan, A. (2025). Decision making effectiveness through strengthening digital leadership, creativity, knowledge management and organizational support. Dinasti International Journal of Education Management and Social Science. https://www.semanticscholar.org/paper/d7f9a7adc240d5a021a942749f8bc08575dff162 (accessed on 24th September 2025).

51. Valgimigli, M., Bueno, H., Byrne, R. A., Collet, J. P., Costa, F., Jeppsson, A., Jüni, P., et al. (2017). 2017 ESC focused update on dual antiplatelet therapy in coronary artery disease developed in collaboration with EACTS. European Heart Journal, 39, 213–260. https://doi.org/10.1093/eurheartj/ehx419 (accessed on 24th September 2025).
52. van der Heijde, D., Ramiro, S., Landewé, R., Baraliakos, X., Van den Bosch, F., Sepriano, A., Regel, A., et al. (2017). 2016 update of the ASAS-EULAR management recommendations for axial spondylarthritis. Annals of the Rheumatic Diseases, 76, 978–991. https://doi.org/10.1136/annrheumdis-2016-210770 (accessed on 24th September 2025).
53. Vogt, B., & Kroll, E. B. (2025). Attraction to chance in Germany and Australia: An experimental study of cultural differences. https://core.ac.uk/download/pdf/7045247.pdf (accessed on 24th September 2025).
54. Weston, A., Kazimirski, A., Kenley, A., McLeod, R., & Gripper, R. (2017). Global innovations in measurement and evaluation. https://core.ac.uk/download/87085547.pdf (accessed on 24th September 2025).

Chapter 8

Negotiation and Conflict Management Across Cultures

Contents

INTRODUCTION

It is essential to comprehend the subtle art of negotiation and conflict resolution in a global environment, as globalization becomes increasingly influential in shaping intercultural interactions. It is important to realize that negotiation styles differ widely between regions and recognizing this emphasizes the importance of cultural competence in cross-cultural management. For example, some cultures might value directness and assertiveness in negotiations, whereas others might support indirect communication styles that prioritize harmony and relationship building. This divergence in strategy and expectation frequently creates the need for a greater sensitivity to cultural influences, that can both reduce the threat of dispute through misunderstandings or misinterpretations and increase the likelihood of successful negotiation. When looking at the tactics and strategies used in differing cultural contexts, it is possible to see that successful negotiation involves more than the mere application of universal principles. Rather, it is a matter of learning how to react to the particular social and moral frameworks that guide action across cultures. The interactive evolution of negotiation style and cultural values has the potential for great variation in outcomes. Through analysis of theoretical models coupled with empirical study, the debate seeks to expose whether advanced models of conflict resolution can leap cultural barriers or whether contextual factors too often dictate the response. Thus, the cultural dynamics of negotiation practice form a fertile field for scholarly research and practical application in international management. For a successful negotiation environment in cross-cultural conflicts, both sides need to understand the importance of intercultural communication. Development of an appreciation of the ethical issues of diverse engagement may ensure mutual trust and understanding, which are essential in successful conflict resolution. Research findings on students' education while undertaking international negotiation projects reveal that cultural diversity exposure is likely to significantly improve cross-cultural competencies. This suggests that graduates in the international marketplace are required to be capable of understanding and working effectively within these complexities, a fact that highlights the pivotal position of education in shaping future global management leaders (Menkel-Meadow et al., 2003; Thanaraj et al., 2016). Emphasizing the need for significant and comparative modes of conflict resolution, this essay tries to throw some light upon the diverse dimensions of negotiation across cultures, ultimately resulting in meaningful mechanisms of conflict management in the international scenario.

Definition of Negotiation and Conflict Management

A core element of effective negotiation comes from the acknowledgement of various styles used between cultures. These styles tend to shape the form of strategy and tactics adopted by negotiators, significantly impacting the whole negotiation process. For instance, in some cultures, a direct style with an open style of frankness and directness may be preferred, while in other cultures indirectness with a focus on relationship-building and establishing within the context may predominate. These types of cultural nuances are highly crucial in propelling strategy in negotiation activities, as revealed by recent research hinting at rising interest in multicultural negotiation dynamics. Understanding these variations among cultures not only assists in crafting tailored strategies for negotiation but also facilitates an atmosphere that is conducive to effective conflict management (Indu, 2025). As negotiation goes on, conflict typically cannot be avoided, and hence conflict management has emerged as a core part of international management. Conflict management symbolizes techniques for resolving differences, instilling cooperation, and repairing relationships during confrontations. A variety of mechanisms can be applied, ranging from mediation and arbitration to integrative bargaining techniques that seek win-win solutions. Choice of a specific method of conflict resolution is often based upon culture, as what is customary when it comes to confrontation and resolution varies widely between societies (Figure 8.1).

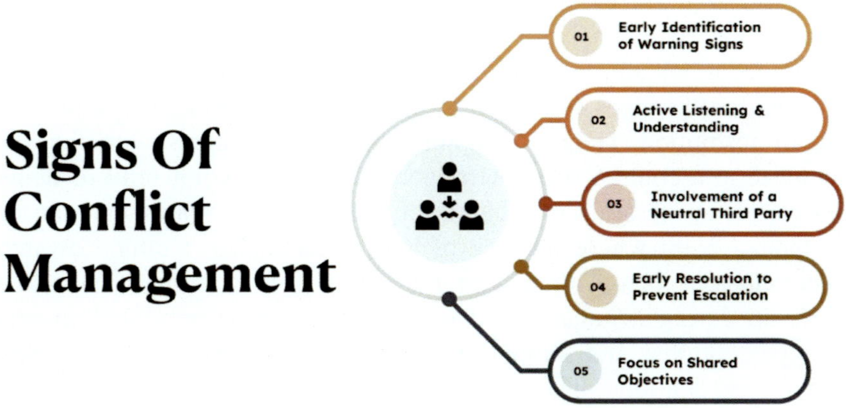

Figure 8.1. The signs of conflict management.

Source: https://kapable.club/blog/wp-content/uploads/2024/06/Signs-Of-Conflict-Management-1024x576.webp.

For example, collectivist cultures may settle disputes in a more harmonious manner, attempting to reach a consensus by all parties. An appreciation of these cultural dimensions is necessary to handle conflicts and optimize negotiation outcomes (Indu, 2025). The mutual relationship between conflict management and negotiation underscores global competence's appropriateness in the more diversified working environment today. Managers and leaders must attain competencies that not only revolve around negotiation strategies but also encompass cultural competence and adaptability in multicultural settings. This kind of competence enables individuals to engage harmoniously with different groups and significantly influences the negotiation processes. Empirical data show that firms are beginning to recognize the value of forming multicultural teams that can transcend differences through efficient conflict management practice. As team diversity grows, the ability to understand and accept divergent styles of negotiation becomes more valuable and constitutes organizational success in global settings (Nishii et al., 2007).

Importance of Cultural Awareness in International Management

With the intricate landscape of international management comes a heightened sensitivity to cultural difference. Negotiation styles are vastly divergent across international borders, influenced by deep-seated tradition, social mores, and patterns of communication. For instance, while some societies might encourage directness and frankness in negotiations, others will place greater value on subtlety and interpersonal relationships. This divergence calls for a delicate appreciation of various negotiation tactics and strategies to avoid miscommunications and facilitate constructive dialogue. Lack of appreciation of these cultural nuances can result in misunderstandings that lead to conflict instead of resolution. Hence, equipping training managers with the ability to recognize and counter different negotiation styles is not only of help but imperative for successful cross-cultural communication, particularly in high-stakes management where the risk of conflict is higher. Cultural awareness also encompasses being attuned to the underlying emotional currents that can flare up during negotiations. The ability to handle emotional situations, observe perceptions, and strategically manage style can be crucial to the success of negotiations. The literature draws attention to the necessity of face-giving and rapport-building as key skills in such contexts, particularly when negotiating in multicultural teams or managing foreign stakeholders. Rehearsing gestures that demonstrate respect and sensitivity towards cultural differences can facilitate ease and build trust, which can result in enhanced cooperation. Such interpersonal skills are particularly required in community appraisals and collaborative settings where the voice of stakeholders matters. A sensitivity to emotional and interpersonal aspects of negotiation, therefore, not only resolves conflicts but also reinforces the cooperative spirit essential for effective international management. A successful international manager also needs to personalize conflict resolution strategies based on the cultural context. Every culture has a different preference in managing and settling disputes, ranging from aggressive to conciliatory. Knowledge of these preferences informs a manager how to manage future conflicts, whether open discussions or being more indirect are appropriate. As per the study by Thanaraj et al. (2016), establishing cross-cultural skills enables managers to solve conflicts better by developing a culture of mutual respect and trust. Furthermore, with negotiation skills, such as creativity and improvisation, managers are able to navigate complex situations with ease. By fine-tuning conflict management strategies to cultural peculiarities, international managers can effectively intervene in conflict and foster harmonious business relationship sustainability within multicultural environments and thereby enhance organizational effectiveness in general.

8.1. NEGOTIATION STYLES AROUND THE WORLD

The intricately carved landscape of negotiation approaches globally is strongly rooted in cultural practice and norms, which guide the manner in which conflict and resolution are managed. In Western societies, for instance, negotiation is likely to emphasize assertiveness and direct communication, with emphasis on needing to negotiate a mutually beneficial deal using open communication. Conversely, in Asian cultures, negotiation has been described as an indirect style that prioritizes respect and harmony with a preference for avoiding confrontation.

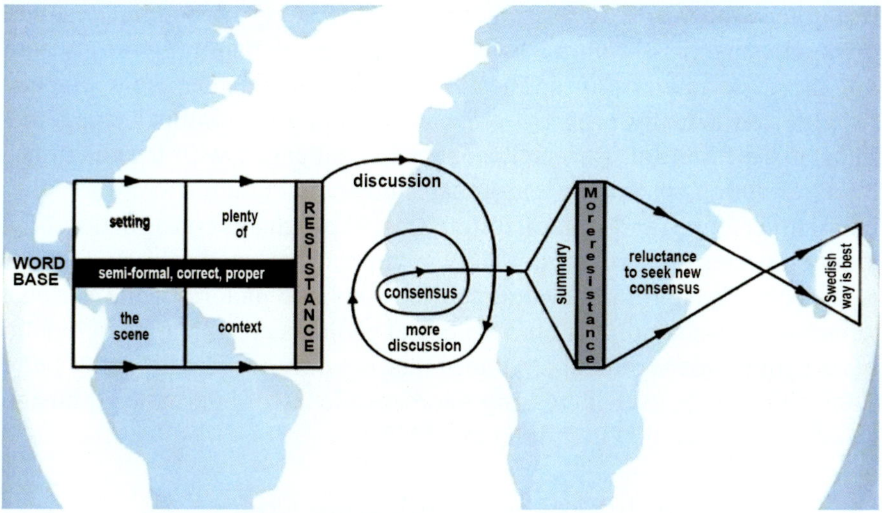

Figure 8.2. The landscape of negotiation styles across the globe.

Source: https://i.insider.com/58a76189dd089506398b487c?width=700&format=jpeg&auto=webp.

This difference in negotiation approaches demonstrates how cultural origins influence conflict management approaches based on differences in communication and decision-making expectations stakeholders bring into the negotiation arena. With rising globalization and the integration of different markets, knowledge about these diverse negotiation styles is a must for global managers who seek to establish effective communication and cooperation in cross-cultural contexts. Cultural influences not only frame negotiators' attitudes but also play an important role in shaping approaches to conflict resolution deployed across different settings. For instance, research has captured the prevalence of conflict evasiveness in Chinese organizational settings, with evasive strategies of leaders found to enhance followers' perceptions of justice and supervisory trust and positively impact their emotional well-being (Figure 8.2).

These results point to a characteristic of Chinese bargaining style where attaining social harmony may override getting to confrontation face-to-face. These results are characteristic of a broader trend in conflict resolution where culturally tailored strategies are shown to be effective in framing leadership dynamics within particular regions. As international managers work against such complexities, it becomes increasingly important to draw upon local practices in presenting effective conflict resolution models that will strike a chord with the anticipation of culture. Moreover, research into negotiation styles around the world highlights comparative study of conflict resolution theories crossing cross-cultural lines. The ongoing debate regarding whether or not there are universally applicable theories, or whether context-specific knowledge can actually progress our understanding of conflict management, remains at the forefront. Researchers remain challenged with the dilemma of conflict resolution, balancing empirical study with pragmatic awareness to identify universalities and cultural differences. Through this concern, the body of negotiation strategy and its applicability in international management continues to be shaped. Through the development of a holistic picture of the variety of negotiation styles that inhabit our world, stakeholders are able to develop more efficient conflict management strategies that not only respect diversity but are also able to meet the ever-increasing interdependency of international business (Menkel-Meadow et al., 2003; Li et al., 2017).

8.1.1. Direct vs. Indirect Communication Styles

The interface between bargaining styles and communication patterns is a reflection of ingrained cultural dynamics that could powerfully influence the success of cross-border deals. It can be conceivable that understanding whether a culture is direct or indirect in communication can provide invaluable insight into bargaining styles that people from various cultures adopt. For instance, in direct communication cultures such as North America, negotiators speak their needs and intentions directly, resulting in more overt expectations and quicker conflict resolution. In the majority of Asian and Middle Eastern cultures, however, indirect communication is most commonly practiced, favoring subtlety and context. This mode tends to prioritize maintaining relations and harmony, inclining to enter negotiation more cautiously, which might clash with assertiveness of direct communication cultures (Adair et al., 2012). The strategic use of these diverse communication styles is appreciated upon reviewing negotiation success across various cultural contexts. Research has shown that negotiators in honor cultures, such as in the Middle East, are likely to apply a more aggressive and affective style, influencing their strategies and overall negotiation approach (Adair et al., 2012) (Figure 8.3).

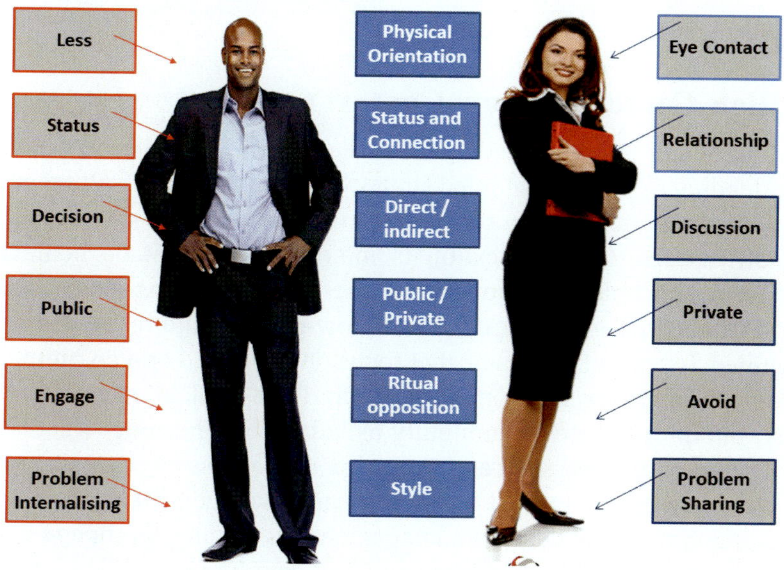

Figure 8.3. The interplay between direct and indirect communication styles.

Source: https://3plusinternational.com/wp-content/uploads/2019/03/Gender-differences-in-communication-1.png.

This competitive mindset is likely to depend on the preservation of face, and this can complicate negotiation with cultures that rely on candid solution and forthrightness. It is then important to recognize the incentives and assumptions underlying these styles in order to manage conflict effectively. Negotiators should be able to understand that the identification of aggressive behavior could be in many forms depending on the culture they are negotiating from, again supporting the use of flexible approach to cross-cultural negotiation. Moreover, the convergence of communication strategies with cultural values in society illustrates the complexity of leadership and negotiation processes in global business settings. According to previous research, incongruence in values between leaders and society can significantly impact the process of communication in negotiations. Leaders must possess proficiency in both the comprehension of their cultural orientations and those of their opposing counterparts to facilitate effective communication and cooperation. The ability to navigate these differing styles not only ensures increased mutual comprehension but puts diplomats in the position for better-quality conflict resolution. By cultivating sensitivity to the broader cultural context, global management practitioners can create ways to bridge gaps between direct and indirect communication with the promise of more effective negotiating and conflict management techniques.

8.1.2. High-Context vs. Low-Context Cultures

Negotiation traditions are deeply embedded within the cultural paradigms' fabric, extending beyond the adopted strategy to influence the resulting outcome as well. Patterns of negotiation style and tactic surround high-context and low-context differences. Communication is indirect, dependent on context, and strongly rooted in context and non-verbal cues in high-context societies such as Japan and China. This is in stark contrast to low-context cultures, as exemplified by the United States and Germany, that focus on expressed oral communication and direct, straightforward communication. High-context negotiators may, therefore, interpret silence or ambiguity as laden with meaning, whereas low-context counterparts view such an interaction as fruitless or confusing. Noting these differences is also critical in international management settings when it comes to negotiation and conflict management. As businesses engage in cross-cultural negotiations, the high-context and low-context communication aspects transcend styles to encompass broader cognitive processes and styles of conflict resolution. Whether questions and answers (Q&A) function more effectively than substantiation and offers (S&O) relies heavily on these cultural chasms. Studies in Poliakova et al. (2020) emphasize the necessity to recognize such mental nuances, demonstrating that S&O methods can yield better outcomes in high-context settings. The interaction among language and cultural expectations may influence whether negotiations yield integrative solutions, based on cooperation, or distributive ones, based on competition. Hence, international managers must be attuned to such cultural variations in a bid to develop specialized negotiation approaches that enhance the relational processes and facilitate conflict resolution. Moreover, the increasing phenomenon of digital negotiations, with global crises such as the COVID-19 pandemic further pressing for the same, underscores the imperative for a more advanced understanding of communication processes in international management. The reliance on virtual spaces necessitates a re-examination of traditional bargaining models, especially with the high-context and low-context cultural divides in perspective. As explained in Poliakova et al. (2020), language cues are ubiquitous in such spaces, posing challenges and opportunities for bargainers alike. This move to virtual interactions makes the poly-contextual behavior more critical, wherein negotiators must adapt strategies based on the linguistic and cultural context in which they are working. The necessity for cultural adaptability in negotiation strategies is, therefore, necessary; it equips stakeholders to effectively de-escalate conflicts dynamically, facilitating long-term partnerships even in the midst of intercultural transactions.

8.1.3. Influence of Power Distance on Negotiation Approaches

Negotiation is a multi-dimensional interaction of strategy and cultural elements that build interpersonal relationships within varying settings. One of the key elements of grasping these dynamics is the concept of power distance and how it relates to different cultures' perceptions of and embrace of power differences in organizations and societies. High power distance cultures have hierarchical frameworks, and this can play a significant amount of influence on the negotiation style. For example, in countries like Germany or the Netherlands, who both have lower power distance, the negotiations can subsequently adopt a more egalitarian mode of communication, that is, open communication and collaborative decision-making. This is a sharp contrast to where there is high power distance with a tendency to negotiate in a more top-down manner, with respect for authority being the general practice. These attitudinal variations at their essence point out the importance of discerning power distance in shaping negotiation styles across different cultural settings since it affects conflict management measures employed on international platforms (Lincke et al., 2025). Power distance effects are also involved in conflict resolution mechanisms where measures adopted closely reflect cultural attitudes towards hierarchy and authority. In high power distance cultures, conflict avoidance by leaders may be appreciated as a way to achieve harmony and respect for their peers, according to Chinese organizational behavior. Avoidance by leaders has been identified as having a positive influence on the sense of justice and emotional states of their followers (Li et al., 2017). This again illustrates the manner in which cultural acceptance of hierarchies can lead to negotiation styles that focus on indirectness and consensus rather than confrontation. The leaders here will engage in negotiations by weakening individual positions to engender a subjective sense of participation, thereby establishing a harmonious setting. This creates a unique intersection of cultural customs and strategic decision-making that ultimately decides international negotiation success. Understanding the nuances of power distance not only enhances negotiation skills but also outlines the approaches to managing conflict by global managers. Through adjusting their negotiation style to the power dynamics that exist in multicultural settings, managers can deal better with any resulting conflicts that may arise. For instance, in power distance cultures where the recognition of power is present, top leadership back-room deals can be more effective than inviting lower-level players to the negotiating table. In low power distance cultures, having everyone at the negotiating table may lead to more innovative solutions and highest buy-in from all stakeholders involved. Lastly, by recognizing and addressing appropriately the power of distance, global managers will be able to conduct more effective negotiations and develop models of conflict management acceptable to cultures everywhere so that they can have successful interactions in a world of globalization.

8.2. CULTURAL INFLUENCES ON NEGOTIATION TACTICS

Understanding the complexity of negotiation is crucial in international management, particularly due to the impact of cultural understanding on negotiation approach and tactic. The diversity in communication habits, values, and norms between cultures necessitates that negotiators adapt their approaches in order to bridge the differences successfully. For instance, while Western cultures often emphasize directness and assertiveness, most Eastern cultures prioritize indirectness and relationship maintenance. This divergence poses a problem in cross-cultural negotiations since misinterpretation of intentions becomes the cause of conflict rather than resolution. Negotiators must therefore foster a sympathetic awareness of these cultural differences to facilitate successful dialogue and cooperation. In this regard, the inclusion of cultural intelligence within negotiation planning can facilitate smoother exchanges and lead to mutually beneficial outcomes. Cultural background of the negotiators significantly influences tactics, including negotiation behavior as well as perceptions of success. Research has shown that national and organizational cultural distances may affect the efficacy of communication in the negotiation process. In cases where the negotiators belong to different cultures, value differences and communication differences may lead to conflict or miscommunication. For example, in cross-border mergers and acquisitions, varying organizational cultural differences are put in the foreground, by making simultaneous negotiation stage difficult, as can be seen from the findings which show national cultural distance to moderate communication-negotiation outcome relationship (Figure 8.4).

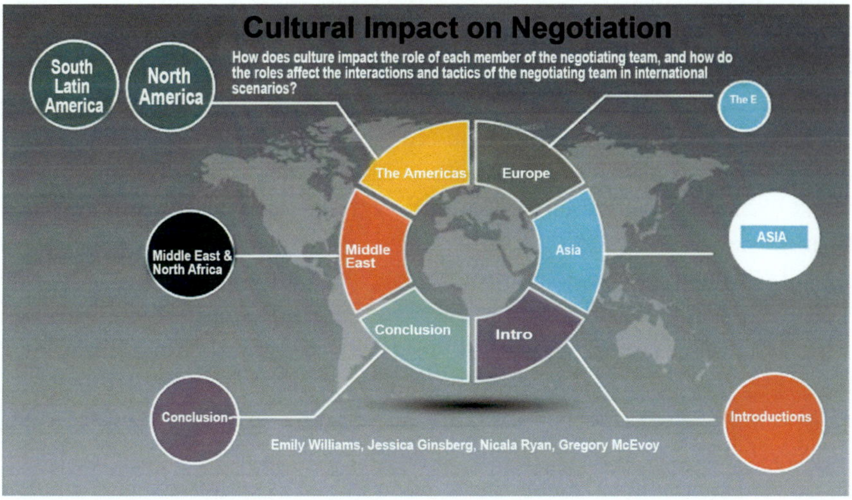

Figure 8.4. Culture impact on negotiation.

Source: https://0901.static.prezi.com/preview/v2/26cqoxg3yub657sw5nqdzxu3j76jc3sachvcdoaizecfr3dnitcq_3_0.png.

It is thus imperative that negotiators not only be sensitive to these cultural dimensions but also make a conscious effort to reduce the differences between them to the maximum extent in an effort to maximize the opportunities for successful agreement. Conflict resolution mechanisms must be calibrated accordingly to account for the profound impact culture exerts on negotiation procedures. Mediators, as in case studies of mediators such as George Mitchell and Lakhdar Brahimi, have difficulty in cross-cultural situations where their own cultural identity can shape perceptions of neutrality and ethics in mediation.

A mediator's ability to be able to understand and respond to the cultural expectations of all parties is critical in establishing legitimacy and trust. The intricate dance between cultural expectation and the strategic use of negotiation technique therefore highlights the importance for negotiators and mediators to be culturally sensitive. By doing so, they can manage complex intercultural interactions better and therefore their efficiency in management and conflict handling in multicultural settings across the globe is enhanced, as summed up in the findings obtained based on critical examinations surrounding ethical standards in mediation processes (Katsoris et al., 2016) and the result of the negotiation phase of cross-border activities (Ahammad et al., 2015).

8.2.1. Role of Individualism vs. Collectivism

Cultural forces play a major role in shaping negotiation styles and strategies in different regions of the globe, which is embedded deeply in individualism and collectivism. In individualist cultures such as America and the majority of Western European nations, personal autonomy and self-expression are promoted and most likely to be reflected in negotiation styles that revolve around personal goals and assertiveness. On the other hand, collectivist cultures that exist in Japan and China, among others, prefer group harmony and relational methods. In their cases, negotiators can follow strategies that build consensus and guarantee that the interest of the group is satisfied. A grasp of these cultural underpinnings is critical for successful negotiation in global management. When one approaches the negotiation with a sense of understanding whether a culture is more collectivist or individualist, one is able to more effectively adapt one's approach to meet one's counterpart's standards and modes of expression. Implications of individualism and collectivism also extend into conflict management styles. It is in cultures that value individualism that individuals tend to employ adversarial approaches when engaging in conflict, focusing on competitive strategies towards individual victory. The same can be justified from studies of negotiation behavior with a focus on how integrative and competitive approaches are more prevalent depending on the cultures that individuals come from, as referenced in a study of Taiwanese and Hong Kong negotiating styles (Christopher et al., 2025). In comparison therewith, collectivist cultures lean toward cooperative approaches, seeking solutions which maintain interpersonal relationships and group unity. Conflict resolution processes, thus, significantly differ, where individualist cultures have a higher tendency to employ formal mediation procedures, while collectivist cultures apply informal conversations and consensus-building. Knowing these varied techniques, global managers are capable of effectively managing conflicts and creating negotiation frameworks taking into account the cultural contexts of all stakeholders. In addition, studies suggest that national cultural dimensions significantly influence organizational responses to disruptions and challenges, hence the need to examine individualism and collectivism in international business (Demirag et al., 2016). For instance, companies from collectivist societies can have stronger alliance-building behaviors and prioritize long-term alliances when facing supply chain disruptions. On the other hand, firms in individualistic cultures can focus on rapid adaptation and entrepreneurial creative variations, at times at the cost of short-term results over enduring relational processes. The divergence also points to not just the extensive variance in negotiation and conflict management but also how cultural indicators can be applied as predictors for organizational competence in scenarios. With more globalization, it will be of utmost significance for managers to recognize and adapt to these cultural differences as a way of enhancing their negotiation and conflict resolution abilities in multicultural global environments.

8.2.2. Impact of Uncertainty Avoidance on Negotiation Strategies

Within international negotiation, cultural dimensions play significant roles in shaping strategies across various contexts. Uncertainty avoidance, which is among Hofstede's cultural dimensions, plays a critical role in how negotiators plan for interaction, decision-making, and conflict resolution. Cultures with high uncertainty avoidance tend to prefer structured bargaining frameworks and elaborate planning to shun potential risks in the bargaining process. These cultures often place a premium on explicit communication and prescribed procedure to cut out vagueness, and tend to want security through comprehensive agreements.

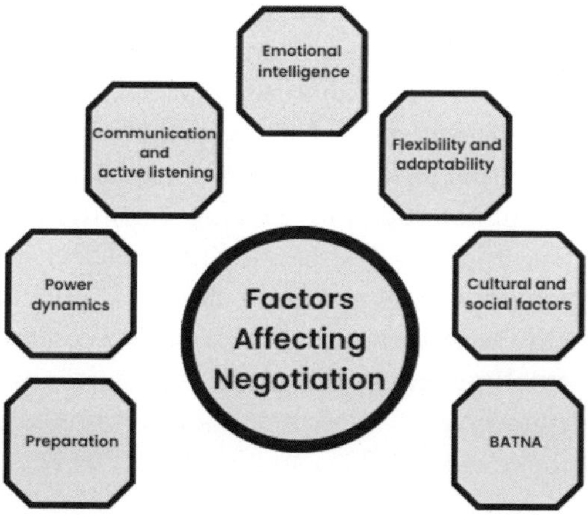

Figure 8.5. Factors of uncertainty avoidance on negotiation strategies.

Source: https://www.theknowledgeacademy.com/_files/images/Factors_Affecting_Negotiation.png.

For example, in Germany, negotiations tend to manifest a careful attention to detail and a sequential structured approach, in opposition to low uncertainty avoidance cultures that can be accommodating of spontaneity and adaptive negotiation methods, resulting in a diverse world landscape of negotiation approaches across international boundaries, as discussed in Lincke et al. (2025). The uncertainty avoidance ramifications extend far beyond individual styles of negotiating, touching upon relationship patterns that are crucial to effective conflict management in multicultural contexts. In high uncertainty avoidance societies, a need for surety shapes a more cautious negotiation style. High uncertainty avoidance societies may regard surprises—such as changes in offers not anticipated or unexpectedness in negotiating tactics—as threats, which justify a defensive strategy. Such a culture can introduce additional layers of tension to negotiations, suppressing collaborative ethos and creating distrust among parties. Low uncertainty avoidance cultures, conversely, are flexible and innovative in negotiations and consider uncertainty as a gateway to innovation and innovative ideas (Figure 8.5).

As the discussion of leaders' avoidance behavior in Chinese environments emphasizes, even the style of leaders has the ability to elicit followers' perceptual differences and emotions and therefore exemplify the overall impact of cultural characteristics on negotiations, as proposed in Li et al. (2017). Uncertainty avoidance implications at the strategic level reinforce the need for culturally tailored models of negotiation in global management. Negotiation styles that can accommodate varying levels of uncertainty avoidance can enhance the success of negotiation, create trust, and lower conflict. For negotiators who find themselves in between high and low uncertainty avoidance cultures, it then becomes critical to understand the expectations and tolerance of the counterpart. This could involve underscoring openness, establishing zones of agreement, and staging negotiations to develop constructively consensus and comfort over time. By employing strategies that respect and embrace these dimensions of culture, negotiators are more capable of managing complexity. Lastly, understanding the ramifications of uncertainty avoidance equips cultural negotiators with the intelligence to tailor their strategies, making interactions smoother and more rewarding on varying cultural terrain, validating the claims herein authored by Lincke et al. (2025) and Li et al. (2017).

8.2.3. Time Orientation and Its Effect on Negotiation Processes

In cross-cultural negotiation, the conception of time influences the strategies employed in negotiating. Cultures have different levels of past, present, or future orientation, and that difference can impact their reaction to negotiation processes. For instance, high future-oriented cultures may emphasize consequences in the long run and building relationships to the detriment of immediate gains, potentially setting a cooperative atmosphere. Conversely, present-time oriented individuals would want immediate solutions and concrete benefit, inclined to generate competitive tactics that drive a tougher bargain. Such considerations are significant for organizations that span cultural divides because incompatible time orientations can lead to confusion and conflict that can impact the efficacy of negotiation attempts in international management. Of special interest is the effect of cultural models that define how time is controlled in negotiating contexts. Research indicates that Middle Eastern negotiators, such as Iranians, are able to employ a competitive mode based on the honor-dignity cultural dimensions and focus on short-term results over long-term relationships. This is likely to create strategies that focus on winning rather than cooperation, thereby affecting the success of negotiations. In contrast, however, North American negotiators, even though competitive in style, tend to balance their styles with a mix of cooperation because they also possess a longer time horizon incorporating possible futures. These cultural differences reflect the need to understand negotiators underlying assumptions and motivations framed by their respective cultures, which also influence both their negotiation scripts and final bargains (Adair et al., 2012). Moreover, cross-cultural negotiation involves not only the acknowledgment of diverse time orientations but also the consideration of relational patterns to improve or sabotage the negotiating result. Relational self-construals (RSC) come in handy while measuring how pre-negotiation conditions affect tactical maneuvers. Relational-mind cultures facilitate collaborative approaches, which could be more fruitful for achieving mutually beneficial outcomes. Where cooperation and interdependence are underscored, actors can find that creating a rapport and gaining trust enables more effective negotiations. Awareness of this advances the negotiator's role to ensure that their strategies adapt based on the relational dynamics at play so that there are enhanced chances for effective conflict management as well as cooperation in international settings (Gelfand et al., 2006).

8.3. STRATEGIES FOR EFFECTIVE CROSS-CULTURAL NEGOTIATION

The negotiative field is usually influenced by the cultural contexts people originate from, and this decides the overall strategy and outcome. Different cultures produce different styles; for example, the negotiator from honor-dignity cultures such as the Middle East can become more competitive in their style, typically prioritizing the demonstration of emotions and distributive tactics. This aggressive competitive mindset can result in combative dialogue, not just affecting the negotiation outcome but the relationship formed through it as well. As has been discovered in studies involving Iranian and North American negotiators, the latter's tendency to be competitive can result in lower joint gains than those of Canadian negotiators. Therefore, international managers need to be aware of such cultural influences so that they can negotiate successfully in complex negotiation situations and minimize the scope for adversarial dynamics (Adair et al., 2012). Much of successful cross-cultural negotiation involves developing intercultural communication competence. Such skills enable negotiators to recognize and appreciate cultural differences, possibly cutting back on conflict and boosting mutual knowledge. To foster a productive environment, negotiators can take time to build deep trust and rapport with counterparts who hail from diverse backgrounds. Investment typically leads to combined efforts that yield productive outcomes. Targeted programs designed to enhance sensitivity to cultural diversity, such as international negotiation projects, have been effective in fostering the cultural abilities of students. These endeavors push individuals to break through and conquer 'barriers' in intercultural communication, ultimately equipping them with the skills needed for professional communication in multicultural environments (Thanaraj et al., 2016) (Figure 8.6).

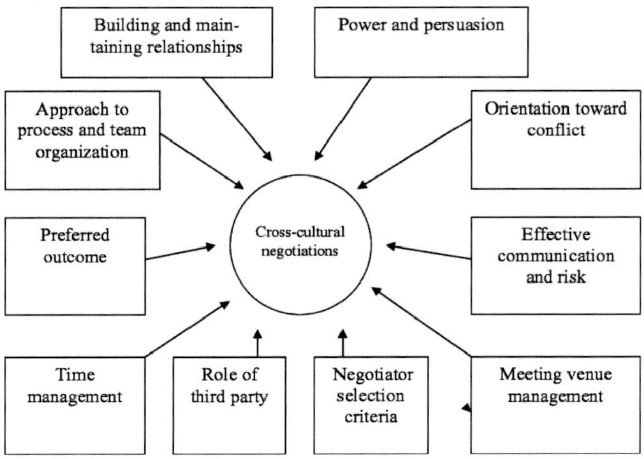

Figure 8.6. Influences of cultural differences on negotiations.

Source: https://www.researchgate.net/profile/Malgorzata-Rozkwitalska-Welenc/publication/299858573/figure/fig1/AS:348234443706368@1460036969444/nfluences-of-cultural-differences-on-negotiations-Rys-3-Wplyw-z-roznic-kulturowych-w.png.

In all negotiation scenarios, the adaptability of strategy adaptation in line with cultural sensitivities is essential. Global managers must be cautious to appreciate the mechanism of conflict resolution that is typical for other cultures. These mechanisms may be quite different; some cultures would emphasize consensus and relationship maintenance, while others would tend towards more confrontational direct strategies. Identifying these nuances allows negotiators to tailor their styles, thus producing cooperation and enhancing general effectiveness. Additionally, identifying the moral challenges that arise in various cultures allows negotiators to approach situations with compassion and direction. Utilizing these techniques not only leads to more efficient results but also facilitates long-term partnerships built on trust and respect in spite of cultural differences, cementing the fabric of international business relationships.

8.3.1. Building Rapport and Trust Across Cultures

Establishing harmonious communication in negotiation contexts usually needs a delicate awareness of diverse backgrounds, as such complexities shape relational dynamics. A central part of successful negotiation is establishing rapport and trust, which act as the pillars of cooperative interactions. Establishing rapport in intercultural contexts involves awareness and appreciation of differences such as communication styles, values, and social expectations. For instance, collectivistic cultures may emphasize harmony and group unanimity, whereas individualistic cultures may emphasize assertiveness and personal achievement. Understanding these cultural variations enables negotiators to establish an atmosphere that is conducive to open communication and avoids misconceptions likely to arise during negotiations.

Figure 8.7. Building trust and relationships across cultures.

Source: https://fastercapital.co/i/Cultural-awareness-skills-The-Role-of-Cultural-Awareness-in-Building-Successful-Startups--Building-Trust-and-Relationships-Across-Cultures.webp.

Establishing trust by repeated respectful interaction not only assists in overcoming initial obstacles but also lays the groundwork for longer-term collaborative effort, and therefore cultural competence is an asset to international management. Furthermore, the role of rapport is more than mere interpersonal attachment; it must also be a key part of the negotiation process itself. Rapport can be created by deliberate use of initiating moves and response moves, as demonstrated through research into cross-cultural negotiations. For instance, the application of relational initiating moves, which highlight relationship construction, can lead to favorable outcomes during negotiations, particularly when negotiating with Chinese business partners who place high value on interpersonal relationships in business dealings (Figure 8.7).

On the other hand, calling upon transactional moves will most likely be truer in cultures where directness is preferred. This elegant nuance in understanding communication behavior is paramount in successful intercultural alliances. It is via right moves and styles that negotiators not only traverse complex exchanges but also foretell and react to potential conflicts inherent in diverse negotiation processes (Bülow-Møller et al., 2011). The role of cultural awareness extends beyond the establishment of initial rapport and must cope with trust management in an on-going procedure through the negotiations. As observed in the context of international collaborative projects, effective rapport is neither permanent nor an event but a dynamic process that requires constant reinforcement by persistent and unambiguous communication. Understanding the various expectations of trust in multicultural contexts may have a strong impact on the success of negotiations. Ongoing activity and accommodation to partners' communication style and responsiveness are essential to maintaining rapport. Negotiators in this fast-changing environment must be sensitive in detecting changes in relational dynamics, particularly when there are challenges or tensions that may surface. Ultimately, establishing an environment of trust and respect, founded on awareness of cultures, works to enhance not only negotiators' performance but also overall international management success (Ewington et al., 2009).

8.3.2. Adapting Negotiation Styles to Cultural Contexts

Under international management, it becomes an important competency to understand the richness of negotiation styles across cultures. Cultures deeply influence not only the negotiations' style but also the underlying strategies and tactics used by negotiation parties. For instance, some cultures would emphasize more on relationship- and consensus-building while others would emphasize more on directness and assertiveness. Thus, a good negotiator must be culturally astute to recognize and adjust the style according to different cultural environments. Experiments have shown that being sensitive is key to facilitating cooperation and avoiding conflicts resulting from misunderstandings. With negotiations becoming increasingly complex within multicultural environments, learning the art of adjusting one's negotiation tactic depending on culture can yield more productive outcomes. Besides, the dynamics of conflict resolution mechanisms are greatly determined by cultural values and beliefs. Cultures vary in how they understand conflict as well as what it ought to be resolved with, and such can influence their negotiation approach. Collectivist cultures, for example, have a preference for cooperation and compromise, while individualist cultures prefer competitive strategies that are aimed at maximizing personal gains. This divergence can lead to tension if the negotiators are poorly positioned to satisfy the expectations of the other party. Empirical research shows that improving one's cultural intelligence helps improve one's ability to successfully negotiate conflict resolution because it enables one to comprehend how personality, culture, and norms cross-interact with conflict management. Thus, translating negotiation techniques to local cultural contexts not only avoids misunderstandings but also enriches the process of negotiation and ultimately enhances interorganizational relationships and outcomes. In addition, problems due to long-duration negotiations, particularly in geographically distant locations, underscore the importance of flexible negotiation techniques. Interdisciplinary research into interpersonal interactions in confined environments shows that psychological factors can significantly affect negotiation processes. With individuals experiencing longer interactions, cultural sensitivities will fuel conflicts due to stress and interpersonal tension, where they must be highly sensitive to cultural variations. Skills of critical negotiation emerge as a priority for learning, not only to protect oneself but also to facilitate effective communication and collaboration in multicultural groups. Negotiator training for increased cultural flexibility is thus an investment worth making that can bring harmony and efficiency, excluding the prospect of maladaptive tendencies that undermine the negotiation process (Goncalves et al., 2025; Galarza et al., 2007).

8.3.3. Utilizing Active Listening and Empathy in Negotiations

In the complex dynamics of international negotiations, active listening and empathy emerge as the vital ingredients that would go a great distance in yielding improved outcomes in intercultural communication. Both these interpersonal skills empower negotiators with the ability to establish a culture of trust and understanding, which is a powerful force that works in diverse cultural contexts where miscommunication could lead to escalation of conflict. For instance, active listening not only entails hearing the words of the counterparty but also comprehending the underlying feelings and cultural context, thus ensuring more open communication channels. Further, when bargainers employ empathy, they are not merely demonstrating respect for the counterparty's objections or concerns but are equally employing genuineness of feeling, thus enhancing interpersonal rapport and resulting in more collaborative negotiations. Moreover, active listening and empathy can be effective in breaking down conflicts that may have been generated out of cultural misunderstanding. Evidence indicates that the ability to read subtle differences between various styles of negotiation will prevent disagreements from surfacing in the first place (Standish et al., 2015). For instance, there are certain cultures where relational harmony is respected more than confrontation, and thus, one's negotiation techniques must be shifted accordingly. The application of empathy enables observers to notice nonverbal cues, which can say a lot about the emotional status of the counterpart—something that is normally determined by cultural backgrounds and communication styles. That implies that the inclusion of these skills not only assists in conflict resolution but also enhances the ability to deal with the complexities that come with cross-cultural negotiations effectively. Lastly, the integration of active listening and empathy in negotiation approaches proactively encourages the pursuit of adaptive and culturally sensitive conflict resolution mechanisms. As explained in many studies, effective de-escalation and conflict management efforts are likely to be founded upon the communicative capacity of negotiators in creating cooperative dialogue (Dickens et al., 2017). Therefore, by keeping in mind a listening and comprehending culture, international negotiators are able to more readily identify underlying causes of disputes and work towards developing mutually beneficial solutions. Not only does this resolve present issues, but it also lays the groundwork for future collaborations based on respect and cooperation, crucial elements in international management. These skills are not only helpful—necessary to successful international negotiations.

8.4. CONFLICT RESOLUTION MECHANISMS

International management dilemmas require a wide array of skills in working through the complexities of various negotiation forms, which are often influenced by cultural orientations. Under such circumstances, conflict resolution mechanisms become imperative to act upon disputes and facilitate cooperation among parties. Different cultures have their own styles for resolving conflict; for instance, Western cultures prefer direct styles of negotiation and confrontation communication, while Eastern cultures prefer indirect styles built on harmony and consensus. This culture difference affects the choice of mechanisms used in the international setting to eventually guarantee the success of negotiations. So, recognition of these cultural differences is imperative for international managers to come up with responsive strategies that encourage cooperation and comprehension during confrontations and address the key questions that set conflict resolution on (Menkel-Meadow et al., 2003). As businesses start expanding their operations globally, they are confronted by diverse conflict scenarios that call for response-based resolution mechanisms. Effective conflict resolution procedures must consider and embrace these cultural factors to enable productive negotiations. For instance, interest-based mediation—seeing beneath the surface to needs and not positions—can resolve opposing conflict styles of culture. Focusing on relational dynamics, particularly in collectivist cultures, makes a space that is receptive to resolution (Figure 8.8).

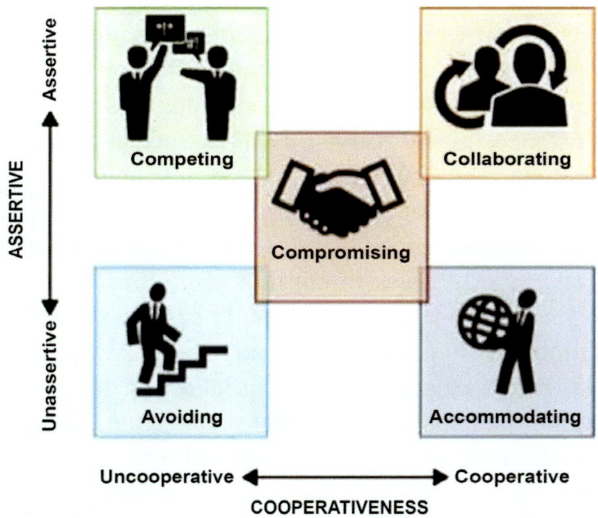

Figure 8.8. The role of conflict resolution mechanisms.

Source: https://b1890761.smushcdn.com/1890761/wp-content/uploads/2016/06/conflict-resolution-strategies.jpg?lossy=1&strip=1&webp=1.

Merging mechanisms that enhance active listening, empathy, and cultural sensitivity not only enhances the efficacy of conflict management but also enhances trust among the stakeholders. These multi-purpose mechanisms serve to bridge cultural differences and facilitate effective negotiations, responding to the call of comparative studies and prudence observed in the conflict resolution debate (Woodhouse et al., 1999). Lastly, choosing mechanisms of conflict resolution highly affects international negotiation results. A one-size-fits-all approach is seldom effective; a multi-faceted model that incorporates several paradigms for various cultures is needed. By examining the processes through which conflicts are created and resolved in various environments, international managers can develop a fuller understanding of the processes at play. That is the key to selection of useful strategies, allowing for more effective modes of conflict management responsive to local norms and expectations. The pursuit of academic research in these multidisciplinary approaches to resolving conflicts should continue to elicit debate, as the integration of experiential wisdom and empirical analysis is the foundation upon which promoting cooperation among cultures and diminishing potential conflict within the global business community is built (Menkel-Meadow et al., 2003).

8.4.1. Mediation and Its Cultural Variations

Understanding mediation within its cultural context brings to the forefront the subtleties of bargaining styles globally. Cultures differ on their preferences and methods when resolving conflict, and these can significantly impact mediation processes. For instance, in collectivist cultures such as exist in most Asian cultures, mediation is conducted from a harmony and consensus approach where relationship maintenance is of prime concern. On the other hand, individualistic cultures, like those of most Americans, may emphasize direct communication and assertiveness in conflict resolution. Mediators thus need to adjust their techniques to accommodate such cultural differences so that the process of mediation not only becomes effective but also culturally appropriate and sensitive. This examination of cultural variations in styles of mediation can enhance international managements conflict management capacities, fostering greater harmony, fruitful solutions in multicultural settings. The role of mediation as a process of conflict management also varies significantly across cultures, largely shaped by indigenous custom and legal traditions. In some fields, mediation rests on customary norms of society, and there is a collective approach to conflict resolution that harmonizes national values and traditions (Figure 8.9).

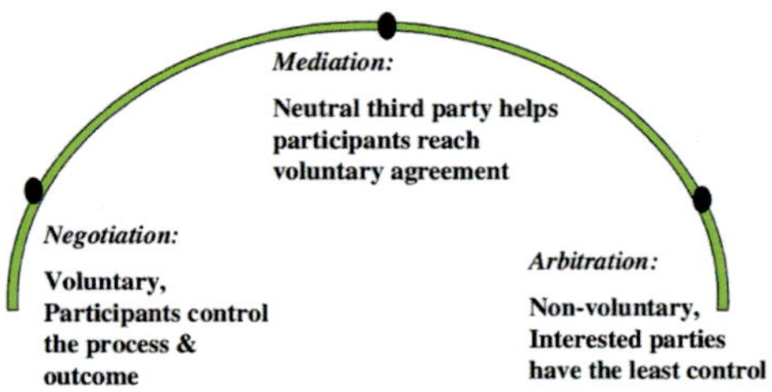

Figure 8.9. Continuum of conflict/dispute resolution mechanisms.

Source: https://www.researchgate.net/profile/Derick-Brinkerhoff/publication/ 253212278/figure/fig9/AS:752351723917314@1556386037236/Continuum-of-Conflict-Dispute-Resolution-Mechanisms.png.

For example, customary mediation within indigenous communities can involve participation of elderly persons who are key in directing the negotiations, a procedure that mirrors collective decision-making within such communities. By comparison, where legalistic brains dominate, e.g., the United States, other than dispute resolution (ADR) methods may be formalized and institutionalized, and this would lead to co-optation of mediation practices. This change, defined in recent literature, raises ethical issues for access to justice and the possibilities of privatized processes of dispute resolution that could be designed for individuals with means, shifting the ethical landscape of mediation (Menkel-Meadow et al., 2013). With the business operations of companies across the world becoming increasingly intertwined, understanding the implications of different mediation strategies is essential to successful international management. Cultural intelligence has to be developed by managers and leaders to navigate the intricate terrain of conflict resolution across various environments. That means recognizing how cultural settings shape one's perception of authority, justice, and negotiation tactics. Not only does it enhance the mediation process but also develops a culture of respect and inclusivity among diverse groups. But as pointed out in the new conflict resolution literature, cultural differences' demands need to be met by ongoing dialogue and cross-cultural research to refine our practice and theory (Menkel-Meadow et al., 2003). By focusing on collective wisdom and experiential learnings, institutions can become increasingly capable of resolving conflicts in a way that honors cultural differences, leading to more sustainable and effective solutions.

8.4.2. Arbitration Practices in Different Cultural Settings

In an increasingly globalized world, the mediation and arbitration practice across different cultures is in need of close examination. Complex negotiation approaches dictate the way parties react to conflict resolution, often the work of deeply entrenched cultural beliefs as well as social norms. As an illustration, harmony and relationship are matters of over-riding concern in collectivist cultures and therefore, arbitrable procedures that center on reconciliation are favored as opposed to adversarial approaches. Conversely, individualistic cultures would be efficiency- and assertiveness-oriented and thus prefer arbitration processes that enable fast settlement and have stringent rules. Such sensitivities highlight the need for managers negotiating across borders to have a profound understanding of the cultural dimensions involved because confusion of these practices will not settle disputes but escalate them. The mechanisms employed in negotiation are strongly influenced by local legal and cultural settings. For example, in some cultures, Elders of the community may have an authoritative role to play in settling disputes outside of formal channels, while arbitration may be formalized by state-run institutions and formalized agreements. Understanding these configurations is essential for effective conflict resolution between cultures. Furthermore, the effectiveness of various mechanisms of conflict resolution will be contingent upon the participation of properly positioned stakeholders. For example, within arbitration settings, involving local representatives who understand the cultural context will help in establishing trust and generating more acceptable resolution for all parties involved. With growing globalization, being able to negotiate these cultural complexities within arbitration is increasingly necessary now for international managers who want to establish cooperative and effective relationships. Besides, comparative examination of arbitration processes can contribute to the development of broader conflict theory that is inclusive of cultural differences. Whether or not universal principles are properly applicable across different cultures remains a critical area of study. Some contend that basic aspects of equity and justice in conflict resolution can cut across specific cultural mores, thereby establishing a universal basis for effective methods of arbitration throughout the world. Others caution against pursuing this line of argument, but instead maintaining the relevance of thick descriptions of cultures to comprehend the complex dynamics of negotiation and conflict resolution. Dealing with this duality is not only capable of expanding the perspective of arbitration practice but also enriching a more fruitful debate encompassing empirical research along with experiential knowledge within the context of conflict resolution (Menkel-Meadow et al., 2003; N/A, 2011).

8.4.3. The Role of Negotiation in Conflict Resolution

Negotiation is a key tool in conflict resolution, particularly within international management's multicultural setting. Since various negotiation styles emerge from divergent cultural contexts, understanding these differences becomes crucial for successful conflict resolution. Collectivistic cultures, for instance, may prioritize consensus-oriented negotiation styles, whereas individualistic cultures may use more confrontational styles. It needs an enormous knowledge of how cultural impacts shape negotiation tactics and strategies. Successful negotiators must not only possess a large number of strategies but also be able to identify and insert themselves into the cultural systems of their counterparty. By building a culture of trust and mutual understanding, negotiation becomes a bridge that enables conflicting parties to collaborate and resolve their conflicts while developing solutions that respect and recognize their respective differences in cultural heritage. Given the more interdependent nature of today's global economy, the necessity for tailored negotiation approaches is even more pressing. Differences in outlook often lead to disagreements due to misunderstandings, and the reason why negotiators need to build intercultural competence. Not merely an understanding of one's own cultural bias, but also understanding others' values and their modes of communication is a part of it. Such awareness of cultures can minimize potential barriers in negotiation and enhance the effectiveness of conflict resolution mechanisms. Simulation activities, such as international negotiation simulation projects, can significantly increase graduates' ability to recognize and appreciate cultural diversity, as well as establish trust and rapport with negotiation counterparts. Therefore, developing this intercultural competence, in addition to improving better negotiation outcomes, enhances a climate for cooperative conflict resolution on and across cultures, ultimately maximizing organizational effectiveness and harmony. Lastly, conflict resolution's negotiation role demonstrates shifting proportions between communicative efficacy and cultural sensitivity. As seen in current debate, questions emerge regarding the relevance of conflict resolution theory to a variety of environments. For some researchers, it is only through richly descriptive, contextually nuanced accounts that subtleties of international negotiation are accounted for, as questioned in Menkel-Meadow et al. (2003). Others contrast by holding that transferable theories can assist practitioners in comprehending and navigating intercultural conflicts. The truth is more than likely a combination of the two approaches, where central tenets serve as the baseline with a realistic acknowledgment of the necessity for contingency-tailored strategies contingent upon particular cultural dynamics. Understanding this complex relationship forms the basis of practices that aim not only to resolve disputes but also cultivate long-term relationships, ultimately contributing to a more harmonious and efficient multicultural environment in international management and negotiation situations.

8.5. CASE STUDIES OF INTERNATIONAL NEGOTIATIONS

Understanding international negotiation processes entails a keen awareness of cultural influences that drive negotiation strategies in parts of the globe. Each culture negotiates distinctively with different tactics, strategies, and underlying values that may influence outcomes profoundly. Collectivist cultures, for instance, are known to focus on relationship and on consensus-building, which may lead to a more collaborative style of negotiation. Individualist cultures, conversely, can take on a more competitive style with directness and assertiveness. This variation can be difficult since negotiators are confronted with countervailing expectations and approaches. Nevertheless, the fulfillment of such variations enables parties to define strategies properly, establishing an environment conducive to cooperative outcomes. Therefore, a case study review reveals the influence cultural origin exerts on negotiation outcomes, demonstrating the use of empathy and adaptability in global practice of negotiation. Conflict management mechanisms are a core principle of international negotiations, dictating how actors manage and contain disagreement that might occur in the process of negotiations. Various approaches such as mediation, arbitration, and facilitation might be employed, depending on the context and actors involved. For instance, mediation can be particularly beneficial in multi-stakeholder negotiations with members coming from diverse cultural backgrounds through facilitating a third-party mediator to help navigate difficult dynamics. Further, understanding of the ethical principles that underpin these frameworks is significant in building trust and relationships (Figure 8.10).

Figure 8.10. Understanding the changing aspects of international negotiations.

Source: https://procurementtactics.com/wp-content/uploads/2025/02/International-Negotiation.jpg.

As seen in case studies, the negotiator who is aware of the ethical challenges will be able to facilitate a settlement better, thus enhancing their capacity to operate in multicultural environments. Such awareness may help promote increased cooperation and mutual knowledge transfer, which are also key in preventing the escalation of conflicts. Studies on the educational dimension surrounding international negotiation methods also support the need to establish cultural competency in negotiators. With the increase in international contacts, individuals must be equipped with skills to recognize and respect cultural differences influencing negotiating behavior. Thus, institutions of higher learning are mandated to design curricula that offer sensitization to cultural diversity in spite of the challenges involved in intercultural communication. International negotiation project study can be an effective learning instrument to create cross-cultural skills in the students to make them capable of handling the complexities of international negotiations. This knowledge, as well as providing students with confidence to negotiate, also promotes ethical conduct that favors long-term collaborations in diverse environments and, in the end, their occupational performance in global management contexts (Menkel-Meadow et al., 2003; Thanaraj et al., 2016).

8.5.1. Successful Cross-Cultural Negotiations

Cultural effects significantly shape negotiation styles, leading to diverse international management approaches. In nations such as East Asia, for instance, negotiations will incorporate indirect communication and a focus on harmony, as actors prefer to escape conflict and preserve relationships. This is completely at odds with Western styles of negotiation, especially in the United States, where assertiveness and directness are typically preferred.

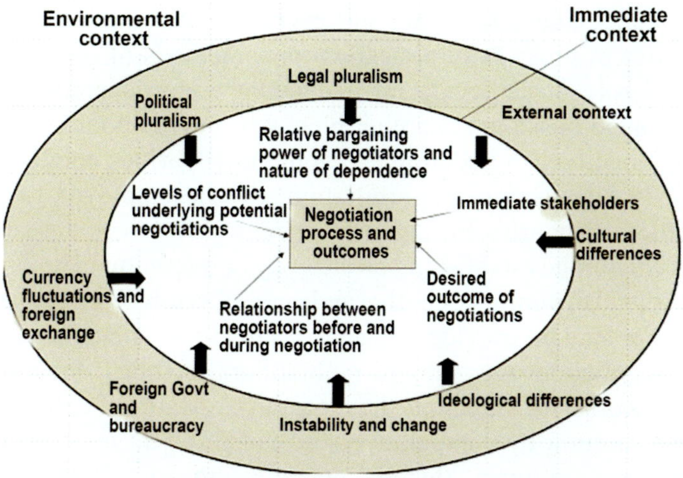

Figure 8.11. The implications of cross-cultural negotiations process.

Source: https://lh3.googleusercontent.com/proxy/-AR6rNByFiZjtpjO19hvO-PL0vJPSyDfBH8f79Nq-AYWYYTXo8PoLyAvh90s4H7fK1tFK4QSkMB-K68jKRns-mnbgc9CPCf3czRWETvdAzZ8tPPWonEatrYtWGvQ.

Recognition of these differences is essential for successful cross-cultural negotiations as insensitivity to distinct styles may result in miscommunication and conflict. In addition, the ability to adjust based on the culture can enhance the quality of negotiations. Practitioners must cultivate cultural intelligence, which entails recognizing and reacting to the subtleties of different negotiation styles in a manner to create favorable dialogues and ultimately come to mutually beneficial terms. Successful negotiation facilitation is not just dependent on cultural style awareness but also on the use of adequate tactics and strategies within specific situations. For instance, a culture that likes to negotiate consensus and integration of views through cooperation may adopt a different one that follows a competitive approach with a focus on getting individual optimal results (Figure 8.11).

The impact of these cultural perspectives can be achieved at negotiation, as they influence how offers and counteroffers are bundled by parties. Also, trust development provides a basis that is required, particularly in relationship-oriented cultures, where reciprocation is highly valued and open communication is preferred. Trust can be created by negotiators being good listeners, empathizing, and making relational commitments over the long-term. By aligning their approaches with the cultural competence of their counterparts, negotiators can not only lower the risk of potential conflicts but also enhance the prospects of achieving successful results that suit everyone. When attempting to solve the complexities of cross-cultural negotiations, methods of conflict resolution play a pivotal role in achieving understanding and cooperation. One must detect and manage possible stumbling blocks in intercultural communication as miscommunication can undermine negotiations. Various conflict resolution mechanisms, like mediation and arbitration, can be employed to tackle and resolve conflicts that arise during negotiations. Moreover, researchers and practitioners encourage establishing proficiency in intercultural communication because it is crucial to minimize conflict and maximize relationship management. Past negotiation studies provide valuable insights into elements contributing to effective negotiation outcomes in multicultural settings. Practitioners can develop frameworks for directing their conduct toward effective negotiation and conflict resolution by comparative study of different methods of conflict resolution between cultures, thereby guaranteeing success of international cooperation (Menkel-Meadow et al., 2003; Thanaraj et al., 2016).

8.5.2. Failed Negotiations and Lessons Learned

Negotiation dynamics shift easily whenever cultural differences are not adequately recognized, typically in a manner that will result in failure. For instance, Western negotiation tactics typically include direct communication and assertiveness, whereas Eastern cultures predominantly value relational harmony and indirect communication. This incompatibility tends to create misunderstandings and frustration during the course of negotiations, with parties misunderstanding intent and strategy from the other. Doomed negotiations often mask broader cultural disjunctures, making cultural competence more salient in such a scenario. Inability to overcome the contrast between opposing modes of negotiating can undermine successful resolution of conflicts, mirroring the broader implications of cultural factors in global management. By analyzing such failures, negotiators can more fully realize that varying cultural settings need to be tailored to avoid adverse repercussions. Menkel-Meadow et al. (2003) refers to the necessity of understanding these cultural differences in order to enhance the efficiency of negotiating strategies within a global context. What can be gleaned from unsuccessful negotiations tends to reveal the imperative of selecting a strategy for conflict resolution founded on multiplicity. The experiences of mediators such as George Mitchell and Lakhdar Brahimi are testimonies to the challenges of cross-cultural mediation. Both were severely tested by conflicting expectations of ethics and perceptions of being impartial from society, leading to their eventual resignations in frustration. Their experiences highlight how it is crucial to understand cultural backgrounds when mediating; failure to comprehend local expectations is capable of undermining negotiations and damaging trust, rendering resolution ever more unattainable. This recognition of cultural basis for negotiation processes suggests that more finesse in the sensitivity to local values and norms can significantly enhance negotiation result. The incorporation of cultural analysis not only generates increased empathy but also shapes strategies attuned to respective parties' context and agendas, ultimately enhancing prospects for successful negotiations (Katsoris et al., 2016). Moreover, failed negotiations are a good learning experience and an opportunity for global management practice to learn and better itself. Each failure is a pending case study waiting to be employed in approaching future negotiation tactics, particularly in cross-cultural negotiation. With careful consideration of what has failed—i.e., miscommunications or cultural sensitivities—managers can construct more sophisticated models of negotiation that can learn to conform to varying expectations. For instance, learning from past failure can lead to the development of precautionary measures, such as increased cross-cultural negotiation training for bargaining teams. These learning opportunities, together with knowledge of basic conflict resolution principles, can result in more effective negotiation strategies by organizations. It is only by failing that organizations learn most of the revolutionary practices, forcing them to develop a more responsive and culture-sensitive model for international negotiations (Menkel-Meadow et al., 2003).

8.5.3. Analysis of Cultural Missteps in Negotiation

It is through understanding the subtleties of negotiation patterns that conflict management is effectively conducted in the varied cultural settings. Cultural blunders frequently occur when negotiators impose their tacit presuppositions regarding what behaviors are appropriate, varying widely from culture to culture. For example, some cultures practice direct communication and assertiveness while others prefer indirectness and maintenance of harmony rather than confrontation. This gap not only facilitates miscommunication but can also hinder the building of trust, which is critical to successful negotiations. As evidenced in literature, intuition and common assumptions can mislead negotiators, turning good intentions into traps that propel unwanted consequences (Lempereur, 2025). Therefore, global managers must develop cultural sensitivity and flexibility to adapt their negotiation approach to the prevailing culture. While some negotiation mistakes are brought about by communication tactics, others arise due to conflicting conflict management tactics prevalent in other cultures. Different cultures have different dispositions toward where a negotiation is supposed to conclude, ranging from a win-lose to a cooperative win-win approach. For instance, Western individualistic methodologies focusing on personal benefit might clash with collectivist cultures emphasizing group harmony and shared benefit. Such inherent difference may cause friction at the bargaining table since the two sides try to align their means and ends. Sensitivity to such contrasting approaches is necessary for global negotiators in order to avoid cultural errors and create productive dialogue. As diversity resources explain, combining different negotiation styles can produce a more unified environment where parties are able to navigate complexities and reach agreement (Bormann et al., 2001). Misconceptions of cultural cues may also be reflected in non-verbal signals, further destabilizing negotiations. Postures, gaze, and even silence may mean something entirely different in different cultures. For instance, while direct eye contact in certain Western societies is a sign of honesty and confidence, it may be viewed as a display of aggression or disrespect in other Asian societies. Such misreads are bound to increase tension, escalating to a collapse in negotiations and lost trust among counterparts. To circumvent such dangers, negotiators must acquire cultural intelligence and enhance their observational abilities, allowing them to rectify interpret and respond properly to non-verbal communication. With the globalized negotiation setting, it is important to be aware and accept such cultural differences so that one does not commit errors that can sabotage even the best-planned negotiation plan (Lempereur, 2025).

8.6. THE ROLE OF TECHNOLOGY IN CROSS-CULTURAL NEGOTIATION

In the current era of globalization, the dynamics of negotiations have been significantly influenced by advancements in technology. Digital media bring instantaneity that generates a moment-to-moment exchange of ideas across cultures, with the negotiators' capability to communicate and interact with various counterparts in real time. This real-time interaction can overcome cultural misalignments and allow quick resolution of misunderstandings, which is critical in cultures that are highly reliant on non-verbal communication and context. For instance, nations such as Germany, whose negotiation styles tend to be more conflict-based in nature, can be confronted with opposition when negotiating with cultures that prioritize the development of relationships, e.g., in Asian regions. Consciousness about these stylistic inclinations, aided by technology, enables negotiators to adjust their approaches accordingly, thus optimizing overall outcomes in cross-cultural negotiation (Lincke et al., 2025). The ability to access technology for instant feedback and iterative bargaining stimulates a more tacit process of bargaining, which consequently reaches more constructive agreements. Technology's fusion also facilitates greater availability of information and materials influencing bargaining policies. Through the support of virtual conferencing tools and data analysis tools, bargainers can prepare more effectively by accessing cultural insights and past facts relevant to the parties involved in bargaining. These riches of information enable negotiators to foresee prospective challenges posed by differences in cultures, for example, differing styles of handling authority and decision-making procedures (Figure 8.12).

Figure 8.12. Dynamics of negotiation by technological advancements.

Source: https://cdn.iveybusinessjournal.com/wp-content/uploads/2004/09/iStock_000040383088_Large.jpg.

Here, technology not only serves as a communication tool but also serves as a tool of deep analysis (Menkel-Meadow et al., 2003). By having these technological tools integrated into their preparation, negotiators are able to create strategies that not only suit the culture but also strategically innovative. This dual nature of perception also enriches negotiation process by allowing more successful resolution of conflict and more opportunities for mutually beneficial agreement. Moreover, the role of technology is played in the field of conflict resolution as well, where internet-based forums can provide an environment of virtual mediation spaces. With an increasing number of organizations spanning geography, there is a need now to resolve conflicts that may arise in cross-cultural environments. Technology provides the means through which dialogue between opposing sides can be facilitated across geographical locations, opening a channel for cooperative resolution. Through video conferencing platforms, for example, negotiators are able to simulate an environment of discussion that is typically instrumental in resolving culturally-based misunderstandings. This capacity not only mediates access to mediation services but also trains negotiators to weave the nuances of various conflict resolution approaches in other cultures into their negotiation strategies (Menkel-Meadow et al., 2003). Hence, technology not only makes communication more effective but also improves the arena of negotiations, thereby indicating its role in providing a necessary service towards responsible and reflective cross-cultural contact.

8.6.1. Virtual Negotiation Platforms and Their Impact

In contemporary global management, virtual negotiation platforms have greatly changed the nature of cross-cultural interactions. Virtual negotiation platforms have facilitated the ability to experience real-time communication and collaboration among diverse stakeholders, enabling differentially oriented cultural parties to engage in negotiations without being constrained by geography. By utilizing technology, companies can access a greater reservoir of talent, promoting innovation and collaboration that can enable global market competition today. The integration of virtual negotiation platforms not only supports the negotiation process but enhances conflict managing and resolving as well. This fallibility is highly significant since different cultures have distinct negotiation approaches and styles that demand precise proportioning of methods that can be navigated more aptly through digital media (Gresse et al., 2025). The ability to tap into virtual negotiation tools also transcends ease of logistics; they fundamentally redefine the boundaries of negotiating. Negotiators can take advantage of features such as video conferencing, which offers the possibility of exploiting non-verbal cues in negotiation to play a role towards tacit understanding that tends to be lost in text communication. Further, these interfaces can be made flexible so that they accommodate multiple cultural negotiation styles, whereby users have the option to select modalities of communication favoring their counterparts' styles. This adaptability significantly enhances cross-cultural negotiations by making the environment more diversified, a fact that is essential for effective outcomes. Moreover, as businesses develop to adapt to cycles of innovation at a high level, the requirement for efficient, flexible, and culturally sensitive negotiation processes increases to be in high demand, necessitating the application of virtual platforms in today's conflict resolution processes (Ahmed et al., 2009). As businesses increasingly employ virtual negotiation platforms, the effects on negotiation processes need to be understood. Dealing virtually calls for a unique skill set for negotiators that includes expertise in using digital platforms, cultural sensitiveness, and ability to build rapport across screens. Technology has the potential for offering impersonal contact that could discourage trust building essential to successful negotiations. On the other hand, the instant dissemination of information and collaborative decision-making supported by such platforms can encourage a more active resolution to disagreements. As firms continue to face complexity in overseas settings, the role of virtual negotiation platforms as drivers of conflict settlement appears as an important component of effective international management, shaping better outcomes through counsel-led negotiation planning that considers multicultural settings (Gresse et al., 2025).

8.6.2. Cultural Considerations in Digital Communication

In global management, the nuances of electronic communication are primarily responsible for causing differences in negotiation styles across cultures. It is of paramount importance to understand these style differences since they dictate the way messages are written and interpreted. For instance, high-context cultures in the Middle East or Japan might rely on subtle hints and tacit understandings, whereas cultures in Germany or the United States might use direct and explicit communication.

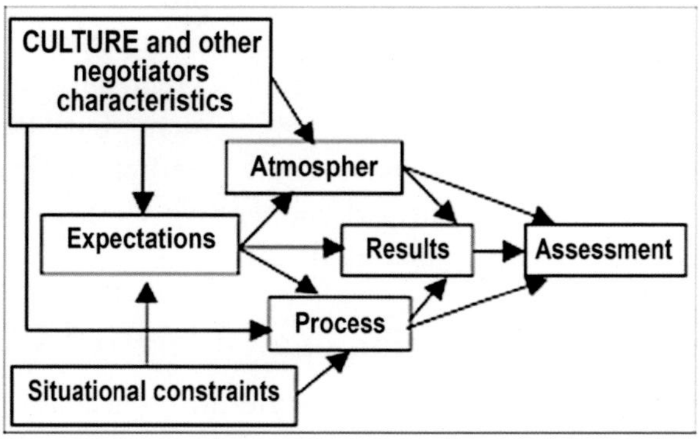

Figure 8.13. Digital communication influence negotiation styles that vary across cultural contexts.

Source: https://encrypted-tbn0.gstatic.com/images?q=tbn:ANd9GcS-l-GXQjJ-QwFNg9uc-MTpsnflOWE0hdGgHwg&s.

The varying ways in which this happens can lead to misunderstandings unless negotiators realize the underlying cultural drivers that create such disparate communication patterns. Thus, successful negotiation is not only a matter of recognizing one's own cultural predilections but of hypersensitivity to the different sets of assumptions on which their interlocutors will likely be operating. Successful negotiating strategies are often themselves culturally and socially conventional in the context of digital communication. In Western cultures, for example, assertiveness and directness of approach may take the lead, risking confrontation with the greater priority put on relationship-building in collectivist cultures (Figure 8.13).

The impact of such divergence is most strongly realized when approaching mechanisms of conflict resolution, when cultural factors can make divergent perceptions of things and their resolutions. Conflict management in this context then becomes a sensitive walk of an artful nature that calls for flexibility as well as sensitivity. Cultural competence allows negotiators to ensure a perception of trust and understanding necessary for the resolution of differences and the attainment of productive results in international settings. To develop such skills, professionals must undergo intercultural communication training that highlights the importance of being flexible in their approach. To address these problems, models of teaching must be developed to create foundational career skill sets in students through experiential learning. Courses utilizing negotiation and conflict management simulations can help teach useful lessons about the complexity of cross-cultural communications. These programs bridge theory and practice gaps, inculcating students with appreciation for cultural diversity while they learn behavioral skills. For example, integrating project management practice with intercultural communication modules allows students' ability to handle the intricacies of global negotiating environments. Such a holistic approach not only stimulates greater sensitivity to cultural elements but also equips future professionals with the competencies to settle conflicts amicably on global platforms, thereby promoting a fair and cooperative work environment in the future (Thanaraj et al., 2016; Kanabar et al., 2018).

8.6.3. The Future of Negotiation in a Globalized World

In a highly globalized world, negotiation style differences are being strongly reflected, influenced primarily by cultural values and precepts. Negotiators from across the globe like to take to the negotiating table whatever is special to them, based on their culture of location and also their histories. For instance, Western negotiators would want assertiveness and directness to obtain quick settlements, whereas Asian counterparts would emphasize harmony and consensus to create long-term relationships. The intricacy of these different styles requires an enhanced comprehension of the influence of culture on negotiation approach and strategy. With the expansion of businesses all over the world, recognizing and adapting to these styles becomes imperative in achieving triumph in negotiations so that parties may effectively close gaps in cultures and create mutually beneficial agreements. This cultural sensitivity is essential in navigating the subtle landscapes of international business transactions. Conflict resolution systems also shift their function in the context of globalization because organizations are increasingly confronting disputes bearing international undertones. The traditional negotiation methods might not be sufficient to handle various cultural assumptions and legal traditions among global counterparts. Interestingly, the advent of alternative dispute resolution (ADR) methods, such as mediation and arbitration, offers flexible solutions to handle varying cultural conflict styles. Therefore, integrating ADR in the negotiating process enables parties to establish cooperation while restricting future cultural misunderstandings. This change reflects the general trend towards hybrid negotiating styles combining elements of formal and informal resolution mechanisms to enhance their effectiveness in a globalized world. Increased acquaintance with these mechanisms can give negotiators the strength to achieve more sustainable agreements in the context of cross-cultural relationships. In the future, it is essential for negotiators to learn to acquire a global mindset with a mix of both flexibility and cultural awareness. As impediments to global cooperation continue to dwindle, the capacity to engage with various stakeholders will play a critical role in shaping effective negotiation. Both field experience and theoretical research should guide the interaction as seen in the rich literature in the labor management and industrial relations fields. For example, the data in books like An Introduction to U.S. Collective Bargaining and Labor Relations put the spotlight on collective representation and global labor rights issues' influence (Colvin et al., 2017). Furthermore, ongoing scholarship still informs readers about successful negotiating strategies crafted for the various cultural settings, further establishing negotiators toolkits as they navigate the future of international business relationships (Cornell University ILR School, 2016).

SUMMARY

In today's more globalized world, success in negotiation and conflict resolution within multi-cultural settings relies on familiarity with the nuances of differences in communication style and approach and cultural outlook. Negotiation style analysis illustrates the necessity of adapting approach to suit the circumstances under which it is being applied. For instance, differences in negotiation styles—ranging from the cooperative styles prevalent in much of the Western world, to the more hierarchical styles employed within some Asian societies—demonstrate the requirement for negotiators to modify their styles to the cultural environment. Awareness of these differences not only enhances the likelihood of favorable outcomes but also encourages respect for the opposing team. By embracing cultural diversity, international managers can foster an environment supportive of conflict resolution effectively and harmoniously, highlighting the mutual evolution of cultural practices while evolving to behavior and context (Indu, 2025). The intricacy of international negotiation calls upon experts to develop not just technical skills but profound cultural sensitivity. Academic studies of intercultural communication emphasize the role of empathy and adaptability in minimizing miscommunication and promoting successful negotiations. By subjecting themselves to special training and experiential education, managers can acquire the skills necessary to navigate the intricate web of cultural forces influencing negotiations. Training programs modeled after authentic situations such as international negotiation projects enhance students' sensitivity towards the diversity of cultures and its application in conflict resolution. This approach is aligned with future professionals possessing cross-cultural skills that can enable them to perform well in a multicultural environment, thereby enhancing their management effectiveness in international management (Thanaraj et al., 2016). Last but not least, sound international management negotiation and conflict resolution rely on a constantly evolving interface of cultural sensitivity, adaptation of strategy, and relationship building. As international interactions become increasingly complicated, the ability to comprehend and accept differences in cultures is increasingly significant. The implication of ongoing research demonstrates that an environment of trust and cooperation, driven by ethical sensitivity, can result in more effective negotiations. In addition, the integration of effective conflict management tools, tailored to the unique nature of various cultures, ensures conflict resolution at a fast pace while developing long-term alliances. In short, future conflict management and negotiation hinges on embracing the intricate mosaic of cultural influences which shape actions, thus making international management practices more effective and longer-lasting (Indu, 2025; Thanaraj et al., 2016).

The negotiative complexities in different cultures reveal not only the diversity of strategies employed but also underlying values that shape these strategies. Each perspective has unique styles of negotiation based on their history, society, and economy. For instance, while Western negotiators might prioritize direct communication and assertiveness, Eastern culture negotiators prioritize relationship building and indirect communication. These differences necessitate a consciousness of cultural norms; the absence of these can lead to conflict or miscommunication. Bridging these incompatible styles requires suppleness and sensitivity to the interpersonal context involved. Building an effective cross-cultural negotiation style, therefore, involves not only using techniques but comprehending the cultural norms that govern interaction. The analysis of these diverse styles and their consequences provides an important building block for effective negotiations, particularly in global management settings. Through an analysis of tactics and strategies utilized in negotiations in cross-cultural contexts, it is seen that they are heavily shaped by dimensions of culture such as power distance, individualism versus collectivism, and uncertainty avoidance. Negotiators would usually select their style based on their cultural orientation, which dictates their perception of authority, risk, and group dynamics. Top-down hierarchical structures in high power distance cultures, for instance, might dictate decisions and hence dictate how the negotiations should be initiated and finalized. In egalitarian cultures, consensus-building approaches would instead be favored. Such differentiation not only affects the result of negotiations but also affects the extent of participation and the expectations of the participants. In an effort to navigate successfully the various tactics involved, international managers must develop a toolkit of culturally sensitive approaches and adaptive strategies so that negotiations are effective and sensitive to the underlying cultural values that are part of the interaction. Conflict resolution skills also vary widely among cultural landscapes, reflective of varying social priorities and expectations regarding harmony and conflict. In relation-maintenance-valuing societies, such as most Asian societies, the avoidance of head-on conflict may be central, and facilitation and mediation would be employed as preferred means of conflict resolution. In societies that value individualism, however, as in some Western societies, confrontational strategies where parties negotiate terms person-to-person and openly vent their grievances may be preferred. It is essential for global managers who want to establish effective cooperation and minimize conflict in multicultural teams to understand these various mechanisms. Effective conflict resolution techniques need to be applied based on an in-depth understanding of cultural environments to work efficiently. As international business operations become more reliant upon collaborative efforts across borders, the need to adapt conflict resolution approaches in accordance with diverse cultural backgrounds cannot be overstated, ultimately leading to more stable partnerships and alliances in global management practices.

REFERENCES

1. Adair, W. L., Lewis, M., Semnani-Azad, Z., Sycara, K., et al. (2012). Being tough doesn't always payoff: The culture of honor vs dignity in negotiation. https://core.ac.uk/download/12215367.pdf (accessed on 24th September 2025).
2. Ahammad, M. F., Cooper, C. L., Glaister, K. W., Liu, Y., et al. (2015). Exploring the factors influencing the negotiation process in cross-border M&A. https://core.ac.uk/download/186324744.pdf (accessed on 24th September 2025).
3. Ahmed, S., Ale Ebrahim, N., & Taha, Z. (2009). Virtual teams for new product development: An innovative experience for R&D engineers. https://core.ac.uk/download/pdf/332903.pdf (accessed on 24th September 2025).
4. Ariño, A., Doz, Y., Lorenzoni, G., Ring, P., et al. (2025). Process issues in alliance management: A panel discussion. https://core.ac.uk/download/pdf/6536393.pdf (accessed on 24th September 2025).
5. Bormann, T., Brooks-Cooper, C., Farley, J., Fuerstenau, D., et al. (2001). *Resources for Workplace Diversity: An Annotated Practitioner Guide to Information.* https://core.ac.uk/download/5127328.pdf (accessed on 24th September 2025).
6. Bülow-Møller, A. M., Paik, Y., Planken, B., & Zhu, Y. (2011). Building intercultural alliances: A study of moves and strategies in initial business negotiation meetings. https://core.ac.uk/download/15111007.pdf (accessed on 24th September 2025).
7. Colvin, A., Katz, H. C., & Kochan, T. A. (2017). *An Introduction to U.S. Collective Bargaining and Labor Relations.* https://core.ac.uk/download/219377052.pdf (accessed on 24th September 2025).
8. Cornell University ILR School. (2016). *ILR Faculty Publications 2015–2016.* https://core.ac.uk/download/127599623.pdf (accessed on 24th September 2025).
9. Demirag, O. C., Kumar, S., & Liu, J. (2016). National culture's impact on effectiveness of supply chain disruption management. https://core.ac.uk/download/144553636.pdf (accessed on 24th September 2025).
10. Dickens, G. L., & Hallett, N. (2017). De-escalation of aggressive behaviour in healthcare settings: Concept analysis. https://core.ac.uk/download/228178030.pdf (accessed on 24th September 2025).
11. Ewington, N., Reid, S., Spencer-Oatey, H., Stadler, S., et al. (2009). *The Global People Tool Book: Managing the Life Cycle of Intercultural*

Partnerships. https://core.ac.uk/download/46446.pdf (accessed on 24th September 2025).

12. Furner, C. P., Chang, L. C., & Zinko, R. (2025). A study of negotiations within the ethnic Chinese community between Taiwan and Hong Kong. https://core.ac.uk/download/pdf/6276609.pdf (accessed on 24th September 2025).
13. Galarza, L., Holland, A. W., & Hysong, S. J. (2007). A review of training methods and instructional techniques: Implications for behavioral skills training in U.S. astronauts (DRAFT). https://core.ac.uk/download/pdf/10538462.pdf (accessed on 24th September 2025).
14. Gelfand, M. J., Major, V. S., Nishii, L. H., O'Brien, K., et al. (2006). Negotiating relationally: The dynamics of the relational self in negotiations. https://core.ac.uk/download/5127384.pdf (accessed on 24th September 2025).
15. Goncalves, G., Ramos-Organbidez, A., Reis, M., Santos, A., et al. (2025). Cultural intelligence and conflict management styles. https://core.ac.uk/download/42478293.pdf (accessed on 24th September 2025).
16. Gresse, C., & Slowak, A. P. (2025). *New Knowledge in Global Innovation Teams.* https://core.ac.uk/download/pdf/6802336.pdf (accessed on 24th September 2025).
17. Kanabar, V., Messikomer, C., & Thomas, A. (2018). Enhancing project-related behavioral competence in education. https://open.bu.edu/bitstream/2144/29016/1/Enhancing%20Project-Related%20Behavioral%20Competence%20in%20Education.pdf (accessed on 24th September 2025).
18. Katsoris, M. (2016). Does nationality influence neutrality? The ethical standards and expectations of international mediators. https://core.ac.uk/download/144231257.pdf (accessed on 24th September 2025).
19. Lempereur, A. (2025). Identifying some obstacles from intuition to a successful mediation process. https://core.ac.uk/download/pdf/6536180.pdf (accessed on 24th September 2025).
20. Li, M., & Yang, I. (2017). Can absent leadership be positive in team conflicts? An examination of leaders' avoidance behavior in China. https://core.ac.uk/download/151161261.pdf (accessed on 24th September 2025).
21. Lincke, A., Ulijn, J. M., & Wynstra, J. Y. F. (2025). The effect of Dutch and German cultures on negotiation strategy comparing operations and innovation management in the supply chain. https://core.ac.uk/download/pdf/6501211.pdf (accessed on 24th September 2025).

22. Menkel-Meadow, C. (2013). Regulation of dispute resolution in the United States of America: From the formal to the informal to the 'semi-formal.' https://core.ac.uk/download/70375135.pdf (accessed on 24th September 2025).
23. Mustafa, G. (2015). The emergence of leader-society value congruence: A cross-cultural perspective. https://core.ac.uk/download/144552158.pdf (accessed on 24th September 2025).
24. N/A. (2011). Book Entries Alphabetized by Author Last Name. https://core.ac.uk/download/159577768.pdf (accessed on 24th September 2025).
25. Nishii, L. H., & Özbilgin, M. F. (2007). Global diversity management: Towards a conceptual framework. https://core.ac.uk/download/219376625.pdf (accessed on 24th September 2025).
26. Poliakova, E. (2020). Language strategies in international business: New prospects for negotiation and conflict management. https://core.ac.uk/download/362511994.pdf (accessed on 24th September 2025).
27. Rao, I. (2025). The behavioral equivalence of organizational culture. https://core.ac.uk/download/pdf/6443708.pdf (accessed on 24th September 2025).
28. Sharkey, S., & Sharples, A. (2008). From the beginning: Negotiation in community evaluation. https://core.ac.uk/download/76704.pdf (accessed on 24th September 2025).
29. Standish, K. (2015). Looking for peace in the Australian national curricula. https://core.ac.uk/download/51077241.pdf (accessed on 24th September 2025).
30. Thanaraj, A. (2016). Internationalizing education: Evaluating the growth of intercultural communication and competency in students through an international negotiation project using an online law office. https://core.ac.uk/download/43757997.pdf (accessed on 24th September 2025).
31. Woodhouse, T. (1999). International conflict resolution: Some critiques and a response. https://core.ac.uk/download/6037.pdf (accessed on 24th September 2025).

Chapter 9

Human Resource Management in Global Organizations

Contents

INTRODUCTION

In a time characterized by increasing interconnectedness, organizations must be compelled to shift their human resource management (HRM) strategies to embrace a global orientation. This is crucial as businesses expand globally and become active in various geographical settings, which require them to acquire and implement various cultural contexts. The complexities involved in managing a global workforce demand that HRM practices not just hire the best candidates but also effectively integrate and engage across various settings. While competition intensifies, it is up to organizations to create new ways of recruiting, training, and retaining based on the expectations and their corresponding characteristics of their global workforce, which reflects the demand for a customized talent management approach to these global environments. Moreover, proper expatriate and repatriate management becomes a significant HRM function in global organizations. Expatriate postings could be useful but fraught with traps, especially when it comes to adapting foreign cultures and adapting back home. Companies need to create elaborate support systems that are geared toward expats' requirements and provide them with the means and training to thrive in multicultural environments. Similarly, efficient repatriation policies are imperative, and faulty handling of this phase leads to the loss of talent and lower organizational morale. Thus, organizations must keep in mind the importance of establishing a caring network to facilitate employees' working across borders amidst the intricate interplay of global HRM issues. Further, managing DEI stands as the priority area in the case of global organizations. As companies recruit from a pool of culturally diverse backgrounds, it is necessary to know the effect of DEI practices on team collaboration and organizational culture. Not only does a diverse workplace increase employee engagement, but it also leads to innovation and creativity due to different perspectives. Companies must put in place systems that guarantee fair treatment where employees feel empowered and appreciated irrespective of their backgrounds. The use of DEI in global HRM practices not only increases employee satisfaction and retention but also puts the organization on the right track with expectations from contemporary society, further establishing it as a leader in efficient and ethical human resource management. This hybrid model of talent management is crucial to long-term competitive success in an age of globalization and cultural complexity.

Definition of Human Resource Management (HRM)

The contemporary situation of Human Resource Management (HRM) is entirely different, particularly in the case of multinational companies. It showcases the need for effective recruitment, training, and retention methods aimed at a global multicultural workforce. Here, HRM transcends traditional parameters by incorporating practices that aid multicultural norms and standards. Emphasizing the importance of a diverse workplace, not only do organizations expand their pool of talent but also drive creativity and innovation. The practice is instrumental in ensuring a diverse work environment where individuals with different backgrounds can flourish, in turn, contributing to the global success and competitiveness of the organizations. Further, understanding and handling the specific problems posed by cross-cultural relations becomes critical as international organizations seek long-term development in overseas markets.

Expatriate and repatriate management constitutes another significant aspect of HRM in international firms. Workers regularly relocating from overseas assignments temporarily to their own nations, international organizations must implement integrated support systems so that expatriates may acculturate into host nations (Figure 9.1).

Figure 9.1. The concept of HRM.

Source: https://community.nasscom.in/sites/default/files/media/images/HRM.jpeg.

Cultural competence, language education, and local business education are essential in mitigating the risk of cultural confrontations and maximizing overall performance of a globally dispersed workforce. Effective repatriation practices are also just as essential in order to reintroduce repatriated expatriates to their home organizations without hiccups and help them leverage their international experiences to the fullest. In doing so, organizations can use the extensive knowledge of expatriates, which can be utilized to shape strategic decisions and organizational learning and play a dual role in talent management. Due to globalization, the definition of HRM has broadened to encompass the need for building diversity, equity, and inclusion within the workplace. Since businesses now function globally, their workforce consists of a diversified group of cultures with varying work attitudes, thus this complexification is an obstacle to traditional HRM practices. In order to deal with such intricacies, an HRM system is required that not only recognizes these differences but attempts to integrate them into business culture. With the centrality accorded to it by the accelerated globalization of the economy, organizations have an imperative need to adapt their HRM practices to be fair and inclusive to all employees (Iyiola et al., 2012). Such inclusivity not only enhances employees' job satisfaction and morale but also general organizational success in achieving sustainable competitive advantages in the global economy. Proactive addressing of diversity reshapes human resource practices in accordance with the broader organizational strategic goals and addressing the evolving desires of the modern workforce.

Importance of HRM in a Global Context

In addressing the complexities of an international marketplace, organizations increasingly come to realize the significance of efficient Human Resource Management (HRM) in crafting a diverse and inclusive workforce. The recruitment, development, and retention of talent cannot be overemphasized, because the diversity of skills and ideas brought to the table by employees with different cultural backgrounds enhances innovation and adaptability. A successful HRM plan not only emphasizes the recruitment of a multicultural workforce but also training initiatives that address cross-cultural skills. These promote workers to work optimally in multicultural groups and respond to an ever-changing worldwide environment. Lastly, the success of global organizations hinges on their ability to construct a work environment where diverse talents may flourish and develop a culture that is aligned with company values while optimizing performance and commitment. Management of repatriates and expatriates is another important challenge that highlights the necessity of integrated HRM practices at the global scale. This entails the complex process of getting employees prepared to work overseas, having them successfully adjust to a foreign setting, and integrating them back into home soil smoothly after international postings. Firms that invest in developing expatriate policies and support systems have enhanced job performance and employee satisfaction. In addition, these practices nicely reduce the risks of expatriate failure, which is costly in terms of wasting talent and financial expenses. Effective HRM considers the specific needs of expatriates and repatriates and offers tailored programs for their professional and personal concerns, which aligns individual capability with organizational objectives. In addition, the adoption of Green Human Resource Management (Green HRM) practices is gaining importance in global HRM context due to the growing issues of sustainability and environmental impact. Now, the organizations are not only required to adopt environmentally friendly practices by law, but also to ensure corporate social responsibility to be perceived positively by a global audience. Sustainability policies that promote sustainable practices demonstrate the seriousness of the organization in respect to both its workers and the public. As the case analysis of Green HRM illustrates, embracing such practices can promote sustainable growth in the long term and improve a positive corporate image (Md. Khan, 2023). The push toward sustainable management is linked with global acknowledgment and acceptance, since business organizations that promote a pledge toward the stewardship of the planet resonate both with capital and clients who are sustainability-oriented and enhance their competitive advantage in the global marketplace.

Overview of Key Challenges Faced by Global Organizations

In the global human resource management scenario, talent recruitment, training, and retaining are significant concerns. Global companies must contend with differential cultural expectations and various labor markets, and as such, the recruiting process is a difficult one. With diverse worker populations come the necessity for tailor-made training programs that not only address technical proficiency but also address cultural awareness so that employees can thrive in the global setting. Failure to invest in these areas will lead to faster turnover and disconnection from business aims that, subsequently, affect organizational performance. Expounding on this argument, Laroche (1998) states that global organizations need to adopt new management fashions that address such issues, ultimately facilitating easier talent integration across different cultural environments. Without strategic and adaptive recruitment and retention, international organizations risk losing their competitive edge in the growing globalized market. Efficient expatriate and repatriate management is also a global organization's main challenge, which seeks to leverage the talent beyond borders. Expatriate assignments are normally preceded by major investment and risk, with companies having to be assured that their employees are sufficiently trained for the overseas assignments. The issue of transferring workers is also exacerbated by unique cultural influences, which can have an effect on the overall success of the assignment and the worker's individual and professional satisfaction. Moreover, even the experience of integration for returning repatriated workers can be equally challenging, as they become vulnerable to reverse culture shock and fail to adapt into the corporate environment. Addressing these issues effectively is essential to achieving the return on investment in expatriate assignments. Therefore, organizations must create comprehensive support systems that benefit not only transition but also ongoing development, thereby making the experience of the global workforce smoother. Promoting diversity, equity, and inclusion (DEI) within global firms is another key challenge. As organizations become global, the need to develop an inclusive culture becomes most critical in order to take advantage of the benefits of a diverse workforce. Effective DEI programs require businesses to confront embedded prejudices and cultural variation that may stall teamwork and productivity. Without any attempt at making the workplace more diverse, institutions risk losing employee morale and creativity, ultimately compromising their overall success. Besides, these efforts can also be a major catalyst of promoting equal opportunities for all the employees, emphasized in the context of philanthropic engagement in the context of worldwide equity (Dadrawala et al., 2004). Challenges of DEI being addressed not only enhance the satisfaction of employees but also create sustainable business practices, again emphasizing the function of inclusive human resource management in the current globalized environment.

9.1. RECRUITMENT OF GLOBAL TALENT

In the modern world of business, organizations increasingly need to source talent that can deal with the complexity of an international market. This is particularly useful as companies aim to maximize their competitive edge through end-to-end recruitment strategies that not only ensure the acquisition of high-quality candidates but also the long-term management of talent.

Figure 9.2. Recruitment of global talent of a global marketplace.

Source: https://goglobal.com/wp-content/uploads/2025/01/Global-Talent-Market.png.

The recruitment process, therefore, extends beyond the placement itself; it is a strategic approach to finding people whose abilities and cultural fit resonate with organizational aspirations. Such investment in tailor-made recruitment processes, therefore, helps to significantly increase the organizations potential for success in new markets, ultimately towards improved performance and innovation, as the comments on talent management within European SMEs confirm (Kohont et al., 2019). Moreover, the integration of diversity, equity, and inclusion (DEI) principles into recruitment practices has emerged as a crucial factor in talent identification at the international level. By offering an inclusive culture, businesses can enhance their appeal to more diverse pools of candidates, complementing their pool of talent further. DEI-oriented practices not only align with ethical responsibilities but also bring measurable benefits, including greater employee engagement and productivity. As business increasingly recognizes the value of diverse perspectives, it is crucial to implement recruitment practices that operate actively to eliminate biases and barriers to entry. By establishing frameworks that are focused on DEI, business places itself in the position where it can unlock the full potential of its employees, fostering rich and creative organizational culture (Doherty et al., 2012) (Figure 9.2).

Repatriate and expatriate management also complements international talent recruitment as a fundamental vehicle for knowledge transfer and cultural adjustment in international organizations. While the recruitment process establishes the stage, effective management addresses the unique expatriate challenges like acclimatization to new environments and ultimate reintegration upon return. Tailored support systems with targeted training and mentoring will enhance the experience of expatriates significantly, reducing turnover and enhancing firm loyalty. In addition, repatriation programs for reintegration of returnees maximize the value derived from foreign experience and provide for knowledge sharing learned abroad throughout the organization across teams. Thus, the entire management of repatriates and expatriates is essential to the greater aim of developing a resilient and responsive workforce for multinational companies.

9.1.1. Strategies for Attracting International Candidates

In terms of human resource management, proper selection of global talent needs a multidimensional approach that appreciates the intricacy of a globalized workforce. Organizations must first create a sound employer brand that is appealing to different cross-cultural backgrounds. This involves identifying the companys commitment to diversity, equity, and inclusion as an attractive magnet for global talents seeking workspaces that value their individual perspectives. Furthermore, customization of recruitment strategies to localized marketing can boost market visibility. Unique cultural sensitivities can be acquired and utilized by organizations to personalize the message that appeals to prospective candidates since the shift of organizational dynamics due to globalization calls for human resource strategies to be tailored (Iyiola et al., 2012). One of the major strategies in luring global candidates lies in relocating with complete relocation packages. These packages should address the logistical and emotional difficulty of expatriate mobility between countries. This may include housing support, integration packages, and cultural orientation, all of which reduce the stress of relocation overseas (Figure 9.3).

Figure 9.3. Human resource management, the successful recruitment of international candidates.

Source: https://www.aihr.com/wp-content/uploads/Recruiting-Strategies-social.png.

In addition, organizations can become more desirable by offering career prospects for the international recruits, particularly through formalized channels that guarantee professional growth and belong to the business culture. Since organizations have a dynamic and complex environment to operate in, emphasizing these features not only gets the right candidates but also ensures that they are properly taken care of in transitioning, eventually resulting in their long-term maintenance and achievement (Florea, 2025). Lastly, cultivating a positive and embracing corporate culture is one prime consideration in keeping global applicants interested. Companies need to engage current employees in the hiring process, the diversified ones in particular, to get their input and experience, which can assist in making the new recruits feel more accepted. Employee networks and referral schemes are also effective tools in aiding recruitment. By empowering the employees to market the firm, companies are able to reach global networks of potential candidates. With firms seeking to conduct business in ever-more difficult global markets, implementing these strategies not only aids in attracting the most qualified talent but also enhances organizational culture, enhancing overall staff job satisfaction and performance (Iyiola et al., 2012).

9.1.2. Utilizing Technology in the Recruitment Process

With the advent of accelerating technological improvements, organizations are now more aware of the important contributions technology can make to optimizing the recruitment process. Utilizing online platforms enables organizations to tap into a wider pool of potential talent while optimizing their overall efficiency. The adoption of applicant tracking systems, for example, not only streamlines the aggregation and sorting of resumes but also facilitates data-driven decision-making for HR professionals. This becomes especially important in international organizations where the necessity to have a diverse workforce demands strong processes for finding potential candidates over different geographical regions. Furthermore, using technology to post jobs on various channels guarantees that organizations can select talent from different backgrounds, which creates diversity and ensures equity in the labor force. Remote recruitment tools have transformed the manner in which organizations make interviews and hiring assessments more convenient and efficient. Video conferencing tools enable HR staff to connect with candidates anywhere globally, thereby reducing the logistical issues involved in face-to-face interviews. These technological advancements not only result in cost savings and time efficiency but also improve the candidate experience by offering flexible means of interaction. In addition, these tools support instant feedback and collaboration between recruitment teams, which results in faster decision-making. This movement towards virtual interaction mirrors wider globalization trends, as organizations need to reinvent the way they recruit to stay ahead of a fluid marketplace. Flexibility is crucial, as global business operations depend more on agile human resource management to tap the right talent and hold on to it (Figure 9.4).

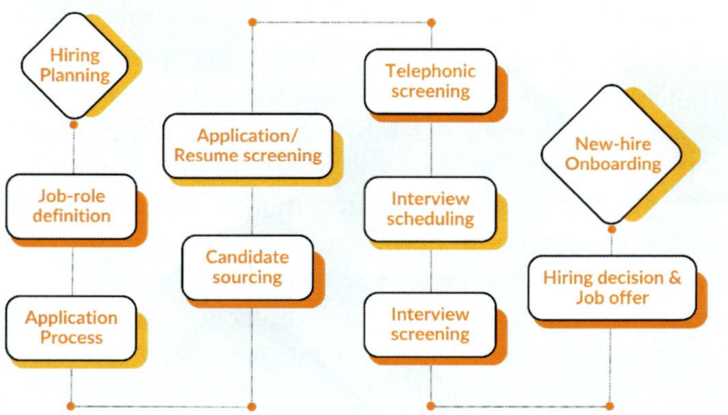

Figure 9.4. Improve your technical recruitment process.

Source: https://techjobsfair.com/wp-content/uploads/blog-images/2023/jan/technical-recruitment-process/general-hiring-process.png.

The strategic use of technology for hiring also plays a major part in building relationships and trust with potential employees. As Nilson et al. (2009) explains, effective human resource practices can significantly enhance relationship dynamics, particularly in environments where working virtually is most critical. Through the utilization of technology in providing an efficient hiring process, organizations can create a positive first impression, which is essential in building a solid employer brand. Moreover, repeated exposure to recruitment using technical tools is an indicator of ongoing interaction with employees even after they get on board, especially for coordinating expatriates and getting them to settle down in new conditions. With the quest for diversity and inclusiveness by organizations, the continuous changing nature of their recruitment process through technological advancement will not only improve their talent hunt but also contribute to the overall efficiency of human resource management across the world.

9.1.3. Legal Considerations in Global Hiring Practices

Nimbly traversing the maze of international employment practices demands a virulent sensitization to the variances in legal regimes. As companies endeavor to extend their operations outside the boundaries of nations, they are faced with a plethora of regulations safeguarding the conditions of employment in different jurisdictions. Ranging from anti-discrimination laws to labor practices, issues of law are at the core of ensuring compliance and mitigating liabilities. For instance, American business companies operating outside the country are required to reconcile their own legal obligations with host-state regulatory controls and local tradition. This is yet more complicated when hiring the disabled, as business companies must act both on international human rights agreements and domestic disability law, which can differ extensively in reach and implementation. The outcome of failure to comply with these legal specifications not only affects workforce morale but also results in costly litigation and loss of reputation. Furthermore, recruitment procedures must be harmonized with several legal factors to ensure the development of an inclusive work environment. Employee rights and protection laws vary in different states; thus, human resource managers must understand the relevant laws so that they can defend their organizations as well as employees. For example, federal law in the US provides critical protection against discrimination with compliance mandated under the Americans with Disabilities Act. However, in other international markets, such legislation may not exist, and so these considerations are not merely about regulatory compliance; they shape corporate culture and influence talent recruitment directly. Efforts directed at employment hindrances within groups that are underrepresented such as the disabled, can make organizations employers of choice within regions, which enhances their competitiveness in the global talent pool. Finally, the legal landscape under which international recruitment practices take place underscores the need for planning and investment of resources in order to create an environment that is inclusive. Organizations must assess their preparedness within the company to engage with diverse groups of workers, particularly in the implementation of activities to assist individuals with disabilities as workers. Evidence shows that inclusive practices not only lead to improved hiring success but can lead to increased overall employee satisfaction and productivity. However, even after federal initiatives for equality, longstanding employment gaps remain, indicating the necessity for ongoing assessment and improvement in hiring practices. Implementing measurement frameworks to measure success, as purported by the Conference Board Research Working Group, is essential in tracking progress and making all the staff excel in their professional lives. An active response to legal matters can thus be a driver towards organizational performance improvement and compliance, hence qualifying as an imperative to modern human resource management practices in multinational organizations (Barrington et al., 2013; Bartram et al., 2015).

9.2. TRAINING AND DEVELOPMENT

An organization's ability to keep up with the rapid evolving needs of markets greatly relies on its training and development initiatives. With companies expanding overseas, they are confronted by a set of issues, such as cultural differences and varying working practices. In order to successfully address these complexities, it is increasingly important to have the right training program in place. Not only do such programs make employees technically competent but also equip them with people and cross-cultural competencies needed to work in multi-ethnic teams. The connection between human resource management and training becomes evident here; as firms practice concurrent engineering, they must make sure their people are trained not only to perform technically but also to communicate their messages effectively across cultures. Consequently, investing in large-scale training programs promotes organizational success because it guarantees the flexibility and elasticity of workers in the current globalized world (Jadhav et al., 2016). Furthermore, expatriate and repatriate management is a unique challenge that underscores the importance of quality training and development. International assignment staff must receive expert preparation to function in new cultural environments and norms. Expat-specific training can help them adapt, enhancing their likelihood of success in global markets. The programs must also address repatriates who may have re-entry challenges upon return to their home country (Figure 9.5).

Figure 9.5. Implementing robust support systems in trainings.

Source: https://uknowva.com/images/13297318_5192058.jpg.

Through implementing robust support structures, including mentorship and continuous professional development programs, it is possible to give these employees a highly valued chance to leverage their overseas experience towards improving the organization upon repatriation. By recognizing that training is an integral aspect of the expatriate process, companies can create a globally capable workforce as well as one that is ready to spearhead organizational goals (Iyiola et al., 2012). Along with focusing on operations and culture in training and development, organizations also need to make diversity, equity, and inclusion (DEI) a priority.

In a global environment, being attuned to the complexities of different cultures is essential; therefore, training programs need to intentionally integrate components that encourage inclusivity and respect for diverse perspectives. Effective training in DEI not only serves office harmony but also innovation since diverse teams of employees carry a wide variety of minds to tackle issues. Additionally, organizations that adopt these values are well placed to select and retain the best employees with varying backgrounds. This commitment to fostering an inclusive workplace resonates with training and development strategies to build workforce capabilities while offering equal opportunities for every employee. Therefore, the inclusion of DEI in training initiatives is crucial for developing an overall strategy to human resource management in cross-cultural organizations (Jadhav et al., 2016).

9.2.1. Cross-Cultural Training Programs

The character of diverse workforce management demands a robust training strategy superior to conventional practices. In cross-cultural enterprises where employees are heterogeneous in origin, the effectiveness of cross-cultural training programs is the most essential element. Such programs will equip employees, especially expatriates, with the competence to manage cultural differences and build inclusive workplaces. By encouraging a deeper cultural appreciation of differences, organizations can reduce potential conflicts and increase cooperation among team members. Consequently, these programs not only assist expatriates on assignment, but also influence the overall organizational culture, promoting a culture of respect and understanding in accordance with diversity, equity, and inclusion values (Bormann et al., 2001). The final aim is to facilitate the effective performance of employees in multicultural environments, ultimately increasing overall productivity and workplace harmony. Incorporation of cross-cultural training into the broader human resource management framework indicates its strategic significance in global organizations. Influenced by the difficulties brought about by globalization, HR departments are required to innovate practices to address the multivariate demands of their workers (Figure 9.6).

Figure 9.6. The aspects of cross-cultural training.

Source: https://www.collidu.com/media/catalog/product/img/0/c/0c2aaf5cf9f8e943a6c5fcb94d15cd6e6eb24992008f98aac271831292f2999c/cross-cultural-training-slide1.png.

For instance, companies that undertake cross-cultural training typically witness a reduction in expatriate failure rates caused by cultural miscommunication and communication breakdown (Iyiola et al., 2012). This proactive measure not only saves money in turnover but also makes employees feel nurtured in their overseas assignments. Finally, developing an effective cross-cultural training program is more than mere compliance but a strategic investment that contributes to building the organization's competitive advantage in the international market. With culturally competent employees, organizations can better deal with the subtleties of international operations. Moreover, the effectiveness of cross-cultural training programs hinges greatly on regular monitoring and adaptation to future trends and cultural shifts. As the world globalizes, so do organization HR processes, such as how they train. Having discussions with employees to seek their opinions on whether training has been effective can lead to more specific and successful programs that are appealing to different groups. Through this ongoing process, the training remains relevant to the specific cultural challenges employees face at work (Bormann et al., 2001). Also, incorporating views of several stakeholders, e.g., people with different cultures, enriches training materials and promotes ownership on the part of participants. In this way, cross-cultural training transforms from a passive normative necessity into an engaged means of enhancing job performance and creating a culture of respect and diversity in international companies.

9.2.2. Continuous Professional Development Initiatives

With the rapid pace of the global organization, never in the past have there been so many imperatives to adopt continuous professional development programs. The programs give employees the information necessary to navigate through complex issues, as well as creating a culture of long-term development. A study covering multiple programs exemplifies the success of these development initiatives, indicating that organizations strongly improve their operational performance when they make continuous learning and professional development a top priority among their employees (Newman, 2001). The integration of these programs with the organization's superordinate goals ensures that employees are not only engaged but also flexible towards the shifting marketplace dynamics, which is vital in order to retain the best global talent. Furthermore, the use of continuous professional development programs is a critical role in expatriate and repatriate management—crucial pillars in international human resource management. With businesses spreading their wings globally, it becomes imperative to have good training programs suited especially for expatriate employees. Such programs allow ease in placing workers in overseas cultures, enhancing their productivity and job satisfaction. Also, repatriate programs can mitigate the challenges of reverse culture shock, thereby reducing turnover rates.

Such programs emphasize the importance of organizations making investments in integrated training models that not only encompass technical competence but also cultural skills required for expatriate assignments. Concerning fostering diversity, equity, and inclusion, continuous professional development programs are instrumental in creating an inclusive workplace culture. By emphasizing diversity training and space for equitable growth, organizations can create a more robust, innovative workforce. The treatment of virtual models of HR illustrates how emerging technology facilitates these development programs, allowing flexible and accessible training experiences (Lepak et al., 2001). Such structures enable organizations to create alliances that facilitate learning and development across geographies. Ultimately, integrating these strategies into human resource planning not only enhances the extent of employee engagement but also optimizes the firm's ability to adapt and thrive within a more globalized business environment.

9.2.3. Evaluating the Effectiveness of Training Programs

Within the new geography of global organizations, training programs are important engines facilitating cultural and working differences. Not only are they designed to enhance workers' capabilities but also foster an environment of tolerance and inclusion within multicultural workforces. As businesses expand globally, they are unable not to encounter employees from diverse cultures with their respective values and expectations. These differences need to be addressed; therefore, training programs need to be carefully planned to consider cross-cultural issues that play a serious role in influencing organizational dynamics. Using properly structured assessments, organizations can guarantee that their training programs are properly addressing their objectives of skill building and cultural incorporation. This is supported further by the necessity to become engrossed in continuous feedback processes that tie the training objectives to the fast-changing global marketplace, finally justifying (Iyiola et al., 2012)'s assertion of the necessity for up-to-date management trends. A central theme in assessing the efficacy of training schemes is co-ordination of these schemes with the general strategic objectives of the firm. This entails a good understanding of the specific competencies and cross-cultural skills to thrive in the global arena. Application of diverse training methods—e.g., e-learning, on-the-job training, and cross-cultural training workshops—can enhance learning while addressing the multicolored needs of a global workforce. Furthermore, as the companies work towards a balance between global efficiency and local adaptability, they must identify whether training initiatives are efficacious in educating workers to cope with intricate, culturally diverse scenarios. The models put forward by Boudreau et al. (2002) suggest that embedding business processes in a product and cultural matrix gives valuable information on the effectiveness of training interventions so that firms can concentrate strategically on talent building. Furthermore, training program effectiveness measurement needs to expand from competencies to encompass long-term employee performance and retention impact. An effective evaluation plan would involve tracking key performance measures, employee surveys, and retention after training. A correlation of these metrics with associated training interventions enables organizations to identify which programs yield the best return on investment. The notion of developing global key talent pools, presented by Boudreau et al. (2002), is an affirmation of the necessity of alignment of training programs with the overall strategy of the organization. This holistic solution not only helps in the development of skills but also builds an organizational culture devoted to diversity and inclusion so that employees feel able and empowered to make significant contributions to their work in a globalized setting.

9.3. RETENTION OF GLOBAL TALENT

In global talent management, businesses face the double challenge of not just attracting but also keeping quality staff in a highly competitive workforce. Global talent retention hinges on strategic human resource management strategy that entails wide-ranging recruitment, training, and development schemes to support the requirements of a diverse labor force. Effective retention strategies must consider the unique aspirations and drivers of employees, particularly for overseas assignments. This is echoed in firms that include personalized career management and mentoring programs to give expatriates a feeling of belonging where they are highly valued and supported. These investments in talent management can significantly enhance the satisfaction and loyalty of employees, which in turn results in improved organizational performance while mitigating the risks and costs associated with high levels of turnover. Additionally, proper expatriate and repatriate management is a key factor in retaining international talent (Figure 9.7).

In-out or coming in and out of foreign assignments can be fraught with complications, from cultural adjustment to reentry issues upon return. Seamless expatriate management needs elaborate support systems, from pre-departure orientation to cultural immersion processes, and ongoing assistance in the assignment cycle. Organizations that understand the importance of such assistance not only facilitate easier transitions but also show their dedication towards their talent. This strategy solves the problems generally faced by expatriates regarding career development and job security upon repatriation to their home country. By engaging employees actively at these key moments, organizations are able to create a caring culture that creates long-term commitment among their global talent pool. Diversity, equity, and inclusion (DEI) programs further support the model for retaining global talent in organizations. A DEI emphasis not only enhances worker commitment but also generates innovation, for diversified thinking brings greater energy to the workplace.

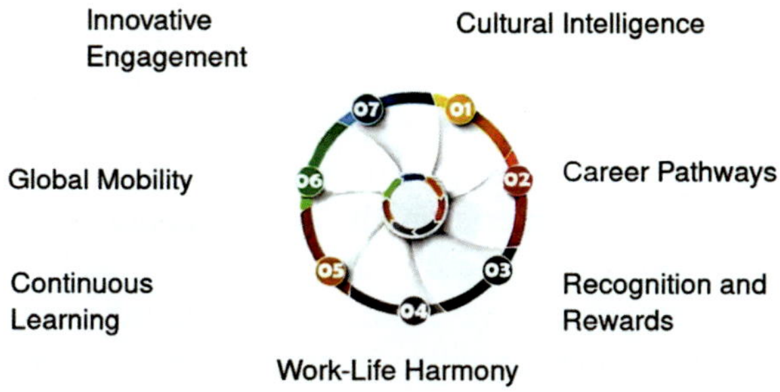

Figure 9.7. The retention of global talent management.

Source: https://fastercapital.co/i/Global-talent-management--Effective-Talent-Development-in-a-Global-Business-Environment--Retention-and-Engagement-of-Global-Talent.webp.

By fostering an inclusive culture where everyone feels valued and enabled, organizations can develop their ability to attract and keep top performers in diverse backgrounds. Second, identifying and addressing the particular issues of diverse talent management enhances the organization's general institutionalized commitment to workplace equity. This is particularly crucial in settings where talent management practices intersect with diverse local norms and expectations. While stressing European research, SMEs must learn to modify their talent management policies to react to local circumstance in a manner that responds to the singular needs and expectations of their employees in a sustainable fashion (Kohont et al., 2019). Through building an inclusive culture of respect, organizations are better positioned to take advantage of retaining global talent (Center for Advanced Human Resources Studies, 2004).

9.3.1. Competitive Compensation and Benefits Packages

In the context of global organizations, effective human resource management is contingent on the dynamics of compensation and benefit schemes that can attract and retain a pluralistic workforce. The evolving dynamics of globalization necessitated a critical reassessment of traditional models of compensation, which have revealed that tried-and-true methods are increasingly subjected to market forces and cultural diversity. For instance, the existing trend from rigid remuneration systems normally prevalent in some cultures, such as lifetime employment in Japan, reflects a growing need for flexibility in developing remuneration strategies. With international companies still facing the conflict of building integrated global systems and conforming to local heritage, the use of competitive pay packages is required in addressing such challenges. The flexibility embedded in domestic contexts greatly influences managerial decisions concerning remuneration, a departure from the imposition of uniform techniques to a more advanced technique that is sensitive to variations at regional levels (Bloom et al., 2000). Furthermore, competitive remuneration analysis must take into consideration the socio-economic environments on which international organizations operate. As traditional pay conventions disintegrate, businesses have to re-evaluate their strategies to make them new in competing for the top-performing talent in diverse environments (Figure 9.8).

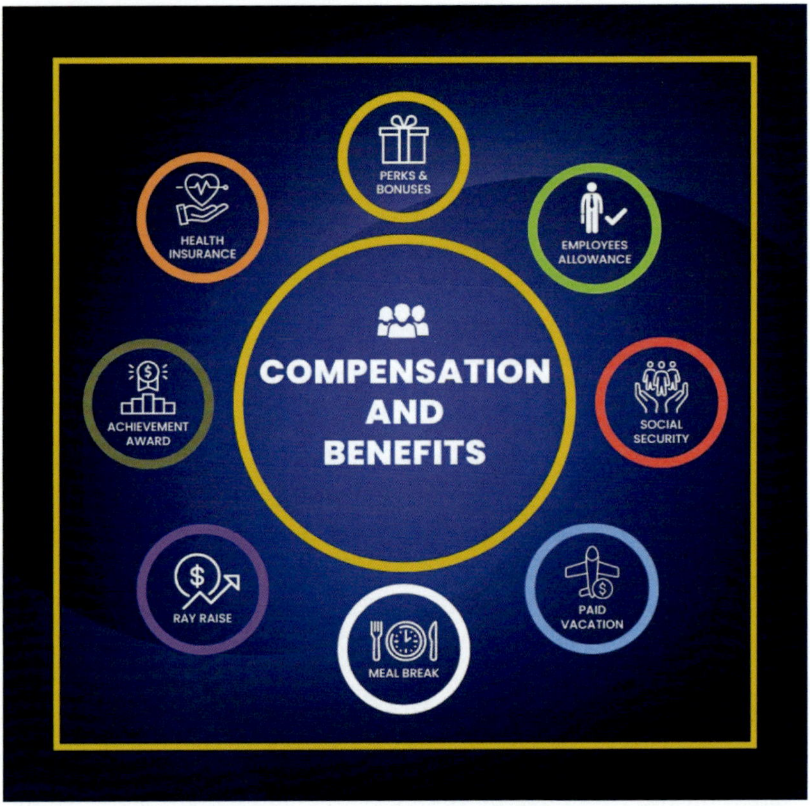

Figure 9.8. Importance of compensation and benefits for employees.

Source: https://gfoundry.com/wp-content/uploads/2024/08/Compensation-and-Benefits-gfoundry2.png.

The concept of host country pay connecting to host countries' cultures is increasingly under scrutiny as corporations wrestle with the demands of a globalized world calling for adaptability and responsiveness. This change provides an impetus for multinational enterprises (MNEs) to design compensation packages that are not only financially equitable but which also reflect an obsession with diversity, equity, and inclusion. Such a plan not only enhances the firm's reputation but also enhances employee satisfaction by specially aimed benefits, thereby enhancing retention rates in a competitive market (Bloom et al., 1997). Overall, competitive compensation and benefits schemes are central to creating a globally fit workforce to contend with the complexities of global operations. By applying a strategic alignment of remuneration practices to regional expectations and global norms, organizations can establish an environment that stimulates collaboration and innovation. Furthermore, the introduction of innovative benefits such as flexible working arrangements and career development opportunities renders organizations desirable employers. It becomes essential for human resource managers to be adaptive to the changing trends in the compensation models while evaluating their performance in attracting talent, as well as creating career growth of repatriates and expatriates. In this manner, not only do organizations enhance their competitive edge, but they also contribute positively to the overall socio-economic situation, paving the way for a more sustainable employment practices future for the world (Bloom et al., 1997).

9.3.2. Creating a Positive Organizational Culture

In this era of global organizational competition, building a positive organization culture emerges as the ultimate pillar to success. Not only does it enhance the morale of employees but also greatly influences rates of retention and productivity overall. By creating a core of an emphasis on an inclusive and caring culture, organizations can build loyalty and motivation among employees, which is especially critical in retaining skilled workers in spite of high turnover. Implementing sustainable motivational practices aligned with individual employees' personal values can have a significant role in fostering such a culture. By aligning organizational and individual goals, organizations can profitably harness the full potential of their employees, thereby making the employees feel valued and engaged, hence propelling the organization's success (Gulchuk et al., 2019). Aside from that, the search for a positive organizational culture demands active effort in workforce diversity management, especially in the context of globalization. Businesses can benefit enormously from an energetic mosaic of ideas that come with diverse workforces. Not only does diversity enhance creativity and innovation, but it also enables businesses to interact more authentically with a broader clientele. Materials with a purpose to cultivate workplace diversity are vital instruments for practitioners who seek to create an inclusive workplace. Through actively utilizing training and development solutions designed for diverse cultures, organizations become more versatile in fulfilling changing market requirements while cultivating a sense of belonging among all employees (Bormann et al., 2001). Finally, successful integration of repatriates and expatriates into the organizational fabric is important in ensuring a positive culture. Such employees bring worthwhile experiences from various cultural exposures that can contribute immensely to organizational growth. Their adaptation and retention, however, require concerted efforts in the area of mentorship programs and support mechanisms that focus on their culture reintegration. Having a platform through which international employees can engage in discussion and exchange of experiences can really enhance cross-cultural understanding and collaboration. As business organizations navigate globalization-related challenges, catering to expatriates becomes essential not only to retain best brains but also to make the organization competitive in the global landscape (Gulchuk et al., 2019).

9.3.3. Career Advancement Opportunities for Employees

In the context of international organizations, development of career growth opportunity is not a secondary theme of Human Resource Management, but is crucial to ensure a competitive edge in talent sourcing and employee motivation. As corporations extend internationally, they encounter a multiplicity of diverse workforce culture that calls for tailored career paths that resonate with a multicultural workforce. The career development strategies must be aligned with the organizational culture and local practice so that the employees are made to understand the career path that they are supposed to adopt. If these cultural considerations are met, organizations can improve the sense of belongingness and motivation among the employees, which is critical in retaining talent across regions. The incorporation of well-considered career progression opportunities serves to enhance the employer brand and attract top talent seeking to develop within the organization. The effective management of employee career progression in a global context necessitates the application of a multi-faceted strategy involving robust training programs, mentorship programs, and open promotional avenues. Organizations who are serious about building their talent tend to introduce systematic programs aimed at investing in workers and giving them the skills they need as well as experience of new roles in the organization. This not only improves their competencies but, at the same time, builds loyalty and engagement. Looking into effective strategies used by top firms, it is obvious that investing in workers' professional development has broad implications. By offering competitive incentives and fostering an internal mobility culture, organizations can reverse entry-level turnover rates while creating a reservoir of leaders for the future (Hanleybrown et al., 2017). An effective career advancement strategy is therefore a key consideration in realizing optimum worker potential at the global level. Further, organizations must understand that diversity, equity, and inclusion (DEI) programs play a significant role in shaping career progression opportunities. An acceptance of diversity in the workplace fuels innovation and creativity because diverse viewpoints provide stronger decision-making. But it is essential that DEI strategies are not tokenistic but rooted in the corporate culture and career development strategies. Organizations that actively promote equitable career growth opportunities for the underrepresented groups will likely have an active workforce who seriously think the organization's values. This emphasis on equity can decrease turnover and boost employees' satisfaction, leading in the end to a stable and productive workplace (Center for Advanced Human Resources Studies, 2004). Integrating DEI principles within career development strategies is thus not only an ethical imperative but also a strategic imperative in the global employment marketplace.

9.4. MANAGING EXPATRIATES

Effective management of expatriates is critical to the success of international companies, particularly in today's dynamic changing global landscape. Companies are increasingly acknowledging complexities involved in expatriate assignments where caution needs to be exercised during recruitment, training, and support mechanisms. The methodology must be integrated so that expatriates are not just equipped with the technical expertise of their work but also with the cultural wisdom to deal with mixed situations. Furthermore, organizations must develop mechanisms that facilitate knowledge transfer and ongoing learning, enhancing the ability of expatriates to share their knowledge and experience. This strategic focus on expatriate management not only improves individual performance but also drives organizational performance, creating a competitive edge in international markets across the globe. Compensation frameworks for expatriate management cannot be overstated. As globalization continues to gain momentum, traditional compensation frameworks are being pushed to the brink, calling for an overhaul of how organizations address expatriate requirements. The assumption that expatriates are economically neutral at assignment has been challenged as there is a push towards more compensation systems that respond more to locally aligned market conditions and individual expectations. As was said, even highly embedded employment culture norms are changing due to global economic pressure (Bloom et al., 1997). This requires a high level of understanding local and international compensation systems to attract and retain top performers in multiple regions and make expats feel rewarded and motivated while on assignment (Figure 9.9).

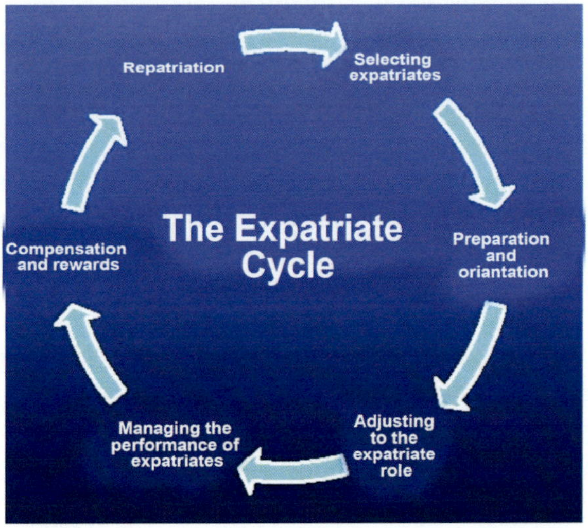

Figure 9.9. The expatriate's role in the success of global organizations.

Source: https://www.ivoryresearch.com/wp-content/uploads/2021/12/260.jpg.

If repatriation happens, expatriates return to their home countries with valuable knowledge and new ideas that can provide significant inputs to organizations. However, the transition from being an expatriate to being repatriated typically creates major setbacks, which are professionally obstructive and prevent the effective implementation of such learned knowledge. As per studies, organizations must bridge the gap between expatriates' individual learnings and organizational knowledge to make the most out of their experience (Antal et al., 2025). The majority of expatriates do not implant their knowledge in organizational culture because they lack enabling structures. This deficiency is intended to highlight the need for organizations to enhance not only their expatriation policies but also to create an organizational culture that is diverse and encourages information sharing by all levels of employees. Through creating a learning-conducive atmosphere, businesses can take advantage of the skills of back-to-home expatriates, thereby strengthening their global strategy as a whole.

9.4.1. Selection Criteria for Expatriate Assignments

The sophistication that is involved in expatriate placement in overseas jobs necessitates that the selection criteria be interpreted in a nuanced manner to affect the outcome of these assignments. Careful and exhaustive selection encompasses multiple dimensions, including job skill, cultural adaptability, and interpersonal skills. Organizations have also prompted HR departments to seek applicants who, in addition to having technical abilities required for the profession, possess a very high level of emotional intelligence required for survival in multicultural environments. Various cross-cultural adjustment theories emphasize the importance of pre-training expatriates for what they are likely to face while adjusting to foreign cultures, postulating that effective training and support mechanisms can minimize expatriate failure rates considerably (Singh, 20205). The firms therefore must adopt an integrative candidate selection strategy, selecting individuals with whom they can have a seamless transition and who can contribute positively to their foreign assignments.

Additionally, the expanding intricacies of global business environments have compelled multinational firms to review their expatriate selection standards stringently. Globalization of business at lightening speed has spurred the need for change-oriented, culturally aware employees who grasp the intricacies of international markets. Research shows that organizations are able to place greater significance on candidates who not only hold technical skills but also arrive with already existing global experience, language proficiency, and a well-established understanding of the cultural context in their destination countries (Linehan et al., 2003). This emphasis on a broadened skill set serves to highlight the importance of selecting employees who will be capable of projecting well the values of diversity, equity, and inclusion—those which are most essential to organizational cohesion in an increasingly international world. By so doing, companies are able to leverage their global management strategies and enhance their overall competitive advantage in the marketplace. Finally, expatriate assignment selection criteria also cover examination of personal considerations, including family status and support systems. Expatriate performance and adaptation are most likely dependent on their families willingness and ability to adjust to new circumstances. Organizations need to screen candidates from a comprehensive perspective by evaluating their families readiness to relocate and adapt to other cultural settings. This approach aligns with the argument that having a good family environment can largely decrease the risk of expatriate failure (Singh, 2025). Therefore, the inclusion of family issues in the selection process can encourage greater commitment and enhance the success of expatriates to their new jobs. Consequently, the development of an inclusive expatriate selection model incorporating professional certification as well as personal circumstances remains paramount to the quest for effective human resource management in multinationals.

9.4.2. Support Systems for Expatriates and Their Families

It is important to have a robust support system that helps not only the expatriates but also their families transition properly to new surroundings. The emphasis on providing complete support justifies provision of preparatory and training needs for expatriates as well as their families in order to minimize the likelihood of failure in relocation. This is particularly crucial when considering that expatriates are generally deployed outside their countries to manage critical business activities or projects in foreign markets. Existing studies highlight the significance of formal support systems, such as cultural orientation and on-the-job support, leading to seamless integration by the expatriates, as well as their families. Since companies are increasingly conscious of the high costs of expatriate failure, developing tailored programs that meet the individual and family-specific issues is a priority (Linehan et al., 2003). No less significant is identifying the part played by the expatriate's family dynamics in expatriation success. Studies have indicated that the emotional and psychological well-being of an expatriates family has a direct impact on the expatriate's adjustment and work performance in the host country. Various support systems, such as family therapy, networking, and provision of education to spouse children, facilitate the adjustment process. Providing a climate where expatriate families feel supported, companies can raise retention rates and overall satisfaction, leading to better performance results.

Additionally, identification and consideration of the issues of family members foster a feeling of responsibility and belongingness, thus increasing expatriates' motivation to excel in their foreign assignments (Singh, 2025). Finally, the development of effective expatriate support systems and families entails an interdisciplinary model that integrates various dimensions of human resource management. This entails serious thought being devoted to cross-cultural training, which protects expatriates from the nuances of different social mores and business standards. Furthermore, organizations must recognize the value of continuous support throughout an expatriate assignment, from homecoming in the host country to returnee repatriation when the expatriate returns. By focusing on the welfare of expatriates' families, organizations are able to make expatriation a strategic asset, thus resulting in organizational effectiveness and competitiveness in overseas markets. The combination of customized training programs, family support systems, and continuous resources demonstrates an emphasis on total human resource management at the global level (Linehan et al., 2003).

9.4.3. Performance Evaluation of Expatriate Employees

The complexities that come with managing a multicultural labor force can sometimes influence the efficiency of expatriate employees. Organizations aspiring to reap the benefits of globalization pose unique challenges in international talent acquisition and management. Such challenges demand delicateness in understanding cultural differences and local business culture, which considerably influence performance management processes. The performance of the expatriate workers is not only a matter of individual capability but also closely associated with organizational support systems, acclimatization in the local environment, and integration into the culture. According to Laroche (1998), economic activity globalization creates a scenario under which cross-cultural difficulties may arise, further complicating the evaluation process. Thus, companies must adopt comprehensive evaluation systems that incorporate quantitative measures and qualitative insight to ensure equitable and effective assessment of their expatriate workers. When designing performance appraisal systems for expatriate workers, companies must focus on incorporating native practices along with strategic international human resource management (SIHRM) concepts. This integration is required for the formulation of a uniform performance appraisal strategy that fulfills the requirements of global uniformity without losing local sensitivity. Writers suggest that SIHRM can provide valuable insights into how multinational enterprises involve employee assessment in various cultural contexts (Cieri et al., 1998) (Figure 9.10).

Figure 9.10. Performance evaluation of expatriate employees.

Source: https://fastercapital.co/i/International-human-resource-management--How-to-Manage-Your-International-Human-Resource-and-Talent-Development--Managing-Expatriates-and-Global-Assignments.webp.

By using this systemic approach, businesses can craft appraisal systems that not only quantify expatriates work performance but also appreciate their contribution to cultural adaptation and organizational alignment. Through these systems, expatriate motivation and job satisfaction are enhanced, which inevitably leads to better performance in foreign assignments. Finally, an effective expatriate performance appraisal process must have feedback mechanisms that will allow career development and retention. As businesses strive to come to terms with the intricacies implicated in expatriate assignments, performance appraisals must shift their emphasis beyond overt economic indicators. Incorporation of elements such as cultural acclimatization, teamwork, and leadership competence is an imperative. Such a holistic outlook forms the cornerstone of a diverse and inclusive workplace, where every expatriate employee can thrive. Organizations need to go an extra mile in acquiring ideas from expatriate employees regarding what they have to say concerning their experience and perceptions of the appraisal process. The two-way communication is a measure of its commitment to full-fledged talent management and helps to eliminate potential dissatisfaction, thereby long-term international talent retention aligned with ideas propounded by Laroche (1998) and SITHRM frameworks.

9.5. REPATRIATION PROCESSES

One of the most significant areas of concentration for human resource management in multi-national corporations is the process complexity of repatriation. Repatriation of the workers returning from overseas assignments needs thorough planning and intentional effort on the part of human resource experts. Repatriates also face difficulty adjusting to their home offices, with potential culture dissonance and career disruption. Organizations, therefore, have to create a knowledge-friendly environment allowing it to happen. Successful communication, customized development programs, and value placed on the unique experience acquired abroad can contribute greatly to the experience of repatriation. These initiatives not only facilitate the return of valuable talent but also foster organizational commitment, thus a steadier workforce in the face of the dilemma of globalizations, the sophistication of whose dynamics tends to make the workers more difficult to manage (Iyiola et al., 2012). In addition to this, expatriates' complexities extend beyond their international assignments and significantly affect repatriation processes. As the global environment continues to evolve, the typical perception of career growth is redefined, and hence organizations need to establish systems that can accommodate the unique needs of repatriates. Existing studies have indicated that organizations must address individual as well as organizational factors in this transition. With the inclusion of cultural sensitivity in repatriation processes, organizations can create a whole-person process that values the rich experiences that expatriates bring with them back into the organization. Not only does this recognize their efforts but also positions the repatriation experience as a key strategic component in global talent management. Accordingly, here, enhancing the repatriation process becomes a must for sustaining employee motivation and developing sustained organizational development amidst globalization diversification (Cappellen et al., 2025) (Figure 9.11).

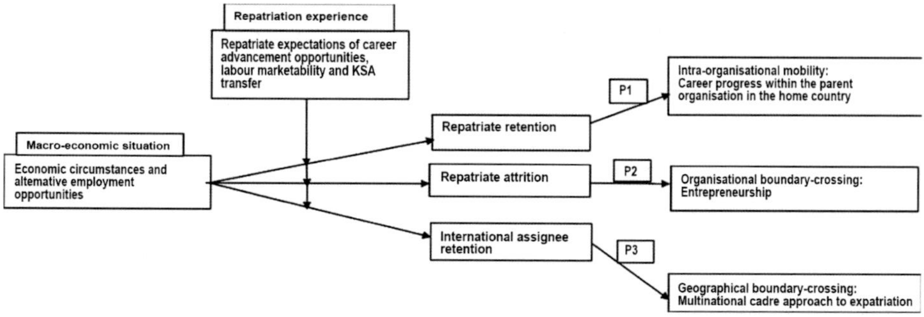

Figure 9.11. The repatriation process model.

Source: https://www.researchgate.net/publication/282199816/figure/fig1/AS:1075282702237697@1633378782208/The-repatriation-process-model.png.

To facilitate effective repatriation, organizations can implement comprehensive training and mentoring programs that cover the various dimensions of career development. These programs must be designed to help repatriating expats close the gap between international experience and the organizational context into which they are returning. Experienced counselors and mentors with extensive knowledge of both domestic and international dynamics can be assigned the task of easing this transition. In addition, organizations must ensure the performance measurement standards take into consideration the unique skills and knowledge that repatriates gain from the international assignment, thus validating the repatriates worth. This thoughtful management of the repatriation not only boosts the loyalty of returning employees but also builds a powerful organizational culture that embraces diversity, equity, and inclusion as fundamentals of human resource strategy. Lastly, effectively conducting repatriation procedures readies organizations to leverage the complete worth of their global human capital in the contemporary globalized world (Iyiola et al., 2012).

9.5.1. Challenges Faced by Repatriates Upon Return

Repatriation, which is the return trip for expatriates, typically involves a lot of challenges that can have far-reaching effects on returning to their home company. Repatriates can also undergo a feeling of culture shock similar to what they experienced abroad but now in their home environment. Adapting back to an organization that has most likely changed while they were away can be disorienting and frustrating. Unless adequate support frameworks are in place, including career planning and mentoring, repatriates may struggle to return to their previous roles or deal with new organizational politics. Research indicates that training specifically to deal with these transitions should be provided, with a strong force that organizations need to build a facilitative environment for reintegration to improve retention and satisfaction levels for repatriates (Ming et al., 2016). Despite skills and experiences gained during time spent on international assignment, repatriates are under-valued when they return home. This incompatibility between their skills that they have newly acquired and organizations' expectations leads to disenchantment and disengagement. One of the prime reasons for this is that the special skills repatriates possess with them are not being properly recognized, like cultural flexibility and global experience. Moreover, studies highlight that women repatriates will most likely experience additional challenges due to social and organizational biases that render their visibility and advancement as compared to men invisible (Linehan et al., 2002). In an effort to effectively manage the expertise of returning expats, companies must understand the unique challenges they face and come up with strategies that make their experience and knowledge visible and valued. Furthermore, the psychological cost of repatriation is typically overlooked in the broader expatriate management rhetoric. For most, the expectation of seeing loved ones and friends is continually thwarted by the worry of adapting to a pre-existing routine, one that becomes alien upon extended stay abroad. This is what it is to come back, and alongside loneliness especially where much is not known about their journey, can also amplify the readjustment pressure back in the workplace. Empirical studies indicate that home-based mentors and peer support groups play a key role in enabling this move, allowing repatriates to share their own stories and reinstate themselves as members within the organization (Linehan et al., 2002). Through creating an environment of inclusiveness and meeting the emotional needs of the repatriating employees, organizations are able to overcome these difficulties and contribute immensely towards integrating repatriates into their corporate culture.

9.5.2. Strategies for Successful Reintegration

Reintegration to a work or community environment is a multifaceted process that requires a strategic plan that includes experiences and exposure to support systems. Effective transitions are based on establishing connections; reintegration narratives attest to the importance of family, faith, and community connections. These connections provide not just emotional support but also the reformation of trust and identity. Strategies employed to enhance community engagement activities can be utilized to a large degree in this context, allowing reintegrating individuals to establish social relationships that guarantee their welfare and integration into the job market. By the individualized narratives, Human Resource Management can subsequently better tailor programs and activities to ease the transition and prompt retention of global talent, particularly in organizations that manage expatriates and repatriates (Hlavka et al., 2015). Organizations are greatly tested in reintegration of returning international assignment employees, particularly in addressing the special needs of these employees. Providing extensive orientation programs and mental care can facilitate the transition process, thereby increasing the overall success of the reintegration. As emphasized by different stakeholders in veteran services, effective communication between different service providers and effective outreach can be highly beneficial in improving access to needed resources. The same models can be extended to global organizations by ensuring that returning employees are educated on available support, job requirements, and organizational changes during their absence. This pro-active manner of managing expats and repats helps in minimizing loneliness and allowing a smoother reintegration into the company culture, finally leading to higher retention (Eaton et al., 2015). Furthermore, integration of varied perspectives within organizations is the most important aspect of successful reintegration programs. This includes understanding and appreciation of the individual skills of returnee employees, which can be a combination of foreign-borne professional skills and cultural experiences. Encouraging diversity not only enhances the feeling of belonging among the returnees but also leverages their diverse backgrounds to enhance innovation and creativity. Active participation in diversity, equity, and inclusion initiatives can also lead to improved team performance and collaborative work among employees. International organizations must be mindful of the risk of fragmentation while re-integrating; hence, a structured framework with a focus on integration, support, and communication yields a comprehensive system to achieve effective outcomes in re-integration processes (Eaton et al., 2015).

9.5.3. Importance of Knowledge Transfer from Repatriates

The worldwide organization dynamics call for a more nuanced evaluation of the knowledge transfer mechanisms, especially among repatriates returning from international assignments. The repatriates bring with them volumes of experience and knowledge gained in overseas destinations, which can significantly add to knowledge capital in their local organizations. Knowledge transfer is susceptible to various organizational and personal variables, however. Recent studies have established that while expatriate return can yield valuable knowledge, reverse knowledge transfer is typically impeded by the lack of proper systems to facilitate this. For maximum benefit from this knowledge transfer, organizations must institute formal processes for repatriate reintegration in their home offices so that their experiences are actually transferred and utilized within the organization (Cappellen et al., 2025). This consideration places additional significance on the role of incorporating strategic knowledge management practices into global HR models. In light of modern careers, the role of knowledge transfer by repatriates cannot be overstated. An integrated career management approach appreciates that organizational and individual variables govern the efficacy of such transfer. For instance, repatriates get stuck between the crossroads of not being able to translate their foreign-acquired abilities into useable knowledge within their home organizations (Cappellen et al., 2025). The incompatibility of the acquired skills in the foreign country with the needs of the home office can lead to underutilization of these assets. Therefore, human resource management (HRM) within global organizations must actively design settings that not only facilitate knowledge sharing but also generate the unique strengths of repatriates. Enabling a learning and adaptation culture will enhance the organization's capacity to absorb and utilize the new knowledge repatriates carry. Furthermore, the significance of knowledge transfer by repatriates is not solely to enhance operations but also has a direct impact on market competitiveness. Under today's knowledge economy, success in innovating and responding to changes in the market is reliant on firms' capability in utilizing tacit and explicit knowledge acquired through overseas experience. Whereas much of the earlier research had treated the knowledge spillover from the headquarters to the subsidiaries, it is important to recognize the reverse process—repatriates sending knowledge to the home organization—as critical as well (Magliocca et al., 2025). Proper control of this cycle of knowledge flow maximizes organizational learning and organizational agility. Thus, human resource initiatives must focus on sound training initiatives for preparing repatriates for their reentry, as well as mentorship programs that harness their unique insights, turning probable knowledge silos into fountains of organizational growth.

9.6. DIVERSITY, EQUITY, AND INCLUSION (DEI)

In the contemporary arena of international organizations, the integration of DEI initiatives is paramount in the development of a productive working culture that can accommodate a wide range of voices. Not only do they advocate for demographic representation, but they also aim to create equitable opportunities for every employee, thus enhancing their productivity and level of engagement. A DEI approach can push competitive edge because companies which promote diversity within their workforce are better positioned to offer solutions to a more global customer base. Research indicated that multicultural teams generate more innovative solutions, and hence they are a valuable resource for multinationals. Thus, the DEI policies applied in a systematic manner direct recruitment and retention strategies such that companies can retain and recruit top talent on offer from various backgrounds (ILR School, Cornell University, 2004). This makes diversity not only in numbers but in a culture of inclusion at all levels in the company. Training sessions that emphasize the awareness of implicit bias and cultural competency are critical tools in this endeavor (Figure 9.12).

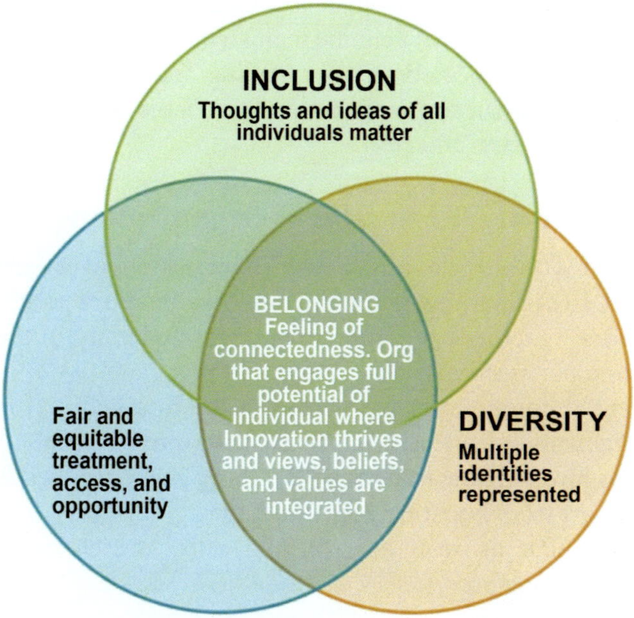

Figure 9.12. The phenomena of integration of diversity, equity, and inclusion (DEI).

Source: https://www.diaglobal.org/en/-/media/diaglobal/images/about-us/dei-definition-graphic-1024x576.jpg.

Through the delivery of learning material and continuous workshops, organizations can instill a culture of inclusivity, resulting in effective communication and team-building between employees from various backgrounds. Furthermore, such training enables the alignment of the organization's objectives and employee objectives, thus boosting morale and job satisfaction in general. According to resources compiled in the guide by The Workplace Diversity Network, professionals are encouraged to tap into both traditional and contemporary literature regarding DEI to inform policies capable of effectively addressing specific global organizational issues (Bormann et al.,

2001). Retention programs must embody the promise of diversity and inclusion by also paying attention to equity in professional development activities. Employees should have well-defined paths for development that are equitable and transparent, and that all people regardless of their status have the potential for advancement within the company.

This can involve mentorship for groups that are underrepresented, access to leadership training, and contribution-based merit performance evaluations instead of bias. Measuring progress on these initiatives through metrics and feedback mechanisms holds companies accountable for DEI commitments. It also emphasizes the notion that a genuine inclusive workplace is one where each employee feels valued and celebrated for making one-of-a-kind contributions, thus creating collective success and innovation in the global economy (ILR School, Cornell University, 2004).

9.6.1. Importance of DEI in Global Organizations

In the context of a more globalized world, inclusion of diversity, equity, and inclusion (DEI) principles is crucial for organizations that are globally operating in order to achieve a competitive edge. Diversity in the workforce provides multiple perspectives and experiences that can drive innovation and creativity, essential components of success in the international marketplace. Besides, if organizations prioritize DEI as their utmost goal, they will be more inclined to hire a diverse talent pool, taking in employees from various backgrounds. Apart from boosting recruitment programs, this also maximizes employee engagement as well as retention rates, which are essential in ensuring an active workforce.

Thus, integrating DEI into the organizational culture becomes a part of the overall human resource strategies needed in order to effectively manage the global world, ultimately reflecting an organization's social responsibility and ethical leadership. In addition, effective management of expatriates and repatriates largely depends on a DEI-centered approach. International firms often have trouble in relocating employees across nations, particularly in cultural acclimation and assimilation in multicultural settings. By making DEI the top priority, organizations can build supportive structures that address the individual requirements of expatriates and provide an inclusive environment that enhances transitions. This is particularly important since expatriates are likely to feel lonely and experience culture shock, which will have a detrimental effect on their performance and well-being. By providing training that is culturally competent and inclusive, not only is it preparing the expatriates for new positions but also enhancing the organizational climate overall (Figure 9.13).

Figure 9.13. Principle of DEI in global organizations.

Source: https://encrypted-tbn0.gstatic.com/images?q=tbn:ANd9GcRJ2otUZdCgJwDOb0z15aWgG18BbregY9ckhg&s.

As such, integrating DEI values into such human resource management enables the right management of international assignments as well as an organization's success on a global scale. Lastly, continuous development of DEI programs within international organizations becomes a key aspect in reputation development and client loyalty among heterogeneous customers. Today's consumers are more aware of business ethics for social justice and diversity, and they prefer companies who hold their same beliefs. Therefore, businesses that encourage DEI proactively not only enhance employee morale but also enhance their external reputation, building trust and loyalty in the marketplace as a whole. Literature identifies that organizations perceived as inclusive and diverse in nature are likely to gain competitive advantage in various regions of the world. Putting DEI at the forefront of human resource management practices can thus lead to long-term growth and prosperity. Synching organizational values with DEI principles can result in long-term success for companies, safeguarding their positions in a dynamic and changing global context.

9.6.2. Strategies for Promoting Diversity in the Workplace

With the rapidly evolving context of global organizations, having a diverse workforce entails strategic efforts to introduce initiatives particular to building an inclusive culture. A successful method is through building a pipeline of diversified talent through targeted recruitment. Organizations can benefit from reaching out actively to underrepresented groups, taking advantage of partnerships with institutions of higher learning and professional organizations to tap into diversified candidates. Through embracing overall recruitment strategies that go beyond traditional approaches, companies not only enhance their diversity but also gain access to the innovative potential that results from diverse perspectives and contributions to problem-solving and decision-making. This alignment into the strategic goals of workplace diversity is essential to creating a culture of celebration and leveraging differences and organizational success. Diversity, equity, and inclusion training workshops are necessary to ensure the reduction of prejudice and the enhancement of cultural competence among employees. These workshops must be designed to enhance awareness of unconscious bias, foster empathy, and enable open communication about diversity issues. When these workshops become part of the orientation program and continuous learning opportunities are offered, companies make their employees sensitized towards the essence of diversity. Furthermore, organizations can utilize available resources, such as those outlined in the updated edition of Resources for Workplace Diversity, which provides practitioners with hands-on guidance and information on how to capitalize on their diversity initiatives (Bormann et al., 2001). Emphasis on continuous learning assists employees' abilities to perform effectively in diverse groups, thereby enhancing collaboration and building team performance. Retention initiatives are a final, yet crucial, component of enhancing workplace diversity, ensuring that diverse hires are not merely attracted, but also remain motivated and satisfied within the company. Creating mentorship and sponsorship programs has the potential to foster professional development while obliterating potential obstacles facing minority workers. In addition, fostering an atmosphere of inclusiveness by employee resource groups and affinity networks provides a shared platform where people are free to share their experiences and get comfort. Research conducted by institutions like the ILR School highlights that for an organization to maintain successful diversity and inclusion strategies, it is blessed with improved employee engagement and lower turnover (ILR School, Cornell University, 2004). By focusing on overall retention strategies, businesses are able to enhance their diversity objectives and create a more productive and dynamic workforce that reflects the global marketplace in which they serve.

9.6.3. Measuring the Impact of DEI Initiatives

The effectiveness of Diversity, Equity, and Inclusion (DEI) initiatives in global organizations is largely contingent on their ability to formulate measurable outcomes that correlate with the broader objectives of human resource management. Formulating effective measures for DEI initiatives is crucial as it informs recruitment patterns, staff commitment, and organizational culture. For instance, businesses are able to track the demographic makeup of employees in order to measure if DEI initiatives are effectively attracting a pool of diverse talent. Moreover, learning about minority groups' retention percentages will give insights into how inclusive actions are perceived by employees. Through holistic measures, organizations are not only capable of measuring the effect of their DEI strategies but also identify areas of improvement, ultimately resulting in a more inclusive and equitable environment in which talent is nurtured in all dimensions of diversity (Anaya et al., 2017). As organizations take a closer look at DEI, incorporating measurement tools becomes an important aspect of strategic planning. These tools can be applied in a number of ways, including employee surveys, performance evaluations, and feedback systems designed to measure employee attitudes towards inclusion practices. Results from such forms of assessments can guide the leadership in identifying the underlying causes of systemic obstacles blocking the achievement of DEI initiatives. Additionally, evidence-based decision-making aids accountability so that organizations can apply intervention strategies that address uncovered issues. By using a data-based approach in evaluating the success of DEI programs, organizations can achieve a long-term diversity excellence model that aligns with their overall human resource management objectives (Horton et al., 2025). Moreover, involvement in DEI programs must move beyond mere compliance and become a part of organizational culture. Successful DEI efforts can create cultural shifts that have important consequences, driving greater collaboration and creativity among different groups. The impact of building an inclusive climate goes beyond the level of individual satisfaction to result in improved organizational performance, with different groups more likely to demonstrate higher creativity and problem-solving. To quantify this cultural shift, repeated measurement tools, such as longitudinal studies or focus groups, are quite effective to identify the evolving landscape of organizational commitment to DEI. Finally, repeated measurement and fine-tuning of DEI programs reinforce the value of inclusivity as one of the core values of human resource management practices for worldwide organizations (Anaya et al., 2017).

SUMMARY

The landscape of human resource management in multinational firms is marked by the requirement for flexibility to adapt to multicultural, economic, and political scenarios. This uncertain context requires an overarching strategy that addresses effective recruitment, training, and talent retention across borders. Increased globalization of the labor market necessitates that organizations not only source candidates with the right qualifications but also those who can handle the sophistication of multicultural societies. Organizations who place a premium on gaining an understanding of employees' cultural influences will have a competitive edge. This emphasis on diversity and sensitivity will eventually enhance organizational performance and staff satisfaction. Therefore, investment in effective training programs that emphasize cultural competence is central to the long-term success of human resource practices worldwide. Expatriate and repatriate management is also an extremely significant part of human resource management in international companies. The expatriate experience can have a significant effect on the performance and image of an organization as well-trained employees are representatives of their organizations abroad. Strong management at this phase of transition is required so that expatriates can adapt to new environments but still effectively represent their home firms. Repatriation also poses its own set of challenges, as the returning workers might feel detached or irrelevant. Organizations must systematically address these problems so that useful expertise and knowledge are not lost. As has been noted in recent research, strategic talent management needs to react to variation in regional context to enable companies to implement tailored solutions that reflect local custom while maintaining one global strategy (Kohont et al., 2019). In summary, interdependence of knowledge management and talent retention forms the basis for effective human resource management within multinational firms. As firms more and more come to appreciate the significance of intellectual capital as a valuable asset, constructing, transferring, and possessing such knowledge assumes the limelight. Organizations that utilize effective processes for managing stocks and flows of knowledge not only enhance competitiveness but also contribute towards a more sustainable future for the organization and its employees. By targeting a culture that promotes sharing knowledge and collaboration, new solutions and better organizational performance can be achieved. Merging alternative perspectives and practices, firms can overcome globalization challenges and address organizational goals and employee aspirations alike (Boudreau et al., 2002).

With expansion of organizations to global markets, recruitment and selection, talent development, and retention are the most crucial aspects of effective Human Resource Management (HRM). With the varied cultural settings, effective recruiting is essential in ensuring that one selects those possessing not only required skills but also organizational culture. Under these circumstances, talent management must break away from the traditional models and embrace technology-enabled and data-driven methodologies that align with global standards. Training modules must also be modified to align with cultural factors and enhance the capability of employees to respond effectively to work environment challenges of foreign environments. By creating a sound infrastructure for finding and nurturing talent, organizations are in a stronger position to boost their worldwide competitive advantage, thereby aligning human capital strategy with overall business objectives. Management of expatriates and repatriates is yet another subject of world HRM often plagued by issues that need to be comprehended in its sophisticated and skilled manner. The repatriation process of an employee requires sophisticated support systems that help them adjust to new surroundings and job responsibilities. This requires organized orientation programs, continuous mentoring, and furnishing the necessary equipment to facilitate the readjustment process. The repatriation phase is also very important, wherein the incoming employees struggle to cope with the home organization's culture. Companies have to actively address these challenges in order to minimize turnover and optimize the return on international assignment. Ultimately, an effective expatriate management strategy optimizes the employee individual experience as well as the return on the company's investment in worldwide talent (Boudreau et al., 2002). Institutionalizing DEI practices in HRM is essential in creating a conducive workplace that thrives on diverse perspectives. A commitment to DEI not only increases organizational culture but also spurs innovation and performance, particularly in global organizations where diverse workforces are the typical norm. Lenses of level practices in recruiting, profession development, and compensation assist in creating an environment where all employees feel valued and are urged to contribute meaningfully. In addition, creating forums for dialogue can enhance awareness and appreciation of diverse backgrounds, furthering cooperation and shared objectives. By placing DEI first, businesses position themselves to capitalize on the dividend of diversity, thereby achieving a more homogeneous and energized work environment in line with a globally focused vision for HRM (Boudreau et al., 2002).

REFERENCES

1. Anaya, T., & Maxey-Harris, C. (2017). SPEC Kit 356 diversity and inclusion. https://core.ac.uk/download/305123198.pdf (accessed on 24th September 2025).
2. Antal, A. B., Stroo, I., & Willems, M. (2025). Drawing on the knowledge of returned expatriates for organizational learning: Case studies in German multinational companies. https://core.ac.uk/download/pdf/6653947.pdf (accessed on 24th September 2025).
3. Barrington, L., Bruyere, S. M., Figueroa, I., et al. (2013). Leveling the playing field: Attracting, engaging, and advancing people with disabilities. https://core.ac.uk/download/19957979.pdf (accessed on 24th September 2025).
4. Bartram, D., Derous, E., Golubovich, J., Inceoglu, I., et al. (2015). Trends in testing: Highlights of a global survey. https://core.ac.uk/download/55809531.pdf (accessed on 24th September 2025).
5. Bloom, M. C., & Milkovich, G. T. (1997). Rethinking international compensation: From expatriate and national cultures to strategic flexibility. https://core.ac.uk/download/5131309.pdf (accessed on 24th September 2025).
6. Bloom, M., Milkovich, G. T., & Mitra, A. (2000). Toward a model of international compensation and rewards: Learning from how managers respond to variations in local host contexts. https://core.ac.uk/download/5131305.pdf (accessed on 24th September 2025).
7. Bormann, T., Brooks-Cooper, C., Farley, J., Fuerstenau, D., et al. (2001). *Resources for Workplace Diversity: An Annotated Practitioner Guide to Information.* https://core.ac.uk/download/5127328.pdf (accessed on 24th September 2025).
8. Boudreau, J. W. (2002). Strategic knowledge measurement and management. https://core.ac.uk/download/5118424.pdf (accessed on 24th September 2025).
9. Boudreau, J. W. (2003). Sustainability and the talent ship paradigm: Strategic human resource management beyond the bottom line. https://core.ac.uk/download/5121274.pdf (accessed on 24th September 2025).
10. Cappellen, T., & Janssens, M. (2025). Reviewing global career dimensions: Towards a future research model. https://core.ac.uk/download/pdf/6468351.pdf (accessed on 24th September 2025).
11. Center for Advanced Human Resources Studies. (2004). *CAHRS hrSpectrum (September–October 2008).* https://core.ac.uk/download/5127193.pdf (accessed on 24th September 2025).

12. Dadrawala, N., & Viswanath, P. (2004). Philanthropy and Equity: The Case of India. https://core.ac.uk/download/71359833.pdf (accessed on 24th September 2025).
13. De Cieri, H., Cox, J. W., & Fenwick, M. (1998). Representing strategic international human resource management: Is the map the territory? https://core.ac.uk/download/5124432.pdf (accessed on 24th September 2025).
14. Doherty, L., Gannon, J., & Roper, A. (2012). The role of strategic groups in understanding strategic human resource management. https://core.ac.uk/download/46597458.pdf (accessed on 24th September 2025).
15. Eaton, D., Hornbach, R., Marcotte, L., Read, J., et al. (2015). An assessment of mental health services for veterans in the State of Texas. https://core.ac.uk/download/211340027.pdf (accessed on 24th September 2025).
16. Florea, N. V. (2025). Linking marketing and human resources recruitment to obtain organizational efficiency. https://core.ac.uk/download/pdf/6327671.pdf (accessed on 24th September 2025).
17. Gulchuk, B. (2019). Non-monetary motivation in the nonprofit sector. https://core.ac.uk/download/213463698.pdf (accessed on 24th September 2025).
18. Hanleybrown, F., & Gilsdorf, K. (2017). Investing in entry-level talent. https://core.ac.uk/download/84911919.pdf (accessed on 24th September 2025).
19. Hlavka, H. R., Jones, R. S., & Wheelock, D. (2015). Exoffender accounts of successful reentry from prison. https://core.ac.uk/download/213078809.pdf (accessed on 24th September 2025).
20. Horton, D., & Watts, J. (2025). *Institutional Learning and Change: An Initiative to Promote Greater Impact Through Agricultural Research for Poverty Alleviation.* https://core.ac.uk/download/pdf/6617930.pdf (accessed on 24th September 2025).
21. Iyiola, O. O., & Osibanjo, A. O. (2012). Assessing the value of international workers: A case of Shell Petroleum Development Company in Nigeria. https://core.ac.uk/download/18294986.pdf (accessed on 24th September 2025).
22. Jadhav, D. S., & Patil, M. V. (2016). Analysis of interconnection between concurrent engineering and human resource management. https://media.neliti.com/media/publications/239730-analysis-of-interconnection-between-conc-6c4c106a.pdf (accessed on 24th September 2025).
23. Khan, M. S. A. (2023). Green human resource management (GHRM):

A strategic framework of doing basic HRM functions. https://core.ac.uk/download/624121370.pdf (accessed on 24th September 2025).

24. Kohont, A., Skoumpopoulou, D., & Stalker, B. (2019). Talent management in European SMEs: Case analysis between Slovenia and Poland. https://core.ac.uk/download/288430588.pdf (accessed on 24th September 2025).
25. Lepak, D. P., Snell, S. A., & Stueber, D. (2001). Virtual HR departments: Getting out of the middle. https://core.ac.uk/download/5129603.pdf (accessed on 24th September 2025).
26. Linehan, M., & Scullion, H. (2002). An empirical study of the repatriation of female managers: An emerging issue for European multinationals. https://core.ac.uk/download/9017292.pdf (accessed on 24th September 2025).
27. Linehan, M., Morley, M., & Scullion, H. (2003). The Management of Expatriates: Contemporary Developments and Future Challenges. https://core.ac.uk/download/9017194.pdf (accessed on 24th September 2025).
28. Magliocca, P., & Canestrino, R. (2025). Managing expatriation, repatriation and organizational learning in MNCs: An integrative framework. https://core.ac.uk/download/pdf/6314764.pdf (accessed on 24th September 2025).
29. Ming, C. H. (2016). Contingent expatriate training strategies with examples of Taiwan MNEs. https://core.ac.uk/download/225241601.pdf (accessed on 24th September 2025).
30. N/A. (2004). ILR Research in Progress 2003–04. https://core.ac.uk/download/33597631.pdf (accessed on 24th September 2025).
31. Newman, A. (2001). *Built to Change: Catalytic Capacity-Building in Nonprofit Organizations.* https://core.ac.uk/download/71346270.pdf (accessed on 24th September 2025).
32. Nilson, T., & O'Neill, B. S. (2009). Achieving high performance outcomes through trust in virtual teams. https://core.ac.uk/download/213076497.pdf (accessed on 24th September 2025).
33. Singh, S. (2025). The journey of expatriates from pre-expatriation to post expatriation. https://core.ac.uk/download/pdf/6314801.pdf (accessed on 24th September 2025).

Chapter 10

Technology, Digitalization, and Virtual Global Work

Contents

INTRODUCTION

In this increasingly globalized world, the nature of global management is evolving fundamentally. Technology spread and digitalization have revolutionized traditional forms, compelling organizations to innovate and adapt forever. With remote and hybrid work becoming more prominent, the necessity for effective management practices in an online environment is more acute. This shift demands greater cross-cultural understanding, with diverse teams working together in geographies and time zones. Virtual global work also presents new challenges that generate new ethical concerns, led by data privacy and cybersecurity. While countries navigate the complexities of digitalization, insights gained by authorities, including those at a recent roundtable of authorities, throw light on the unforeseen consequences that could result from such changes in managerial techniques and organizational schemes (Garcia et al., 2020). Besides that, application of artificial intelligence and digital platforms has revolutionized the business process on a globalized scale. Modern technology makes it possible for higher communication, higher productivity, and never-before-possible information availability, allowing companies to compete in global markets effectively. Simultaneously, the exploitation of these technologies is followed by a complete set of difficulties related to ethical requirements and data management. The need for comprehensive frameworks governing cybersecurity and data ethics is of utmost importance for international operations. Evidence indicates that successful management in such an environment requires a reinterpretation of traditional approaches in order to develop novel practices responsive to the unique needs of a digital workforce. As highlighted in the research of augmented reality in retailing, consumer motivation and involvement are now central to deciding management practices, reflecting the overall experiential value creation trend in virtual worlds (Alexander et al., 2018). The implications of these changes extend beyond mere technology adoption; they demand new organizational cultures and leadership. While organizations struggle to transcend the intricacies of international management practice, flexibility and inclusiveness are essential to make homogeneous virtual teams. Prioritizing continuous learning and improvement is essential, as leaders struggle to navigate the challenge of leading through quickly changing technology advancements and shifting market landscapes. The intersection of these factors raises important questions about future management practice that challenge scholars and practitioners to explore the intricate dynamics between technology and human behavior in international environments. Through discussion of these topics, the debate about technology, digitalization, and virtual international work is made more relevant as organizations strive to optimize the opportunities of digital transformation while limiting its attendant problems (Garcia et al., 2020).

Definition of Technology and Digitalization

In the era of rapid technologies, terms of technology and digitalization have dramatically evolved, affecting various aspects of worldwide management. Technology can be defined as the applied science in industry, which has a significant influence on innovation and productivity. Digitalization is the process of integrating digital technologies into everyday processes, essentially changing the way in which companies do business and interact with customers. Above all, digitalization provides the emergence of remote and hybrid teams where companies can reach out to worldwide talent. Through this change, businesses can target several geographies simultaneously, hence gaining a competitive edge in international markets. This transformation also necessitates the overhaul of management methodologies and cultural aspects of working across multiple digital platforms that hinder or enhance collaborative works between distanced teams. Besides this, an awareness of how digitalization and technology are interconnected is needed for managing cybersecurity and data ethics at the global level. With the propagation of digital instruments and tools, organizations face greater vulnerabilities and challenges in defending secret data. Digitalization also enables the harvesting and processing of large amounts of data, but there are ethical concerns regarding privacy and the handling of data (Figure 10.1).

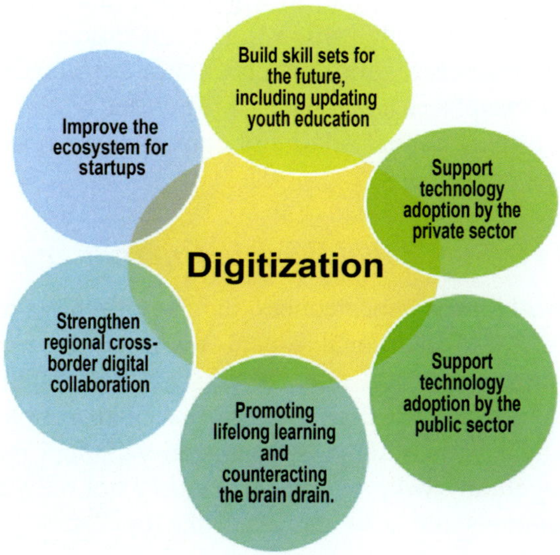

Figure 10.1. Digitalization and business activity.

Source: https://pub.mdpi-res.com/sustainability/sustainability-11-02204/article_deploy/html/images/sustainability-11-02204-g001.png?1571369771.

Effective global management practice, therefore, must integrate good cybersecurity practices into their web strategies to ensure they safeguard organizational integrity and instill confidence in the stakeholders. In addition, as companies embrace technologies such as artificial intelligence (AI) to automate functions, ethical considerations surrounding AI adoption become paramount. That with the ability to make ethical decision-making habits alongside AI technologies can enhance corporate responsibility as one navigates the realities of a networked world is small to debate. The implications of their conceptualization of technology and digitalization are also experienced in their role in organizational culture and workers' experience in virtual global workplaces. As telework and blended teams become prevalent, the need for quality technological support systems and digital platforms is given precedence. Not only do organizations have to provide advanced technology tools but also build a culture of inclusiveness that encourages openness and collaboration among the employees regardless of their location. The success of these programs largely rests on the ability to engage the workers through experiential technologies such as augmented reality (AR) applications, which enhance the engagement and interaction of the users. Studies indicate that the incorporation of such technologies can have a positive influence on employee satisfaction and motivation, leading to a general productive workplace. The fusion of technology and digitalization thus is of crucial significance to the evolution of an international workforce capable of exceling in a dynamic and intricate digital marketplace, as indicated by current research examining the potential benefits of experiential retail and consumer trend in digitally driven markets (Alexander et al., 2018).

Importance of Virtual Global Work in International Management

With this era of world interconnectedness, the rise of remote and hybrid teams has come to transform traditional global management practice, allowing organizations to leverage world talent diversity. It is facilitated in part by advances in technology and digital platforms that simplify cross-border communication and collaboration. As organizations adopt such frameworks, they realize that operating with a virtual workforce not only gives them more flexibility in operations but also increases the opportunity for innovation. By incorporating AI-based solutions and digital tools, organizations can enhance project management, make workflows more efficient, and promote productivity. However, success of such emerging work patterns depends to a great extent on the ability of managers to develop a uni-cultural team spirit as well as effective communication. The implications of such arrangements extend beyond logistics, in the sense that they require leaders to make sure all members of a team anywhere in the world feel committed and valued in the organizational cause. Utilization of AI and digital platforms contributes to the necessity for efficient international management across virtual global workplaces. These technological developments allow managers to sort through vast amounts of data, which can aid in guiding strategic choices and enhancing responsiveness to market dynamics. Beyond this, AI systems also help team members through customized work experiences, needs anticipation, and efficiency driving. As corporations embrace these innovations, though, they must also remain cognizant of the ethical aspects of data use and the residual threats posed by cybersecurity breaches. Handling sensitive information on a global scale emphasizes the importance of sound data governance procedures, such as adhering to various international laws and ethical standards. Sustaining technological benefits with the honor of safeguarding information is necessary to ensure organizational integrity and trust in the context of a globally dispersed workforce. As the importance of virtual work worldwide increases day by day, the issue of cybersecurity as well as ethics of data is more critical than ever before to global management. The reliance on the virtual world demands an adequate understanding of what is at risk, as cyber-attacks not only risk individual companies but also national economies and security. Organizations thus need to establish robust cybersecurity protocols that involve technological safeguards as well as employee training. The integrated approach is used to equip employees with the ability to operate securely within virtual environments and build a culture of responsible data handling. The challenge of nation-specific divergent regulation is among the factors that fuel the increased complexity in demanding that international managers remain ahead and continue to adapt. By taking this route, the nexus of technology, ethics, and security in virtual global work is not merely a logistics issue; it is an intrinsic aspect of sustainable international management needed to construct long-term development and innovation in an ever-evolving digital age.

10.1. THE EVOLUTION OF TECHNOLOGY IN INTERNATIONAL MANAGEMENT

The revolution brought about with the digital revolution has greatly influenced global management dynamics, particularly in team structures. Hybrid and remote teams have dominated organizational structures in the past few years as organizations attempt to benefit from the global talent pool. Not only can businesses tap into a broader talent base with this transition, but it also guarantees flexibility and adaptability in operations. Nevertheless, it presents unique challenges because team members often work across time zones, cultures, and regulatory environments. The repercussions of those challenges are far-reaching, demanding advanced communications tools and collaboration methods that can effectively integrate conflicting opinions. The imperative of developing strong interpersonal relationships and team harmony in such a virtual setup is highlighted by the imperative of innovative management strategies that reshape traditional practices to suit the challenges of virtual workplaces. The symbiosis of artificial intelligence (AI) and virtual platforms has become a turning point for global management strategies. Such technologies empower organizations to streamline their operations, enhance decision-making processes, and drive innovation. For instance, analytics based on AI can offer real-time insights into global demand and consumer trends, and companies can promptly change their strategies to cater to global demand. Further, digital channels facilitate seamless data transfer and communication among global stakeholders and hence enhance collaboration and operational efficiency (Figure 10.2).

Figure 10.2. The proliferation of digital platforms for technological advancements.

Source: https://businessmap.io/wp-content/uploads/website-images/Agile/what-is-digital-transformation.png.

However, the reliance on such technologies also raises pertinent questions concerning data ethics and privacy concerns, particularly since organizations operate within several different legal systems across different nations. It is crucial that AI applications and platforms are not merely efficient but also ethical and compliant with local authorities in sustainable international management. While businesses expand their international spans, the question of data ethics and cybersecurity has risen as a major concern in global management. With greater reliance on digital platforms, danger to cyberattacks and data breaches has multiplied, leading businesses to adopt a proactive approach to cybersecurity. Businesses must devise robust plans to protect sensitive information and adhere to a myriad of regulatory controls that significantly differ from one region to another. Moreover, the ethical issues regarding the use of data, particularly with regard to artificial intelligence and consumer privacy, require an advanced understanding of cultural differences and legal regulations. Organizations are thus compelled to embrace strong cybersecurity architectures that not only safeguard their resources but also establish trust from consumers as well as stakeholders. Addressing these challenges holistically adds to the general stability and integrity of global operations and fosters a culture of accountability and transparency in the era of digitalization, as brought out in the conclusions of Garcia et al. (2020) and Alexander et al. (2018).

10.1.1. Historical Context of Technology in Business

The technological evolution of business has been at the forefront of economic growth, influencing various modes of operation over the years. The introduction of mechanical innovations during the time of the Industrial Revolution initially revolutionized manufacturing processes via an improvement in efficiency and output. With the evolution of businesses based on machinery, it initiated the transformation of the dynamics of labor, propelling urbanization via the migration of the workforce to industrial cities. This technological expansion paved the way for more advanced systems, enabling businesses to enlarge operations exponentially. With the arrival of digital technology during the latter half of the 20th century, a new era began; firms increasingly made use of computers and, subsequently, the Internet, transforming communication and operational abilities, accentuating the seminal role played by technology in defining contemporary business strategies as they started to shift towards more decentralized and internationalized operations in the marketplace. With the 21st century ushering in an era marked by fastened digitalization, companies were also faced with both challenges and opportunities of technological innovations (Figure 10.3).

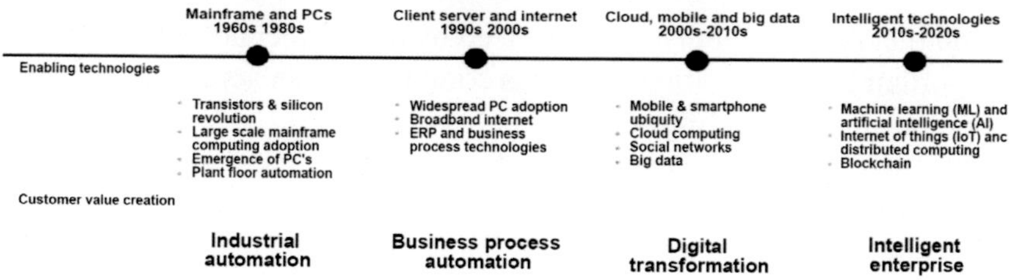

Figure 10.3. Evolution of information technologies (IT) from digital era into the intelligence era.

Source:: https://www.researchgate.net/profile/Luca-Toldo-2/publication/329624902/figure/fig1/AS:728723011682307@1550752513564/Evolution-of-Information-Technologies-IT-from-digital-era-into-the-intelligencc-era.png

The popularity of the internet has particularly facilitated the growth of remote and hybrid teams, enabling organizations to tap into a worldwide reservoir of skilled professionals. The transformation calls for an advanced form of global management conduct, as cultural variations and communication style differences necessitate more sophisticated types of team interaction. In such a situation, companies have to take on the complexities of virtual teaming and integrating artificial intelligence (AI) technologies to maximize decision-making and operational efficiencies. Such technology integration says volumes about the need for flexible strategic management that can adapt to multiple global business situations while upholding high-quality deliverables and sustainable operations in a digital global economy. Besides, the history of technology business is also interwoven with serious matters such as data ethics and cybersecurity. As companies keep relying on online platforms to carry out their activities, ensuring the security of sensitive information has become the top priority. This field of technology management is especially complex in international settings, given that varying governance and cultural beliefs around data privacy make it an enormous challenge. A solid understanding of ethical priorities and issues—paired with emerging technologies—has to become the beacon that guides firms if they are to maintain stakeholders' trust. Consequently, approaches involving concepts from both circular economy thinking and AI optimization techniques, as such detailed in emerging research, provide valuable lessons for achieving sustainability and addressing ethical issues that accompany digitalization. These historical lessons regarding technologys impact on business not only define contemporary practice but also shape future direction for international management.

10.1.2. Impact of the Internet on Global Communication

In a world that is increasingly characterized by digital technologies, the internet is an important link facilitating seamless communication across global borders. With organizations adopting remote and hybrid work arrangements, having the ability to communicate with members of their staff regardless of their location becomes critical, defining international management conduct. Having multiple communications platforms available facilitates the exchange of ideas and collaboration among remote staff, promoting inclusivity and engagement. However, the success of such interactions generally relies on digital literacy and digital resource accessibility, exposing the complexity of the digital divide for most of the world. Redressing such inequalities is important to develop an environment that enables effective communication and cooperation, hence enhancing organizational performance across the world. With the recognition of the inherent ability of the internet to transcend geographical boundaries, organizations have the option of capitalizing on this benefit and using it strategically to enhance their management strategies. The reach of internet-enabled communication is wider than mere connectivity. These advancements also necessitate reconsidering cybersecurity methodologies and information ethics in a transnational environment. Organizations are confronted with the challenge of protecting confidential data and staying compliant with multi-faceted international regulations. As communities engage in real-time discussions and share sensitive data, the likelihood of compromise and the risk of ethical dilemmas increases. Dealing with this situation requires an extensive understanding of the legal implications of data exchange within borders, which can be significantly different from country to country. Moreover, as international management entails increasing levels of artificial intelligence and virtual platforms, implications for communication become even more profound. A fine balance between technology advancement and moral accountability must be achieved if firms are to build trust and uphold the integrity of their operations in a more globally interconnected environment. Augmented reality (AR) and other experience-based technologies are reshaping the manner in which individuals interact with one another in the global marketplace, once again transforming communication patterns. For instance, AR technologies can enhance virtual meetings and presentations by creating immersive experiences that go beyond the traditional approaches to communications. These innovations are especially relevant in handling hybrid teams, wherein visual interaction produces a sense of presence and belonging among distant members. Their impact is neutralized by users hedonic motivations, highlight the importance of grasping consumer action in todays internet age. As businesses are refining their digital strategies, they need to think about how these experience-based tools can make connections in virtual spaces more meaningful, improving collaboration and project results. By successfully incorporating state-of-the-art technologies, organizations can utilize the potential of the internet to fundamentally redefine cross-country communication in the realm of international management conduct, presenting possibilities for more impactful and engaging interactions across cross-functional teams (Garcia et al., 2020; Alexander et al., 2018).

10.1.3. Role of Mobile Technology in International Operations

The evolution of mobile technology has transformed communication frameworks fundamental to global operations. More organizations are turning to virtual and dispersed teams, making real-time discussion across geographical distances invaluable. Mobile technology bridges geographical gaps, creating fast coordination between team members and management. Furthermore, AI and digital platform advances improve these teams to function smoothly and make innovations and increases efficiency. Hence, businesses can be agile in dynamic global markets, responding instantly to changing customer demands and global challenges. However, the application of mobile technology also accompanies complexities, particularly in cybersecurity. Businesses must remain watchful, installing strong security measures to protect sensitive information while maintaining open communication. As businesses traverse these virtual fronts, the relationship between technology and operations becomes even more central to sustaining global competitiveness. Aside from communications, mobile technology is also an operational effectiveness enabler in global management. By integrating mobile apps, teams can access critical resources and information remotely, enhancing decision-making processes. This feature is particularly beneficial to businesses operating in different markets, where local expertise could influence overall strategies. Additionally, mobile technology provides analytics tools through which organizations can derive insights from their operations around the world and improve resource allocation. With these abilities, international businesses can improve cultural understanding and modify marketing accordingly. Beyond operations, the effect of mobile technology extends to changing business models by allowing direct interaction with customers. As managers embrace digitalization within business, they must also consider the implications on human resource management, whereby the role of the HR manager is adjusted to accommodate new patterns in worker engagement and working flexibility (Chytiri et al., 2019). Such intricacies embedded in mobile technology over-reliance carry over to ethical matters, primarily data security and privacy across global operations. Organizations must comply with competing regulatory spaces in order to protect sensitive organizational and customer data. This requirement is a testament to the need for integrated management practices that address cybersecurity threats, which subject companies to risk of corporate reputation and integrity. Besides this, there are moral issues arising as companies employ mobile technologies to gather and analyze individuals' private information in order to provide better services. Maintaining a balance of innovation and ethical accountability is paramount, especially for international markets characterized by multicultural regulatory settings. While organizations pursue digital transformation, building a culture of cybersecurity awareness and ethical data management becomes absolutely necessary. Overall, integrating mobile technology into foreign ventures calls for a strategy that not only preserves operational efficiency but also prudent management and ethical conduct (Garcia et al., 2020).

10.2. DIGITALIZATION AND ITS EFFECTS ON WORK CULTURE

This change in work culture caused by digitalization has also developed at a substantial speed with the advent of remote and hybrid teams. These structures offer organizations greater flexibility since employees are able to meet their career and personal needs better. The use of digital platforms and AI in such teams has enabled companies to maximize processes and enhance communication despite geographic distances. But this flexibility comes along with challenges of maintaining the employees' enthusiasm and creating a cohesive team morale. Organizations must navigate through the intricacies of remote work arrangements while making sure that fundamental workplace values are preserved. Balancing this art involves innovative methods, as managers cleverly develop virtual environments that promote collaboration and participation, which are essential ingredients in constructing an effective workforce in the face of evolving situations. In addition, with organizations increasingly reliant on digital assets, cybersecurity and data ethics issues have taken center stage. Dealing with sensitive information in a virtual setting necessitates not only stringent security measures but also ethical reflections as a corporate culture. The pervasiveness of cyber-attacks has placed data breach issues at the forefront of everyone's mind, so companies are spending a lot of money on cybersecurity training and methods. Moreover, businesses must react to the broader ethical dimensions of data utilization, particularly in terms of staff surveillance and privacy. A clear and responsible approach to data ethics raises trust levels in the workplace, a key element of employee morale and efficiency (Figure 10.4).

Figure 10.4. Impact of digital transformation on company culture.

Source: https://media.licdn.com/dms/image/v2/D4D12AQFcgPJbzLdSZA/article-cover_image-shrink_720_1280/article-cover_image-shrink_720_1280/0/1718264444418?e=2147483647&v=beta&t=JN58M01pEamHiCuXP2JdlUcx5reIT59qMclWXTSCZsI.

This serves to emphasize the connection between paradigms of ethics and technological innovation, revealing digitalizations impact upon work culture to extend beyond operational efficiencies to encompass significant corporate values. In addition to addressing technical and ethical matters, recognition of cultural dynamics is fundamental in reducing the incidental effects of digitalization. As appears from debates over the problems of different regions, for instance, South America, the digital divide remains a significant problem; not all have equal access to digital resources or education (Garcia et al., 2020). This can make it challenging for remote and hybrid forms of work to be productive, worsening inequality. Cultural sensitivity is active in global management as businesses strive to build inclusive environments that respect and celebrate diverse backgrounds. By embracing and leveraging cultural subtleties, managers can simplify communication and collaboration between globally dispersed teams, creating a platform for a more harmonious and productive working culture accepting globalization. As has been noted, acknowledgement and responsiveness to such cultural nuances are necessary in order to successfully navigate the opportunities and dangers of a more virtual workplace (Winangsih et al., 2001).

10.2.1. Shift from Traditional to Digital Work Environments

The work dynamics have been fundamentally transformed by technological shifts, and this has opened a window to allow remote and hybrid teams to flourish. With the world adapting to the virtual office, the traditional office setup is increasingly being replaced by different flexible options that leverage digital methods of communication. Through these reforms, companies can attract talent from across the world, bypassing geographical constraints and allowing heterogeneous groups of people who can collaborate effectively regardless of their location. The transition is not without its pitfalls, with organizations now having to consider how they maintain engagement and productivity within the virtual setting. The fusion of communication platforms, project management software, and virtual collaboration platforms is critical to ensure that interactions are smooth. Specifically, they call for a reconsideration of leadership strategies to create inclusive team cultures that are able to thrive in digital media since knowing about such dynamics is essential to successful international management behavior. As digital platforms become more integrated into international management, the role of artificial intelligence (AI) becomes more significant. AI-enabled solutions enhance decision-making, automate procedures, and provide insights into global consumers' actions. However, embracing such advanced technologies will imply that organizations must suitably prepare their workforce with the necessary skills to drive this digital world. Digital literacy and AI literacy training programs will be needed to harness the potential of digitalization. Also, the application of technology raises serious issues of data ethics and cybersecurity, which require proactive measures to protect sensitive information. Companies must implement robust cybersecurity and ethical practices to protect against cyber-attacks while maintaining international data compliance. This intersection of technology and management highlights the role of strategic management in providing an environment in which digital innovation flourishes while remaining committed to ethics (Figure 10.5).

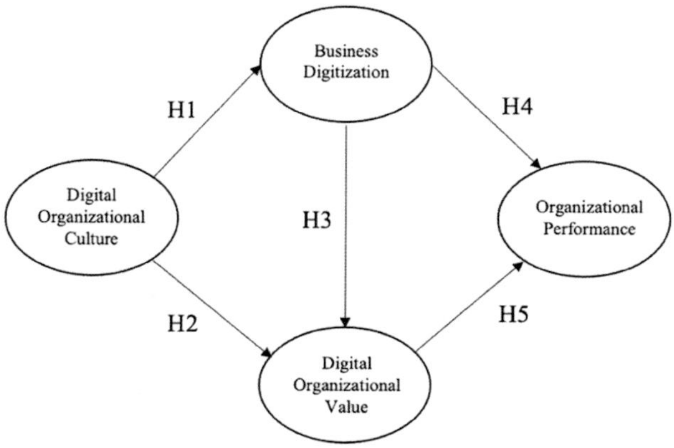

Figure 10.5. The transition from traditional to digital work environments.

Source: https://images-provider.frontiersin.org/api/ipx/w=1200&f=png/https://www.frontiersin.org/files/Articles/840699/fpsyg-13-840699-HTML/image_m/fpsyg-13-840699-g001.jpg.

The transition to digital workspaces comes with some inherent challenges, primarily in the field of cybersecurity and data ethics. As remote and hybrid work arrangements spread, organizations become vulnerable to cyber threats, as the employees interact with various digital software and platforms. This demands an overall approach to cybersecurity that not only entails technical measures but also fosters security culture among team members. Employee training on best practices in protecting data is critical in risk management. It is also necessary at the same time to deal with ethical concerns of data use, especially in international settings where data regulation could significantly differ. Companies must deal with such complexities in instilling stakeholders' confidence. As has become apparent in recent controversy over the unintended effects of digital transformation, organizations must remain vigilant with regard to the effects of their technology choices to offer sustainable and ethical management practices for their increasingly interconnected employees (Garcia et al., 2020; Alexander et al., 2018).

10.2.2. Influence of Digital Tools on Employee Collaboration

The advent of digital solutions has revolutionized the dynamics of employee collaboration, particularly for remote and hybrid teams. Where workers are physically far from each other, the application of digital platforms facilitates communication and collaboration, hence enhancing productivity and collaboration. These tools enable individuals to communicate in real time, share documents instantly, and exchange ideas seamlessly, all of which have a significant contribution towards maintaining organizational alignment. Moreover, digital technology provides an experience of virtual presence that helps to mitigate the feeling of isolation that most remote workers experience. This shift towards more interactive digital interfaces underscores the necessity of organizations to modify their management style in order to leverage these technologies to maintain staff involved and connected across time zones and geographies, which is essential in global management environments (Special Libraries Association, 2004). The incorporation of artificial intelligence (AI) in digital collaboration platforms has further transformed how employees engage with one another in international management. AI-based tools can gauge team operation and suggest optimal collaboration strategies, allowing managers to respond more effectively to the changing global workforce requirements. Consequently, this technological advancement allows organizations to personalize collaboration experiences, aligning with the specific tastes and work habits of individual members of a team. Moreover, AI can execute routine tasks so that workers can focus on value-added collaboration work, thereby optimizing overall productivity. As the workplace standard becomes virtual, an appreciation of AIs role in value addition to collaborative activities is important for managers who desire to build creative working environments and maintain competitive advantages in a globalized world (Special Libraries Association, 2003). Yet, the use of digital tools also presents serious challenges in the area of cybersecurity and data ethics that require close management oversight. As the number of online collaboration platforms continues to grow, organizations become increasingly vulnerable to risks that involve data breaches and invasions of privacy. Workers who exchange sensitive material across digital channels must follow strict protocols to help eliminate such risks while being able to maintain a security-conscious culture. Also, good ethical practices in data collection and usage remain of critical concern, especially for multinational corporations that deal in various legal and cultural frameworks. Placing high-priority cyber security practices and establishing good ethical guidelines for online behaviors, organizations can not only protect their data resources but also build employee trust, which is necessary to generate teamwork in the expanding digital workplace (Special Libraries Association, 2004).

10.2.3. Changes in Management Practices Due to Digitalization

With a more interconnected world, organizations are increasingly moving from conventional management paradigms to more dynamic methods that capitalize on the advantages of digitalization. As remote and blended teams become more prominent, management has to evolve to support interaction among various geographical locations. The use of digital solutions facilitates real-time interaction and project management, supporting productivity and engagement among workers who may never be physically present. In addition, this transformation requires reforming organizational models, with flatter, more responsive hierarchies enabling teams to react quickly to dynamic marketplaces. This shift overcomes the traditional assumptions of authority as leadership now includes facilitation, enablement, and building trust, necessary for adapting to sophisticated virtual realms. These changes are not problem-free; they demand leaders to manage issues like company culture retention and employee welfare in a digital environment. Another, more widespread shift induced by digitalization is the application of artificial intelligence (AI) and digital platforms to global management practice. Companies are increasingly making use of AI systems to develop insights from large data sets, improving decision-making and operational efficiencies. This paradigm transformation not only makes routine functions easier but also allows managers to focus on strategic plans that promote innovation and expansion. Cross-border collaboration is facilitated through digital platforms, allowing organizations to engage with communities and stakeholders globally, regardless of geographical frontiers. However, the advent of these technologies necessitates re-evaluating ethical issues as data privacy and security move to the forefront of management concerns. Practices in management must evolve so that they function according to country laws while maintaining levels of transparency and ethical conduct, hence safeguarding business reputation and consumer trust. As a result, the role of managers is evolving into technology coordination with strategic emphasis on ethical management. As a result of the new complicacies introduced by digitalization, management of cybersecurity and data ethics across borders has emerged as an integral component of new management practices. Firms must conduct business within a sophisticated structure with varying global regulations, domestic sentiments regarding privacy, and the technology that their employees have at their disposal. All of these aspects must be thoroughly understood in order to establish measures that will minimize risk but enable trust and accountability to take root. Additionally, as firms go digital and deploy cybersecurity policies, integrating their cybersecurity policies with their global business strategies cannot be overstated. While AI integration enhances the operational efficiency, it also introduces vulnerabilities capable of weakening organizational integrity. The management should, therefore, accord training and awareness programs high priority, ensuring that all employees are well aware of their role in safeguarding information and ethical practice within the digital space. This proactive cybersecurity management is a further extension of the general change in management practice dictated by digitalization based on demands of a highly educated and vigilant workforce.

10.3. REMOTE AND HYBRID TEAMS IN INTERNATIONAL MANAGEMENT

Work patterns altered through technology have immensely reshaped the organizational structures of today's companies. The emergence of remote and hybrid work teams has enabled organizations to tap a wider pool of talent, unencumbered by geography. This shift has profound ramifications in global management, where cross-border collaboration capacity has become invaluable.

Figure 10.6. The effective governance of remote teams hinges on the appropriate utilization of technological advancements.

Source: https://imageio.forbes.com/specials-images/imageserve/6447981d0971efa9dea821c1/0x0.jpg?format=jpg&height=900&width=1600&fit=bounds.

With the integration of artificial intelligence and digital platforms in business activities, organizations are not only more efficient in performing their tasks but also develop innovative attitudes to respond to diverse market needs. Provision of access to remote and hybrid team modes requires a greater level of cultural awareness, communication sensitivity, and ethics awareness related to data handling. As leaders navigate these complexities, it is more crucial to incorporate frameworks that ensure harmony and cooperation, which ultimately drive fundamental business objectives. Under global management, effective management of remote teams depends on effective utilization of technology advancements. Electronic platforms not only facilitate real-time communication but also make project management easier, with increased accountability among team members. The pandemic has accelerated this digital shift at breakneck speed, forcing the organizations to rethink their models of operation in totality. However, technology dependence has to be complemented by a robust framework of cybersecurity and data ethics. With remote workers handling sensitive information from multiple jurisdictions, adherence to varying standards of law is imperative (Figure 10.6).

Organizations therefore must invest in safe digital infrastructure and cultivate a culture of cybersecurity consciousness among employees to stem risks. Emphasis on safeguarding data can allow companies to gain the confidence of stakeholders and ensure their enterprise continues to flourish in an increasingly digital world. Integrating virtual and hybrid teams into global management has opportunities along with it but also challenges that call for introspective leadership. At its core is the recognition of how cultures influence team performance and behavior. To effectively lead such teams, leaders must have versatile communication styles and build a sense of belongingness even while away physically. Organizations must also be mindful regarding ethical concerns triggered by digitalization. Prioritizing the management of sensitive information and adherence to ethical standards in the use of data should be maintained to ensure credibility in global operations. This triple method, encompassing strategy, technology, and ethics, is critical to the attainment of a sustainable and high-performing virtual workforce. Working with these components holistically leads to competitive advantage in today's highly digitalized business environment, where flexibility and global collaboration are requirements to be successful.

10.3.1. Benefits of Remote Work for Global Teams

The entry of technology and digitalization has brought with it a paradigm shift in the team collaboration dynamics, particularly for remote and hybrid teams. By using high-tech communication platforms and collaboration tools, organizations can overcome geographical limitations, and a diverse workforce brings in different perspectives. This heterogeneity not only sustains creativity but also sustains innovation, with unique ideas from team members from different cultures coming into the picture, generating competitive advantage in the globalized economy. Besides, telecommuting enables companies to tap into a greater reservoir of talent, hiring experts from across the world—a priceless asset in today's knowledge economy. With the rise in remote work popularity, it's clear that employing digital tools enhances efficiency, which ultimately contributes to higher productivity levels for global teams. Apart from improving talent availability, remote work encourages flexibility to workers, and as a result, improved job satisfaction and retention. The flexibility provided by remote working arrangements allows staff members to achieve a more balanced personal and business life, resulting in overall improved employee well-being. Improved work-life balance can have a significant impact on organizational culture, resulting in a more committed and motivated team. Those organizations that prioritize flexibility can create strong loyalty among employees that can result in reduced turnover and associated expenses (Figure 10.7).

Figure 10.7. The emergence of technology and digitalization for remote and hybrid teams.

Source: https://assets-us-01.kc-usercontent.com/469992e5-7cbd-0032-ead4-f2db9237053a/319e1483-8dd2-4e02-bf5c-cd62dcd973f7/2021-07-14_social_how-to-lead-hybrid-team-5-best-practices.jpg.

Moreover, as telecommuting becomes ubiquitous, companies can better align their business strategies with those of employees to create a more robust and elastic corporate environment in a rapidly transforming world. However, working from home also has challenges that must be addressed with utmost care, particularly the realm of cybersecurity and ethics of data. Global teams must adhere to complex regulatory environments while maintaining sensitive information across borders. With increasingly more organizations placing their collaboration efforts on digital platforms, they must impose robust cybersecurity measures to safeguard against the leakage of data. That same demand carries with it increased ethical sensitivities, and firms hence must impose standards of data usage and conduct in an online environment. These multiple challenges overcome can make global teams not only efficient but secure as well, providing potency to trust among members and stakeholders alike. By having these issues integrated into the remote work structure, organizations can achieve long-lasting success within global management conduct in terms of the standards of today for both operational excellence and ethical conduct.

10.3.2. Challenges Faced by Hybrid Teams

With the new trend toward hybrid teams in the international management landscape today, several key challenges have emerged that can negatively affect overall performance and teamwork. Among the major challenges is ensuring that communication is effective throughout different channels and time zones. Hybrid teams tend to include members based both on-site and off-site, and this can create inconsistencies in how information is transmitted and received. Miscommunication can cause misunderstandings and trust eroded within team members, ultimately affecting the outcome of projects. Additionally, relying on digital tools and platforms to bridge the gap leaves one susceptible to collapse in case there is an issue with the technology.

As companies adapt to such dynamics, they need to invest in building resilient communications infrastructure and establish a culture that encourages open communication and feedback within the limits of physical as well as virtual domains. Hybrid teams also have another pressing issue related to the harmonization of new practices in the context of advanced technology. Open innovation methods are involved here, wherein the teams must grapple with the intricacies of bringing about collaboration both within and without the organization. Teams are able to lose pace in realizing and applying innovative concepts effectively, particularly when they are not collocated to have impromptu ideation mechanisms or relaxed conversations. This is further aggravated by the potential for knowledge silos, where the distant participants are isolated from the source of creativity. Therefore, organizations must embark on frameworks that incite grouped R&D projects, institutionalize knowledge-sharing and practices, and provide avenues for external input, while they ensure team players constantly feed an ever-flowing stream of innovation (Brandenburger et al., 2006). Additionally, the handling of cybersecurity and data ethics poses significant challenges for hybrid teams operating across geographies. Since team members can access sensitive information with various devices and platforms, the threat of breach of data is higher, heightening stakes in maintaining confidentiality and integrity. Governance controls must be in place to regulate the way data is handled and exchanged in hybrid work environments. Teams must also be knowledgeable about various legal regimes for data protection in various geographies, which complicates compliance. With the growing reliance on digital technologies in international management, the need for regular training and education on cybersecurity best practices comes to the forefront. With the cultivation of an accountable and skilled culture in data ethics, companies can mitigate risks and make the best use of technology to help drive more effective collaboration in hybrid teams (Biros et al., 2016).

10.3.3. Strategies for Effective Management of Remote Teams

With the present-day, hurried pace of work, teams now often work from disparate locations and thus, remote team management becomes a fundamental task for organizations. Open communication channels are essential to establish the rapport among members who may never see each other. Effective communication at times relies on myriad online tools so that channels remain open and accessible. By having access to real-time collaboration platforms, such as video conferencing and project management software, managers can assist in establishing a sense of belonging for remote employees. Establishing relationships is significant because it works to counteract the sense of isolation that many feel comes with remote employment. Such practices not only foster team unity but also contribute to generating higher levels of productivity, affirming that management of remote teams has a direct connection with effective communication principles.

Another central practice in managing remote teams involves the implementation of artificial intelligence (AI) and digital platforms as a way to enhance workflows and guide decision-making. Applying AI technologies can make it possible for managers to track performance and engagement of employees in a more effective manner, creating vital information about team dynamics and individual contribution. Electronic platforms enable easy sharing of data and collaboration irrespective of the location of team members. With such tools, an organization can automate its processes and cultivate a performance culture that motivates individuals to be accountable and self-improvement oriented. Aside from this, managers may use predictive analytics to predict any probable issues and create preparatory actions in that regard, thereby ensuring stable and productive remote team dynamics. The union of technology and remote management is an evidence of going toward a data-driven strategy, which again emphasizes the importance of international management practices requiring modernization. Data ethics and cybersecurity issues are critical in the field of remote team management that reflect the necessity of comprehensive strategies to safeguard organizational integrity. As remote teams become increasingly reliant on digital tools for communication and project collaboration, data breaches and ethical concerns rise exponentially. Organizations should assign high priority to implementing robust cybersecurity technologies, such as encryption and multi-factor authentication, to protect sensitive information. No less important is the creation of a culture of data ethics, through which the staff members are informed about their role regarding confidentiality and acting ethically with data. Having proper guidelines and training programs in place can make employees vigilant and proactive in dealing with data security. With this cyber world, being at the top of the cyber threats not only saves organizational capital but also inspires trust among remote staff, reminding them of ethical conduct that is in agreement with global management standards.

10.4. THE ROLE OF AI IN INTERNATIONAL MANAGEMENT

In present-day organizational settings, team structure has evolved significantly with more common remote and hybrid arrangements. The complexity and dynamic of work demand advanced approaches to maintain these teams in line. As companies react to global markets, they need to take advantage of digital platforms that facilitate effortless communication and collaboration among members working in different geographic locations. This transformation is a testament to the inherent significance artificial intelligence (AI) holds in worldwide management. By leveraging AI technologies, organizations can analyze team dynamics, increase productivity, and address special issues related to virtual collaborations. Besides, AI will assist in the identification of best practices for leadership in virtual settings, as companies learn how to deal with the intricacies of motivating and engaging workers across cultures, thus enhancing overall team performance and cohesiveness (Bell et al., 2002). Integration of AI in global management gives organizations effective tools to streamline operations and improve decision-making processes. Online platforms with AI functionality have the capacity to process large volumes of data to gain insights that can guide strategic pathways (Figure 10.8).

This capability is particularly valuable in virtual and mixed team management, where such traditional control and face-to-face interaction may be limited. AI-based technologies can predict project outcomes, assess risk, and synchronize workforce deployment with real-time data analysis. AI-based technologies also allow managers to tailor the employee experience by providing tailored communication and assistance mechanisms according to individual needs. As organizations grow more reliant on digital solutions, effective deployment of AI not only builds operational efficiency but also fosters inclusive culture that celebrates diverse points of view and builds a culture of innovation in global teams (Bell et al., 2002). However, the liberating potential of AI in global management is fraught with significant challenges, particularly those associated with cybersecurity and data ethics. The reliance on digital platforms opens up an array of cybersecurity risks to be addressed preemptively by the organizations, especially when dealing with sensitive data across different jurisdictions. The design for managing the risks must include robust data protection measures and ethical considerations for deploying AI. In addition, employee awareness on issues of cybersecurity must be cultivated to enhance the human element against threats. In the context of ongoing geopolitical competition and hybrid conflicts, as exemplified by the experience of countries like Ukraine, businesses should be vigilant in protecting their staff and data privacy. Lastly, the ethical embedding of AI in international management functions is vital not only for business excellence but also to defend trustworthiness and integrity in international cooperation.

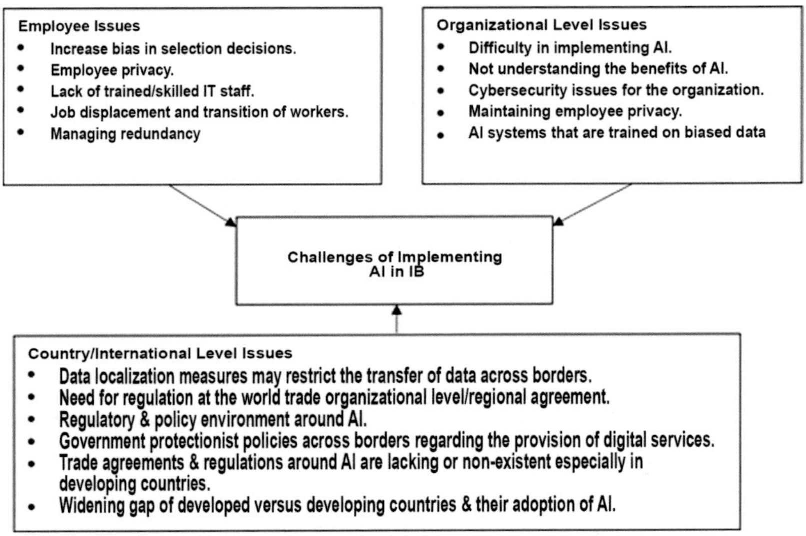

Figure 10.8. Challenges of implementing artificial intelligence in international businesses.

Source: https://onlinelibrary.wiley.com/cms/asset/6fe1354a-3fcf-45c6-8d77-44d0a5751be3/tie22370-fig-0003-m.png.

10.4.1. Applications of AI in Decision-Making Processes

In an era marked by technology and digitalization, artificial intelligence integration into models of decision-making is transforming the globe's management landscape. Organizations are increasingly applying AI-enabled analytics to interpret complex data sets, which enables managers to make informed decisions that optimize the efficiency of work in remote and hybrid teams. The potential of AI to examine voluminous amounts of data at breakneck speed makes it possible to track real-time performance metrics and worldwide market trends. Such companies, therefore, stand to foresee shifts in customer conduct and adjust their strategy accordingly. This situational decision-making facilitates flexibility in a fast-changing worldwide setting, pointing to AIs contribution toward establishing viable management modalities. But the same technologies' complexities also demand strong governance structures to hold in check the dangers of data ethics and cybersecurity—a challenge managers would have to manage acutely as they utilize AI tools to achieve competitive advantage. As global management practices are increasingly emulated by organizations, the cooperation facilitated by AI and digital platforms presents special opportunities and challenges. The ability to learn cultural nuances and adapt business strategies accordingly facilitates cross-border interaction, allowing for more integrated collaboration among geographically dispersed, heterogeneous populations (Figure 10.9).

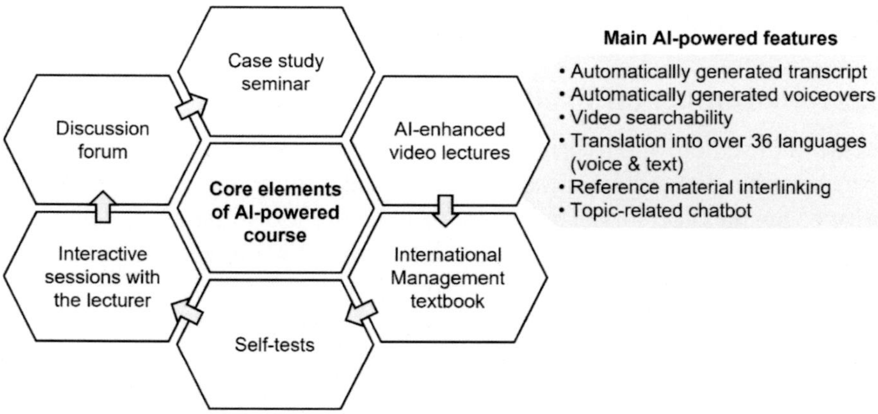

Figure 10.9. The use of AI in teaching international business.

Source: https://s3.amazonaws.com/production.scholastica/public/attachments/e9cfbf9a-92b5-428f-9151-dd7aac533593/large/figure_1._core_elements_of_the_ai-powered_international_management_course.png.

Artificial intelligence-powered tools are also able to assist managers in recognizing patterns, tendencies, and even the triggers of disputes that could arise among virtual teams. This information is important in assisting organizations in creating an inclusive organizational culture conducive to contribution from every geographical and cultural environment. Additional research into AIs application in comprehension of behavioral dynamics serves to guide leaders in making preparations against possible mishaps, such as the repercussions of digital transformation on employees. In this context, the seamless integration of AI into decision-making is as much an efficiency strategy as it is a building block for socially responsible global management. But the road to reaping the rewards from AI in making decisions is strewn with implementation challenges. The concept of the Bionic Radiologist demonstrates the potential for AI to augment human ability without diminishing essential aspects of patient interaction in clinical settings, a broader trend that can be translated across industries. By mixing AI-enhanced decision-making with human monitoring, organizations can enhance the quality of their outcomes while reducing concern regarding the loss of human judgment. This dualism is, nonetheless, ethically problematic when it comes to data usage, especially in an era when security and privacy issues are paramount. Optimizing AI applications calls for reorienting corporate cultures to prize continuous learning and adapting to achieve a culture of trust and innovation. Finally, the collective push to tap the full potential of AI within decision models can significantly improve performance and resilience with a rapidly changing world.

10.4.2. AI's Impact on Productivity and Efficiency

In the world of remote and hybrid work, the integration of artificial intelligence (AI) has spearheaded a dramatic increase in productivity and efficiency in the majority of business sectors. The ability to leverage tools that are based on AI allows companies to automate repetitive tasks, thereby allowing employees to concentrate on higher-value tasks that require critical thinking and creativity. AIs analytical power also enhances decision-making capabilities, with real-time inputs being able to help bring about wiser strategies in international management. This is particularly beneficial for international teams based in different time zones and cultural settings because AI-enabled platforms are able to speed up communication and collaboration and bridge gaps that might otherwise slow down workflow. Lastly, such efficiencies are passed on to a dynamic working place where flexibility becomes paramount in catering to the complexities of the global market. The ongoing digital revolution is accompanied by opportunities as well as challenges to businesses, particularly SMEs striving to take advantage of advancements such as AI. As organizations implement new technologies, with that comes the need for end-to-end digital capabilities as well, emphasizing the need to invest in training and development alongside implementing technology. AI can create operating efficiencies, but teams won't be able to take advantage of its true capabilities without the skills they need, which can lead to growth slowdowns and operation bottlenecks. Secondly, differing levels of digitalization across the European Union point to differences that can undermine compliance and adoption rates by businesses of differing sizes. Against the background of these challenges, the transformational role of AI is a challenge to strategic planning that aligns technological investment with staff development programs that promote an inclusive and more productive platform as cited in Ristuccia et al. (2019). But with the rapid infusion of AI and digital platforms in worldwide management comes the very real problems of cybersecurity and data ethics. As ever more sensitive information flows through these AI systems, the size of the threat base increases, and stringent measures must be taken to protect data integrity and confidentiality. Organizations must treat cybersecurity as a priority to repel new threats, even greater in a world environment where regulations and compliance rates are very far apart. The argument over whether AIs are responsible for productivity cannot overlook these points because gains in productivity seen may be compromised by vulnerabilities unless they are dealt with very carefully. Thus, establishing a culture of responsible data practices and reinforcing cybersecurity structures becomes significant to organizations which want to navigate the complexity of digital transformation ethically, so productivity increases are not at the cost of ethical values and security issues as presented in Garcia et al. (2020).

10.4.3. Ethical Considerations Surrounding AI in Management

The introduction of artificial intelligence to management has also raised important ethical concerns, particularly for hybrid and remote teams. As more and more companies employ AI software in decision-making processes, the likelihood of unintended biases and hiring discrimination emerges. The biases may be embedded in the data that is used to develop AI, reflecting embedded inequalities. Thus, managers should remain vigilant in questioning the ethical implications of implementing AI to make sure it promotes inclusiveness, rather than inequalities. The vigilance is in questioning transparency in AI algorithms and accountability in decision-making through these technologies. Ultimately, ethical stewardship requires that leaders not only impose AI as a means of efficiency but also actively promote environments that welcome equal opportunity in global management practices, understanding the diverse character of global teams operating under digitalization. The ethical framework for AI in management is also trapped by data privacy and cybersecurity complexities, especially globally. The reliance on digital platforms for global team collaboration increases the need for robust data ethics, in which sensitive information is stored away from breaches and unauthorized use. Companies must deal with varying regulatory landscapes, with changes to various degrees of data privacy in various nations. This is problematic, and even more so the need to maintain stakeholders' trust as breaches of data ethics result in enduring reputational damage. Fostering ethical data practices not only benefits the organization but also the overall integrity of the use of AI in management. As much as corporations are embracing the promise of AI, they must at the same time develop strong mechanisms that weigh heavily on ethical issues in data management and cybersecurity as a means of safeguarding organizational and individual rights under this networked digital era. The AI disruptor capacity can also be extended to process optimization in management practice with the appeal to appreciate ethical reasoning in the presence of innovation by organizations. Digital technology, such as predictive analytics and AI-based decision systems, can significantly enhance operational efficiency. Its use, however, is based on compliance with ethical behavior, particularly regarding data use and the decision impacts arising from algorithmic influences. Organizations can mitigate ethical risks by establishing clearly defined guidelines for the ethical usage of AI, fostering a culture of responsibility, and developing ethical training among employees. This proactive approach allows corporations to take benefit from AI without addressing the ethical implications arising due to its usage. By making ethical issues a priority, management will better position itself to ensure that AI is an instrument for good, ultimately enhancing organizational effectiveness and towards broader societal and operational objectives under the purview of global business practices.

10.5. DIGITAL PLATFORMS AND THEIR INFLUENCE ON GLOBAL BUSINESS

The development of digital platforms has irrefutably reshaped the business environment on a global level, generating new dynamics and challenges for managerial practices worldwide. In remote and hybrid work environments, digital platforms have enabled effortless collaboration and communication across different geographical locations. Through the use of tools such as video conferencing, cloud storage, and project management software, organizations can create environments that improve productivity and creativity. Concurrently, this transformation is accompanied by complexity, such as the possibility of miscommunication and loss of organizational culture. The necessity to establish close interpersonal relationships and make expectations clear in virtual environments cannot be overstated when companies are striving to have an engaged workforce. Awareness of such complexities is important for future practice and research in international management behavior, as discussed in recent studies on digital transformation (Garcia et al., 2020). Besides, the intersection of artificial intelligence (AI) in online platforms has led to significant increases in decision-making capacity and process efficiencies in global business environments. AI-powered analytics enable companies to take advantage of enormous amounts of data to make inferences that inform strategic actions and operating improvements. Meanwhile, reliance on AI is accompanied by ethical concerns regarding data privacy and algorithmic bias, which companies have to navigate with extreme caution. As data ethics continue to raise concern, there is a need to address these risks for multinational corporations (Figure 10.10).

Figure 10.10. The capacity digital platforms challenges for management practices across the globe.

Source: https://miro.medium.com/max/1400/1*Q03I9axxtClf5mYt6WC42g.jpeg.

The capacity to draw and respond to data-driven insights in an effective manner, yet being aware of potential ethical implications, guides a path towards obtaining competitive advantage as well as establishing trust among stakeholders. The intersection of AI and digital platforms in international management, hence, necessitates culturally adept insight that balances technology innovation with responsibility (Schlegelmilch et al., 2020). Lastly, with increasingly global business networks relying on web-based platforms, the subject of cybersecurity takes a central role among all other issues affecting organizations today. The proliferation of digital tools has enhanced access to information and made sensitive information vulnerable to cyber-attacks. Organizations must implement robust cybersecurity measures and create a culture of caution among their workers in order to effectively mitigate these risks. Also, the requirement for harmonized data governance practice across multi-jurisdictional arrangements complicates the cybersecurity strategy, and hence the need for management direction through a strategic perspective is needed. Emphasized in the topic of digital transformations collateral effects, business organizations must consider potential consequences of cybersecurity breaches for their reputation and capacity to carry out activities (Garcia et al., 2020). Therefore, as businesses continue to venture into the virtual world, innovation and security remain essential to the sustainability and success of global operations.

10.5.1. Overview of Popular Digital Platforms Used in Management

The global management environment has undergone a huge transformation through the utilization of many digital solutions aimed at augmenting collaboration and productivity in distributed and hybrid teams. Such solutions, such as Slack, Microsoft Teams, and Asana, enable effortless real-time communication notwithstanding geographical locations. Through integrating modules for project management, document sharing, and virtual meetings, such programs provide an environment that is team-centric. They serve to do more than complete the gaps in communication but also enhance stakeholder engagement on various sites, enabling effective project handling. High stakes prevail, particularly as organizations implement such technology to ensure that remote teams are able to work effectively and therefore embody a more agile management approach that transcends the traditional (Garcia et al., 2020). One of the most important aspects of such a transformation is applying artificial intelligence (AI) integrated into digital platforms being used in management. AI functionalities are increasingly being added to the platforms to assist decision-making capabilities, automate business processes, and search vast amounts of data for actionable intelligence. Tools such as Trello and Monday.com use AI-driven analytics, which allows managers to predict project congestion and deploy resources better, thereby increasing total productivity. Moreover, with the quest for global competitiveness by business firms, it is also imperative that AI skills are set in tandem with company goals. This technological improvement calls for ongoing training and fine-tuning by management to benefit from the benefits generated by AI platforms to remain pertinent in a changing digital landscape (Schlegelmilch et al., 2020). While the advantages of digital platforms in international management are tremendous, they also foretell major challenges of cybersecurity and data ethics. As companies increasingly rely on digital spaces for confidential data and communications, cyber-attacks pose palpable threats. Ensuring that digital spaces remain secure against data breaches is most important, necessitating investment in sound cybersecurity. Furthermore, ethical data usage, privacy, and compliance with data protection laws like GDPR should be the driving force in utilizing such technologies. Therefore, management must create a comprehensive approach that integrates cybersecurity practices and ethics into the organizational culture and organizational systems, establishing trust and accountability as the building blocks of good management in the digital age (Garcia et al., 2020).

10.5.2. Integration of Digital Platforms in International Strategies

With a shifting global market, the shift to remote and blended teams has required a rethink about how digital platforms are integrated into international strategy. Companies are looking to these platforms increasingly to enhance collaboration, simplify communication, and facilitate project management across geography. The use of digital tools not only facilitates real-time engagement but also supports heterogenous team management, promoting inclusivity and innovation. Besides, the use of platforms for specific activities, such as cloud collaboration platforms and project management solutions, enables organizations to provide a responsive way. As the groups operate between various cultures and time zones, the role of such digital technologies becomes more critical in enabling coordinated and effective operations, thereby enhancing organizational performance in the global competitive market. The application of artificial intelligence (AI) on these online platforms is a game-changer aspect of international management activities. AI-based software is capable of automating various business activities, enhancing decision-making processes, and providing predictive analysis that influences strategic decisions. For instance, AI-driven algorithms are capable of scanning large amounts of data to identify market trends and consumer behavior, allowing companies to tailor their strategies in foreign markets accordingly (Figure 10.11).

Such integration of cutting-edge technology not only increases efficiency but also allows organizations to have increased capabilities to tackle intricate business environments. Secondly, the integration of AI within digital platforms can enable deeper interaction with customers worldwide, enhancing stakeholder relationships as well as creating brand image in foreign markets. While these technologies get adopted by organizations increasingly, it will be crucial to realize their implications on management behavior to drive maximum opportunities for growth. Yet, digital integration into global strategy must address legitimate challenges of cybersecurity and ethics of data. As companies more and more build their operations around digital platforms, threats associated with data breaches and ethical considerations of data use come into play. Managers must navigate the complexities of varying regulations within nations, which complicate data management practices. This dual challenge requires an across-the-board approach where organizations prioritize cybersecurity strength as their primary objective along with creating an ethical culture for data utilization. Furthermore, cybersecurity best-practice education and training are essential in securing sensitive data, as well as building trust among global clients and partners. Addressing these challenges proactively not only reduces risk but also enhances the organizations reputation and international market credibility, ultimately leading to long-term sustainability and growth in global management practices.

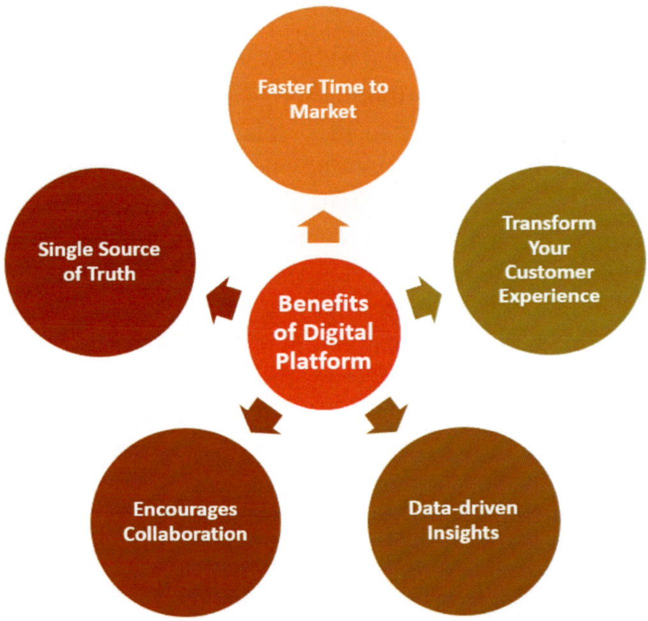

Figure 10.11. Benefits of digital platform.

Source: https://credencys.com/wp-content/uploads/2020/09/Benefits-of-Digital-Platform.png.

10.5.3. Case Studies of Successful Digital Platform Implementation

In the aspect of global management behavior, digital platform utilization is an integral area of concentration in promoting collaboration among distant and dispersed teams. Eminent case studies illustrate the ways organizations apply digital tools to overcome physical boundaries and facilitate effective communication. For instance, a worldwide multinational organization integrated a digital platform that enabled seamless information sharing among various teams spread across various time zones. This program not only brought greater productivity but also fostered an innovative and inclusive culture. Such digital platforms have the potential to support the dynamic character of global markets by helping organizations react very fast to changes and as a consequence, enhance their competitive edge.

Further, the success attributed to these deployments underscores the significance of technology as a core component of contemporary management techniques, hence setting a precedent for future adaptability in an ever-evolving digital landscape. Current research from thought leader forums offers insights into challenges faced through digital transformation, notably regarding unpredictable effects that may arise. For example, a South American roundtable highlighted various unseens that trail the deployment of digital platforms, such as the digital divide affecting small enterprises that are finding it difficult to keep up. As companies navigate the intricacies of incorporating digital platforms, they must be mindful of the broader societal and development stakes involved. The research indicated that there is a need to stay informed with regards to vulnerabilities such as the risk of exclusion of specific demographic groups from the digital economy. Lastly, case studies examining successful implementations and resultant challenges provide key insights into the complexity of digital transformation, such that a multifaceted approach is necessary for thorough understanding and effective management.

The application of circular economy thinking and digital platform design shows the high level of potential for encouraging sustainable management practices on the global business landscape. New conceptual models have attempted to integrate such principles in digital transformation agendas, which require firms to rethink their operation paradigms. Employing an Eco-Holonic Architecture in the design of circular business models effectively enables firms to manage the complexities of sustainability while enhancing their operating competence. This integrative approach not only resolves the issues of resource allocation but also encourages a holistic understanding of the relationship between technology and social systems. As businesses apply this all-embracing vision more and more, they are able to help temper the metabolic rift between economic processes and environmental sustainability. These programs not only fulfill company social responsibilities but also set the importance of green practices in an attempt to maintain a competitive advantage within the new global marketplace.

10.6. MANAGING CYBERSECURITY AND DATA ETHICS GLOBALLY

In the ever-evolving landscape of teleworking and remote teams, companies are faced with relentless challenges in tackling cybersecurity and data ethics. With digital platforms increasingly infecting global management methodologies, the risk of data leakage and ethical complications around privacy is compounded. With employees distributed across various geographic locations, cloud-based systems and electronic messaging tools enhance the vulnerability of sensitive information. Thus, establishing robust cybersecurity protocols and ethical standards becomes imperative for organizations to safeguard their information and build trust. Integrating training modules emphasizing the importance of data security and ethical decision-making in such a virtual setting can contribute significantly to lessening potential risks associated with virtual cooperation. The role of education toward conceptualization of cybersecurity and data ethics cannot be overstated, especially as industries set their eyes on understanding the nuances of Industry 4.0.

Figure 10.12. Implementing and identifying the challenges in cybersecurity and data ethics.

Source: https://eu-images.contentstack.com/v3/assets/blt69509c9116440be8/blt8ffb90a2f64bacfa/6776f4544b281ca5e2bc465a/cybersecurity_NicoElNino-AlamyStockPhoto.jpg.

Through such endeavors as the Industry 4.0 Technologies Laboratory at the Technical University of Catalonia, emphasis on engineering education can play a very significant role in the formation of competencies transferable to cybersecurity. The intersection of operational technology and information technology opens new avenues to innovation but also demands a well-considered methodology towards ethical practice and data governance. All such academic programs are equipped to train future managers and engineers not just to handle imminent security threats to cybersecurity but also inculcate an ethic of responsibility that can bridge geographical divides (Prieto et al., 2019) (Figure 10.12).

Hereby, the dynamic dialogue between education and industry is of primary importance in shaping pro-active cybersecurity management in the fast-evolving digital world. Secondly, fostering innovation within small and medium-sized businesses (SMSTEs) is of paramount importance to their capacity to succeed in a high-velocity world driven by technological transformation. An assessment of how technologies facilitate innovation can assist SMSTEs in developing feasible strategies for data security management and ethical concerns. As have been identified in recent research, key areas of governance, technology, and sustainability are enablers of SMSTEs innovation capacity and directly impact their cybersecurity posture (Mercadé et al., 2020). Embracing an innovative mentality and allowing ethical use of data, these firms are able to more effectively contend with the complexities of global markets as well as adopt responsible application of technology. In this way, cybersecurity and data ethics worldwide become not just a problem but also an opportunity, inviting big corporations and SMEs alike to allow ethical practices lead them along the way of digital transformation.

10.6.1. Importance of Cybersecurity in International Operations

With increasing digitalization of international operations, remote and hybrid workforces can only be employed through an efficient cybersecurity mechanism to protect valuable data and maintain operational integrity. When businesses become increasingly interconnected in operations through digital platforms, they are more vulnerable to cyber attacks that violate data integrity and disrupt coordination between global teams. The intricacy of cybersecurity management in a dispersed workforce is also compounded by diverse cybersecurity laws across geographies. This international dimension highlights the imperative for companies to frame integrated cybersecurity strategies that take into account regional nuances with a view to unified protection. In addition, with (Garcia et al., 2020) having noted, the beginning of digital transformation brings unexpected effects that can enhance already-present vulnerabilities, necessitating international managers to adopt a proactive stance towards risk assessment and mitigation in their businesses. Artificial intelligence (AI) and cybersecurity interactions in international management evolve into a double-edged sword (Figure 10.13).

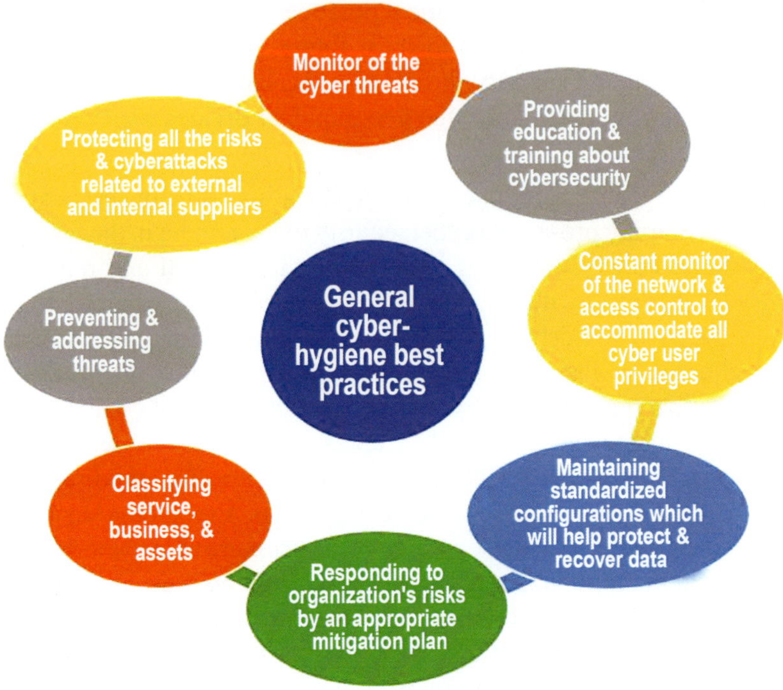

Figure 10.13. Necessitates a robust cybersecurity framework to protect sensitive information.

Source: https://www.mdpi.com/applsci/applsci-13-03410/article_deploy/html/images/applsci-13-03410-g001.png.

While AI technologies enhance operational performance and decision-making excellence via analysis of data and automation, they also introduce unique vulnerabilities that can be taken advantage of by cyber attackers. Businesses must navigate this tight rope with care, capitalizing on AIs strengths while instituting strong cybersecurity measures to safeguard their digital landscape. For instance, as indicated in Bertagna et al. (2022), shipping and shipbuilding sectors are increasingly discovering AI-based solutions, which require robust cybersecurity systems to shield supply chains and operational networks against potential disruptions after a cyberattack. Such systems not only characterize dominant vulnerabilities but also evaluate ripple effects of threats, meaning that it takes center stage to maintain an integrated plan to managing global operations' cybersecurity. Lastly, ethical aspects of data management in the realm of cybersecurity cannot be overlooked. In an age when personal data is generally the target of cyber-attacks, international organizations must prioritize data ethics in their approach to cybersecurity so that stakeholder data is managed in a responsible manner to protect it. This becomes even more so in multiculture and multijurisdictional settings where varying degrees of data protection exist. Ethical data management promotes trust and transparency, important catalysts for client and partner relationship longevity in a globalized economy. By embracing ethical principles in their cybersecurity strategies, organizations not only meet regulations but also demonstrate responsibility to their stakeholders, and in doing so, enhance their reputation and operational efficiency in a world driven by technology.

10.6.2. Data Privacy Regulations Across Different Countries

The most recent technological innovations and digitalization have brought about an excellent change in the way organizations manage data privacy regulations in different countries. As remote and hybrid employees increase, companies must grapple with a complex global regulatory landscape that can significantly differ from one country to another. At the center of this issue is the implementation of policies like the General Data Protection Regulation (GDPR) in Europe, which has heightened expectations for data privacy protection. Countries all over the world are increasingly appreciating the importance of privacy in order to enhance user trust and are being challenged to re-examine their regulatory approach. The difference in laws does present challenges to international management, where companies must comply with several legal expectations as they establish a culture of data ethics and security in their virtual workplaces (Mayer et al., 2018). An understanding of the complexities of data privacy laws is significant to organizations, especially where there are industries like connected health, in which substantial volumes of sensitive personal health data are being generated. For example, studies of user attitudes to the sharing of personal health data in four European countries uncovered varying levels of willingness to share data depending on country-based legislation and cultural contexts. This acts to support the need for cross-border managers to make their strategies congruent with not only legal stipulations but also employee and customer attitudes and practices wherever they happen to be based. As interconnectivity continues to be driven by increasing globalization, success in handling personal data depends on comprehending such local opinions while balancing adherence to wider organizational norms (Audrey et al., 2019). Also, the evolving data privacy and ownership environment, as expressed through calls for more transparent principles of ownership, underscores the need for a robust paradigm in handling digital property. Latest discussions on conceptualizing data as a new class of property are reflective of a growing perception that effective data regulation should be able to facilitate cooperation among individuals and organizations. By creating models that are centered on ownership rights, organizations can promote trust and accountability among users, which is essential in risk management in respect of data breaches and privacy violations. As global virtual work increasingly takes center stage, the maintenance of different national laws as well as the support of ethical data practices will remain the cornerstone for successful international management and sustainable competitive advantage in the market (Mayer et al., 2018).

10.6.3. Best Practices for Ethical Data Management in Global Contexts

With the world economy nowadays being more intertwined than ever, data ethics is no longer a simple task with different regulatory landscapes per jurisdiction. In this arrangement, businesses must develop and follow best practices that are appropriate for ethical data handling in an environment of diverse cultural and legal backgrounds. One important aspect to this is to encourage transparency in data processing procedures, which will further enhance stakeholders' confidence. For instance, companies are required to implement clear data governance policies that specify how employee and consumer information is gathered, kept, and utilized, especially in remote and hybrid workplaces. Transparency can diffuse potential misinterpretations and enhance collaboration, allowing businesses to unlock the full potential of AI and digital platforms. Overall, such practices not only promote ethical responsibility but also enhance the organization's credibility within global management circles. Addressing cybersecurity challenges is of the highest priority in the practice of ethical data management, particularly given that businesses increasingly rely on cyber systems for global operations. Telecommuting, fueled by the pandemic, has increased vulnerabilities to cyber-attacks, and therefore adequate cybersecurity measures are requisite to protect sensitive data. The use of multi-layer security frameworks like encryption and access controls becomes necessary in avoiding probable incursions that can destroy data integrity and confidentiality. Apart from it, regular employee training and awareness programs may allow teams to detect and manage cyber threats in a suitable way. By embedding security culture within their organizational values, companies can achieve complete leverage of technology and digitalization and secure their data handling processes. This, apart from adhering to ethical standards, helps in ensuring operating continuity and resilience in global operations. Besides, it is necessary to consider the implications of technological advancement on ethical data management in global environments. As digital transformation continues to grow, business organizations must be sensitive to the unintended consequences of adopting new technology. For instance, the digital divide in global markets can deepen inequalities, which can stimulate ethical issues regarding data availability and representation. To combat this challenge, businesses have to assume rigorous examinations of the way in which their data practices affect underrepresented communities, especially in underrepresented regions. This includes impact assessments to better help identify probable biases in AI algorithms and data analytics tools so that they reflect global populations reasonably. By prioritizing such ethical dimensions, companies not only enhance their own management culture but also contribute constructively to broader social impacts that arise out of digital innovation. Such a shift further solidifies their values of applying technology responsibly in international business strategies.

SUMMARY

The profound transformation that digitalization and technology have initiated in global management practice underscores a requisite modification of organizational structures, particularly in the context of distant and hybrid teams. As the geographical limitations of traditional offices dissipated, firms increasingly adapt to global collaborations enabled by advanced digital platforms. The change comes with new management challenges, including maintaining unity within teams and ensuring effective communication across diverse cultural environments. Digital technology has enabled real-time collaboration but, in turn, necessitates rethinking managerial practices to establish an open culture that welcomes diverse cultural backgrounds and work styles. Moreover, the adaptation of leadership styles to enable virtual dynamics is also essential. Organizations thus need to utilize technology solutions strategically that aim at the multi-dimensioned complexities introduced by dispersed and blended working setups. No less important is the application of artificial intelligence to worldwide management, which enables enhanced decision-making and business efficiency. AI technology is capable of processing gigantic sets of data, allowing managers to have access to insights no longer available before, thereby reducing wasteful use of resources and improving strategic planning. However, its application raises pressing concerns of cybersecurity as well as data ethics around the world. Organizations must deal with the risk of exposure of sensitive information in a networked environment, which requires robust cybersecurity controls and ethical data management practices. As corporations continue to construct their presence globally, they are faced with the challenge of coping with differing regulatory frameworks that may vary significantly across jurisdictions. Consequently, it is imperative that managers establish a culture of responsibility while being anticipatory in order to neutralize potential cyber threats to the organizational integrity and stakeholder trust. In brief, the intersection of technology, digitalization, and virtual work necessitates a rethink across the board of international management behavior toward sustainable development and ethical behavior within the global economy. The implementation of circular business models, as outlined, can provide an entry point for more sustainable management practices that harmonize with changing economic models and social expectations. The incorporation of circular economy principles into digital transformation models not only improves operational effectiveness but also works to mitigate adverse impacts of traditional linear practices. By leveraging both technological innovation and new business models, organizations can better buttress themselves against the uncertainties of the digital world. As previously observed, paying attention not just to the benefits technology offers but also to the resulting societal impacts of such innovations is paramount, with the final objective of creating a balance between innovation and morality in global management strategies (Garcia et al., 2020; Aguayo-González et al., 2020).

The change in work practices globally has seen an unprecedented growth in the use of remote and hybrid teams, a trend driven by digitalization and technological developments. The change requires a global management culture focused on flexibility and agility in team setups. The union between AI and digital platforms enables collaborative environments that are larger than geographical borders. As practices of management evolve, they have to acknowledge the distinct challenges offered by these emerging ways of working. Central arguments to come out of recent debate emphasize the importance of having clear protocols of communication and accountability within distributed teams, which form the pillars of maintaining productivity and team coherence. Furthermore, organizations must create a culture of trust so that they can effectively manage increasingly software-mediated communication-based diverse teams. The use of AI and digital platforms as components of international management systems is another key area that requires attention. The benefits provided by these technologies are numerous, including improved decision-making, automated processes, and improved customer experience. But such inclusion is with associated cybersecurity and data ethics threats. As companies navigate these challenges, it is vital they develop good cybersecurity practices that protect sensitive information across different platforms, especially in managing global data regulations. The debate on the topic emphasizes global managers' need to remain informed about upcoming cyber threats and data security regulations. Furthermore, understanding the ethical dimension of AI deployment is important since organizations have the double bind of leveraging technology and data handling. In exploring the unplanned consequences of online transformation, it is clear that there are many vulnerabilities, or unseens, which need to be taken seriously. They may span from digital divide issues, where disproportionate access to technology takes precedence over organizational performance, particularly in less developed nations. The recent roundtable session of experts concentrated on 15 interrelated causal mechanisms for the above-discussed unseens, indicating critical issues of concern for the overall societal impact of technology. Development drivers of government organization, geographical constraints, and technological readiness of the labor force are needed to tackle these challenges through transdisciplinary intervention. Organizations must realize the place of inclusivity in their digital projects so that everyone is given equal access and opportunities so that the dividend of digitalization is available to all and leaves a positive influence on worldwide management practices (Alexander et al., 2018; Garcia et al., 2020).

REFERENCES

1. Abedsoltan, A., Abedsoltan, H., & Zoghi, Z. (2024). Future of process safety: Insights, approaches, and potential developments. https://core.ac.uk/download/622196256.pdf (accessed on 24th September 2025).
2. Aguayo-González, F., Lama-Ruiz, J. R., Martín-Gómez, A. M., Ávila-Gutiérrez, M., et al. (2020). Eco-Holonic 4.0 circular business model to conceptualize sustainable value chain towards digital transition. https://core.ac.uk/download/299807283.pdf (accessed on 24th September 2025).
3. Ahmed, S., Ale Ebrahim, N., & Taha, Z. (2009). Virtual R&D teams in small and medium enterprises: A literature review. https://core.ac.uk/download/pdf/332902.pdf (accessed on 24th September 2025).
4. Ahmed, S., Ale Ebrahim, N., & Taha, Z. (2010). SMEs; virtual research and development (R&D) teams and new product development: A literature review. https://core.ac.uk/download/pdf/107707.pdf (accessed on 24th September 2025).
5. Alexander, B., Salavati, L., & Watson, A. (2018). The impact of experiential augmented reality applications on fashion purchase intention. https://core.ac.uk/download/287582322.pdf (accessed on 24th September 2025).
6. Ast, M. P., Bini, S. A., Chung, C. C., Kalore, R., et al. (2020). Digital orthopedics: A glimpse into the future in the midst of a pandemic. https://core.ac.uk/download/323308683.pdf (accessed on 24th September 2025).
7. Audrey, S., Fishbein, M., Girardin, F., Han, Y., et al. (2019). Connected health user willingness to share personal health data: Questionnaire study. https://core.ac.uk/download/269021381.pdf (accessed on 24th September 2025).
8. Bell, B. S., & Kozlowski, S. W. J. (2002). A typology of virtual teams: Implications for effective leadership. https://core.ac.uk/download/5121145.pdf (accessed on 24th September 2025).
9. Bertagna, S., Bucci, V., Diaz, R., & Smith, K. (2022). Digital transformation, applications, and vulnerabilities in maritime and shipbuilding ecosystems. https://core.ac.uk/download/614218304.pdf (accessed on 24th September 2025).
10. Bini, S. A., Jäger, M., Maslaris, A., Patel, N., et al. (2020). Equivalent mid-term results of open vs endoscopic gluteal tendon tear repair using suture anchors in forty-five patients. https://core.ac.uk/download/323073887.pdf (accessed on 24th September 2025).
11. Biros, G., Bungartz, H., Corones, J., Cramer, M., et al. (2016). Research and education in computational science and engineering. https://core.ac.uk/download/148025463.pdf (accessed on 24th September 2025).

12. Brandenburger, A. M., Campbell-Kelly, M., Chandler, A. D., Chesbrough, H. W., Conant, J., Freedman, D. H., et al. (2006). Challenges of open innovation: The paradox of firm investment in open-source software. https://core.ac.uk/download/70426037.pdf (accessed on 24th September 2025).
13. Burov, O., Krylova-Grek, Y., Lavrov, E., Lytvynova, S., et al. (2020). *Cybersecurity in Educational Networks.* https://core.ac.uk/download/322373029.pdf (accessed on 24th September 2025).
14. Chytiri, A. P. (2019). Human resource managers' role in the digital era. https://core.ac.uk/download/228199176.pdf (accessed on 24th September 2025).
15. Cuevas, M., Dohler, M., Laya, A., Lema, M., et al. (2017). Business case and technology analysis for 5G low latency applications. https://core.ac.uk/download/96762095.pdf (accessed on 24th September 2025).
16. de las Heras García de Vinuesa, A., Luque Sendra, A., Zamora-Polo, F., Ávila-Gutiérrez, M., et al. (2020). ADAPTS: An intelligent sustainable conceptual framework for engineering projects. https://core.ac.uk/download/322844241.pdf (accessed on 24th September 2025).
17. Delgado Prieto, M., Fernández Sobrino, Á., Fibla Biosca, P., Romeral Martínez, M., et al. (2019). Active learning-based laboratory towards engineering education 4.0. https://core.ac.uk/download/294830056.pdf (accessed on 24th September 2025).
18. Dewey, M., & Wilkens, U. (2019). The bionic radiologist: Avoiding blurry pictures and providing greater insights. https://core.ac.uk/download/228064788.pdf (accessed on 24th September 2025).
19. Dover, P. A., Manwani, S., & Munn, D. (2018). Creating learning solutions for executive education programs. https://core.ac.uk/download/286269636.pdf (accessed on 24th September 2025).
20. Garcia, F. C. O., Cardona, D., Chesñevar, C., Collazzo-Yelpo, C., et al. (2020). South American expert roundtable: Increasing adaptive governance capacity for coping with unintended side effects of digital transformation. https://core.ac.uk/download/286359460.pdf (accessed on 24th September 2025).
21. Gong, H. (2016). Places and spaces in the weightless economy. http://hdl.handle.net/10419/147972 (accessed on 24th September 2025).
22. Kettunen, P., & Laanti, M. (2017). Future software organizations – agile goals and roles. https://core.ac.uk/download/146449838.pdf (accessed on 24th September 2025).

23. Matos, J. F., Pedro, N., Santos, M., Soares, A., et al. (2008). The use of learning management platforms in school context: A national study. https://core.ac.uk/download/12425065.pdf (accessed on 24th September 2025).
24. Mayer, A., & Ritter, J. (2018). Regulating data as property: A new construct for moving forward. https://core.ac.uk/download/213019991.pdf (accessed on 24th September 2025).
25. Mercadé Melé, P., Molina Gómez, J., & Sousa, M. J. (2020). Technology, governance, and a sustainability model for small and medium-sized towns in Europe. https://core.ac.uk/download/322918717.pdf (accessed on 24th September 2025).
26. Ristuccia, C. (2019). Industry 4.0: SMEs Challenges and Opportunities in the Era of Digitalization. ZEI Discussion Paper C 252/2019. https://core.ac.uk/download/223242116.pdf (accessed on 24th September 2025).
27. Schlegelmilch, B. B. (2020). Why business schools need radical innovations: Drivers and development trajectories. https://core.ac.uk/download/323315652.pdf (accessed on 24th September 2025).
28. Special Libraries Association. (2003). Information Outlook, September 2004. https://core.ac.uk/download/129538078.pdf (accessed on 24th September 2025).
29. Winangsih, N. (2001). The image of public relations in Indonesian 2001: Myth and reality in multicultural approach. https://media.neliti.com/media/publications/154734-EN-the-image-of-public-relations-in-indones.pdf (accessed on 24th September 2025).

Index

D

J

K

L

M

N

O

P

Q

R

S

T

V

MIX
Papier | Fördert gute Waldnutzung
FSC® C083411

Kolibri 360 GmbH
Ferdinand-Jühlke-Straße 7
99095 Erfurt, Deutschland
produktsicherheit@kolibri360.de